THE BOOK OF SAY

THE BOOK OF SAY

BENJAMIN SHEPHERD

Tampa, Florida

This book is a work of fiction. The names, characters and events in this book are the products of the author's imagination or are used fictitiously. Any similarity to real persons living or dead is coincidental and not intended by the author.

The views and opinions expressed in this book are solely those of the author and do not reflect the views or opinions of Gatekeeper Press. Gatekeeper Press is not to be held responsible for and expressly disclaims responsibility for the content herein.

The Book of Say

Published by Gatekeeper Press
7853 Gunn Hwy., Suite 209
Tampa, FL 33626
www.GatekeeperPress.com

Copyright © 2024 by Ben Shepherd

All rights reserved. Neither this book, nor any parts within it may be sold or reproduced in any form or by any electronic or mechanical means, including information storage and retrieval systems, without permission in writing from the author. The only exception is by a reviewer, who may quote short excerpts in a review.

The cover design, interior formatting, typesetting, and editorial work for this book are entirely the product of the author. Gatekeeper Press did not participate in and is not responsible for any aspect of these elements.

Library of Congress Control Number: 2023952711

ISBN (paperback): 9781662947728
eISBN: 9781662947735

TABLE OF CONTENTS

Introduction		vii
1.	"Father, forgive me for I have sinned"	1
2.	"Before you were born, I set you apart"	3
3.	"You are worth more than many sparrows."	8
4.	"Keep your tongue from evil and your lips from telling lies"	13
5.	"Her children arise up and call her blessed"	20
6.	"Everyone that Loves is Born of God"	38
7.	"God shall let me see my desire upon mine enemies"	65
8.	"Come and See the works of God"	82
9.	"Love is Patient, Love is Kind"	98
10.	"Perfect Love Cast Out All Fear"	117
11.	"Fear Not I am with You"	146
12.	"I have loved thee with an Everlasting Love"	170
13.	"And the Child grew and became Strong in Spirit"	206
14.	"Speak to the Earth, and it Shall Teach Thee"	228
15.	"My Flesh and my Heart may Fail"	274
16.	"He satisfies the longing soul."	300
17.	"But my God shall supply all your need"	323
18.	"See how the flowers of the field grow"	341
19.	"To be full and to be hungry, to abound and to suffer need"	372
20.	"Draw me, and I will run after Thee."	400
21.	"I have compared thee. Oh, My Love"	428
22.	"What Mean These Stones?"	469
23.	"Who walketh upon the Wings of the Wind"	530
24.	"Use Your Freedom to serve one another in Love"	540
Epilogue		550
Credits		555

INTRODUCTION

The Blueridge Mountains were pushed up from the ocean floor over one billion years ago when the African continent collided with North America. The Glaciers' slow march from the Great Lakes to the Chesapeake Bay removed their once lofty peaks in the last ice age. The coat of Pine and Hemlock reflects the color of the deep sky, giving it the name Blue Ridge.

Individual tribes of the Cherokee nation prospered here. Artifacts of early inhabitants date back twelve thousand years. The Cherokee did not feel they owned the land any more than they could own a spirit. When Europeans came, they made space. Thinking they owned the land, immigrants pierced its granite walls with iron and staked out plots and fences; the Cherokee gave them space. Moving ever higher to the plateaus of the peaks, they eventually were forced to face famine and death in their relocation to Oklahoma. Panther Mountain is one of these places.

CHAPTER 1

"Father, forgive me for I have sinned"

"Finn, what's he asking?" "The boy leaned over his fevered Father in the backseat of the Delta eighty-eight. "I can't hear him, Marlene." As she stared at him in the rearview mirror, the dash lights flashed in her eyes. "It's Mamalene, and if you had any decency, you'd call me Mother. Now, what's he saying?" The boy moved from the recesses of the back seat and crawled upon the blankets covering his Father. The heat of fever filled the car, and Marlene rolled down the window. Finn could see the sweat-beaded face in the glow of the dash lights and a tongue pass and slip behind parched lips. "Did it work?" "What, Daddy?" "Did it work?" "The Preacher's anointing, Daddy?" The heavy head nodded slowly, and Finn glimpsed the wilted eyes of his Father, Reggie. "Did it take?" Finn retreated and leaned towards the driver's seat. "He wants to know if he's healed. If the Preacher's anointing worked." Marlene turned her face for fresh air. "What was that oil the Preacher was using?" She twisted the chrome knob of the radio, and the antenna began to lift in front of the windshield. "It's called Olive oil. It's rare, I guess. We don't use it in the South." "And it's biblical and all? I mean, Jesus used it?" She twisted her head. "I know they sell it in the Bible store in Greer."

She raised two fingers from the steering wheel. "Little bottles for anointing." "That's all it takes?" "It takes faith, Finn. You pushed your Daddy to the front of the church, and you weren't listening to Preacher Skelton?"

"Jesus save me!" Finn turned quickly back to his Father, Reggie. He had lifted his thin arms and bolstered his chest in the back seat as if preparing for currents of Jesus's power to run through him. "He's delirious. See if you can feed him some of the ice chips." "He ate 'em. I rubbed them over his lips." The boy leaned forward, giving the six-foot man all of the backseat. "I was listening. Everybody was watching and covering their faces from the smell. The Preacher talked about the woman with the blood disease that was desperate for healing. He said Jesus could heal you if you had enough faith, but you still had to pay the debt." He glanced at his Father, and his arms had fallen. "But if Daddy is healed, how much more do we have to pay?" Marlene looked at the boy in the mirrored dash light. "Hush now, Finn. President Reagan is about to speak on the radio."

CHAPTER 2

"Before you were born, I set you apart"

"Reggie, you cannot just leave, we have two children, and I am six months pregnant with a third. " Pansy Kindhart pleaded with her husband of ten years. Her skin was tan from the walks with the kids up the gravel road. "And I'm all alone in this trailer and scared, Reggie. You disappear all the time, and I hear nothing from you. My family is all back in Greensboro, and I can't go to them, Reggie. I can't go to them and ask them for help. I'm trying to feed Suzanne and Stephen, but I don't have food for myself or this baby growing inside me. Reggie, are you listening to me?" She moved from behind the kitchen table towards the brawny man she'd married, him with dreams and confused ideas.

Reggie's scowl intensified, and he pulled away. Pansy reached for those familiar arms, but they were no longer open. He stood up against the mobile home door and puffed out his chest. His clothes were new, and he had worn them because they made him feel good, and he wanted his future ex-wife to know that he was better off without her, that he had always been right when he said that she was holding him back, that they didn't belong with each other. She knew that his mind had silenced the metered truth in his heart. Reggie looked at the door. "I want to be free. I've told you, Pansy, I told you when I took you over to Greer and left you with those people. I love you, but I can't do this any longer; it's been nearly ten years. I am suffocating. You are suffocating me. You can't know, or maybe you don't want to know what a wife should be to a man."

Weeping, she moved close to him, reaching to the hands that covered his face. He went quickly towards the door, and Pansy cried out to stop him. He turned and shouted in her face, "You never had a mother to teach you how to love a man. Your Momma never said a good thing to your Daddy, always on his case about the house and money. Why do you think he died in that steel mill, Pansy? Aneurysms don't just happen to healthy young men when they're forty-one. Your Momma killed him, creating some, some kind of cancer in his brain. She was always worrying him so much about money and the kids. And now, and now, you are doing it too. For ten years, I'm not enough. You said all you wanted was marriage, so we got married. You say all you want is a baby, so I give you that boy over there. You say you want me to get an education so I can leave the garage and have a real job. We pack up, go to Missouri to college, and you cry every day, missing home. We move back East, and I start running the maintenance garage, making good money, and buy you a big ole house, and it doesn't stop. It is not enough! Do you know why? You know why?"

Pansy crumbled to the kitchen floor, her pregnant belly keeping her upright on her knees. Weeping, she covered her face. Reggie leaned over her, the yellow dress matching the linoleum. "Because I'm not good enough for Daddy's little princess." He paused. "I just want to be free, Pansy."

She looked up at him, done weeping. Her body felt like a love spear had run her through, and then she was surprised when the love spear withdrew. "I never needed solutions. I need support from you.

I don't have anything, Reggie. I don't have anything. You left us, in some stranger's driveway, eight months ago with three hundred dollars, and you haven't given us anything since. I'm trying to raise these kids, send them to school, work a job, and keep that old station wagon running. I'm leaving the kids with strangers so I can work and do the chores when I get home ." She lost all steam, exhausted from reality, spiritless from this boy-man in front of her, with his new clothes, cologne, and newfound freedom. "Reggie, you've got a good job at Milliken. You got a new car and home, and we want is some help. This baby." She rose slowly, her housecoat wrapped around her, and the tears dried across her cheeks. "Our baby needs us," she whispered, trying desperately to connect him. Reggie's face flashed red with hate. "Our child? Our child?" He moved his hands back as if they were passing strangers as if they didn't feel the thin rings still circling their fingers with never-ending vows. "That's some bastard child, Pansy. You are not passing that on to me. We haven't been together; we are in divorce." "You don't have to be so ruff Reggie. Stop before you wake the children." "Stephen told me about the black man working at the shoe store. You got some bastard inside of you?"

Pansy burst into tears. She turned away from him, this man she once loved, when love was simple. When he was sweet, they'd lay in the green fields. But now sweet love had soured and melted away like crayons on the station wagon dash. Violet and brown wax melting, dripping hot, down the heart that still felt the sting of it but knew there was no way to recollect it, and if it could be recollected, how could only one of the old lovers remold it? What were the chances of it breaking cleanly from the mold? Would it continuously be deformed, a reminder that true love's reincarnation was best left in the box, in the drawer, in the room that no one entered too often? "Reggie, you are the only man I have ever been with. You were my first, and I always thought you'd be the last." She wished that she could cry, that she could fall on the love spear, and that the tip would pierce some reserve of tears and want and truth. But there was no love weapon of war when you were fighting for love, there were only weapons of personal destruction, and in the dryness of her tearless soul, she found utter exhaustion and collapsed onto the floor.

When Pansy woke up, she was lying in her bed, and Reggie was beside her. She turned her head and looked at his large frame, the heavy arms that used to lay across her breasts, remembering what it was like nestled into that chest, her man's chest. Reggie lay with his arms stretched out above his head, asleep. Pansy lay still, her body feeling abused like the love spear had run her through, and when its end came through her body, she looked down upon it and touched it softly. She smiled down at it like some dove had lighted upon it because the love spear was the last expression of the once-innocent love she'd known, even in its gruesome form. This blood-soaked love spear was inside her—right where it was supposed to be, where the passion for Reggie had always been. Don't move sharp one, she thought, knowing that it would. I can stay here; we can live this way. I can walk more carefully. I don't need to lie down to rest as long as you are content with me. Suddenly her nightmare was realized, and the spear was kicked violently back through her womb. She felt all love leave her, and the cavity that remained was breathless, thoughtless, dumb, a drum beat continually in her ears. Her mouth opened to clear her ears, but all that came were silent screams and tears.

" Don't you have to go to work?" Pansy whispered.

"It's Saturday, no, I don't have to go to work," Reggie said while sitting on the bed. His shoulders cast a shadow over Pansy from the rising sun.

"Reggie, I want you to know that I get it . . . I want you to have your freedom." She looked up at the trailer's bedroom ceiling. "I just can't, I mean . . . Reggie . . ." She breathed deep and exhaled raggedly. "I just can't do this." She held her pregnant belly like an offering for a pagan god. She started to cry again; she opened her mouth wide but had no breath to scream. She started speaking slowly, one word at a time, the agony and grief pushing her mind so close to insanity that she could no longer control or hide the revulsions of her heart. "I . . . can't . . . keep . . . this . . . child. I can't. I can't." She rolled away from him and buried herself in lonely grief. Her mind and heart separate, coming apart, thrashing together and apart like love birds in a hurricane. Her heart swore to always fight for the love in her womb, and her mind swore to always fight for her preservation, saying in sensible meter, A fairer season, a fairer child; a fairer season, a fairer child. Then the drum stopped. Pansy's heart calmed. She remembered she had to work today and had a grocery list to make. She thought her two children would need to eat soon. She needed to move on from this—the drum had stopped beating. She needed to get up and move on today. The tear residue cleared, focusing; she realized Reggie had come around the bed and knelt in front of her; his hand was resting on her arm. She looked up at him, surprisingly clearly. He was about to speak and then stopped. She looked more intently at him and leaned her head forward, and he said, "Those people over in Greer, they've never been able to have a child."

CHAPTER 3

"You are worth more than many sparrows."

"Jon, are you sleeping?" "Of course not; the sun's too bright out here." "Well, here, take my hat then. There you go. Don't you look cute now? Wow, I'd say you're meant for wide brims and sunflowers. Can you sit up? I want you to see this photo." "You got my readers? Let's see what you got here. Well, hmm, look at that! Looks like you lost your shirt in this one, Betts!" "Photos back then gave you a healthy tan." "I actually thought someone stole this out of the Sawmill." "Yeah, me." "Let me see that again." "The date's on the back, it was fifty-three." "Sounds about right. I bought that big machine to build this pond. And look, here we are, still picnicking in our field of Queen Anne's lace." "Hmmm, you getting lost in it, Jonny?" "Hard not to, right? When you sit here and look at the pond, you remember how it used to be just in trees and those boulders over there." He looked at his wife. "I remember the chipping clay." She rubbed her fingers together. "It felt ancient, like foundational?" "Like Africa?" "You really think that, Jon? Hard to wrap my mind around it." "That's what they say. A billion years ago, the Blueridge was created by the African continent colliding with the Americas. The impact lifted this whole range." "Well, it does make me feel some kind of way."

"Jon?" She lifted her hat from his resting face. "Did we sin?" A squinted eye observed the beloved silhouette. "What's this now, Betts?" "You, know, the Mountain. Living here and all, have we sinned against it?" "Did the Cherokee, Betts? I mean, they lived here for a thousand years before us. Look at the staircase carved out of the rock and the washing pools by the spring. They were Caretakers, too, Betts. In my mind, we've done a pretty good job." "But, I'm saying, Jonny, like with the cabin and all. Just building our home where we wanted in the meadow by the small pond and fountain. Did we ignore or disgrace their history?" On elbow, the man lifted from the rug and laid upon the field grass. "Elizabeth, the Cherokee built their homes in the meadow, too. Are they there now?" "No, well, maybe deep down." "Yes, and one day, Betts, our home will not be there either, but the meadow, the fountain, and this Mountain will be." "Will they remember us?" "You talking about the trees and the Ancient leaves." She nodded her reply, and he nodded his. "Maybe." They sat together. "Come here, Betts." "I just love our story, Jon." "Hmm. Have I ever told you that you're mostly good?" "Moi?" "Oh yeah, no. After nearly fifty years, I think you've finally got the top spot in my book." "That's nice of you to say, Jon. You're writing again?" "My journal, you know someday someone will find it and roll the finest lyrical cigarettes from it." "Umm, a cigarette does sound yummy, but one rolled from your pages sounds a bit, well, inky. Might stain these lips." "Stain your soul, rather." He touched her. "You know, Betts, the doctors are saying now that smoking may kill you." "Dying's just a part of growing up, Jonny. Doctors should tell people that." "Hahaha. It would scare the hell out of them. Scares the hell out of me, and I'm fearless." "You are fearless, a regular Skyuka." "Was fearless, big difference."

"Jon, tell me again about the chipping clay and the night we had the bonfire in the bottom of the pond before it was filled with water." "You mean, the night all we all camped out, all friends and their kids were riding the horses around the basin, and Bobby was playing music?" "Yes! The standpipe, remember dressing it up and painting our faces and worshipping it like some God. Hooping and hauling and dancing all about." "That might have been Bobby's Apple wine. Sounds like you remember that night just fine." "I want to hear your version of it. I can dream it all anew when you tell it." With head in his lap, he saw the delicate heart. "You need this hat back?" "I'm not crying." "Yes, you are." These are good tears. Like salt water." He held the hat, blocking the last intense rays of the sun. "I feel like I'm in the night season of my life." "What? The night season? I don't feel that way." "That's why I need more stories, Jon. I want to dream the day seasons again in this dusky light."

"I know you wanted kids, Betts, but I just couldn't after what I saw in France." "Shhh." She touched his lips. "Nothing to do with that past but hurt yourself. Our children are all the fish in these ponds and all these Queen Anne's Lace.

The last rays of sun disappeared behind the canopy of trees. "Let's take the staircase back down; I want to visit with all the trees." "Okay, kiss me."

A small stream flowed from the upper pond and intertwined itself amongst the stones and ferns that covered the earth. Not speaking but carefully making each step, they reached out to touch the leaves as if hands extended to them. Two root cellars marked the end of the trail and the beginning of the raised wooden walkway over the moss yard to the cabin's porch.

"I will be in directly; just going to wash up, Darlin." "Don't be long." Watching her movements in the night. He splashed his face with cold water from the spring and talked aloud. "The Night Season?"

With the kettle hissing on the cast iron stove, he fumbled and found Elizabeth's lighter under a church bulletin. "Oh, I was just lighting candles out here." "No matter, I think I found 'em?" "Found what?" "They were jumbled in my hat boxes." "Your filing system." "That makes me sound unorganized, Jon. I just like the thrill hunt; got it from my Father. Where should I set them?" "Yonder on the Corn barrel, and then pull out what you want and bring them over." "Let's start here. Move; I want to sit on your lap." The two lovers set in candlelight flickered with memory at the cabin's porch table. "Pictures?" "I think letters, but I don't know; they're all mixed in. The man moved the hair back that fell across her face. "I found it, I think. Here, you see." He took the letter and then looked back to check her certainty. "Will you read some to me? I just…". Head against flannel, she kissed his neck.

"Betts, up by the pond, you said that you felt this was the night season of our lives. What did you mean by that?" Jon felt the warm tears start running down his neck and chest. She cried for some time, and Jon held her closer. "Dying is not scary, but the thought of you watching the fireflies alone breaks my heart."

He took the envelope and brought it into the candlelight. It was brown paper, and he pulled out the few sheets inside. "Will reading this bring up old things? "Don't matter, I want to hear it."

December 25, 1944, Bastogne, France

My Dear Elizabeth,
I'm alive and writing to you with my hand and from my heart. The gas shell knocked me out and over an embankment that saved my life. Trust me when I say that I'm fine and just missing you.
My hospital room overlooks a French Valley. Small birds visit each morning and sing songs as the sun rises. I spill bread crumbs there, and they come, not

minding my presence but playing and teasing each other. I place my hand on the warm stone amongst the breadcrumbs, and they perch and play across my fingers, singing and saying what could only be described as lovely, tender things. They are precious to me because I see them from this diminished freedom. I wonder why they would return each day to play for an injured man, but they lift my heart with the softness of their wings, and joy emanates from every beating heart.

I long to lay my hand amongst your beating heart. You are worth more than many little sparrows; you are worth more than many songs. I want to spend each day with you in our window and in a nest under the moon each night. To wake each day, feed with you, and whisper tender, lovely things.
Elizabeth, will you marry me?
Love, Jon

Finished, the envelope was tear-stained. He placed it in the palm of her hand. "You ready for bed?" "Our nest?" She smiled. "Elizabeth, hey, thank you for." "Oh, oh, my special man. Don't." "I do Bett's." "Jon, my heart never gave me a choice with loving you." Hands intertwined, they snuffed out the candles and ascended the stairs to rest.

CHAPTER 4

"Keep your tongue from evil and your lips from telling lies"

"Daddy, why are we driving my truck to the courthouse?" "Take Church St. Jamie." "This whole thing is embarrassing, Daddy." The Father's knees were against the dash, and his belly touched his knees, and he endured the ride like enduring his son's questions.

"Police come to your house, walk up that huge staircase and say they were there to arrest you? Did you tell them you were a former Cop? The son let the clutch out against the granite curb. "Sorry, Daddy, I haven't entirely gotten used to this standard transmission." "Ugh, Jaime, it is embarrassing for us all to be here, but this is how the devil works. Now, we've got to show this judge that this old lady was just fickle. One minute saying one thing and the next minute changing her mind."

The son nodded. "Just like a woman, am I right? Say, you prepare anything, Daddy? You got papers or a briefcase, you know, since it's court and all?" The man's door opened and the fabric strap caught it. "This Bible here, Boy. You see, in times like these I just saturate myself in the word, and when I find I'm saturated, the Holy Spirit just speaks. My word is God's word." The son let the word drip from his lips, " Saturation."

They walked inside the courthouse. "Ain't this the Devil? "What now, Daddy? A woman judge? Ohhhh, lord, help us; the devil is doing his best this morning," Two deacons from Beau Pre Baptist Church waited in the Court room.

"Shane Keith Skelton . . ."

"Yes, Your Honor, good morning to you. I'm happy to finally address this minor misunderstanding with the family of Mrs. Ledbetter." The judge looked down from her desk over a thick pair of reading glasses, taking in Shane.

"Mr. Skelton, the prosecution has accused you of stealing five thousand dollars from the wardrobe of Mrs. Edith Ledbetter, and once confronted, you became violent? Care to explain your side of this story?"

"Your Honor, I appreciate your time today. Thank you for coming together with us to straighten this matter out. I am a pastor, you see. A leader of a flock, if you will. Mrs. Ledbetter and her late husband have been part of our congregation for a few years after brother Ledbetter retired from the ministry. I must look after the Beau Pre people, and after the departing of Richard Ledbetter, I was checking in on her, you see."

"Beau Pre People?" the judge asked.

"Uh, yes. I am the ordained pastor of Beau Pre Independent Baptist church in Taylors, South Carolina, Your Honor."

"Okay, Mr. Skelton, let me see if I'm following you. The Ledbetters have been attending your church for a few years. Now, I know Mr. Ledbetter had been in a wheelchair for the last couple of years of his life, and apparently, the last months of his life were a complete shut-in. Is it your practice to regularly visit the elderly and shut-ins that belong to your congregation?" The Man looked down as if there were papers or clues to find.

"Your Honor, my congregation is tremendous, and we host two large, week-long camp meetings every year that host about two thousand people. In addition, we have a monthly youth meeting on the second Saturday of each month that draws in, say, thousand people or more." Confidence grew with oration.

"So, you don't get much time to visit the elderly? Is that what you're saying, Mr. Skelton?"

"Your Honor, most people call me Pastor or Brother Skelton. I do have an honorary doctorate degree, as well."

"Okay, Mr. Skelton. You are not my pastor or my brother; you are not my spiritual advisor. You are in my courtroom, arrested, and now being tried for being a thief. I will refer to you as Mr. Skelton." The son's reaction to the Judge brought Shane's emotions back into focus.

"Is it your practice, Mr. Skelton, to take cash from the wardrobes of the elderly widows in your congregation?" The Judge matched the former Cop's stare.

"Uh, Your Honor, Your Honor, now, please. I feel like we've gotten off on the wrong foot here." He flashed a giant grin at the Judge. "Mrs. Ledbetter requested I take the money as a love offering to put into our missionary fund. You see, we support some 130 missionary families. It is not uncommon that people bestow a love offering anonymously to these various funds in our church."

The Judge just looked at him. He expected her to pick up the next leg of the conversation, but she didn't. She just stared at him with a look of doubt and disgust. "Your Honor, does it appear that I have not been sufficiently taken care of? Our camp meetings bring in nearly two hundred thousand dollars in-love offerings. Why I have even been referred to as the kingpin of the South.

"You're the kingpin of the South?" the Judge said.

"It references the connection between God's will and works in the Southern states. Brother James Jones referred to me once like that, and it stuck. Brother Bruce Styles also uses that term for me, so it gets used amongst the South circle quite a lot."

"Mr. Skelton, the term 'kingpin' is a mafia reference, and you are in my courtroom today trying to defend yourself against theft charges. Furthermore, I don't know all of your brothers that you are referencing, and the things you are saying are confusing when a court is trying to determine your innocence."

"Oh, I guarantee a hundred percent that I'm innocent; you don't worry your little self about that now."

"Mr. Skelton, do you have any character witnesses in the courtroom today?"

"Why yes, Your Honor. I have my three deacons of Beau Pre right here."

"Mr. Skelton, would you perhaps like to call upon one of these witnesses for testimony?"

"Um, I suppose, Your Honor. He's right there; you can call him."

"Mr. Skelton, that is not how this works. He is not my witness. I am not on trial for larceny. Your witness. You are on trial; you will have to call him. Mr. Skelton, is there a reason why you have not hired counsel for yourself today? Why do you wish to represent yourself?"

"Your Honor, I feel that the Lord Almighty is my judge, so whom shall I fear?"

"Mr. Skelton, call your first witness."

The Son cranked the truck as it rolled back from the curb. "God showed up, Daddy! Moved in and troubled the waters. That woman couldn't do anything but obey God! Not enough evidence to convict!" Jubilant, like Christian soldiers were marching and beating drums following his pickup. The Father loosened his necktie and slouched in the seat, victorious. "You know, Daddy. I bet that woman wasn't even a judge. There ain't no way Greenville County will make a woman a judge. God would strike a woman dead for ruling over a man like that. That woman will give account one day. She's going to bust hell wide open." He spit from the window. "Whore."

"Hurry up now and get me back to Edith Drive."

"Okay, what's going on, Daddy?"

Removing a white handkerchief he rubbed his face. "I left that Kindhart boy at the house, picking onions out of the front lawn."

"Daddy, you left Reggie Kindhart's boy pulling wild onions out of your yard all day while we were in court? Your front lawn is five acres of grass. That boy might be dead." "He's been my Haint for three weeks now. Reggie Kindhart just came up after church and said God hadn't been blessing his family, and they couldn't feed him no more, so he was going to let him live with me. I just figured the man was fevered, and someone would take the kid before the service was over, but the kid was standing beside my truck and wouldn't move."

"Oh you ain't saying, Daddy? "The kid's name is Finn. He showed up with this fireman's bag, except it was nearly empty. He's never even had a pair of sneakers in his life. Just work boots and church shoes. What is he ten or eleven? How's that happen?"

"Listen to this, he's been staying upstairs in the white room for three weeks, and you go in that room, and there is nothing out of place. It doesn't look like anyone has slept in the bed or used that bathroom." The man realized what he was saying and straightened up in the seat. "I just mean that it is hard for a man of God to work when you got this kid around you all the time. I have secret ministries that God has me doing, and I can't really do those with him around, Jaime. I stuck him in a well for two days over there at Marty's house, and when I pulled him out, he just asked me what I wanted him to do with the trash."

"Daddy, you stuck that boy in a well for two days?"

"I pulled him out at night. Ain't as bad as it sounds."

The son had no care. He hated the boy for being around his father all the time. "So, umm, just so I know how to pray for the boy's father. As I understand it, from the prayer rooms, of course, is that they have him on the AIDs wing of the National Institutes of Health? Isn't it strange that they'd have a married man on the AIDs wing when the papers say it is a homosexual disease?" The two locked eyes. "God probably wants that family to move on. You know, to another church somewhere. I just feel that if Reggie has sin in his life that he's not willing to give up, and God sees fit to judge him, Beau Pre really can't be in the way of that. We have a much broader ministry to thousands of people in the South, and our name can't be tarnished by that kind of sin."

They rode in silence, then, turned on the gravel of Edith Drive. "Daddy, do you remember Jon Joines, that old man who did all the grading work for the new tabernacle, and then at the dedication, he and his wife, Elizabeth, came and started handing out candy and dollar bills to all the children?" "Dollar bills? Yeah, I remember." "Well, they live above the state line on some mountain the man owns. Rumors say he owns the whole thing. Anyway, I just thought that is near where Reggie Kindhart lives, and if I'm correct, Reggie knows Jon Joines because he sold him some equipment once or worked on some equipment for him." "Make your point, Jaime? I got to piss."

"Just call Reggie and tell him that he's got a fine boy, but he's getting in the way of you doing the Lord's work, and just delicately put a bug in his ear that these old people, who he already knows, might just be a good fit. You know, a place for the kid to live during the summer. Because Lord helps us, you are probably going to kill him. Oh dear, is that Finn? That wheelbarrow heaped with onions." "Bring my Bible when you come, I got go."

The son stepped from the truck. "Hey, Finn! He's got you working hard. Want some water?" The boy set down his hoe against the wheelbarrow and walked over. "This water will get cold in a minute. Feels about right. You try it?" The boy drank from the hose and then wiped his mouth on cotton. "Say that's some hard labor you've been doing." "I don't mind the work. It is right warm, Today." The Son smiled. "Uhm, you know, for a boy, you sure have a soft voice and a gentle soul. How did you get a spirit like that?" The boy looked side-eyed to Jaime as if peering into the sun to find the correct answer, "How do you tenderize a piece of meat?"

CHAPTER 5

"Her children arise up and call her blessed"

Marlene Pethel took Reggie Kindhart's last name when she became his second wife nearly a year after his divorce from Pansy and their three children. She didn't exactly like the name Kindhart, but it stuck like dough to a baker's fingers. And like dough made up of things like flour, butter, and oil, the last name came to her in small, clinging parts: a different state, a smaller house, insecurity, a strange religion, and a total of five children to mother.

You see, the Baker has certain expectations, as undoubtedly the thirty-one year old Marlene did. Both the Baker and Marlene asked questions of themselves, as they should. Is today a day for baking? Is the hearth evenly heated? What shall I use to garnish my creation? Should I infuse the butter with salt, rosemary, or honey? Will my patrons rise up and greet me happily with hungry faces and loving accolades? Will they feel the warmth of my hearth, see the flour on my face, and know that I've tried hard for them? Will they tell others about my abilities? Will they all rise up and call me blessed? Yes, of course, they will. And so, Marlene, like the Baker, tells the man and owner of the building that she will throw her lot in with her husband and says, "Dear husband, I will rise early and the knead the bread and bake it too. I will feed the hungry and set aside a table for you each day. If I can, I will sit and share and take my portion with you. And yes, I will keep your building, and your bread, and your children and mine too, and not just your dreams but our dreams will rise, like yeast, set aside and covered, and in the end, this bakery, which I started, for love, and the families we've intertwined, will all rise up and call me founder, creator, and Mother kind."

But what if the man and the building owner should have stated their expectations clearly? What if he didn't have a warm hearth, well-seasoned, with butter and oil, but a cold, yellow, electric stove. What if the bakery was not in a novel city, with cobbled streets and candled windows, but stood alone, on a wheat hill, beside a tree and an empty well? What if he said, "My Dear, there will be days when I will not be at your table because, you see, I need other food than bread, but this tree, this tree, is good for nutting, and the wheat fields will bare flour for your bread. The well, the well is a gift, my dear. Use it all you like. Needs to be cleaned; fools have filled it with the waste of leftover hopes and dreams, but clean it, dear. Sand is good for scouring, but wear gloves because you know I love your painted nails and delicate hands. Employ the children to your liking. They will bear your will, pull up the trash, and divine where the good water hides. Soon this bakery will flourish as you do now. However, the patrons, my dear, there will be few; only me and the two youngest of my children will be here to notice. The older other children will find warmer and better places to live, and while I've got you here, I should really tell you that I've not got very long to live."

Marlene moved to Reggie's farm, sight unseen, save for the image Reggie had drawn in her mind. The wedding was witnessed by hopeful well-wishers and a fake diamond ring. Marlene's family had shown up to persuade her to think again, but how could she? This was her second marriage, her first having ended devastatingly as the first ones often do. She needed a home, a car, a person's arms around her, and, most of all, hope. Reggie did give her hope. He was always loving and caring, holding her hand, begging her to sit closer to him, and running his hand over her knees. She touched his arms and intertwined his chest hair in her fingertips. When he spoke, when he looked at her, she had no doubts that all he promised was going to come true in time. She needed to be patient and wait.

"Listen, Darlin, I know this farmhouse is small, but I've got big plans for us and this property. Look now; all the kids are here to say hello." "You've got a baby boy?" "Surprise, Sugar! Oh, my goodness, the joy on your face is just too much! You are exactly the Mother these children need. Come here; you're exactly the change I need. You are going to complete me."

Marlene's two children, being older, were shocked and startled by the day's events. Waking early, driving to an unknown state. Arriving at an unfamiliar church, their Mother could marry a man they had only met once. Now, after the wedding, they were brought to what they had thought was a large farm with a large house, to a place that, though it was pretty, was not what they could've imagined or could even see themselves living in or their Mother. Where they had come from, there was a community and neighbors, baseball fields and sidewalks, paved driveways for skateboarding, heat in the houses, and bedrooms of their own, and familiar, loving faces, and this place had no resemblance of that. Back home, they would ride their bikes to their grandfather's potato field and walk with him through the deep rich soil as he leaned over and dug up the new potatoes with his hands. This place was not fertile, it was not warm, it did not smell of good earth but of harsh chemicals, and misunderstandings and confusion and the kindness of their grandfather were so far away. But as kids do, being tender plants, they smiled and embraced the day and followed Mother's lead.

Marlene opened her arms, welcoming three new children into her life as her own children watched.

Just as her father planted potatoes in his garden, knowing with certainty that, when he reached his hands into the tilled earth, he would discover new life, a swelling of feedable things, so was the hope of Marlene. She could grow where she was planted, as new potatoes would grow from old potatoes in any state, whether North Carolina or South Carolina. Given enough time, the season would change, and she would prosper once she acclimatized to it.

The house on the wheat hill was built beside a lonely pecan tree. The wheat on the hill was thin because decades before, all the topsoil had been stripped and sold because red clay was believed to be best for peaches. These trees would bear fruit every season, so a man came and planted the trees, and as they grew, he returned and pruned out their central leader so the tree would thrive in a bifurcate shape. Fertilizers, and weed killers, were sprayed with regularity. When the trees blossom in the early spring, everyone stares in awe at the beauty of the blossoms that would last only a day or two and would cover all the rolling hills like a blanket to the blue mountains. But then the crops stopped producing, the poisoned soil would not grow anymore, and the barren ground, with the old house and the only tree for several miles, was sold. Reggie Kindhart had bought the land; he drove by the lonely hill down to the crossroads and then turned around and returned again. He pulled into the gravel driveway that encircled the house like a giant horseshoe, going between the corner of the house and the tree and old well which stood side by side.

Clay colored fieldstones lined the gravel drive. Weak and untamed patches of grass surrounded the house, the tree, and the well.

Marlene realized when she married her new home, with new kids to raise, her hourglass was turned over and slowly began to drain. All her expectations, financial stability, youth, beauty, self-awareness, sense of integrity, and parental caring began to drain away. She married the situation, the patch of earth that Reggie had said was a garden that needed attention. The tiny house, the lonely wheat hill, the yellow stove, a towheaded boy.

At first, she didn't mind that her time was slipping away. She assumed that was normal, that first, you worked and were rewarded, that the sand would drain out as time, but even then, one could add more. More money, experience, laughter, joy, and by the end, one would have a glass vessel full of time well lived, well desired, and well-admired.

But the coupling of this hourglass, this thin band of gold, was decaying from within. There was a virus in its fibers, so the precious sand of Marlene's life was being exhausted, slowly, at first. Then a funnel appeared in the pool of her time, her morals, her self-worth, and her self-awareness, and soon nothing was left to do but sink into Reggie's sphere of time.

Reggie was rarely at her table. Her two children had returned to the familiar home in North Carolina, having spent one night and then insisting on living with her ex-husband. Reggie's oldest son was gone, leaving home at sixteen, knowing even at that age he could provide better for himself, but that was okay because there was just enough room in the low-ceilinged wheat hill house for who was left. Reggie had been sick several times, with fever and chills that lasted a day or two. It had worried Marlene, but Reggie was relatively young and still strong, so she just assumed it was something seasonal and let it pass. His self-employment bought and sold tractor-trailers and heavy equipment. With this trade, he traveled often, but consistently he visited Charleston.

As they had come to be called between themselves, the attacks of fever and chills had become more frequent. The fevers were so intense that Marlene could feel the heat, like a strong fire, from his body when she entered the bedroom. And yet, he would be delirious, freezing, and covered with blankets. Reggie was hospitalized during the attacks and would be out of work for a week or more. All of this she coped with, but the concerning thing was that when he was well, he would disappear for two to three days without any notice or call.

As the sand swirled from Marlene's sphere, she poured herself into a world that was altogether different and much worse than she could have imagined. The house was not getting any bigger, Reggie was not getting more robust, and her children were not returning. The mortgage was continually her biggest worry. She would go to bed at night, and in the darkness, she would look toward the blind-covered windows and whisper, "please help me" to no one.

Reggie viewed their circumstances in life as beyond their control. God was the only thing to heal and restore his body to health. To Marlene, God was the only thing that could replace the grains of sand in her hourglass. God was the only thing that could restore her relationship with her kids. God was the only thing to make this poisoned hillside grow. God was the only thing that could allow her life dream of being a mother whom all adored come true. God was the only thing that could allow none of it to happen, and all those people still call her honored mother, holy one. So, Reggie and Marlene began seeking a church and a group of believers. Reggie, who had never really been able to get victory over specific issues in his life, thought that a legalistic, conservative faith would undoubtedly do it. Marlene, who, over the years, had become more desperate than Reggie to survive, thought that this brand of faith would certainly give her time value again, in a new way, a righteous way.

Marlene stopped wearing pants and would now only wear dresses below her knees, which was the biblical attire for women.

That was okay dresses were easier to find at Thrift Stores or to make herself. They stopped listening to secular music other than a few Christmas carols during the holiday season. There was no television in the house, no alcohol, no bathing suits, no shorts, no t-shirts with graphics, no magazines, and no newspapers. They started praying over every meal and a family devotion of Bible reading and prayer before bed, wherein each person in the family would take a turn praying out loud. Marlene began carrying a leather Bible, a merit badge of difference, everywhere she went. This Bible went to the grocery store, bathroom, and outside to do yard work and bed. God and church meant more than her children as her hair turned prematurely gray, so her aspirational dreams turned loose and fell away.

"Hello? Preacher Skelton? Oh, oh, yes, of course, he's outside working. Let me call him, hold on a second, have a blessed day, Preacher." Reggie was working on a truck in the yard beside the pecan tree. "Reggie! Phone, it's Preacher Skelton!"

"Who'd you say, Marlene?"

"Preacher Skelton wants to talk to you; don't keep him waiting." Reggie had lost so much weight that his work clothes were now too large for him. The mechanic's pants were cinched about his waist with a leather belt, and the gatherings of extra material looked like large pleats running down his legs. His leather work boots now looked clown-sized on slender legs as he came to the phone. Reggie took the phone, covered the receiver end, and momentarily pecked a kiss on Marlene's lips like they were about to receive the winning lottery ticket. "Well, praise the lord," Reggie said.

"This is Reggie." He beamed from his emaciated face. "Ah, uh, it sure is a blessing to hear your voice, preacher; thank you for calling." Marlene clung to his forearm.

"Well, Preacher Skelton, if you like his work, you can keep him. He can do the work of any man. He's homeschooled, so Marlene can figure that out. I feel so bad that I cannot be there and help you with all the work around the church, so it makes us feel better knowing that Finn is there working with you. We just hope he's not a burden."

With his sickness, many people looked at him like he was dirty, something of reduced worth. Shane had told him after he had anointed him with oil and prayed over him that if he were to have an attack again, it would be in his mind and not the body because God had healed him, and it was up to his faith to make it so.

"You know, Preacher Skelton. We sure do appreciate you letting Finn stay with you. We thought that would be a great influence on his life."

"Yes, yes, preacher, I will pray about that. I do want to be in the Lord's graces. Yes, okay, sir. In the meantime, right, okay, I will send Marlene to pick up, Finn."

Reggie hung up the phone, walked past Marlene, and sat down at the head of the table, his work boots slowly taking their place beneath his seat. Marlene sat down and took his IV-bruised hands. "What did he say, Reggie?"

"He said Finn was a good boy and worked well, but it was difficult for him to find the alone time to prepare and lead the church with Finn around. However, now listen to this!" Reggie leaned closer to his wife. "Nobody knows this but us. He said that the lord had been leading him to start a Christian school, and if the lord opened the door for that school, then they'd need a new building, and the man who's going to do the grading work is Jon Joines, that old white-haired fellow that comes to church with his wife. You know the one? That's the man I sell equipment to."

"Preacher said Finn may be able to stay with them. They live on a mountain near Tryon." Marlene fell slowly back into the dining room chair, knowing where Reggie's mind was going and that any response other than what he wanted to hear would turn out badly. "What's the matter?"

"Finn has been gone for a while, Reggie. He has chores to do here. He also has schoolwork to complete, and he could be working and helping you." The illness made Reggie's emotions unstable. At times he could be laughing heartily and, in the next few minutes, experience pains of deep depression. His passions could be as hot as red steel and then quenched in a dark pool of water. "Reggie, hear me now, we love Finn, and you adore him, and he adores you. He sits at your feet and listens to your stories every night after dinner. I'm just saying, can't I just go get him and have him home for a while?"

"Well, I feel pretty empty now." "Reggie, I know your relationship with Finn is more special than the other children. It could be good for you now, you know, to have him with you each day like in the beginning." Reggie's first significant health scare had come in 1985 when Finn was five years old. Reggie had gone to the National Institutes of Health and did not leave that hospital for an entire year. Several times that year, he had been on the brink of death, and a doctor would call the house and speak to Marlene and then each of the kids. The doctor would say, "Your father has five minutes to live; you need to tell him that you love him." Five-year-old Finn would try to make sense of this, and when the phone would be laid by his father's head, all Finn would hear was a man sobbing and delusional with fever. Finn would wait for the man to stop so he could say, "I love you," but the time would never come, so he would end up just saying it over and over into the phone until, not realizing it, he was shouting into the phone, "I love you; I love you; I love you," and then he burst into tears and ran to his bed. Throughout the young boy's life, he had gone through the grieving of losing his father dozens of times, only to find out that he lived again. This gave Finn and everyone in the family, especially Reggie, hope. "Just let me get him and bring him home." "Yeah, fine."

Finn was covered in a thin layer of red dust from being in the cow pasture. The pastor had stopped earlier and was sitting on his back porch in a rocking chair with his black Labrador, Lady. Finn saw the burgundy car of his stepmother, Marlene, coming up the gravel road of Edith Drive. It was the feeling of being paralyzed in your sleep, unable to stop the oncoming nightmare. He watched, horrified, as the car turned into Preacher Shane's driveway. Finn had not seen Marlene for a couple of weeks and instantly wondered if he was in trouble and, if so, how bad the punishment would be this time. He thought for a second of hiding, but it was too late; she saw him. Still, the boy didn't move. Shane stood up from his rocking chair and spread his arms across the painted banister. "Finn, your mother, is here; guess you better get your clothes together."

Finn walked up the back stairs of the home, but once he got to the rocking chair where the pastor had been sitting, he noticed that his red fireman's bag was already on the porch. "You're quite dirty, I don't want you in the house." He looked at the prominent pastor in his white dress shirt, wrangler jeans, and black and gray hair and just nodded like one man to another at the end of a day, at the end of an agreement, or at the end of a prison sentence. Finn walked to the car, and Marlene was there with her arms open wide. Finn hugged her around her waist though this had always seemed awkward to him. He didn't trust her and didn't understand why she insisted he called her Mother when he had a mother; even though he didn't see her much, she was still alive and was his Mother. A woman who gave birth to him and raised him until he was two years old.

He got into the car's back seat, even though the front seat next to Marlene was open, and they started the long drive back to the wheat hill house. Marlene turned the rearview mirror to see Finn sitting in the back seat. She kept flashing smiles at him, and Finn awkwardly smiled back. He felt it was best to play along. If he could put in the effort and just get home close to his father, this would turn out alright. "You know, we sure have missed you," Marlene said. Though driving, she was mostly looking at Finn.

"I missed you all too," Finn said appropriately.

"Is there anything I can make special for you for dinner, one of your favorites?"

Finn thought for a second. He knew this could be a trap. If he asked for something special, it could be thrown back in his face later. "I like the homemade pizza you make; that's probably my favorite, but I know that's a difficult one because you need yeast for the crust, so if that is too much work, then I really like spaghetti."

Marlene flashed another smile at him, and then it seemed like she was about to tear up. Finn looked at her, not knowing what to do. She made this expression often, but sometimes it could mean extreme hurt or disappointment, and other times it could mean intense joy. Marlene suddenly picked up her red Bible and placed it across the steering wheel of the moving car, and holding it with her fingers, she began to turn the pages as if searching for a verse. Once found, she whispered it to herself, and finally, looking back at the road, she repeated it repeatedly. "Spaghetti is good," she said.

She always put bay leaves in the spaghetti, which was always overcooked, making the noodles soft. Finn nodded. The car turned by the Lake Cunningham fire station, and Finn knew they were halfway home.

"You haven't been doing your work around the house or schoolwork." Finn could feel the oxygen in the car being sucked away. Here it was. It was there all the time. She looked at him again, straightforward with no smile. "Did you hear me?" she said sternly. Finn looked straight at her, knowing this was what she wanted. "When you hear me say something, you have to acknowledge it. Whether by making eye contact and nodding or responding loudly enough, I can hear you clearly. You've missed a lot of school while you were on vacation, and it will have to be made up this summer." Finn connected eyes with her, nodded his head, and said clearly, "Yes, ma'am." The rest of the ride was silent.

The car pulled into the driveway lined with the red fieldstone, and Finn quickly got out of the backseat and walked forward to open Marlene's door. She said nothing and made no gestures to him as if she was entitled to this service. They entered the house, and Finn quickly went down the narrow hallway into his bedroom. He closed the door but did not push it fully closed because he knew the sound would resonate throughout the house, and it would trigger Marlene, fracturing the cracked eggshell. He opened the blinds and looked over the fields to the mountains. The verse he had heard so many times in church ran through his mind, "If you have faith the size of a mustard seed, you can move mountains."

So, what did faith really mean? In his mind, he could hear Shane quote a verse from the pulpit. "Faith is the substance of things hoped for, the evidence of things not seen." Why couldn't someone just say it simply? Finn wanted the mountains to move closer; they were his Promise Land. Reggie wanted his disease to be healed, but did he have enough faith? Either his emotions were lying to him, or the preacher was lying.

Truth sounded like an unknown character in the story of his life. The business definition of Sunshine. The truth was also known as honesty. And now, looking towards the mountain, he had two stepping stones. With truth and honesty, he could move mountains.

Truth and honesty lead to faith, which in turn creates peace. Truth, honesty, faith, and peace would allow him to exercise his abilities of God. "That means I am God, and all those who live in honesty and foster peace are God."

The opening of his spiritual eye had exhausted him. He felt sick at the thought of Shane and Jaime Skelton. Finn lay down and wanted to sleep, but his instincts were acute, monitoring Marlene's footsteps throughout the house. If they entered the narrow hallway, he would have to jump up and look active. Then there were footsteps in the hallway, but they were his father's, and he stayed resting. A minor knock came on the door, and then it slowly opened. "Can I come in?" The familiar smell of his father engulfed him. "I missed you, Finn; things are never the same around here when you're gone. You're quite a working man, aren't you? I even feel that way when you go to your mother's house on the weekends. I feel empty."

"I always miss you when you're gone." Finn never asked why he always was going somewhere or being dropped off at someone's house. He never asked his dad why they went to church or asked him to describe the meaning of faith. He never asked his dad why he had to call Marlene "Mother." Why he had to hug and kiss her and serve her, and why he had to drink the spoiled milk she sat in front of him, Or why he had to bring the paddle when she insisted on beating him. Those were the questions he knew his father did not have enough faith to answer or the strength, to be honest about. Honesty did not have much value in his father's life. It did not have much weight in the church he had wholeheartedly given himself to. Finn had faith that his father would die one day because the Doctors on the phone so many times had told him the truth, and so therefore, Finn promised to do all he could to enjoy his father's last days and to do all he could to bring happiness into his life. If he could not control the storm raging in his father's body and life, then at least he could be there to hold his hand.

"So, how was your time with Pastor Skelton. Did you have a good time?" Finn wanted to tell him the truth. He tried to tell him what he saw the man do, how he behaved. He tried to tell his father how Shane had lowered him into a well and left him there, not knowing if he would return, but Reggie's eyes were so bright, and the sun coming through the window was turning them into blue pools surrounded by the yellow of a failing kidney. So, Finn lowered his value of honesty and said, "It was good; we cleaned out a well, and we fixed some of the bunk beds in the men's dorm at the church. I also fed his cows, and he wants to build a pond on his property. There were some people there clearing out some pear trees."

"What about devotions or prayers with the preacher?"

"Oh, um, we never did that together. We prayed over meals, but as far as devotions, I did that on my own in the mornings. There was a leak in the bathroom that was off my bedroom, and the pastor came to look at it, but it was nothing that I did. That's the only time he came into my bedroom." "Well, it's good to have you back home." "You sure enjoy seeing those mountains, don't you, Finn?"

"I'd like to go up to them sometime, you know, walk around, find the waterfalls, or just look up at them. We don't ever go that way. What's up there? What's it like?"

Reggie turned to Finn and rubbed his back. "I'm going to Charleston, but when I come back, how about we go up there?"

Finn didn't understand why it took days to look at a few trucks to purchase, but he was happy to take some time off to see the mountains, something new. "Supper is going to be ready soon, and I need to get in bed. I've got to leave early in the morning." His father hugged Finn again, and just as he was leaving, Marlene stepped into the room. She was all smiles and looking lovingly at Finn and Reggie as if they were her two favorite people. Marlene sat on the bed and laid her arm across Finn's chest. She seemed so full of love, and Reggie smiled.

The following day Finn could tell that his father was gone. The vacuum started at 5 am, even though Finn and his sister were required to be up at 6 am. The machine covered the house and then would turn into the small hallway and would repeatedly bang on the bedroom doors. Eventually, the bedroom door would open, and Marlene, with the vacuum, would charge in. The light would come on, and she would maneuver around the bed, and on her way out, she would say, "Get up." The light would stay on, and it was expected that you were to dress, read your Bible for morning devotions, and then be at the breakfast table by 6:30 am.

Marlene opened the milk, stuck her index finger inside the jug, and tasted the milk. Declared good, she poured it over the cereal. Finn ate the first bite of the grain, then spit it back into his bowl.

Marlene stared at him in rage. "That milk is good; I just tried it."

"I'm sorry, but it's gone bad," Finn eased hesitantly back from the table. "May I have a piece of toast?" "Finn, the English muffins are mine. I buy them for myself. You have the cereal, and if you are going to be rebellious and not eat it, then you can do without."

Finn left the table and dumped out the spoiled food. "Do you think we could put the milk in the back of the refrigerator where it would stay colder and maybe last longer?" Wanting to make some type of truce with Marlene before starting his homeschool studies for the day. Marlene swung around to face him. Her face flashed bright red, and her lips began to curl. "Finn, the milk is fine. It is you that is spoiled. You've been on vacation and neglecting your chores and work here, and you think you can just come home and nap and demand what you want for breakfast." She stood up now and looked down at him. "That space in the door is for milk. That's where the milk is supposed to be. Now brush your teeth and get back here so we can pledge allegiance to the flags before starting your schoolwork."

When Finn returned, Marlene stood at the back of her chair. Her Bible was open, and she touched a verse and then inhaled deeply with resolve. She looked up at Finn. "We are going to start with a spanking this morning. You've been gone on vacation, neglecting everything. You came home wicked, with rebellion in your heart, and you need to be reset. Maybe then you will hear me and obey."

Finn knew it had been coming. This is how it always was, but still, he hated being beaten and treated this way. It didn't make any sense. His real mother had never spanked him, and his dad had only spanked him once in his life, but Marlene spanked him at least once a day, if not two to three times a day when his father was gone. "I don't understand. Why?"

"Oh, you're asking me why? Why you're going to get a spanking? Well, why are you evil? Why are you arguing with me? I'm the parent here; you are not the parent. Now go get the paddle." Finn walked to the shelf where the paddle stayed above the dirty laundry. Marlene's paddle was a wedding gift that her brother Earl had made out of cedar. It was long and wide with a rope loop through the handle. Drilled with holes so air would flow through the wood and not restrict the paddle's speed. Earl had burned the words on both sides of the tool, "Lookin' for some hot stuff!!"

Finn made one more attempt to appeal her decision. Holding the paddle, he watched Marlene's mouth move with the usual accusations. Knowing his size was enough to overpower her, to defend himself, seemed wrong. He could run away and stay hidden in the wheat fields until his dad came home, but that was probably not good either. He handed the paddle over like a man sentenced to hang, knowing nothing he could say would change the verdict.

"Grab your ankles," Marlene demanded. This seemed over the top for Finn, and he started to question her again, but Marlene pushed his back hard, and he bent over. "Now, I want you to know,

Finn, this is going to hurt you more than it is going to hurt me," and she swung the paddle with both hands into the boy's backside. She did not stop until Finn broke into tears. "God's will has been done, and I have completed the duty that the Bible has demanded of me as a mother. Now Finn, tell me you love me."

Reggie returned home with his stomach and back feeling like he had been beaten with batons. He immediately went to his recliner and covered himself with the blanket. Marlene made hot tea and brought it to him. Everyone's biggest fear was that he would get a simple cold and that it would turn into something larger, something that would take him away. Reggie slept or at least tried to, lying very still, as when his drunken father had come home early and wanted to celebrate Christmas with beatings.

In Reggie's mind, he had lost again. He condemned himself over and over. His body was weak, his mind was tired, and his soul felt in debt to his past choices. In debt to his family that had written him off at such a young age. Why had he abandoned them? Because if he had stayed there, he would have hurt them. A beloved son and brother who couldn't control his nature. The Bible said it was unnatural, the church said it was unholy, and society said those sick were unclean. Conflicted, he tried to understand God's punishment. He asked God for answers, but no reply came. There was only silence, which, nevertheless, thundered, "This is going to hurt you much more than it will hurt me."

Reggie lifted his hands up. "Please help me, please help me, please help me." Marlene rushed over and felt his head, and there was a fever. She asked Finn to help her take his father to bed. His teeth were beginning to chatter. Marlene removed his clothes. Finn saw the jaundiced color of his father's face spread over his entire body, and the scars across his torso from experimental surgeries were blue and purple against the yellow, sagging skin. With Reggie laid under the covers for a rest cure, everyone gathered to pray. The children earnestly prayed that God would work a miracle and heal their father of this unheard-of, rare-blood disease.

The following day Reggie's fever had broken, but he had started throwing up, and it seemed he couldn't stop. The house filled with the smell of sickness. Every few minutes, he went back and forth to the bathroom. At times Reggie cried softly. By the afternoon, things settled down, and as the sun started to set, Reggie came from the bedroom and sat at the head of the table, covered in the blanket. He sat in the chair, leaning forward.

The supper was vegetable soup, toast, and hot tea. The family gathered around the table and waited for grace, but Reggie raised his head, not looking at anyone. "There is sin somewhere in our family's life, either with all of us or just one of us, but God is not blessing us for that reason." Finn pictured God with a paddle of cedar.

"I want us all to pray before this meal and ask God's forgiveness and blessing, please." The family took turns praying, and Reggie was the last to pray over the soup. He quoted parts of Genesis, where Abraham had answered the test of God by binding his only son and preparing him for a burnt sacrifice to God. When Abraham was about to slice his son's neck, God stopped the knife and promised to bless Abraham for his willingness to give the life of his beloved son.

CHAPTER 6

"Everyone that Loves is Born of God"

A knock came at Finn's bedroom door. He didn't have to say "Come in" because he knew that it was his father and that he would wait a moment and then slowly push the door open. Reggie lay beside Finn and said nothing, giving Finn time to let the day spirits whisper and wake up.

"Finn, do you remember asking about the mountains and if we could go up there?"

Finn opened his eyes. "Can we go up there today?"

His father looked over and smiled but said, "No, no, I'm sorry. I didn't mean to insinuate that. I wish we could go together; that would be fun, and I promise we will, sometime. We will all go and take a picnic and play in the river one day. To be sure, we will. I'm asking because I think there might be a good opportunity for you if you feel up to it."

Finn had heard this line before; he knew what was coming now and wondered what the twist would be. One time, it was a family with many boys his age who just happened to be starting a boy's home. Another time, Reggie took Finn with him on a business trip but decided that Finn would have more fun staying on an elderly couple's farm. Last time, so much work needed to be done around the church, and Reggie was too sick to do his part, so Finn went to live with Preacher Skelton and work around the church. Finn was tired of the insecurity and constant awkwardness of being in some stranger's home. Sitting down to eat with Strangers, trying to shower, or use the bathroom in a strange place, tired of wondering how his clothes would be washed or if he, a child, was supposed to pay the people in some way for their hospitality. He was tired of watching his hosts, whether they were families or old people or boy's homes, whisper in quiet voices and cast gazes in his direction and then turn with false smiles and kindnesses when he entered the room. He wondered if the smell of sickness inundated the wheat hill house and clung to him. When could he ever just be a kid? When could he ever run through the wheat hill and peach trees and be free? Could he ever be healed of his father's disease?

"You know Jon Joines and Mrs. Elizabeth that come to the church every now and then? They're the old couple handing candy to the kids and sitting right behind Curtis and Brenda. Finn pictured Curtis and Brenda, the sweet couple from Greer who always seemed peculiarly paternal to him. I don't think they're proper members, but Jon owns a grading business and did all the dirt work for the new tabernacle. I don't know if they are saved, but they seem good-hearted. Preacher Skelton believes that God is using them to help the church. God can use anyone, whether sinner or saved. Anyways, the old couple has a cabin up in the mountains, the ones you've wanted to see and, uh, well, I thought that you might like to go up there and spend a few days, and, you know, get to see the mountain?" Finn turned to look at his father lying on his back and addressing the ceiling. He turned to Finn. "Whatcha think?" "That sounds really nice. Can you come up there and stay with me?" Finn touched his father's chest.

Reggie touched Finn's hand. "I wish I could, I really do, but I've got to stay here and work, you know. But it will only be a couple of days, and then, I promise I will come up there and get you, okay? Okay, I will come up to get you, and you can show me everything you've learned." He nodded as if they had reached an agreement. Reggie stood up from the bed and looked down at Finn. "Listen, the old man has run a lot of equipment, but I don't think he's ever had, children. My point is you need to watch yourself. I've always tried to warn you about what's safe and what is not. Still, if you're up there, that's someone different, who may not be watching out for you, so you've got to watch out for yourself, and If you don't feel comfortable with something, don't do it for any reason. Promise me that. Promise me you will watch him and yourself and be careful."

"I promise, Dad."

"Okay, he's going to be here in about an hour. Get your things together for a couple of days; you'll be back before the weekend." Finn's bag was never unpacked. He lived out of it like a Bedouin roaming the Arabian Peninsula. He never kept a toothbrush in a bathroom cabinet; he never had to look for a suitcase or wonder what he would need for an overnight trip or even one lasting weeks.

"Dad, hey, Dad." Finn caught Reggie's attention as he was about to walk out of the bedroom. "You think I could bring my axe, the one you got me for my seventh birthday? The small one with the redhead."

"Yeah, I guess so. Why?"

"I don't know. I just thought since it was the mountains and the trees that maybe I could bring it with me, in case we go in the woods or hiking, I don't know." Reggie smiled. "You remember when you bought that axe, Dad? You picked me up from school, and we stopped at the hardware store. It was my birthday, and I knew the hardware store, sold all kinds of things, like harmonicas and slingshots and BB guns. I knew I was going to get something good, and we walked over to the tools, and you took that axe down and put it in my hands and then said, 'Yep, I think that fits.' That was the best, Dad! Time with you and all."

"That was a big deal to you? Sure, I don't think the old man would mind. Listen, um, I've got to get going. I've got to go down to Fountain Inn, and your Momma's gone for the day at the church quilting, so just get your stuff together and wait for Mr. Joines on the porch. Take your axe, take your clothes, don't forget your Bible, and I want you to have a good time up there. You know it's not enough to see a new place with your eyes but you've got to think about what you're seeing and feeling. You keep that in mind while you are up on that mountain. Now, give me a hug." The smell of his Father was palpable, the feel of his clean-shaven cheek treasured.

Finn watched from the front porch as a red Toyota pickup truck pulled up. The truck's color blended almost seamlessly with the red stones lining the driveway. The man getting out had tanned skin and crystal-blue eyes. He simply nodded at Finn, who gathered the red bag and his axe and walked to the passenger side of the red truck. "Bags in the back," the man shouted over the running motor. Finn pulled himself up on the side of the truck tire and placed his cargo in the back, which was filled with refuse of hard labor. The inside of the truck bed had a thin layer of grease and oil spread across it like someone had been preserving it daily from getting old. Finn let himself down and climbed into the cab of the truck. It was nearly as filled as the bed with trash, receipts, and Styrofoam cups embossed with Bantam Chef, Tryon, NC, written across them in bright red, which undoubtedly would have gone well with the color of the truck when it was new. "Not much room in this cab, a small truck and all. I call it the battle wagon. Been using it for years on the mountain. That reminds me, I've got a few stops since I'm down in the Flat."

The truck lurched backward and just as promptly started towards Greer. It roared down the road, the large four-wheel-drive tires humming over the pavement.

"What's the flat?" Finn asked. The man looked at him for the first time since seeing Finn on the front porch. "The flat," He moved his hand horizontally over the Styrofoam cups. "The flat land is all this area down here. You see, I live up in the mountains, where steep hills, rocks, and trees are things you have to negotiate around. The air is cooler. We get more snow in the winter. "The flat land is where you live, you know. You could walk all day around here and never get winded, you know? You'd never get your heart rate up." The man twitched his head as if he was saying something common knowledge. Finn didn't know his heart rate, and perhaps the old man sensed this. "You could walk all day down here, never hear any thunder in your ears, no life pumping through your veins. You play sports?"

Finn recognized the man's rough edges, but a poetic passion oozed through him. Finn nodded to let him know that he understood what he was saying. The old man nodded too. "Listen," he said above the whine of the tires, "when we get up to the mountain, I will show you what I mean." Shifting down, preparing to turn. He raised his hand as if tapping a finger drum. "You'll get it then," the man said, briefly stopping before turning onto highway twenty-nine and heading into town. The old man handed Finn a Styrofoam container from the seat beside him and another set on his own lap. "Ham D-light biscuit, some breakfast. Your dad said you might be a little hungry."

" Finn wondered exactly what his dad had told him, how much awkwardness to expect, going to another stranger's home. What if his dad didn't show up, like so many times before? He'd be faced with another awkward moment of people going through old clothes, trying to find something to fit him. Finn, couldn't wait for childhood to be over.

"What's the matter? You don't like country ham?" Finn opened the Bantam Chef container. The man ate using one hand and drove the small truck at high speeds with the other. Finn bit into the biscuit sandwich, chewing slowly, working through the savory mouthful, and then swallowing. "There's coffee and milk didn't know what you might want." The man raised his eyebrows. "You a coffee drinker?" Finn shook his head. "I didn't think so."

The truck slowed as they reached the more congested part of town, where the car dealerships lined either side of the highway. Finn reached for the cup closest to him. He lifted the small indent in the plastic lid and peered inside. He drank it thirstily, and the man appeared not to notice.

The truck came to a near stop at the Dodge dealership. The man hopped out, "Stay here for a second. I will be right back."

Finn looked around the dealership parking lot at the rows and rows of new Dodge trucks. He had seen them before because this was how his family would drive to church when they came from his real mother's house. His father would say, "It takes money to make money," but Finn didn't fully understand this because he would rake leaves and cut grass for people, and they would pay him for his work; he didn't have to have money to work for someone. Finn heard his father often say that maybe he'd break down one day and just buy a new truck for himself to work out of, but no one thought he ever would.

The old man returned to the truck. "Okay, Finn, we're catching a different ride out of here. Grab your gear." Finn immediately dropped the Bantam Chef trash and got his red bag and axe from the tool-filled bed of the truck. A new red and silver Dodge pickup truck pulled up beside the old faded red Toyota. The wheels were bright chrome, and a gold pinstripe ran the length of the truck dividing the red and silver bands. Finn could hear the loud diesel engine rolling over like beach stones hammering a drum.

"Brand new Dodge Ram, Mr. Joines. This is the nicest truck on the lot." The young, lean salesman rocked back on the heels of his cowboy boots. "I'm glad you called ahead," like he had been preparing the truck for days. The old man opened the door and climbed inside. Finn followed suit. This vehicle was much larger, so there was room for all his gear and him. The burgundy bench seat stretched long, and he could feel the mighty diesel engine rumbling through the core. The man closed the door, and the salesman, looking a little confused, walked up to the driver's side door and motioned for Jon Joines to lower the power window. Jon looked for a moment, then found the power window button on the door and lowered the window. "How's she feel, Mr. Joines?" The old man just looked at the salesman. He reached to put the automatic transmission in drive, and the young salesman got the idea the old man was leaving. "Well, thank you for the trade-in; people love those Toyotas. I bet a fella like you kept the oil changed in that truck like clockwork."

Jon let the truck roll forward slightly and then looked at the young salesman and said, "Son, if there's any goddam oil in that truck, it's what they put in it at the factory." And with that, they left the faded old truck—high miles, breakfast containers, trash, chains, jacks, grease, tools, and all—and were gone.

The diesel motor purred up the steep mountain roads. Gliding passed the railroad tracks and sleepy Main Street of Tryon. The road leading from town was bordered by two rivers and mountain trees. They passed a small cafe on the left, and Finn noticed the sign over the building saying The Bantam Chef and associated it with the Chocolate milk he drank from the Styrofoam cup.

Finn, amazed by this world he had never known. A real town where people moved back and forth. Houses that were different from those he had seen. These houses did not seem squashed or congested but large and stately, with a sense of purpose and design. The trees were delightful shades of green and had different tones of bark. It was like he had just crossed over to a place where plants and people thrived too. He saw the rivers flowing and cascading over huge boulders and rocks and wondered how it would feel to sit under those waterfalls, in all his clothes, and just be covered and soaked by the joy they'd bring.

The truck turned onto Howard Gap Road and crossed one more prominent, fertile flatland. Directly in front of them was the tallest mountain Finn had ever seen. Then he remembered he'd seen it a thousand times from his bedroom window, but thoughts of home, now, had faded, like the old red truck, with all its dirty chains. On the flat, open plain, they had been in direct bright sun, but now they traveled into the dense, cool shade of the mountain. The large conifer trees were hanging limply over the mountain road, and the road began to climb slowly at first, and while it was rising, Finn pushed the power window button. He took in deep breaths of the pine-scented air. "Hey, look over there." The man pointed across a small valley to a brilliant waterfall pouring from somewhere hidden by the green foliage of hemlocks and pines. Finn's mouth dropped and started to open and close like a fish pulled from a stream, tasting the air and finding it dry.

"Welcome to Panther Mountain, son."

Finn watched the falling cascade until he could see it no more. The road began to get steeper, and a pressure that Finn had only felt when he dove deep into the water began to build in his ears, so he started to yawn and work his mouth, and his ears popped steadily. He took in the shapes of the hills, how the sun was warming each tree, and how each tree seemed to sway in thanks in the heat of the sun. They reached a large flat plateau, and the diesel engine noise quieted. The man turned left and started up one side of another blue mountain. This road was gravel, and Finn imagined the granite stones being flung to all sides by the tires. He watched row after row of large tree trunks, in the cool shade, pass by. The bases of the trees were covered in thick green ferns, and a blanket of pine needles covered the bed of earth where their roots slept. The truck suddenly stopped. The old man didn't say anything. He just got out and started up the steep bank on foot. Finn unbuckled his seat belt, pushed the heavy truck door open, and slid down the seat until his butt slipped from it, and his honey-colored work boots stood on the mountain for the first time. It was like a shock wave running through his body, like an ice dam that first cracked and then exploded with a thunderous boom. Finn felt nature for the first time, like a raging crackling fire, all-consuming and all-encompassing. It ran through his boots, his jean-covered legs, and his chest and arms.

He scrambled up the steep hillside in pursuit of the man and, for the first time, grasped the pine needles and the ancient soil under the trees the Cherokee knew. He found the man kneeling on the blanket of pine needles in the glade of trees, beholding a plant with flowers of dark orange and light orange color. The flowers bloomed from woody branches and flowed in a cascade of color. The man motioned for him to come closer, and Finn knelt beside him. "Look, it's a native azalea. They are my favorite flowers up here and quite rare to see." The boy knelt in awe, and something coursed through his veins, something he had never felt before, something that felt warm and good and pure and not fearful and certainly not alone. The man looked at Finn and shared a smile. "I always stop and see them; they're so beautiful. There can't be more than a few on the whole mountain." The man seemed youthful. Like the spirit of ancient tribes, the ether of the glade surrounded them.

The man reached into his shirt pocket, pulled out a small notepad and pencil, and sketched the wild blossom, noting its colors, date, and time. Like it was something he would flip through on cold, rainy days, it would take him back to this moment. Finn had only ever known the azaleas planted around the wheat hill house in the poisoned soil. They were woody and complex and not so pretty, and they didn't bloom every year as if they, too, were beaten or diseased. They lay dying back there, their graves surrounded by red stones, the only companion a nut tree that had produced its last crop years before

"Do you often draw?"

"Qui, Je designne souvent." "What did you say?" Jon glanced at the boy. "It was French for yes; I draw often." "You speak French? Are you French?" "That's funny. No, I'm not French, but I learned it long ago, and somehow it became the language of my heart. You know, the one you speak when you are passionate. The one I dream in at night."

"That's pretty neat. Souvent?" " Yeah, Souvent. It means often.

Finn tried the French word again. With the notepad in his shirt pocket, he got to his feet. "You'll get to meet a lot of woodland creatures up here, but first, let's get you to the cabin. You've got to meet my Betts." They turned and went back down the steep slope to the truck.

The gravel road arced, following the shape of the mountain, steadily climbing. There were no houses, only trees and ferns and the dappled light of the sun cascading through the large canopy and spreading around each tree trunk like fingers. They reached a meadow covered in tall grass. When the wind blew, the grass bent and lifted as an invisible hand passed over it. A weathered split rail fence separated the road from the sea of grass. The driveway turned off the road, and a barn at this intersection was gray like the cedar fence. The barn had what looked to Finn like two shoulders on either side of a taller with one large door in the center with a hay loft door. "Is that your barn?" " Yeah, it's the Old Saw Mill."

Passing the barn, the sea of grass was on the left, and opposite, two wooden sheds were built into the mountainside soil, and pine needles hid their roofs. As Finn's mind was taking in the wonders of the sheds, his attention moved to a cabin nestled into a cove of granite. A small pond was behind the place, and a natural spring could be seen bursting from the gray rocks. Wooden walkways could be seen crossing the moss-covered yard. Smoke rose from a stone chimney into the tree canopy. "Well, this is home, Finn." Jon pulled up in front of the house alongside a burgundy Cadillac Seville Elegante and turned off the truck.

The boy and the man climbed out of the truck and met at its rear bumper. From the side porch of the house came a welcoming voice. A graceful woman with graying brown hair wore gray-blue slacks and a short-sleeved top with a cotton rope tied in a seaman's knot around her waist; she stepped from the side porch and onto the moss. Yellow slippers were on her feet, and she held a thin cigarette. "My dears," she said as a smile crossed her face. She learned over a potted plant and extinguished the cigarette. "I've missed you all day," she said. The old man, blushing, replied to her French. The lady, Mrs. Elizabeth Joines, turned to Finn, her arm still around Jon's shoulders. She took in a deep and excited breath. "Now tell me, you must be Finn, the little man everybody keeps bragging about." Her smile was different than others. She seemed comfortable and happy, and Finn felt at home.

"Finn, I've learned, is a man of few words," "Really now. Well, I like the strong silent types." She winked at Finn and then looked at Jon. "Tell me, did he feed you today, handsome son? Jon's got a way of getting in too much of a hurry and staying in his mind, thinking that he often forgets to feed himself or others around him." Jon grimaced. Elizabeth came closer to Finn, leaned over, and looked into his eyes. "Say?"

He smiled, and his face flushed. There was an immediate peace in his heart. "That's what I thought. Give me a minute, and I will feed you."

"Hey, Doll," Jon said. She turned and looked back at him. "I promised this flatlander I'd take him up and show him the view. I think we can see his old man's place from up there. How about we put some food together, watch the sunset, and have a little appetizer up there? Then we'll make dinner when we come back."

It was the first time Finn had seen a man ask a woman her opinion as if they were equal. She looked at Jon and then over to Finn. "A flatlander . . . a flatlander!" She dropped her head and gave Finn a big smile. "You going to let him call you a flatlander?" She raised her eyebrows. "You don't strike me as a flatlander. No, what do you strike me as? Hmm . . ." She put a hand on one hip, and the other hand she lifted to her chin and tapped her lips with a long finger. "I don't know what you strike me as, right off. I'll have to think about that, but I know you do strike me as something magical, someone I've fallen in love with at first sight. But I'll leave off descriptions until the perfect description for the handsome son comes along." She turned and looked at Jon. "Okay, Special Man, but shame on you; you're too old and know better." She walked backward, her feet knowing when to step up to the porch, the silk slippers sliding across the worn planks of the deck.

"Have a look around," Jon said to Finn, gesturing to the boy. Finn took in the granite boulders, the spring coming from a small place between the stones, and the pond behind the cabin. He had often heard the descriptions of Heaven as pearly gates and streets of gold and mansions for all God's children, but that had always seemed imposing. Knowing that it wasn't possible, but if there was a heaven that would be right for him, this place was it. He walked first to the fountain and wondered where it came from. He had never seen a natural spring; he had never been to an actual waterfall. He was getting splashed by it, but he didn't care. He reached his hand up to the source but could only find a thin slit between the rocks. He followed the water with his eyes as it formed a small stream that flowed from small pool to small pool and eventually emptied into the granite basin of the pond. He noticed corn kernels on the ground and wondered why they were there.

Jon stepped onto the porch with a rolled-up rug under one arm and a few flannel shirts. He looked at the boy, and the image froze him in his tracks. Why hadn't they had a son? He could have stood on this porch and watched him move for hours. It would have been a fulfilling gift for him and Elizabeth to see their love grow and expand in that way. Elizabeth stood behind him, ran her arms around him, and laid her head on his shoulder, and her eyes captured the image of the handsome son, which her mind now held in rapture. "Jonny, I've never seen a more magical being," she whispered in his ears. Their eyes almost filled with tears. "Hey, Flatlanderflatlander, let's go look back into Egypt. Finn turned smiling and knowing well the Bible reference Jon had made to the chosen children of God moving towards the promised land and turning around to see the place that had once held them oppressed and captive.

They all piled into the new pickup, with Mrs. Elizabeth sitting between her two men in the middle of the bench seat. They left the driveway and turned left up the wide winding road toward the top of the mountain. The sun was getting lower on the horizon, and long shadows were cast from the tallest peaks of Panther Mountain and Bird Mountain. After a few minutes, they reached another flat plateau, and here the boy could see another pond with a standpipe at one end and large boulders that dipped their feet in the pond. Finn could see a deer standing, not scared by the passing vehicle. They kept climbing, the road became steeper, and the switchbacks became more frequent, and Mrs. Elizabeth spread out her arms, one hand on Jon's knee and one on Finn's. Finn holding himself high in the seat to take in everything.

They stopped at a flat place, only large enough for a car to turn around. There were wind-swept trees here, and a grouping of granite rocks came up vertically. They reminded Finn of pictures he had seen of bottlenose dolphins jumping together out of the water. One flat boulder sat like a sloping countertop, where Jon unrolled his rug. Finn opened the heavy door with two hands, stepped from the truck, and waited to help Mrs. Elizabeth.

Finn immediately started climbing over the rocks. Looking down across the flat plains, he suddenly realized why Jon had referred to it as the flatland. The mountain peaks in either direction were silhouetted against the yellow, orange, and pink sky. He looked off the cliff, and the drop nearly took his breath away. He turned to look at Jon, and Jon silently gave his permission by raising his chin and knocking back his head as if saying, of course, I was a boy, and now you are a boy. Throw the rock, and shout as loud as you can. Go ahead, be a boy. Finn threw the hand size rock he had found and watched it sail heavy through the air. Lit by the setting sun's rays, he watched it fall, alone and long, and burst on another stone, and then the report came, thwack. He looked back again; the old lovers were sitting on the flat rock as if on a magic carpet that had flown here to this ancient place.

Jon nodded again and gave the boy a huge smile. "If you don't, I will," he said. Finn gulped in a chest full of air and, throwing his head back, yelled out across the flatland as if he were an ancient chief of war, yelling to all the other tribes across the great hunting ground that he was at last at home.

"Bravo, Bravo." Finn turned to find Jon and Elizabeth clapping and cheering him on. He had never had that before. He scrabbled up the flat rock onto the rug, crossed his legs, and surveyed his own Egypt.

"You must be hungry, child." She opened the basket and removed a long thin bottle of wine. Finn looked at the bottle with its chilled appearance and was taken aback. She then pulled out a long, thin loaf of bread. Finn had never seen bread like this, only sliced bread or biscuits. Elizabeth reached into the basket, withdrew grapes and cheeses, dried meats and hummus, and cut carrots. She lifted the corkscrew, and Finn saw a wine cork removed for the first time. She poured the wine into small stemware glasses, and then from inside the basket, she pulled a bottle of chilled water and poured a small glass of water in the same type of stemware glass for Finn. They broke the bread, leaned back on their arms, sipped the wine, spread butter and cheese across the bread, and ate while watching the sunset.

Finn wondered how this could be. The wine was alcohol, and if they were consuming it and Mrs. Elizabeth was smoking a cigarette and wearing pants, they couldn't be Christian. Yet, they had shown him more love in one afternoon than anyone ever had. It was confusing, but his gut told him it was good and okay. "He drew a picture today," Finn whispered in Elizabeth's ear. She turned and smiled at Jon.

"What's that? What'd he say?" Jon said.

"He said you drew a picture today." Jon shook his head, dismissing the comment.

"What did he draw, Finn?"

"He drew this flower that was blooming in the woods. It was all alone, and it had woody stems and broad, coarse leaves, and then, just out of nowhere, it had this orange blossom that just," the boy raised his hand and made a motion of a squid swimming through the sea, "it just kept flowing and moving. It was beautiful."

Elizabeth looked back over at Jon. "What a secret and beautiful man." The flannel shirt draped over her shoulders, and she reached and slipped the notepad from Jon's front pocket. Mrs. Elizabeth opened the journal, and Finn slid his hips closer to her. She opened to the page where Jon had drawn the wild azalea bloom. She traced the lines of the flower that Jon had beautifully captured, careful not to smudge the pencil marks.

"It's beautiful," Finn said and reached his fingers to touch the page and relive the moment of worship in the glade of trees. Mrs. Elizabeth turned the notebook's pages, revealing lines of poetry the old man had penned and renderings of the cabin and the pond. Sketches of Cherokee women washing clothes in the granite pond and children playing with sticks in the moss. With each page, Finn looked up into Elizabeth's gray eyes. He could smell her scent, the light dash of perfume, the sweet hint of tobacco feeling her warmth. The flannel collar grazed his cheek now. The last page of the notebook contained a pencil drawing of the place they were now. It showed the granite dolphin noses, the large flat stone they were sitting on, but ropes were stretched across the rock like something had been held in place upon the great stone table. Under the picture were two words, "Skyuka's Rest." Finn pressed the paper down to take a better look. "What is this?" Finn asked.

Elizabeth smiled at him. "It's his notebook. His thoughts and doodles flow out on these pages. Jon communicates better through his art than in words. That's why he's so moody, so quiet. Small things swirl around inside of him, like birds over prey, until they form a phrase, a poem, a picture, and then they pop up on these pages or in a letter or, sometimes, he will just start talking, like a bird happy to see the sunrise. You would never know it by looking at him or by what he does for a living, but he's tender and artistic and wise on the inside, and, most of all, he's all mine." Finn nestled his head on Mrs. Elizabeth's shoulder. "He's a lot like this mountain and its history, you know. Did you see that fountain in the backyard that just comes out of the stone?"

Finn didn't look up because his head was connected to her soul now. He just shook his head and raised his hand as if to stick it in the small place where the water came. "I often think Jon is like that rock, rough on the outside, yet this flowing stream of artful joy. I don't know where it springs from. I often wondered if it would stop, but it never has."

Jon suddenly stood up like a dream had ended, as if a complex thought had brought the sleepy, comforting moment to a damning close. "You ready, flatlander? Had enough looking back towards Egypt?"

Elizabeth looked at him like he was stealing a lifelong dream from her. "Jon?" He was moving the items from the rug and preparing to roll it up even while they were still sitting. Finn moved, following the old man's lead. "Moody. You see now what I mean; it is embarrassing and distressing. I don't like that, Jon. I don't like when you get in these moods and think everyone is supposed to just jump up and do your bidding. Jon, stop it!" Jon looked at his wife. He stopped rolling up the rug as Elizabeth slowly swung her legs over the side of the rock. She wiped off her slacks and the back of her thighs, then began to pack up the picnic basket.

Jon moved in again, and she stuck her arm out and pointed a long finger. "No, sir!" Finn had never seen a woman talk to a man, especially her husband, like this. He had not been mindful, and she was upset. She picked up the wicker basket, turned, looked into Jon's eyes, and shook her head. She walked towards the truck. "Finn, let's turn our hearts toward home." Finn followed her and opened the truck door, and she slowly lifted herself inside and slid over to the middle of the seat.

They started back down the mountain and soon reached the driveway and the large barn. "Finn, that barn was the old sawmill when we moved up here. We lived in the loft for a couple of years while building the cabin. We sawed all the wood for the cabin and outbuildings. There was nothing up here when we first came, and Jon built all the proper roads on the mountain. Now, that barn, well, it's just full of old things. I haven't been in there for years. Jon keeps tools and most of his books in there. There's an old wagon we used with horses when we worked the vineyard, but mostly it's a storage space for a time now gone. She leaned toward Jon and put a hand on his thigh, "Remember our horses, Jonny? Oh, our babies were so sweet. We had horses, Finn, and we rode them all over this mountain on old Cherokee trails. Seems like a different lifetime, and it seems like just yesterday."

When they reached the house, Finn grabbed his red bag and axe from the back of the truck and waited for them. The old couple sat in the truck a second longer, and Finn saw Jon say something to Mrs. Elisabeth, and then he saw her lean over and kiss his lips. Mrs. Elizabeth stepped out and seemed to be wiping tears from her cheeks. Jon stepped out, and he, too, was obviously affected by the moment. "Let me show you your quarters, get you squared away."

"Jon, I will show Finn around the cabin. Can you split some kindling for the stove? Maybe, feed your children?" "Come with me, child."

"I'll hang on to this," Jon took the axe and held it up in the glow from the porch light. Finn walked arm in arm with the mother figure on the porch.

Finn followed Mrs. Elizabeth into the kitchen. "Let's see. How about we show you where you are going to sleep." She entered the cabin's great room and turned on an overhead light that seemed unnatural for a rustic feel. "This is the main room of the house. It's just full of old things from my family. Jon doesn't have much in that way. A lot of our treasures from traveling the world are here." The room had no business being in a rustic cabin. The carpet was plush under his feet, and the furniture was old and ornate. There were glass cabinets, opulent lamps, gold framed artwork, and a significant elephant leg piano that sat behind a daybed with button-tufted fabric and carved trim. "Here," she said, removing the cushions from the couch. "This is something we brought back from Tunisia."

She walked over to a wooden buffet where Jon had stacked all his clothes and began to open drawers beneath. She removed pea-green sheets and a light cream-colored blanket and made the bed. She placed a brown and orange Afghan on the back of the day bed. "Just in case you get chilly." Finn smiled. He had never seen a bed made so cleanly with layered blankets. "Now, Finn, this is your bed, and right here is a bathroom for you." She moved down the hallway and turned the lights on. "This is yours; you'll have all the privacy you need." She pulled back the shower curtain and showed him how to turn on the water and work the shower. Then she turned and opened the sink cabinets, pulled out soft, matching towels and washcloths, and laid them on the vanity. "Shower every day. Don't let Jon tell you otherwise. You can hang the towels here to dry. And when your clothes get dirty, just place them in this hamper, and I will wash them up for you."

"Our bedroom is right up there, Finn," and she pointed up the stairs to the loft. "We will be right there if you need us. We are so glad you're here, and we want you to feel comfortable and safe, okay?" Finn nodded. "Good, good. Now, my handsome new son, I'm going to fix us some dinner. I bet Jon is probably waiting outside to show you something."

Finn walked back out on the porch, and Jon lit the oil lanterns hanging from the porch eaves to light the patio space at night. Finn watched him work; migrating toward the edge of the porch, he laid his arm on the porch rail. Jon finished hanging the lanterns and tucked his shirt tail back in. "You want to help feed my children? Take the lid off that barrel." Finn looked down in the barrel and saw the large yellow corn kernels he had seen on the moss-covered lawn. Jon flipped a switch, and the pond behind the house, snug to the granite boulders, flooded with light.

The old man scooped corn from the barrel and walked towards the pond. Finn could see the granite cliffs plunging into the dark pool. Nothing moved in the deep. He heard the fountain, ever flowing, and the tree frogs clinging to the trees. The old man threw his offering in two magical arcs across the night sky, and the corn spread out across the water. From the deep, like birds darting, colors of green and purple began flashing, diving, feeding on the corn. The pond's water began to boil and froth. Like plunging arrows, the mountain trout pierced the surface, the old man's children, fed on the kernels like manna from their father above. Hundreds were leaping from the dark water and jumping above each other like birds of the sea. Finn stood in absolute rapture over what he was seeing.

"Come on, get some feed, Son." Finn plunged his arms so deep into the corn kernels that his boots left the porch floor, and his whole body balanced on the barrel's rim. He lifted his head back and, like a scale tipping, resurfaced with corn spilling from his hands. Running to the pond's edge, flung the kernels into the night sky and watched the swirling magic within the pond. Jon put his hand on Finn's shoulder, and Finn put his arm around the old man's waist. Together they laughed and stood amazed at the miracle of nature. Finn thought of the sketch of the Cherokee women washing clothes in the granite pond and the children playing with sticks on the moss where they now stood.

The fish, having fed, returned to the hidden depths of the pool. Occasionally a lone fish would swim the length of the pond, undoubtedly fueled from the feeding. Finn and Jon turned to find

Mrs. Elizabeth had stepped out into the lantern light of the porch with an apron tied around her waist, wiping her hands on a kitchen cloth. She switched off the floodlights, returning the backyard and the cabin to its familiar ambiance. "Dinner's ready."

Jon showed Finn the hand pump and the sink where he could wash his hands, and he showed him the spring box, something Finn had never seen before. "Yeah, so if you want some cold water or tea or ginger ale while you are here, you just come inside and lift the lid of the spring box and get whatever you want. Glasses are on this little shelf." Mrs. Elizabeth had pulled out the small table and set a third chair for Finn. She had placed a plate of roasted chicken, green beans, and carrots on the table, mixed with red onion and shaved almonds. Next was a plate of thick-sliced bread, soft butter, and a stone white cheddar cheese.

"Beer or wine," Betts asked Jon.

Jon thought for a second, taking in all the food before him. "Beer, but just in a small glass. I will probably have some tea later." Betts turned and took out a golden bottle of beer from the spring box and poured it into a small glass.

"Finn, I made us some sun tea. I hope you like it." Finn smiled at her. He had never sat at a table before where someone was drinking beer. He had imagined it differently. Beer was something the church associated with evil and mayhem. He never thought it was something that could garnish a meal. Jon didn't gulp it all down but took small sips after a bite. The biggest shock to Finn was that the old couple did not pray over their food. They sat down, smiled at each other and Finn, and without even acknowledging Jesus, they filled their plates and started eating. Finn paused and lowered his head, and prayed to himself.

After Finn prayed, Elizabeth wiped her lips with a cloth napkin and reached over and touched Finn's arm. "I'm sorry, Finn, uh, we should have said a blessing before the meal. We're not very practiced Christians."

"Nope, just a bunch of goddam sinners," Jon said and slapped a newspaper he had been reading down on the table. "Heathens! Betts here is the ringleader, the very worst of them. Even got a little tattoo of a mouse right down . . . " Jon slid back his chair as if he were about to show where Elizabeth's tattoo was, but she slapped him and then slapped him again. "Oh no, her pussy ate it!"

"You are a horrible man." She looked back at Finn with apologizing eyes. "Finn, we are not good. I'm sure your parents are. But all we can do is mean well. Jon here curses like a sailor, and I smoke, and we don't, or at least we've never really gone to any church, well, because . . . I don't know. I guess, well, I guess because we've felt like we've always lived in God's backyard. We've always felt so near to God or even that we were of God. I don't know; I am making a mess of what I'm trying to explain." She straightened her shoulders, took a deep breath, and looked out into the mountain night beyond the porch lanterns and candlelight. "It just means so much to us that you're here. You are special to us, handsome son, my Skyuka child."

Finn didn't know exactly what to say. Seeing these old people respond to him this way felt awkward, but it wasn't the same awkwardness he'd always known in the boys' home or at Preacher Skelton's house. It felt good. "I like being here. I think this mountain is magical. Thank you for letting me stay here with you." The two elderly people were hanging on his every word. Jon was looking at him from across the table over a crossed leg and the newspaper in his hands and reading glasses low on his nose. Mrs. Elizabeth was smiling, tears forming at the sides of her eyes, and Finn turned his eyes away so he would not start crying. "Skyuka . . . Wasn't that what was written on that sketch he drew in his notepad?"

Elizabeth looked over at Jon, but the old man seemed involved in reading the paper. "Jon, Finn is asking you about one of your sketches."

Jon looked over and then looked at Finn. "Do what now?" Jon had turned serious Finn shied away from asking.

"Skyuka's Rest. Finn is asking about Skyuka's Rest, where we went for sunset. And we also saw the drawing you did in your notebook."

"And you just called me Skyuka's child," Finn said. "Did you finally remember who I reminded you of?" The boy looked at the couple, and they seemed a bit lost for words now as if it had been a long time since they'd had company for dinner.

Elizabeth turned to look at Jon. "Jon, come on, tell him about Skyuka and the rest. I'm sure he would love to know the mountain's story."

Jon put down the paper, took off his reading glasses, and laid them on the tablecloth beside the candles. Jon looked at Finn, who had a full mouth of roasted chicken. He smiled and waited for him to finish the bite. "How old do you think the world is, Finn?"

Finn didn't have to think long. He had been told the answer to this question repeatedly in Sunday school and by his parents. "The world is 2,000 years old," Finn said confidently. Jon's head turned slightly, like a puppy trying to decipher a new sound. Finn began to quote Genesis. "In the beginning, God created the heavens and the Earth." Jon paused.

"Skyuka was a boy not much older than you, born into one of the seven Cherokee Tribes. He was born not too far from here, in Tigerville. When we go back up to the top of the mountain, I will point it out to you. He was playing in the forest and got bit by a timber rattler, and a white man named Thomas Howard saw the snake bite the boy and ran to him, took his knife, and cut an X over the spot where the snake had bit the boy. With careless abandon, Thomas sucked out the poison from the boy's arm. He saved his life. Back then, the Cherokee and white settlers lived together in the same towns and villages. The problem came when the white settlers began to mine for gold or grow crops or raise pigs, and they began to set boundaries for the land they felt they owned." Finn sat forward in the hard wooden chair and listened. "This was a problem because the Cherokee thought differently about owning land. You see, the Cherokee were nonconfrontational; they felt that the land belonged to their God, who they called Elder Fire, and so as the white settlers wanted more and more, the Cherokee just started backing away until the only place they could come was here on this mountain and in this same meadow." Jon spread his hands. "Think about that a whole tribe of Cherokee lived right here beneath our feet." The sketch from his notepad of the women washing clothes in the fountain pool made more sense. This magical place was an ancient, sacred place, and Finn quickly looked around as if all the Cherokee who lived before were now reincarnated into the trees surrounding the meadow. Like guardians, like warriors, like chiefs of peace, like chiefs of God.

"Skyuka grew up to be a natural athlete. He was a skilled hunter, a tracker. He could speak the forest languages of the birds and animals. He became a Chief of War, protecting his tribe from the Shawnee or white settlers who sought to abuse them. As he grew, he never forgot the man, Howard, who had saved his life, and he would bring the man and his soldiers deer, squirrels, and fish. The Cherokee had three types of leaders selected by the people. They had Chiefs of War, Chiefs of Peace, and Priests who explained their God. As a person progressed in wisdom, his roles within the tribe would change, so Skyuka's role changed from a Chief of War to a Chief of Peace, and as a chief of peace, he moved his tribe to this meadow. But the problems with the settlers were still growing, and even so far up here, they couldn't escape it.

"Skyuka learned that some warriors of his tribe were planning on massacring the white settlers. He sought guidance from the Elder fire and the smoke spirit and the priest, but most of all, he asked the god within himself what was the right thing to do. Skyuka decided to defend his friend Howard and fight a battle against other tribes of the Cherokee in a place called Round Mountain; we passed it today, coming up the hill. When Skyuka returned to this meadow, his own people accused him of treason, and they bound him somewhere here in the meadow and marched up that staircase." Jon pointed across the yard with his hand. "You'll see it in the morning. They took him all the way to the rock that we were sitting on for sunset, and they drove great stakes in the ground and tied Skyuka to the rock with ropes made of hemp and grape vines. In their custom, if a man was guilty or had evil within him, then you offered him up to the Elder Fire then buzzards and vultures would come and eat the wickedness out of the man. Skyuka stayed stretched across that rock for two days," Jon raised two fingers to Finn, "and the buzzards came, but something else came too. A great Bald Eagle came and set upon the stone over Skyuka's stretched-out body and guarded the great Chief. Every time a buzzard would fly towards Skyuka, the Eagle would drop from the heavens and, with his mighty talons, would rip the foul bird to pieces. Skyuka had followed his heart and had to deal with the consequences. That's why we call that place Skyuka's Rest."

"Can we go back up there; can you tell me more stories?" Finn asked, barely able to hold back his excitement.

"Yeah, yeah, of course, we will. There's a lot to see here, Finn. How about this. You're only going to be here with us for a few days, so how about we have an intellectual conversation every night at dinner?" Finn didn't exactly know what Jon meant, but if it told more stories, he wanted them. "Every night, you come up with a question. Anything, anything at all. Doesn't have to be about this mountain; it could be about Timbuktu, for all I care. The point is, any question you have in the world, you get to ask over dinner, and Elizabeth and I will tell you everything we know about it. We'll show you proof of everything we tell you in books, dictionaries, or encyclopedias. How's that?"

"Is proof another word for truth," Finn asked, looking at Jon and then over to Mrs. Elizabeth.

"Yes, Finn, the proof is evidence of truth." She stood up from the table and pushed her chair across the smooth planks of the porch. "We have rules in this house, Finn. If you make a mess, you clean it up. Now, everyone helps with dinner clean up. I wash the dishes, and Mr. Moody Pants here dries them and puts them away. He doesn't like drying the dishes, but that's how his cookie crumbles, and he does it, normally, without complaining."

"What can I do," Finn asked.

"Why don't you gather the plates, put the scraps in the trash, and compost. I'll show you." She smiled.

They finished cleaning up dinner, and Jon blew out the lanterns, walked inside, and closed the cabin door, latching it for the evening. Finn went into the yellow bathroom, showered, brushed his teeth, and put back on clothes because he never felt comfortable wearing pajamas in someone else's home or even his own. He only put them on once he was sure he was alone. Jon and Elizabeth said good night and walked up the stairway to their bedroom. The light from their bedroom illuminated the great room and the couch Finn was lying on.

Finn heard the two talking, but he thought they were talking in French as they seemed to do when they were close. Like two doves sitting together on a fence post in the rain. He felt at home for the first time in his life. He wasn't nervous that Marlene was waiting around the corner for him or that his Dad would scream out in the night for God to relieve him of his pain. He lay there thinking about all the many events of the day. The Cherokee women washing their clothes in the granite pond. He thought about Skyuka being bound and led up the stone staircase to flat rock that looked over all the mountains and plains. He thought about what Jon had said, that Skyuka had followed his heart and had to live with the consequences. Was his father having to live with the consequences of following his heart? If his father were to lay on the rest, would buzzards come to eat out the blood disease within him, therefore punishing him for the sin within, or would a great eagle come to guard over him, delivering him and letting everyone know that he was just as pure of heart as they? Is everyone that loves born of God?

Jon and Elizabeth got into bed and turned out the lights, except for the reading lamp on Jon's side. Elizabeth whispered, "Jon, my heart is bursting with love for that boy." Tears filled her eyes, and Jon slid beside her and grabbed her hand. Hands he had held nearly every night, all night, for fifty years. He didn't say anything. How could he? He had robbed her of having a son. Now all he could do was hope from the bottom of his heart that the love of his life didn't hate him. "Jon, he's a god. I'm serious, Jonny, he's like, a god of small things." She raised his hands to her lips and kissed them, and he could feel her warm tears. Jon didn't know how to console his beloved. Jon wrapped his arms around her and pulled her to his chest. He felt the tears start streaming down his chest. "Did you hear how he talks and lifts his hands when imagining something or trying to learn it? How could his Parents just send him away, Jon?" She pushed back against his chest and strained upwards to look into his eyes. Jon shook his head back and forth. He turned out the light and held her while she cried.

CHAPTER 7

"God shall let me see my desire upon mine enemies"

"Jaime..., Jaime," Shane was standing in the flower bed of Jaime Skelton's home, knocking on his bedroom window.

"Yes, Daddy, Yes. What in the good Lord's name are you doing? You're going to wake the children; what's gotten into you?" Jaime, wrapped in a robe, walked out of his house and lifted his hands up to ask why. "Why are you standing on my back porch at six in the morning, Daddy?"

Shane sat back on the porch swing and raised his hand to calm the scene. "Listen, Son, Tuesday mornings I have a silent ministry, you know, one I normally do alone, and no one but God and me knows about it."

"Yes, I know, your thing, Daddy," Jaime moved his hand like he was shooing away a fly, "So?"

"So, Jaime, I've been doing a service for the elderly at Tryon Estates."

"Did you say Tryon Estates? Tryon, Daddy, like that little town, by the mountains, with that toy horse and that pizza place, what's that place called?" Jaime began to snap his fingers as if seeing cards from a Rolodex. "That's like an hour away. Why don't you do something in Greer?"

"Yeah, that's the place. Listen, Son, I'd like for you to come up with me this morning. I know, I know, you got things to do, but the Lord's laid it on my heart, I need you. Normally, some kids, some homeschoolers join the service and play and sing before I deliver the message, but they will not be there today."

"Oh dear, Daddy, you say the Lord laid it on your heart? I know the Lord never intended for you to sing," Jaime raised his eyebrows.

"This is some sort of emergency, Son. It reflects on our church."

"I guess it is," Jaime was mulling over what he had to do today. "Okay, Daddy, I will tell you what. Let me call the bank and let them know I'll visit some of our newly acquired branches in the Western part of the state this morning. Just give me ten minutes." He turned to leave and then noticed his father about to move from the swing to sit on the front porch steps. "No, Daddy, you don't have to sit on the porch. What's the matter with you? Sometimes you just act like a stranger. Come inside quietly; just don't wake Chris and the babies."

As Shane drove his pickup along scenic highway eleven, Jaime listened with satisfaction to the dual exhaust rumble. "Daddy, how come you never tell anyone about what all you do for the Lord? I mean not just this stuff with the silent ministries, even though I am always amazed at how you can pull stuff off. I'm talking about the developing adventures you do. The ways you're able to find these elderly people who are about to lose their land. How you're able to provide for them means they never thought it possible. What was that lady's name that used to own Edith drive? Imagine how desperate she was when her husband died, and then God put you there, and you could come in and strip all the topsoil off the land and get her; how much was it, a dollar per yard? Amazing, and then how you could take it, run it through that sifter, and sell it for nearly thirty times that! The Lord blesses you, Daddy; the Lord blesses you because you put others first; you out serve them. Even after that old lady ran through that money, you bought that stripped land from her. You know that money provided for her until the Lord called her home."

The highway ran along the base of the mountains, and the morning sun stretched out and warmed the hills, creating a slight fog that drifted back up the green slopes. "Most people want a preacher to hold their hands, Jaime. I'm not that kind of Pastor," he took a toothpick out of the visor and stuck it in his mouth, "most people ain't willing to go through what they're praying for."

Jaime gave a deep nod. "That's some truth, Daddy."

"They think a pastor should keep office hours, some church office," Shane pulled the toothpick from his mouth and held it against the steering wheel of the pickup truck. "A place where the guilty conscious can confess can roll around like a dirty pig in filth. They want a Preacher to tell them that God will forgive their sins. Well, here's what I got to say about that . . . There ain't a verse in the Bible that said Jesus was going to be in his office between ten and four to hold your hand."

"No, sir!" Jaime interjected.

"Jaime, people need to learn to depend on Jesus. People have marriage problems, financial problems, and problems with the physical body or mind; they need to take it to Jesus and leave it there. They are the only ones that can keep God from blessing them."

"Amen, Daddy! But people depend on those in leadership to lead."

Shane snapped a quick stern look at Jaime. From the fabric seat of the truck, he lifted a leather Bible. The sun made it glow as if it were holy. "Son, the Bible is the only book a person ever needs to read. It's the inerrant word of God. People don't need me. They just need the word."

Jaime was silent in his thoughts, and only the sound of the truck could be heard following the mountain road. He finally lifted his arm and placed it on the back of the truck seat. "Hmph, well, Daddy, I sure do sometimes wish you wouldn't have sold all the topsoil on Edith drive. Ha, my yard looks like a Clemson tiger pep rally; it is orange clay! Can't get grass to grow for nothing. God knows I wish it did grow. I'd buy a push mower. Chris, she's got a way of thinking that she still needs to eat for herself and them babies." His father rolled his eyes. "Went to Birmingham last week, and when I got home, I found an entire pack of snickers bars under her pillow." "Not the small ones, mind you." He lifted his hands and marked the full-size length with his two index fingers.

They crossed the railroad tracks and pulled into the parking lot of Tryon Estates Nursing home. Jaime followed his father to the far end of the cafeteria, sniffing the air. "Is every piece of furniture covered in plastic or made of rubber?" A woman with a name tag waved to Shane, pulled out a wooden podium, and placed it in the center of the room. Jaime found the bookcase holding sun-faded, yellow hymnals and began passing them out to the residents who were showing up.

Shane began to hug and hold the elderly hands while having intense conversations about their needs. He even knelt in front of one lady. Jaime was shocked to see this unnatural personification from his father and couldn't help but stare, and that is when Jaime Skelton saw her. Mrs. Ledbetter was just pushed through the small congregation to a table in the cafeteria. A nurse covered her clothes and began to feed her. Jaime's face grew warm with anger and stayed that way until the end of the short service. "Daddy, what is the matter with you?"

Shane was pushing Jaime back to the truck. "I could ask you the same boy! I've never heard "Just as I am" played on the piano with sledgehammers. It's like you had boxing gloves on, Son. Like the devil was on your back or some mess."

"Well, Daddy, the devil sure was! The devil was in there!" Jaime pointed over his shoulder, "Did you not see that Ledbetter woman, Daddy? She is in that home. That accusing, lying woman. The very woman that slandered your good name and the name of my paternity," Jaime fumed. "Burns me up that woman would have the audacity to show her face, let alone eat a meal in the very room with the man, the man of God, she set out to destroy!"

"Easy now, Jaime, easy. That woman probably ain't even in her own mind half the time. "She didn't realize we were even in the room."

"How can you say that? The woman accused you of stealing from her wardrobe."

"Son, I said, lower your voice, your blood pressure. Your face is beet red. I can't think while you go on like that. Let's get some lunch, and maybe a bit of sweet tea will calm you down."

Shane pulled into the Bantam Chef for lunch. The front door clanged with a bell as they walked inside. "Good morning," a sweet voice came from the kitchen.

"Morning," Shane replied. He stepped back in his suit and freshly shined ankle boots and looked at the menu. Jaime, still fuming, paced back and forth and could not concentrate. "The Specials are right here," Shane said.

"I don't care. I'm too mad to eat. I'm not hungry."

"Go sit down. I'll order for us."

"Whatcha having, preacher?" Penny Burgess was half leaning over the counter, and Shane admired her outline.

"I say, Penny, your menu is the best I've found in North Carolina. Now, I can't decide between the hot dog special or the Ham D-Light. Any suggestions, Darling?"

THE BOOK OF SAY   69

"Well, you could stop in more often!"

"I wish I could; the lord's work here is fulfilling. You know I drive up each Tuesday just to do a little service at Tryon Estates."

"Ah, that's sweet. I bet the residents love it. So, what do you think about lunch? I will hit the rush here soon, and I've got an order to deliver."

"Uh, yeah, we will have two Ham D-Light specials with chips and two sweet teas..."

"You got it." Penny wrote the ticket and shot him a quick smile.

Shane joined Jaime in one of the booths. "What did you get us?" Jaime was still sulking.

"Ham D-light." You'll like it, its a—"

"I don't care." Jaime waved off his Dad's explanation. "Why were you being so nice to those people, Daddy? Holding their hands, kneeling, and listening to them moan about their diabetes and arthritis? The smell, uh." Jaime feigned, throwing up in his mouth. "I've never smelt so much rotten flesh in my life. Anyways, Daddy, it wasn't like you to act that way. It was strange like I was seeing a different man."

Shane took out his white handkerchief, laid it before him on the table, and mimed cleaning the spot in front of him. "Listen, Son, I raised you; we put you through college. You can wear that big fancy graduation ring and flash it around. I never questioned what you did or took in school, business, okay, no problem. Never question when you wanted to marry that little rollie pollie from Chattanooga. Remember when we went down there to meet her Daddy and them?"

"It's actually just west, Daddy."

"What I am trying to explain, son, is that the work of the Lord is mysterious. He moves, moves me, and works in ways I can't explain. You got to trust that. When you live by faith, you live by God's promise and not his explanation."

"Here are your orders, fellas," Penny set the two sandwiches in baskets on the table. "Miss. Penny, it is Miss, right? You not married?"

"Shit, no." She covered her mouth and laughed.

"Ha," Shane attempted a fake laugh. "We'll chalk that up to farm language and being raised on a farm," he leaned closer and touched her hand.

"Oh, my goodness, you've got such a good memory" she removed her hand from his and placed it on her hip out of his reach. "Goodness, I haven't been on my family's farm in years. It's crazy how time flies by. Enjoy those sandwiches!" Penny disappeared back into the kitchen, and Jaime Skelton watched her leave with a scowl.

"Why, Daddy?"

"Why what?" Shane responded, finishing the bite in his mouth.

Jaime turned in the booth to face his Dad and the sandwich in front of him. He picked it up, then dropped it, took the top layer of bread off, and salted the county ham. He looked around the small cafe. "The orange booths, the gum ball machine, the Kiwanis Club candy display by the door. Everything seems covered in a thin layer of dirt, the countertop and the menus. "Why, Daddy, do you love these places? Please, just get me back to the Bank office in Greer."

"Hmm, the taste of that, taste of that takes me back home. Sometimes, boy, I wish I'd never left West Virginia. Being up there and raised in them hollers was one of God's best things ever intended for a man."

"I don't know about that, Daddy. I hadn't seen many people with teeth up there, much less a college education and pocket money." Jaime snickered.

Shane leaned over the table and placed a giant finger upright on the paper where Jaime's sandwich lay. "What, I'm saying, sometimes, it would've been good for you to have gotten your hands

THE BOOK OF SAY 71

a little dirtier. Your belly every now and then a little hungrier." Shane began to be irritated by his thinner, paler son. "Sometimes, I can't see much difference between your soft hands and your sisters. Working in that bank, like some kind of tenderfoot. Yeah, smart guy, knows the price of everything and the value of nothing."

Jaime sat, taking small bites of the over-salted ham. He looked to the side like a dog that had been scolded and just wanted to slip away. He threw the last of his sandwich back on the paper. "Let's just get out of this town. I can't get that Jezebel off my mind." He dumped his sandwich, the wax paper wrapping, and the tray into the garbage.

"Penny, Sister Penny!" Shane's voice echoed in the small place. "We will see you next week."

"Thank you," Penny said, coming out of the kitchen with a delivery of food.

Jaime Skelton had always thought he would make a career of working for NHB&T. A new bank started on Christian fundamentals with plenty of advancement opportunities, but today he hated it. In fact, he hated everything. Everything was immoral and filthy. Unsaved sinners surrounded him. He looked at his receptionist with disdain. He'd invited her many times to the Beau Pre youth revivals, but she never came. He told her he disagreed with her wearing pants, but she refused to wear dresses. Except for today, she wore a red skirt, a pencil skirt, that was above her knees. A slit up the back showed the inside of her thigh when she walked across the office. And the heels. He didn't know why she should wear those heels. He couldn't handle her demeanor; she didn't respect him like he thought a woman should appreciate a man.

He closed his office door and locked it. He needed to pray, a word with God. He pulled out his desk chair and got on his knees. "Heavenly Father, why do you let the unjust live? Father, strike them down in their sin, or allow me to do it for you. This Ledbetter woman, why do you let her live when she blasphemes your man? Father, Oh God, My God, my heart is yours, my mind is yours." Jaime began to sob. He raised his hands and looked up into the face of Christ on the cross, "My hands, get them dirty, scar my knuckles for your service." He stopped crying and suddenly found something in the fluorescent light crown of God. "You'd send me to deal with this Ledbetter woman? I hear your voice, Father. I will judge the wicked and be a true soldier."

As he drove the Ford Courier pickup home Jaime turned on the radio, but he couldn't hear the songs with the window down and the noise in his mind. He wanted God to give him a purpose in life. Was God calling him to be a Pastor, to lead a flock, to be a Prophet, a teacher, no, a principal? Yes, a principal; would control children and teens with that position. That was a faithful flock that couldn't walk away or thinks for themselves; they would have to come into his office, confess, and pay the price.

Jaime got home, but Chris and his kids were not there, having gone to Chattanooga to visit her parents. He pulled into the upper drive and saw the basement rental apartment tenant was home. The tenant, a nineteen-year-old girl, was from the church. Jaime had set stringent rules for what she could and could not do. There was to be no television because they were sinful. She was not to entertain guests unless they were women from the church. No alcohol, no music other than Christian music, and appropriate dresses, past the knees, no slacks, no shorts. She could leave if she could not abide by these rules; the road went both ways.

In the quietness of the empty house, he heard her shower turn on. He often thought of how he could drill a hole into her bathroom and watch her or hide a camera somewhere in the ductwork, where he alone could see her body. He dreamed of how he could go down there and accidentally catch her coming out of the shower. He could say he didn't realize she was there, and he was just checking the smoke alarms or changing the air filters. No, no, he could scold her about something. Something that he could see would lead to a bad habit and eventually sin. Yes, he would stand on the stairs and look down at her with her wet hair and in a towel. He would tell her that she had disappointed him. She would have to think about it, and thinking about disappointing him, she would work out a way to impress him.

The shower stopped. His eyes opened wide, and he knew now was the moment if he wanted to see her exposed. He walked lightly across the hardwood floors to the door that led to the basement apartment. He touched the gold-plated knob. He looked at his shoes on the hardwood floor. He dropped to his knees; he couldn't sin over her again. "Dear God, forgive me... forgive me, lead me in the path of righteousness for your namesake." He begged God to communicate with him. "Please, God talk to me?" The voice he heard in the alley of moral decay sounded right. "Confront the old lady?" His eyes opened, and he wiped away the tears from his eyes with the sleeve of his flannel shirt. "You've laid in on my heart. Thy will be done."

On Saturday morning, Jaime left his home on Edith drive and started driving the mountain road to Tryon. At times he felt strange driving the small truck to work at the bank. Him in his gray suit and shined shoes, pulling up to work in an old, beat-up, hand-me-down truck. It was a gut punch to his ego. It was not the sort of vehicle a potential bank executive would drive. It was a truck a blue-collar tradesman would drive and probably would appreciate but not him. He had always lived in his father's shadow. His father's hand-me-downs. His father was more significant than him, more potent than him, and more brutal than him. A man who'd never gone to college but surprisingly a head for business. His father had been raised in

West Virginia. That's where he'd met his mother. When they first had Jaime, they decided on a complete change from the hill town and moved to Florida, where his father became one of the youngest and fiercest Motorcycle policemen on the beaches. Many times, as a child, he would be regaled by his father's stories.

The Policeman wasn't afraid to manhandle the filth of Tampa. His father bragged about fights and breaking people's faces in one punch. "The base of the chin..." He could hear his father's voice and see him touch a long finger on the point at the base where he swore the entire face would break and sag. It gave him chills. He had even seen his father manhandle the cows he raised on Edith Drive in his pastures. When a particular cow would not do what his father wanted, he would grab the animal by the ears and punch and beat it in the face until it would behave.

Jaime admired his father for being such a man, seemingly above the law and answering only to God. He saw himself as impotent and standing on the shoulders of his father. Jaime's image of God was his father. His mind and thoughts were a mystery. He was inspired by his ability to manhandle the situation until the non-behaving behaved and the unrepentant repented. Jaime felt that he was somewhat more refined than his father, and though he worked in a bank with people's money, he, too, had the character trait of his father to make people do right. To correct them and, if necessary, physically alter their course. He had often heard his Dad, from the pulpit, say, "I don't believe in divorce, but I do believe in murder." Just as his father was a vessel admired by the congregation, Jaime wanted to be an admired vessel worthy of double honor.

He reasoned that without much problem, he could slip into the nursing home and find Mrs. Ledbetter. He assumed many people would be visiting the elderly on Saturday, and not being in his suit clothes, he would blend in. Anyways, if he was recognized, he would tell them that after visiting with his father, he had felt compelled to do more for the elderly. The parking lot seemed busy. He parked and looked behind him in the rearview mirror. He could see the long line of rocking chairs on the front porch but few people in them. The main entrance passed directly by the nursing station, and he wanted to avoid it. He noticed a nurse opening a door from the cafeteria. She had been feeding people breakfast and then moving them in their wheelchairs outside for fresh air. That was where he needed to enter.

He just wanted to talk to the Lady. Just tune her morality to show her that she was wrong and had sinned. He wanted to hear her confess to him and say how she'd lied. Then tomorrow, on Sunday, he would stand in church, stopping the service, and testify to the congregation how God had brought the old Lady back into the fold. He walked from the parking lot to the concrete walkway lined with green grass. Reaching the columns of the home and then the wide porch. Instantly, he could smell the sweet putrid smell of old age. It turned his stomach. The thought of old flesh. He thought of what he may say to Mrs. Ledbetter, but he knew God would lead him now. The cafeteria emptied out, and the staff was busy decorating for a one hundredth birthday. He slipped through the event room and by the piano he had played for the service. Both the instrument and the people were disgusting. The piano seemed to have a skim of old age.

In the hallway, he turned right without passing anyone. He turned right again, and before the nursing station, he found the room he was looking for. The door was slightly opened. He looked both ways, and no one was there to see him. He pushed the door quietly and slowly stepped into the old woman's room. The curtains were drawn, and the light was dim. He could see her lying tilted in her bed, the tv on. She was awake, and he could hear her breathing. The room had the scent of wilting flowers. Cards from her grandchildren sat on the dresser and window sill. A picture of her husband and her on the steps of his first church in Aiken, South Carolina. The image was black and white, and their smiles and loving embrace showed how much they were in love and happy to be on this new adventure.

"Mrs. Ledbetter," Jaime said, slowly moving from the shadows towards her. "Hi." He smiled. "The Angel of Death is here." He stepped closer to the bed. The old lady slowly turned her head and looked at him. She stared at him and extended her hand toward him. Jaime leaned slightly over her. He could smell her, seeing the withered hand growing towards him. It turned his stomach slightly. He did not want to touch the soft wrinkled hands. He lifted his head and exhaled, "The lord told me to visit you today. You remember Daddy to come to visit your husband?" Jaime picked up the picture of the couple and turned it slowly so she could see it. "Ah, uhh, Daddy came and visited your man." Jaime Skelton nodded his head in unison with the old lady. He began to tap the photo with his finger. With each tap, feeling as if he was being empowered by God. He suddenly set the picture down on the bedside table hard. It tipped over and fell to the tile floor.

The old ladies' eyes turned wide. You remember me?" Jaime said as drops of spit flew towards. Jaime smiled. He was in control, and God's vessel was filled with wrath. He slid his fingers around the wrist of tender flesh. Mrs. Ledbetter shook her head, trying to protest his actions. His prey wanting to flee, he leaned over her, putting his hands on either side of her.

"Satan," she said.

Jaime Skelton's head split. He felt something warm and numbing run up the back of his neck and over the top of his head. "Daddy is a man of God!" he said, pushing hard on her mattress. The old lady's body moved up and down. Her hands tried to make him go away, but it felt like small pinches on his arms. "You're a tramp!" Jaime spoke the words with spit flying into the old woman's face.

"God should kill you; repent to me, Repent!" He began to lift the old lady and shake her. She closed her eyes and lifted her feeble arms to beat at his face. His hair fell over his eyes. The pillow dislodged from behind her head and fell into the confluence of arms and movement, and Jaime, like a rapid dog, thrashed now and covered Mrs. Ledbetter's face, pinning her body to the bed. At that moment, becoming the messenger of God, he quoted a hymn, one that he had played for so many invitations for sinners to repent at the end of services. But it was no longer a hymn but a chant in his frothing mouth.

> Just as I am - and waiting not
> To rid my soul of one dark blot,
> To Thee, whose blood can cleanse each spot,
> O Lamb of God, I come!

The old woman's hands clawed at the tops of his. He removed the pillow, and the old woman gasped for air, but spit filled her throat. He slapped her face, grabbed the old chin, and forced her pleading eyes to look at him. "God sent me for your confession. Pray to me, beg for forgiveness. The forgiveness a bitch like you doesn't deserve." He slammed the head back onto the bed. The old woman, terrified, shook her head. Tears ran down her face. She slapped at his arms that held her. The Dark Angel sang on:

> Just as I am - poor, wretched, blind;
> Sight, riches, healing of the mind,
> Yea, all I need in Thee to find,
> O Lamb of God, I come!

She clawed his face, and a drop of blood fell onto the white pillow. Jaime ripped his head back as her nail clawed the soft spot beside his nose. Enraged, he shoved the pillow over her head and held her back down to the bed. His arms felt strong, like his father's arms must feel.

Just as I am - Thou wilt receive,
Wilt welcome, pardon, cleanse, relieve.
Because Thy promise I believe,
O Lamb of God, I come!

Her struggle stopped. Jaime Skelton came back to himself when there was no resistance. "No, No, No." He removed the pillow and instantly saw the old woman looked a hundred years older. Her head lay back, her mouth wide open, her face contorted at a strange angle. He closed the mouth, and it fell open again. He tapped her face. He called for her. He even thought of pushing on her chest so that maybe she would begin to breathe again, but if she lived again, things would go wrong. He glanced behind him as if he could feel the oncoming inquiries. He looked back at the old woman, and she had not changed. He lifted her head and shoulders, returned the pillow. He saw the blood spot and moved it, so the blood appeared to have come from her nostrils. He started to close her eyes to give rest to the deceased but then thought that would be unnatural. He stepped back and straightened the bedding. He looked at the floor to see if he'd tracked anything into the room. The picture lay there on the floor. What should he do? He looked for another way to exit the room. His heart began to beat wildly. He felt dizzy, not that he had just taken a life, but that he was in a room with a woman that was not his wife, which was against the church policy. His heart began to beat in his ears; what mistakes could he be making now. He looked at his hands, checked his face in the mirror, and saw the panic all over himself. He thought quickly about crawling out the window. He could see himself crawling awkwardly from it, but how would he latch the window again? And what if someone noticed the awkward departure? "No, no, no, what would Daddy do?"

"No, I can't run. I got to control this." He would have to walk calmly, and if anyone saw him, he would act cheerful. He never looked back at the lady. He got to the door and used his shirt sleeve to operate the lever. He listened for a second, opened the door, and moved into the hallway. There were nurses with other patients, but he turned his head and hid his face. He began to walk fast and then remembered his casual pace. He began to count time just like he would for his piano students. One, two, three, and four... One, two, three, and four... The counting of measures lifted his gait. He almost felt free. "Somewhere over the rainbow, skies are blue, and the dreams that you dare to dream of really do come true."

He got to the cafeteria and, for some reason, casually extended his hand and touched one of the yellow hymnals lying on the edge of the piano.

"Mr. Skelton! Jaime Skelton?"

His heart stopped. His mind flashed images of bloody footprints leading down the hall to himself by the piano. The dirty yellow hymnal was an old woman's wrist. He turned slowly. His face felt flushed with blood. He could only hear a drum beat in his ears.

"I thought that was you! I guess I should say, Mr. Skelton, junior. You look like your Dad today; it must be the casual clothes." The woman who had helped with the podium on Tuesday stood smiling at him.

"Oh, ha-ha, my Saturday clothes, no suit Saturday. Oh gosh." Jaime Skelton looked intensely at her smile.

"Is everything okay," she said?

Jaime Skelton felt like a child learning to stand. He leaned against the upright piano for support. "Um…yes, yeah, I'm good. Now, how are you? Is the question," he refocused his attention on her like his father would.

"Oh, I'm hanging in there, working a double, so, you know, I'm a bit tired. Church tomorrow, though," she pointed her finger at Jaime. Was she accusing him? Jaime was coming unglued and starting to sweat. "Just surprised to see you here on a Saturday. Didn't hardly recognize you in your casual clothes. Are you visiting someone or just planning your father's service for next week?"

"Me?" Jaime pointed to himself. He smiled and then shook his head rapidly, "I don't, uh, I don't know anyone here." He shifted his weight and looked down at the hymnal in his cold, sweating hands. "Well, somehow, we took a few of these hymnals home with us. I just thought I would drive up and return them." He held out the book, and it was shaking.

"Well, that's no problem; we got so many; you could've just brought it back next time you were here." Jaime's ears burned with the sense of logic she had just delivered. "Yes, You're right." Was she on to him? Surely any minute, someone would realize that the old woman was dead. "It's, ah, just such a nice peaceful drive up here, and I guess I just needed some time, you know, to connect with God," he tapped the center of his beating chest. "Thought I'd just come by..."

"Well, you and your father are just the sweetest people. You know you're welcome here anytime. She reached for him and patted the hands that had just fulfilled the Death Angel's dream.

CHAPTER 8

"Come and See the works of God"

Finn woke up to the sound of Jon Joines making his way down the stairs and into the kitchen. The sound of the wood stove lid moving and a crumpled newspaper started a fire. Finn dreamed peacefully tucked in the covers, a small blanket and a heavy comforter. He didn't want to stop being there; he was safe, warm, and secure. He pictured Jon brewing coffee and opening the porch door to ease into his day, with the sun coming up, looking over his backyard, hearing the waterfall, tasting the strong coffee, and writing in his notebook.

Finn sat up in the bed and held himself up with his arms. Looking around the great room and then stealing a look upstairs to where Mrs. Elizabeth was still sleeping, he felt safe; no one was watching. He raised his arms above his head and let out a giant, silent yawn. Swinging his feet to the floor, took his clothes to the bathroom and changed. Coming back to the couch, he made it up exactly as he had seen Mrs. Elizabeth do. He spread his hand flat and moved it across the bedding to remove any wrinkles. He wanted Mrs. Elizabeth to come down and be impressed.

He picked up his work boots, which had been stowed neatly under the bed, and carried them to the kitchen with a finger in each.

He sat down at the booth and put them on. The fire in the stove had heated up the kitchen. He could hear it and visualize it burning in the dark space and illuminating it. He could smell the coffee on the stove, but it had not begun to brew or well up in the glass on top of the pot. The door was open to the porch, and he knew Jon would be there. He walked to the door and stopped, waiting for Jon to notice him and invite him out into his space. Jon was sitting at the table that was still drug out from the wall into the center of the porch from last night's dinner. The lanterns still hung from the eaves of the porch, sunlight starting to fill their hourglass globes. Jon was writing in his notepad in a chair that was turned towards the waterfall and the wooden walkways that crossed the backyard of moss-covered rock.

"Good morning," Jon said. "How did you sleep?" Finn took this as an invitation, moved on to the porch's wooden planks, and sat down in a chair across from Jon.

"Good. I had some nice dreams. How about you?"

"Like a fat baby, full of warm milk." "I've never heard that before!" "No? Come on now. I sleep like that every night except for the full moon."

"The full moon?"

The old man looked down at his notepad like he wanted to finish an idea before closing it. He was chewing the pen and crossed his leg. "Yeah, yeah." He closed the book and looked up. "Yeah, things can get pretty crazy around here on the full moon." He looked up at the trees and shielded his eyes from the rising sun. "There's a lot of history soaked into this soil, a lot of memories, a lot of heartaches, which is just a sign of a lot of happiness, you know, great grief is evidence of great love." He looked at the boy. "Crazy, no other way to say it, like this mountain chooses the full moon to bobsled the dead, past the living, down her slopes. It's strange; the trees moan, the earth shakes, and it's like the moon is just trying to appease her grieving children.

"Are you ever scared," the boy asked? The man looked at him. He had never talked about this before. The boy was turning a new page of his life that he didn't know existed.

"I often wonder if I'm in the way. It makes me feel very small and impertinent."

"How so," the boy looked at him in the sunlight. Jon just looked back but didn't seem to really see him.

"Oh, my coffee is bubbling over." He hopped up, and Finn followed him. Jon pulled the percolator from the stove, the coffee welling up inside the glass bubble on top and steam pouring from its sides.

"Good morning," Mrs. Elizabeth said as she met them in the kitchen in a silk robe, pajamas, and periwinkle slippers. Jon set two mugs on the counter. He put one spoon full of raw brown sugar, a little cream, and a dash of cinnamon in each coffee mug and stirred them. "I've never known you to burn a pot of coffee in my life. I could smell it all the way upstairs." She leaned over and placed a long, meaningful kiss on his neck and a squeeze around his waist.

"Good morning, dear. How'd you sleep?"

"Oh, it wasn't a dream," Mrs. Elizabeth said. "Here is my handsome son. I love you being here." Finn reached his arms around her neck without hesitation, placed his head on her shoulder, and hugged her. With a broad smile and an arm around him, she led Finn to the porch and sat down. Jon brought out her coffee and set it down carefully in front of her. They sat quietly, serene at the moment.

"Well, I can't stop crying these last few days." Mrs. Elizabeth took a cloth napkin and wiped her tears of joy. Finn felt like crying, but he just looked down at his hands, stood the hands up on his fingertips, and forced them down the legs of his jeans. "Finn, we need to get you some breakfast; how about some chocolate milk to get started, and then after we have our coffee and milk, I will make some breakfast for us?" Finn smiled and nodded to her, and

Elizabeth got up and went inside. She returned shortly with a glass of cold chocolate milk and then returned into the kitchen and began cooking over the wood cook stove.

Jon opened his notepad again, and Finn, feeling brave after hugging Elizabeth, stood up and looked over Jon's shoulder to the tablet. "What are you working on," Finn asked?

"Oh," Jon shook his head and flipped through the pages revealing small sketches and phrases. "These are just old man's doodles. Probably just proves I've taken leave of my senses." He closed the notepad and returned it to his chest pocket.

"Can you show me that staircase you mentioned last night, the one they took Skyuka up to the rest?"

"Sure, it's right there." Jon pointed across the yard along one of the slatted walkways to a set of stone steps almost hidden by the green vegetation of the mountain ferns, the rhododendron, and the mountain laurel.

Finn hurried across the wooden walkway to the steps. The stone looked worn and polished by thousands of feet moving up and down them. He touched the steps, and the edges were round and smooth, but the corners still resembled squared stone. Looking up and saw that the staircase continued, out of sight up the mountainside, weaving in and out of the ancient trees. Finn's fingers left moisture on the stone that showed in a dark fingerprint, and in front of his eyes, it disappeared; whether it sunk into the history tables of the stone or evaporated into the morning mist, he didn't know.

"Can I go up there?" Finn asked Jon returning to the table.

"After breakfast. You got a watch?"

"No. Those stones are so worn down like they were just gone over and over with a sander."

Jon smiled. "Yeah, makes you feel a bit small, doesn't it?" He returned to his notepad.

"Where does it go? I mean, where does it lead? Does it go to where we were last night, to Skyuka's Rest?"

"Yeah, yeah, it goes all the way up there, winds around, stops, turns, then keeps on climbing, but I don't want you going all the way up there today. We'll go up there sometime together."

The breakfast came. Toasted buttered English muffins and shredded trout fillets with dill and bathed in diluted lemon juice. On the side, there were red grapes and mild cheese. Finn had never seen a breakfast like this. "Tu veux un jus," Elizabeth asked? The boy thought for a moment. "Do I want juice?" "Qui," Elizabeth responded with a smile. "Qui, yes, please." Elizabeth returned with three small containers, one with orange juice, the second apple, and the third grapefruit. Finn was amazed, and Jon took turns enjoying all three with his coffee.

"The path goes to the upper pond," Jon said as he ate. "You can go up there and walk around. You'll see where the standpipe comes out of the back of the dam, and water flows down beside the staircase for a good while."

"Where does all the water end up?" Jon was bathed in the sun, reflecting off his white cotton shirt and through the lenses of his reading glasses.

"Some of it comes down into the pond, over there, beside the fountain, see where it's green and wet, that's Gravity doing its job. There's an artesian well in the center of this mountain. Which is very rare. You know most water runs off mountains, yet this mountain has water bubbling up inside it. Even in the worst droughts, I've never seen that fountain stop running; it just flows. It doesn't give any thought to how much it flows or how much the people that have lived here need it to flow. It just flows.

Finn turned his chair to focus on the fountain. "Is there a secret entrance?" He imagined the chambers of the underground space and the stalactites and stalagmites that would encroach on the waters. " There's more than a few secrets here."

"Like Moses, leading the children of Israel out of Egypt when he struck the rock and water poured out of it. Do you know that story?" Jon wiped his mouth and looked at the boy.

"Why did Moses strike the rock?" Jon asked.

"Because he was mad, he felt he wasn't appreciated."

"He had to strike it? Was it God's intention for him to beat it, to produce a result?"

Finn raised his eyebrows, stretched his hands down the legs of his jeans towards the fountain, and looked over at the old man, who was giving him all his attention. He was thinking before answering. "No, you are right. God told Moses to speak to the rock and water would flow from it, but Moses struck it with his rod. I reckon he felt powerful like he could control it and, in that way, control God's words. Like in his mind, he was God, and the people needed him to reach God, so he could tell them when to drink. Now that I think about it, out loud, Moses saw himself as able to feed or not feed these people. Like in a way, they needed to worship him, their preacher, to worship God." Jon sat quietly, watching Finn. "So, Moses hit the rock, even though God told him to just speak to it. But, I guess, it doesn't matter, it was just a dumb rock, it couldn't feel anything, it doesn't have a soul."

Jon pushed back his chair and leaned forward, his elbows on his knees. " I don't think one person should beat anything in nature. Control is not love." Finn looked over. "Preacher Skelton says only a person that has given their heart to Jesus has a soul."

"That's why he's always hunting and stuff because animals don't have souls. Now that I think of it, he's constantly hitting his cows in the face because they don't mind. They make him mad." " I don't know, Finn. Sounds like a deeper problem to me."

"I'm familiar with the story you're talking about. There were two instances with the stone. Another part of the Bible talks about the story, saying the rock was Christ. I've often thought about how God could take the shape of a stone just to be close to his people. Imagine the children of Israel thirsty and coming to the rock for water. Imagine them touching the stone, praising it, kneeling before it, and being replenished. And the whole time, they were in the presence of their God. Do you think anyone stopped to consider that? Moses didn't; their preacher, as you say.

"What about you?" "What about me, Finn?"

"You got all this equipment that you push over trees, move rocks, and build roads with. You got the sawmill where you take trees and cut them up into boards, and you built this house out of them."

"Let me ask you a question, Finn. Have you ever written a poem, drawn a picture, or made a gift for someone you were really proud of, something that moved you?" Finn nodded his head. "And when you showed this gift to the person, did it move them?"

Finn thought back and remembered a time. "Yes, I made a birthday gift for my Mother, my real mother."

"What did you use to make the gift for your Mother?"

"I took a piece of wood, and I cut the wood, then sanded it down smooth, then I took paint and painted it, and I wrote her name in another color of paint, across the front, and I put nails in it, like three nails, in it, across the front, so she could hang her necklaces and jewelry from it." He held up his hands to show the size of it.

"And when you gave it to your Mother, did she love it?"

"Yeah, she loved it; it was special to her and me."

"You used a piece of wood to make that?" The boy nodded, thinking of how he had taken the piece of wood he found, scraped away the dirt, cut it with the hand saw, and rounded the edges with sandpaper.

"Finn, I've always thought that nature had its own life force, whether it be wood or stone, mountain roads or paints or oils. If someone had good intentions, his life force would communicate with that life force and decide to work together or not. The world is a human being with the same rights. The Cherokee never felt that they owned this land. They saw themselves living on it and respecting it. That everything they harvested from it sustained them, and their refuse returned, and even their own bodies would return to it one day. The English felt like they owned the land. They began to mine it, clear-cut it. That control mentality ruins the ground and, ultimately, its inhabitants."

" I found a stray kitten once. I got low to the ground and whispered to it. At first, it was leary of me, but soon it started purring and rubbing itself against me. You're saying that nature can feel like that. It was my favorite companion."

Jon smiled. " In French, we call a pet - animal de compagnie." " Animal companion?" " Yes, that's right. I like that better. Pet implies ownership, but animal companion is a relationship of mutual care.

"I guess what I'm trying to say is that when someone with good intentions approaches another being in nature in the right way, the collaboration can be art, another creation in the world that everyone finds useful and sees beauty in. Does that make sense?" Finn slid back in his chair. "Like a painter goes out here to the mountains and sits down to paint the picture, but if the picture doesn't want to be painted, it just doesn't work. Or if a sculptor of stone wants to create a great sculpture, but the stone doesn't want to be changed, and if he tries and forces it to change, then it turns out to be deformed, may even break itself or the sculptor. Some stones are soaked in blood. They've seen so much trauma, people killed, tribes massacred. They don't trust mankind. If a man tries to change them, then they resist." "You mean they fight back?" "I think its Free Will."

Finn rested his elbows on his knees. "One time, I wanted to write a poem for my mother, and I thought really hard about words that would rhyme and sound good, and I gave it to her and she read it like it was something from school, but another time I just had been thinking about how much I loved her and couldn't wait to see her and I wrote down these words that came to my mind, and I gave it to her and she cried and hugged me and put it by her bed."

Jon nodded. "Yes, when we take ourselves out of the creating and let the spirit of the creation speak, it becomes true art."

Finn, getting the point the old man was making, said, "Like if the painter just had to paint a picture, but there was no love in it, it would just turn out to be painted on a page, something that was maybe recognizable to someone local but not something that everyone in the world would be moved by." "Yes," Jon said. "Truth is the universal language of every heart."

"Man's attempt to control nature is represented by straight lines. Just look at the houses we build and the skyscrapers. The highways, the bridges, the dams. But nature is not straight lines; it's circles and radiuses, intertwined, a drop of rain, the cresting wave of the ocean, the moon, the breeze. Items like boats and airplanes. They all have rounded features, a sign that man is working with nature to achieve a common goal. Straight lines break under pressure; circles just become stronger. That's why Moses struck the rock with his rod, which was straight, instead of using his voice. He wanted to control nature, but the rock was round and only needed to be spoken to. That's why so many people live in frustration because they have a definite plan for their lives, but our lives are not straight lines. Our bodies are not straight lines. Our souls, our minds, and our emotions, they are constantly changing. In my opinion, the path to God is not straight and narrow but very broad and accommodating.

Finn sat back in the wooden chair and looked around. The world was now completely different because, at a glance, he could tell if something was natural or manmade. He could see attempts to work with nature and where a man was forcing his will upon nature. He wanted to look at art now. He wanted to read now. It was like he spoke a new language, an international language that let him understand the world and interpret every part of the world in a new way. "Does that mean a letter or book could be that same way?" " Yes, written or spoken words are very powerful."

" I think God is in all things, and all things are made up of God. That's just how Elizabeth and I have always lived our lives. Some trees want to be formed into houses, furniture, or paper for books and learning. I see places on the mountain that it wants to let itself be shaped into a road so people can enjoy the views that the mountain sees every day. Michelangelo said he could see the sculpture inside the stone before he ever started carving. He also said he could see the depiction of the Sistine chapel before painting it. Nature speaks to people, who slow down enough to touch it, communicate with it, and, most of all, respect it. It's not wrong to shape a piece of wood or stone; It is wrong to not respect or abuse it. The sculptor never strikes the stone out of malice. It would be like slapping the face of God."

Finn was again struck when the old man evoked the name of God as a stone. "How do you communicate with nature?"

"How do you communicate with God, Finn?"

"I talk to him. I think about him every morning that I wake up and every time I eat, and every time I see something beautiful. I'm thankful, my heart is thankful, and my soul is thankful. I'm thankful Jesus died on the cross to save my soul from hell."

Jon nodded slowly, listening as Finn poured out his love for God. "How do you think the cross felt against Jesus's back, Finn?"

Finn had never thought about this aspect of Jesus' crucifixion. He had always heard Preacher Skelton talk about the nails that pierced his hands, the crown of thorns driven into his head, the

Roman centurion's spear being thrust into his side, and a mix of water and blood pouring from the wound. He had never thought about the old, rugged cross touching the back of Christ. He did now. In his mind, he went back to when Jesus would have been laid down on the cross, his first place of rest in days, and how his racked and beaten body must have felt just to lay down. Even when the nails pierced his hands, they would have pinned him closer to the wood. The wood that would have been hard and cold but would have warmed with the touch of his skin would have protected his back and spine, the only place where no one could reach him now, all else being vulnerable. Alone, the cross, a piece of shaped wood, was his protector, his support, and at that time, his only source of comfort, his only connection to something familiar, his only connection to something akin to his soul. "You touch it, don't you?" he said.

Jon nodded his head. "Yes, you do; you touch it, and touching it makes you mindful of it."

"How?" Finn asked Jon, almost pleading for his heart desperately needed connection. "How can I touch nature?"

"With your feet, with hands, with eyes, with your mind, with your ears, with every breath, son." Finn felt so close to the old man now. This distant, odd being had become real to him. "I will show you; take off your boots." Finn looked at him like he was joking. "No, no, listen, take off your boots, alright? I will do it with you."

Jon got up from the table and stepped over to the old church pew that sat to the right of the porch door. He slipped off his work boots and socks one by one, revealing his pale feet. Finn pushed back the wooden chair from the breakfast table, untied the laces of his honey-colored boots, and pulled them off along with his socks. Jon rolled the cuffs of his pant legs up, and Finn followed suit. Jon walked to the edge of the patio and onto the wooden walkway, and Finn moved beside him. They looked at each other, and Jon stepped from the walkway onto the moss-covered granite of the backyard. Finn stepped too and could feel the soft moss warm in the morning sun press up into the arch of his feet. He could feel the cold stone beneath the moss, and he could feel how hard and how strong it was, and with each step, the strength of the rock seemed to travel up through his feet, up his legs, to his hips, as if the stone were part of his skeleton. Finn said, overwhelmed with the connection to the earth, "This is how giants must feel."

"You feel it? Good." Jon squatted down and laid his hands on the stone. Finn walked over, knelt on the stone, and put his hands on the granite, feeling its soul and the rough places of the rock connected to each of his fingerprints. He felt it recharging him like his battery cells were empty and the ancient rays of the sun, soaked up by the stone, were flowing like waves into his skin.

"I'm going to put my feet in the pond, but I think you should go check out the small pools of water over there, between the fountain and the pond. Go step into them and tell me what you see and feel." Finn walked slowly, barefooted, across the granite rocks, mindful now of each step as not wanting to hurt the being but wanting to learn from it and communicate with it. He stopped at the small pool edges, each not more than four feet around. Full of water to various depths and rounded shapes, their edges polished, smooth, just like the staircase steps. Finn thought back to the sketch of the Cherokee women washing clothes in front of the fountain and the children playing on the boulders with tiny sticks. Could this really be? That the edges of the pools were worn and shaped by the hands, feet, and clothes of the Cherokee for hundreds of years? Could his bare feet be stepping in the same places as their feet? Could he be sharing in a moment that was older than Christ? Older than what Preacher Skelton knew? Was this proof, alone, that the world was more than two thousand years old and hadn't started when Jesus was born?

Finn reached out his hand, touched the smooth sides of the pool, and found a lip towards the bottom that seemed as if it could have been the result of someone pushing, almost kneading bread in one direction over and over. He let his hands run over it, and his mind and eyes wandered about from clear pool to clear pool. How magical was this connection to ancient humanity? He looked over and saw Jon sitting on the pond's edge with his feet in the water. Finn walked over and sat beside him.

"What do you think?" Jon said.

"The pools are worn smooth, just like the steps."

Jon looked at him and smiled. "Yeah, humanity should not have to spend so much time figuring out things when so many have lived before us, yet everyone thinks they are the first son of Adam."

Finn was quiet now. Nature had just shown him tangible truth, and the Bible never had? "They weren't straight lines."

"What's that?"

"They weren't straight lines, the sides of the pools, they weren't straight lines. The fountain and this pond have been here for thousands of years. They are smooth with a lip at the end like people had washed clothes there for thousands of years. There are no straight lines; they are all signs of God."

"Everybody through with breakfast?" Finn turned from the pool and saw Elizabeth standing on the porch. She had dressed in slacks, a simple top, and another rope belt for the day. She slowly gathered the items off the table and laid them over her outstretched arm. Finn turned to Jon. "We better give her a hand; I don't want to break the house rules." Finn stood up.

"Hey," Jon said, holding out his hand. Finn reached over and helped Jon to his feet. "Thank you, sir. How about you go up the staircase and check things out, and I will help her clean up."

"Are you sure?" Jon nodded. "Can I go barefoot, or do I need my boots?"

"You can walk up the staircase barefooted, but if you go around the pond, you will want your boots." Finn rushed back to the porch to grab his boots.

"Where you headed, little fella?"

"Uh, Mr. . . . uh . . ."

"Try calling him Jon. I know it's hard for you. I'd call him Papa Jon or JJ, but he hates that, especially the JJ thing, so why not just try out Jon? He won't mind."

The boy looked up into her eyes. "Jon said I could go up the staircase to the pond."

"Oh, an adventure! To be a full Skyuka child, you need a little wardrobe change." Finn looked at her, not knowing exactly what she meant. She stepped to the church pew and took out a small rope. "How about this?" She wrapped the rope around his waist, testing the length, and then cut it. "How about you give me that belt, and I will hang on to it." Finn unbuckled his small leather belt with the bronco-busting cowboy on the buckle and handed it to her. And she looped the white cotton rope through his belt loops and tied it in front. Standing back up, she opened the top button of his shirt, and the tanned skin of Finn's chest was slightly revealed. "There you go, now you look at home up here." Finn smiled and hugged her and then took off towards the staircase.

Jon slowly walked to the porch and sat on the church pew to put his socks and boots back on. "Jon, I feel a little out of our depth here, like we need someone else to help, well, to help us answer some of Finn's questions. What do you think?" Jon said nothing, only contemplated what he had told the boy. " I was listening from inside. While I admire how you look at life, it may not be the right time for Finn. "To what? To think? These people are ruining this child's innocent perception of the World. I mean, isn't the purpose of childhood to be in awe of this wonderful World. The kid thinks that dinosaurs didn't exist. He thinks that's a lie because his preacher and family say the World is only two thousand years old and only started right before Jesus was born." " Calm down, Jon. We are just talking." " Yeah." He extended his legs forward on the deck. " It fires me up, Betts." " Listen to me for a second, Jon. Put yourself in his shoes. The only thing this child has any control over in his life is his attitude. He doesn't know from day to day if his Father will be alive. He doesn't know from week to week if he will ever see his real mother again. He doesn't know if he will sleep in his own bed or on some stranger's couch from day to day. Food and heat are on his mind, but they pale compared to his anxiety over his Father or if he will inherit this disease." " But Betts." " No, wait, Jon. That child goes to church three to four times a week. He says they pray over every meal and before bed each night. Jon, the only consistent thing that child has to hold on to, whether good or bad, is his faith in Jesus Christ." Jon looked at her, threw back his head, and then looked back at his boots, his lips forced together. "You're right, Betts. A loss of faith can be devastating at any age." The two sat, searching the yard as if it contained answers. " You know, he probably doesn't have much faith in what his parents say; hell, they haven't even called to check on him. He will probably be up here all summer. Yet he goes to that church, and they tell him that God has a plan that he does not forsake his children. If he found out that his Dad is suffering from Aids." " Oh, Jonny, don't even go there. His little mind and heart couldn't handle that. That's why I'm saying we must be careful and need help." " I get it now, Betts. Me telling him that this mountain is nearly a billion years old, and that the kingdom of God is within him may cause him needless stress." " Yes, Jonny. Even though I know there wouldn't be a better teacher for a boy than you." Jon looked over at her. The woman that would be a Grandmother if it would not have been for him insisting on not facing his fears. " Do you hate me?" " What? What did you say?" " For not having kids. I mean that time in Spain when I promised and then." " God Damn you, Jon." She held her hands and started to cry. " It's ancient history. Let it go. I love you. I love you. Can you hear me? Can you feel it?" She reached out her hand and laid it against his chest.

Jon took her hand and laid it on his heart. She could feel it beating. He started to speak, and she spread her fingers over his lips. "Jonny, I'm just scared, is all, and when I'm scared or uncertain, I lash out, and I always lash out at you because I know you won't leave me, and I know you'll always forgive me, and I know that's horrible that's not what a wife should do to her husband, especially, such a wonderful husband as you, I just feel like we need some help."

Jon kissed her lips and then again. " I get scared too. It makes me feel like what we have isn't enough. Like I've done my best, and there's still something I can't fix, and I can't make it right now." "There's nothing to fix, Jonny. I love our life. My heart finds comfort when I can just speak, and you hear me. Just hear me." He hugged her, and she drew into his embrace, the dish towel still in her fingers.

"We need Bobby, Jon."

"You are right; we need Bobby ." She held his hand like the moment had taken a lot out of them both, and they clung to each other to recharge. "The boy needs Bobby, and we need Bobby."

Elizabeth suddenly burst into tears. "Ruby, Ruby, Jon. Ruby, Ruby." She was whispering over and over through her hard sobs. Tears, too, filled Jon's eyes as he remembered their dear and lovely friend whose life had been stolen from them so long ago. Jon held Betts, picked up the dish towel to wipe his eyes, and then turned to Elizabeth. She wiped her eyes and then blew her nose on the cloth. She pulled her head out of the crook of Jon's neck and looked up at him. "Ruby . . . Ruby was the best of us, the best human I've ever known, Jon. My heart still aches after all these years. My heart could weep for days when I think of what they did to him. Oh, Jon, Oh Jonny, our Ruby."

CHAPTER 9

"Love is Patient, Love is Kind"

Family lore said Elizabeth was born in Baghdad, the Arab State city by the beautiful river, on a night when snow fell and covered the streets, and even the Mullahs of the town, realizing something remarkable had happened, stopped by to bless the child, and kissed their fingers and placed them on Elizabeth's head. They scribbled passages from the Quran and placed them in the hand of her father, and upon leaving, they blessed the house and the milk of the mother. The Mullahs did all of this without being asked because the home that Elizabeth was born in, beside the river, had a rose garden that was visited and loved by King Faysal, and the woman who owned this villa and the rose garden and the heart of the King was Elizabeth's godmother. Gertrude Bell doted on her godchild. Holding her, walking her close to her chest through the Arab night air, whispering to Elizabeth stories of the night she was born and how the snow had covered the old tracks of the mountain wolves. How the Mullahs, the holy men, recited verses of the Quran and kissed their fingers and touched her head, so undoubtedly, she was destined for greatness and romantic love. Gertrude had known and lost love, love that was wonderful and messy, but Elizabeth's love would not be cluttered. Her passion would not be in a time of war, her love would be different, and like always, Gertrude was right.

The only messy thing in Elizabeth's life now was that they had left the beautiful villa in the city she had always known. Now they were in a different country, oddly green, and her father, who had always been so strong and solid, had turned weak and diseased and in need of quieter hours, non-strenuous walks, cooler air, and things called rest cures which were no more than frequent long naps. How could a moist spot in her father's lung disrupt so much of their lives? How could a man who had carried a chest full of medals now only carry one small piece of glass that showed the inside of his chest, the heart one slight blur in this image? How could this vacancy in the image become the only thing to matter? Who could have known that it was not the number of medals on his chest but unseen tuberculosis that would measure her father's courage?

They had been sent to the Veterans Hospital, a Sanatorium outside Asheville, North Carolina. Elizabeth thought her diplomat father and his family would be given a cabin or at least private lodging on the facility grounds in line with his status, but upon arrival, they were shown to the common area, a long narrow porch with a row of one hundred beds. That is where they were expected to live, storing their lives in foot lockers, and exposed not only to the disease of other patients but also to the entire lives of everyone abiding the moist spots in their chest and sleeping side by side at night on the porch of the hospital. Only the terminally ill were taken indoors and separated from the general public to not bring down the morale of the non latent diseased.

This was not going to do for the family of three, so they moved from the hospital and down the mountain range to a place they had seen a postcard of. A place where the family had vacationed for a summer. They arrived at the Oak Hall Hotel in Tryon, North

Carolina, the summer Elizabeth turned sixteen. They stayed in the hotel for several weeks until they could rent a small house near town, and her father was treated by a local physician practicing at the Pine Crest Sanatorium.

Elizabeth became friends with the hotel's owner and was given a summer job there. Each day, she set up the dining room, cleaned windows, organized activities for the guests, greeted new arrivals, and lamented the leaving of people who had spent the whole season on the grounds. Spending so much time working there in the summer that she had her own room in the staff quarters and had become independent, which her godmother would have been very proud of if she were still living. Elizabeth had come to love the hotel, her new home, the mountain air, and the vistas so different from what she knew in the Middle East, Madagascar, Ceylon, and even London, France, and New York. This was a simpler life, where first names were not offensive after getting to know someone. A place where you could dress up and go dancing or dining in the small town or just as quickly hike Pearson's Falls or ride horseback to Glassy Mountain or Green River gorge. The friends that she made seemed quilted together and a genuine family. Her favorite part of her day was walking into town to check the mail along the winding road lined with tall trees, green ferns, and rhododendron at their base. Here she picked wildflowers and mountain laurel blossoms, and in the early spring, magnolia swags to decorate the dining room tables in the hotel.

"Good morning Mr. Bagsby; how are you today?" Elizabeth walked into the post office and over to the wood counter, where a gentleman not much taller than herself was sorting through postcards and pieces of mail in a blue and white apron. He turned and smiled at Elizabeth. "Morning, my dear, such a wonderful day for walking, and here, I have your mail. From the looks of all these reservations pouring in, it will be a hectic summer season for the hotel this year. Say, do they prepay for their lodging and meals, or do you just take it on good faith that they will arrive and arrive with cash?" The last word seemed to squash out of Pleasant Bagsby's gray mustache.

Elizabeth looked at the lovely, portly man with his hedgerow of hair around his ears, the back of his head, and his glasses resting proudly on top of his bald head. "Oh, I don't handle those things, just the flowers and activities. The owner takes care of all the reservations and billing. I just mainly do what I'm told. This reminds me. I was told to drop off this order for the sawmill. PMI Mill? Does that sound familiar? We are starting a renovation and going to add three cabins on the hotel property, so yes, I guess we will have a very busy season. So, do you know them, this PMI Mill?" Elizabeth tapped her lips with her forefinger.

"Oh, oh, those hard-shelled creatures, those chiseled thieves of hearts, the players, the jesters, yes, yes, my dear, I will take this and give it to them, oh what do they call themselves, the wolves, or is it the cougars, the panthers, I'd say it would be the toads, yes my dear, I will present it to the toads."

Elizabeth needed clarification. "This is where the sawmill does their correspondence?"

"My Dear Child of knowledge, everyone in this bleak, forsaken town does all their business here; just look at the board."

Elizabeth was turned by Pleasant Bagsby now, and he pointed to the post office walls covered in cork where people pinned advertisements and notices for any and everything. She walked to the wall looking the items over.

"It's like the town paper!"

"No child, the paper costs money to advertise in. This is just a good ole fashion protestant publication. Roman Catholics are decent enough to pay for publishing."

"So, you'll place the order with the sawmill?"

"Consider it done, Elizabeth."

Elizabeth took out two loaves of banana bread made in the hotel's kitchen and placed them on the counter. "These are for you for being so wonderful in teaching me all the things I need to know about my new home."

"Oh dear, you don't have to do that but thank you. And I hate to ask, but how's your father and Mother's health? Stronger, I hope. Did they get new scans?" It had become fashionable amongst patients to keep a glass image of the X-ray on their person at all times as if one could remove it from a purse or pocket and check the progress of the dark spots of infection on their lungs. In actuality, it just reminded them that it was there, and until it was no longer there, time was still; it had lost its meaning.

"They are doing okay. They take several walks each day and continually monitor their temperatures; they've made friends, at least people they speak to on their walks. Their time needed for healing has been extended another six months, and surprisingly they seem very okay with that, like they've come to enjoy the routine of temperature recording, walks, rest cures, and meals in between."

"Good, my dear, give them my very best when you see them." Pleasant was sincere.

Elizabeth gathered her items to leave as a young man, tall and thin with blonde hair and piercing blue eyes, opened the door and walked into the post office. He was wearing a blue shirt that buttoned in front and open about the neck, revealing skin tanned from working in the sun. Brown leather boots and grey workman's pants, with suspenders running over the handsome young man's shoulders. She took him all in, and he, looking up, met her gaze as she passed him. He kept staring. As Elizabeth approached the door, it swung open, and two dark-skinned, very handsome young men entered, talking to each other. They were beautiful in their features and demeanors and reminded her of the Massai warriors she had seen with her father in Africa. They were tall and imposing with wide cheekbones and intentional eyes. They smiled at her, revealing perfect teeth. They were dressed similarly to the man that had entered just before. They said hello, and she excused herself, and then she said thank you and slipped away.

"Jon, Jon, hello Jon," Pleasant Bagsby said.

Jon was still watching the figure of the girl that had walked past him and his brothers. He turned and looked at the mail clerk. "Pleasant," Jon said, "did you miss me, old man?"

"Oh, of course, stayed up all night crying, wondering when I would see you again." Bagsby rolled his eyes and grasped his chest as if losing his wayward heart to Jon Joines's handsome face. "Oh good, thank god, the sensible ones are here too," Pleasant stretched out his hands and motioned for the other two men to come closer. "Ruby Fry and Bobby Gunn, I have been waiting to see you two. Listen, I want to hire you to play the music for a couple of garden parties this spring."

Jon turned from the counter, walked over to the post office window, and looked down the sidewalk to see if he could see the girl with the wicker basket. He had never seen her before and was curious for some reason; there was something in her way, as if he had come close to his star that would guide him through the rest of his life. He stood watching for some time but, not seeing her, turned back into the store.

"So, my gentleman, the invitations will go out today if that works for your schedule? Good, we agreed. And you will bring all your instruments and be prepared for whatever mood the party takes? Cello, violin, guitars, drums, the gambit?"

"Indeed, indeed, Pleasant, we will bring everything, and we will have a great time!" Bobby said, always the sensible leader of the three. "Jon, hello. If you have to come to the party, will you please

THE BOOK OF SAY

clean up? Wash the sawdust and earth from yourself, maybe comb that swath of hair? Do you own a clean shirt?" Jon glazed his eyes over, dismissing the jabs of Bagsby. Bobby and Ruby laughed and turned to walk away. "Oh, before I forget, this order came for you from the Hotel. It seems they're going to add some cabins on the property. Looks like an order for timber to be delivered."

Jon looked down at the note. It was customary that when people needed something from the Sawmill, they would either leave a message at the Post office or the Hardware store in town. Both places served as a community communication hub, but the central hub of gossip was Pleasant Bagsby. "Appreciate it, Pleasant, say do you know . . ." Jon thought better of asking the gossiper who the girl was. He certainly knew that Pleasant knew who she was, but he didn't need the whole community to know he was asking. "Never mind, we will get on it as soon as possible."

"How's your old man Jonny?" "He's not my Old man Pleasant, and you know that." Jon turned and stepped back to the counter, frowning.

"Well, he took you, boys, out of that orphanage and gave you a place to live, didn't he?"

"Yeah, he did that, Pleasant, but it wasn't some family other than the three of us. He needed hands to run the mill so he could disappear in the holler and make his moonshine. To answer your question, we haven't seen him in a while."

"Is he going to sell you that Mill, Jon?" Jon turned back to the counter again; he liked Bagsby and knew his wife and kids, but he didn't like this part of Bagsby, the man who pried into lives, this part of him that could not hold back the questions burning in his brain.

"I don't know," Jon replied.

"Maybe the whole mountain?"

Bagsby was pushing now. "I don't know, Bagsby." Bobby and Ruby had slipped out the door and were waiting by the yellow sawmill truck. It was just Jon and Bagsby in the post office.

"What would it take to buy the sawmill, maybe the mountain, Jon? A gold mine?

Jon looked into Bagsby's eyes now. "Why are you asking?"

"Just wondering, Jon, that's all. Say, did you ever find that gold? The Jug factory legend people always talk about?"

"I'm sure you've had your brothers, as you call them, running all over those hills and streams trying to find that old Cherokee place. Did you find it, you, and your Panthers, find that confederate gold?" "Say?" Jon looked back from the door, Bagsby had gone too far, and Jon could feel the disgust turning over in his stomach. He hated when people asked him questions that he didn't want to answer. "Sure, we found it, Bagsby. That's why we are still covered in sawdust and sleeping like orphans in the sheds around the mill." Jon took the order for lumber and left the office. There was a poster pinned beside the door of an Uncle Sam in a top hat and pointing a finger. The caption on the sign said, "I want you! Enlist now."

Bobby and Ruby were sitting in the back of the truck; they had purchased bread and a small bag of groceries and were waiting for Jon in the pre-dusk light. They all got in the small cab of the truck, with Bobby, the largest of the three, in the middle. As they drove up the steep grade of the mountain, they talked and laughed, and Bobby pulled out a harmonica and began to play. Ruby tapped his thighs and places around the truck as if playing a drum set inside the cab. And then Ruby began to sing, opening his mouth and letting something deep inside his soul push out, something that was alive and crystal clear. Jon turned the sawmill truck at the top of the steep grade onto a narrow dirt road, and as they turned, Bobby's hand reached out and rested on the leg of Ruby to steady himself. The sun was setting, pink and purple, on the tops of the evergreen trees. Jon leaned over and turned the lights of the truck on. The road in front of them illuminated dimly. It was getting darker by the minute, and reflecting eyes could be seen crossing the road, going up the bank, and into the ancient trees. Ruby was humming softly, and Bobby was harmonizing with his notes. Jon couldn't stop thinking of the girl in the post office, something he felt when he first saw her; he wondered if she felt it too. Why was Bagsby prying into his life? Ask him about what he was reading, MiddleMarch, ask him about swimming in the Pacolet River, but don't ask him about himself. And what about this war? Would he and his brothers enlist?

Bobby's hand was still on the knee of Ruby, and Rueben had moved his hand up in the darkness, taken Bobby's hand, and held it rubbing the large, calloused knuckles. The two had been inseparable from when they first met in the orphanage in Tryon. "Bagsby asking about Paul?" Jon slowly nodded his head. "Reckon he knows that he been gone?" Jon pursed his lips and looked harder into the night. "Gone? I expect him to show up in these in headlights." He looked over at Bobby. "Just as drunk and as dirty as the day he came to town and adopted us. He will someday stumble out of the woods, one day, and need help again." Ruby squeezed Bobby's hand. Bobby forced the memory out of his nostrils, looking over the hood of the work truck. "What if the town folk say we killed him?" Ruby shook his head up and down as if what Bobby was saying had been on his mind too. "Won't be no New Orleans," Ruby whispered. "We didn't kill anybody. The fool was drunk running those steels. He'd go to town once a year and buy copper line and yeast." Jon lifted his hand from the steering wheel. "Listen, he taught us to run this mill, and we have. Hell, we've made it better. If we just keep our heads down. Keep going into town and picking up orders and doing business, then everyone will forget about Paul Taylor." "Bagsby ain't forgettin', Jon. Ruby and I have plans, music plans, for New Orleans. Ruby's going to be famous one day." " Both of us, Bobby, going to be both of us, got to be both of us. Can't nothing tear us apart." So it had been since the first day at the orphanage, they had instantly gone and stood beside each other, undressed, opened their mouths, raised their arms, and been prodded and poked by the staff. The strangers going over their hair, looking for lice with wooden combs. That night they slept beside each other in the same bed because there was no extra room, but as they grew, they continued their lives together, inseparable, their ears stuck to the same radio. Their hands tapped along to the same beat, one finding an instrument and teaching the other the chords he had just learned. Now, as young men still sharing each life's treasures with the other, mending each other's clothes like it was his own, harmonizing the notes of life so the other's voice would be the more beautiful, the clearer, and still they shared the same bed, they made the same bed, they held each other's heads and cares, and hands, and hearts. "Bagsby just needs a piece. We just don't know what piece that is yet."

They came to the large grass meadow, and the Sawmill could be seen in the headlights. The moon was a pale sliver in a cloudless sky, and the mountain seemed to be basking in the radiance of a lover's gaze. They had come to the mountain around the same age, in their early to middle teens. A skinny, dirty man named Paul Taylor went to the orphanage to pick up Jon, who he had been told was his sister's only child. He didn't want the kid or have time for a kid, but he needed help in his Sawmill, and he thought it may be a way to get free labor. So, he drove down the mountain and went to the orphanage to look the kid over. He could always just say that there was a mistake. His sister had never had a kid, especially some Cherokee bastard, but when he got there, he noticed that Jon's eyes were clear, he seemed strong for his age, and he had two friends. He leaned close to their faces. "Well, if it ain't two colored boys, huh?" Paul knew they could become a whole team, like the horses he used pulling timber from the slopes and deep forest of the mountain. He circled the boys, made them talk off their shirts, pulled and whipped their flanks, gripped their muscles and calves, squeezed their cheeks and looked at their teeth and smelt their breath, and decided he could use the stock. So, loaded them and their few belongings in the truck, drove through the town without needing anything else, and started the steep ascent up the mountain to the boy's new home. Jon had brought his few clothes and the books he had managed to borrow. Bobby had got his clothes, a wool hat, a threadbare jacket a harmonica he had been given from the Salvation Army at Christmas. Rueben, the smaller of the three, brought his clothes, an extra pair of boots that he would grow into, a dulcimer that had once been destroyed and thrown out, but Bobby had put it back together with wire and tack nails, and a small brown bottle he blew across to make rhythmic sounds. They were naturally scared, not knowing what to expect of this strange man who lived on a mountain and treated them like cattle. They reached out, with their backs against the headboard of the flatbed truck, and grasped the wooden sides, and sometimes they reached and steadied themselves against the shoulders of one another, carefully protecting their belongings.

Now, pulling up to the Sawmill in the moonlight, things were much different. They were no longer scared boys but men, men who had grown in stature and mind and respect for each other and men that had made the Sawmill thrive and turned the top floor of the barn into their home. Paul Taylor had been a drunkard, and as the boys grew, he had spent more and more time drinking, laying in the drying shed, in his vomit and piss, his hair stringy and his clothes mildewed. One day he was just gone, the boys looked for vultures circling over a dead carcass, but they found none. They walked to the top of the mountain and looked out and down, but there was no Paul like he had disappeared into the underground; a tomb had opened in the mountain and swallowed him. Paul's ancestors had been proponents and instigators in resettling the Cherokee Nation to Oklahoma because they wanted to buy the land, the great hunting ground of the Cherokee, and so they did, piece by piece, as the Cherokee were forced to sell, they bought the whole mountain for not much more than horses and grain. Now Paul was gone, the only heir being Jon, but how would anyone believe the three orphans if they showed up in town saying that Paul, the dirty, drunk, and yet the wealthiest landowner in the county, was dead? The boys talked it over. There was a good chance that Paul was just drunk somewhere or had gone somewhere to stay drunk and would turn up one day. However, there was a certainty that if they went into town and claimed Paul was dead, they would be back in the orphanage or, worst, convicted of his murder. In the years they had been on the mountain, they had learned the wood trade, how to run the mill, select timber, and fix things when they went wrong. They could keep things going. They just needed to go to town regularly, communicate with the customers, and keep people off the mountain. If anyone did show up on the mountain, they would tell them that Paul was in the valley looking for mulberry and should be back in a few days.

The boys had turned the back room of the Sawmill into a woodworking shop where they would make custom furniture for customers and where Bobby and Ruby made instruments for themselves. With clamps and glues, and a box for steaming, they shaped and molded wood for the intricate sound boxes and inlays for their items. Ruby picked up the guitar strap Bobby made for him as a present from the small desk in the corner of the woodworking shop. It was tanned cordovan leather with white inlays that said "Ruby" down the front.

"How's it look, Ruby?" Bobby said. "Want anything added?"

"I like the sparkles; they're going to reflect off the stage lamps when we get to New Orleans." He smiled into Bobby's face.

"Big dreamer you are, New Orleans and all, maybe Chicago."

"Yes, indeed, all we have to do is get on the train." He leaned over and looked at Bobby's reflection in the small mirror.

"It ain't time just yet," Bobby replied. "This war and all, we got to think about that."

"Bobby, what are they going to let a couple of colored boys like us do in some war? Wash some Lieutenant's underwear, peel his potatoes?"

"Jonny, need us here too, Ruby. We can't up and leave; we got to do this with him, and we can." The boys had taken the barn's loft and turned it into a lovely home for themselves. They milled wood planks along the wall vertically, and thinner slats covered the seams. They had inset windows into the tin roof and boxed them out into eaves. They had two wood stoves, two bedrooms, a bathroom, a kitchen with a soapstone sink, an ice box, and a walnut table made of wide slabs. The floor was heart of pine planks that had been sanded and oiled, and there were lanterns with light yellow shades that hung from the center of the ceiling and smaller ones that pulled out from the wall for reading or washing dishes. There was a set of built-in bookcases for Jon, and he constantly rotated the books on shelves that he thought would be to their liking. He never forced them to read, just as they never forced him to play or sing, but out of their love for each other, they both meddled in each other's hobbies. Jon had learned to play guitar and banjo, and Rudy had taught him a baritone note for a song they would all perform together. A staircase was in one corner of the loft, and at the bottom of it was a landing where they all kept their coats, boots, and hats. There was a small door and washroom where they kept their dirty clothes, each man stripping here and going up the stairs in his undergarments when ready to bathe or be done with work for the evening. The three never spoke about God, but Bobby and Ruby did play music and sing at a church every Sunday. Jon would join them because Sundays were a nice day to spend in town and meet and talk to people, and his brother's popularity grew because everyone came to hear their harmony and the songs; most everyone mistook the God-given love in their voices for each other as just talent given from God.

"What's this garden party that Pleasant's got you and Ruby playing for?"

"Oh, you know Pleasant; if he can't have a green thumb, then he'll settle for a finger in everything, Bobby responded. Those two ladies moved down here from up North; they bought that house off of Trade St. Had all those masons and landscapers come in and been working there since time immemorial. I guess they finally got it done. I bet it is going to be nice. I guess Bagsby will want us to use the truck and move tents and tables over there the day before. He gave you some big order for the Hotel today?"

"Yeah, he sure did. I guess they're renovating and adding three new cabins on the property. We've got some of the stuff in stock, but we will have to keep going back and forth as we cut it. Guess we can load up what we have and deliver tomorrow or the next day. It's been a long enough day. I'm going to take a bath and turn in. Good night Bobby, Good night Ruby," Ruby was playing softly beside the wood stove of the loft, his old wire-held, patched dulcimer hung on the wall of the loft like a reminder of where he had come from.

Jon bathed, got into bed, and began to read a translated book of poetry that had been done after an English woman who had lost her lover on service to the Middle East. Translating the poems her lover had read to her in Arabic was her way of coping with her grief. In his bed, with the lantern pulled out from the wall, Jon read and reread the lines like it was a timeless truth. It filled him and comforted him like the mother he never really knew might have.

The yellow sawmill truck rumbled over the gravel river road to the Oak Hall Hotel carrying wood meant for the floor joists of the new cabins stacked neatly under a canvas tarp. The road was broad with a slight grade and a large canopy of trees overhead. There were spaces along the road where the river could be seen, tranquil in some places and deep and cascading in others. Jon, who was driving the truck, was lost in thought. Bobby was sitting in the middle, and Ruby was by the window humming a tune that no one knew, not even him.

Jon's attention was called back to the road when he saw a tall female figure walking a bicycle with a wicker basket attached to the front. He kept studying her as the truck rumbled closer, and he realized with great surprise that it was the girl he had passed in the post office. He watched her pass the truck, their eyes locked again, and his head turned to follow her, and then he stuck his head outside the cab and closer to the side mirror to continue watching her. Jon suddenly turned, realizing he was driving, but Bobby was guiding the vehicle.

"Did, did you see her?" Jon asked for confirmation that the vision that had just passed him wasn't a dream. He looked in the mirror again and could barely catch the outline of her as she was fading into the horizon. "Did you see her?" Jon raised his thumb, pointing back over his shoulder. Bobby and Ruby nodded, smiling.

"I've seen you flirt with girls, but never seen one just come and steal your lunch like that," Ruby said.

"Who is she?" Jon said, looking back in the mirror for answers. He turned and looked into the faces of his brothers. "She is beautiful!"

They delivered the wood to the hotel, and Jon walked around the white structure with the green and white awnings up the steps and across the wood porch to the front office. He was hoping that enough time had passed that the girl he saw would have returned to her nest, but not finding her, he was stalling in hopes that she would return. "No need to pay us today, Mam. I can stop back by another time."

"Pleasant, you really giving us these suits?" The Tailor was about finished hemming Jon's pants.

"What's that, JJ? Can't hear you, JJ; I'm in the back stacking boxes." Bobby and Ruby looked at each other and laughed.

"The name is Jon, and why are you giving us these suits? There's got to be a catch, and I want to make sure they're not going to be deducted from our pay; that's all I'm saying."

"Well, J, a man like me learns to leave very little to chance. I only need to buy two suits for these two wonderful musicians. I need you around in case something goes wrong, the lights go out, or an ice sculpture falls over." Pleasant thought to himself for a moment. "Who did Gatsby get for that kind of stuff? Oh, you're my Nick Carraway!" With his glasses pushed atop his head, he pointed to Jon standing in front of the full-length mirror in a black suit and white shirt. "So, JJ, I need you clean, kind, and eat before you come; that's the price you pay for the suit."

On the night of the garden party, held at the home of two ladies on Glenwalden Circle, the brothers were greeted by the sight of acres of gardens and terraced walls with small footpaths, staircases, various fountains, fishponds, and pools. The guests were greeted by valets, and the vehicles were ushered off to a large open area on the property. They approached the house by one of two stone staircases that flanked either side of the front garden. The staircases progressed in a series of landings, and from each landing, Jon looked over the garden lit by candles floating in the ponds and lanterns hanging overhead from the giant trees.

A large white tent was set up on the back lawn of St. Augustine grass. Two crystal chandeliers were hanging above a long table adorned in a silk cloth, with silver vases and garden flowers spilling out of them, nearly touching the table. Ruby and Bobby, dressed in their black suits and white shirts, played on a stone landing. Ruby played the cello, and Bobby played the violin. Both turned slightly on wooden stools as if they were playing for each other and to one another. Jon had the job of guarding a pyramid of champagne glasses erected on a nearby table. The glasses were mostly filled, and Jon was supposed to saber a bottle of champagne with a sword that Bagsby provided at the appropriate time. He would promptly hand the bottle up to Bagsby, standing on a ladder near the top of the pyramid. Bagsby would then fill the top glass of champagne, causing a cascade down the pyramid.

When the moment came, Bagsby gave everyone the sign and ascended the fabric-incased ladder to the top of the pyramid. He welcomed all the Tryon Garden Club to the evening's festivities. Looking down, he winked at Jon, who, on cue, stepped forward, twirled the silver saber blade in the air, and made sure it reflected the light across the entire tent so everyone inside and outside could see. He thrust the champagne bottle forward and held it to the light to find the glass bottle seam. He then made a show of the blade of the saber running up and down the seam to the cork of the champagne. Satisfied, he had found the right spot, he lifted it slightly and looked down the seam, but this time his eyes did not focus on the cork but on the girl from the post office, who had just stepped under the tent and was radiant in an off shoulder dress and her hair up on her head.

Jon's mind was taken, but his body was in the motion of sabering the cork. It seemed time stood still as the angel he had been searching for suddenly appeared. At the exact moment, his body was in motion to saber the cork; his heart was in action to call out and run to her. So as the silver saber lifted, it fell behind his necktie, and it looked as if Jon was trying to fling himself across the room. He missed the cork entirely, managing only to cut the end of his black tie off, which completed an arc through the air, landing promptly on the grass in the middle of the tent. The movement had propelled Jon forward as if he had drunk all the bottles of champagne it had taken to fill the glass pyramid.

Jon saw the girl giggle and then cover her mouth with a small kerchief. He picked up the saber and tried to smooth out his tie but couldn't with the sword in one hand and the still unopened bottle of champagne in the other. He looked up at Bagsby, and Bagsby returned the gaze, lowered his arm and chin, and said, "JJ?"

Jon reassured, stood back, found the seam, and with great determination and half of a black tie gone, he sabered the champagne bottle and lifted it up amongst the crowd's cheers to a waiting Bagsby. Jon, embarrassed, left the outdoor room and walked away from the sound of music in the air. He stood on a terrace, looking down over the garden, with his back to the house, and the tent, wondering how in the world he could have made such a fool of himself. How long would it take for the party to be over, and they could get back in the truck and head up the mountain and just forget about the night and the girl.

"It's a lovely garden." Jon turned, and his heart stopped. It was her in the glow of the garden light. "I hope I'm not bothering you. I just hoped to see more of the garden and less champagne." Jon was off guard and didn't know what to say. She pointed to his tie and smiled sheepishly. "Nice."

Jon looked at her and smiled, or maybe he had always been smiling, but now he caught his breath, "Yeah, I guess you saw that?" Jon tucked the ragged garment inside his suit jacket. "Masterful performance. Did you practice much?"

"Hours, could you tell?" Jon said. "Are you hiding out here?" Jon looked over the garden and then at her. " I guess I was." Elizabeth turned her curious head. "And what are you now?" Jon looked down at his dress shoes and smiled. " Well, right now, I feel rather found." Elizabeth looked over, and her broad smile covered Jon's anticipating face. " May I show you the garden?" Jon asked.

"I'd love that; it seems my company is enjoying herself immensely; anyway, I will not be missed."

Jon looked back in the direction of the tent. "My name is Jon, by the way," his heart was beating wildly, but he was controlling it;

she did not respond, only took the information in. "Have you ever seen a garden like this, all lit up at night with music playing and candles glowing?"

She walked to the limestone balustrade and looked out over the garden. "Yes, I was raised in a garden like this, by the river, in my old home."

"Was that here?"

"No, no, it was on the other side of the World, in what now seems like a fairy tale, like a different life." Elizabeth turned and looked into his eyes and saw her own soul in the reflection.

"Well, If I promise to give you my full attention. Will you promise to enchant me with the story of your life?"

CHAPTER 10

"Perfect Love Cast Out All Fear"

"Hey Bobby, It's Elizabeth. I didn't know whether to call your house or your office at the church, so I left a message on both. You got plans for dinner? We have a young man staying with us, hopefully for a while, but we wanted you to meet him. I think it would be good for all of us. He's special. Just come up if you get a chance; we'll be around. Love you." Elizabeth hung up the phone. She thought about the boy and Jon in the backyard with their shoes off. Standing at the kitchen door, watching them and hearing their soft voices spilling over the yard. Her heart was heavy now for many reasons, yet some reason was more significant than the others, but she couldn't figure out what that was. It was just there, like a great sadness.

She wasn't remorseful; for not having a child. She couldn't have asked for a more meaningful life or spent it differently. It just seemed like something was coming that would change her life, and she didn't want it to change; she loved every bit of how it was today. It was like she realized that this moment was precious, yet she didn't need to spend it with anyone. She didn't need to tie the moment down or write her thoughts to remember it. She didn't need a cup of tea to make it better or listen to her favorite song. It was perfect.

It was perfect, with her sitting in the breakfast booth and looking around the small kitchen. Taking in all she had seen and all that had been so familiar for so long. It seemed that she noticed all the glasses on the shelf individually, and the fabric curtain that hung under the counter was swaying. She wanted to walk into the great room, look back at the old pictures of her Mom and Dad, and touch the jewelry her mother had left her.

She wanted to spend some time in her mind just remembering the small moments, what it felt like to hold Jon's hand while he was sleeping or blow a kiss through the Queen Anne's lace and watch the petals scatter. What it felt like to lay on the rug in the vineyard and to run her fingers through its stitching. She wanted to hug Bobby again and smell his cologne. To hunt for four-leaf clovers or to peel an orange and see the mist of the peel cover the tips of her fingers. She closed her eyes and could hear Ruby singing while showering outdoors under the fountain. This boy had become the angel of her night season. She looked down at the phone cable plugged into the wall and thought of unplugging it. If the phone couldn't ring, no one would come to take Finn away. He was supposed to have left a week ago, but no one had come to retrieve him, and no one had even called to check on him.

Jon went to the sawmill. It had always been his retreat when thinking or stressed. Going there was like walking back into the past and seeing if you mistakenly left something behind. His roots were stuffed away in boxes or on bookshelves. Some of the items were personal to him, and some things were unique to him and Betts, though she didn't come out there that much anymore. Their vineyard wagon was in the back corner under a canvas. When Jon felt alone or pensive, he always made his way to there, lifted the canvas, and felt the wood of the wagon, the ruff-sawn planks, and it took him back to some of the sweetest memories of his life. Their fiftieth anniversary was coming soon, and Jon was thinking about restoring the wagon to surprise her. He could rent a couple of horses and pick her up in the wagon, and they could ride again around the mountain through the years of their life, just like they were kids again.

"Wow, is this the old wagon Mrs. Elizabeth was telling me about?" "Yep, sure is. Have you ever ridden in one?" Jon looked over to find Finn standing at one end of the wagon. He had not heard him come into the barn while daydreaming.

"No, I don't think so. It reminds me of a johnboat that's on wheels."

"Ha, well, Finn, that's a pretty good analogy. It rides about like a johnboat on wheels."

"Can I sit up there on the seat? Would that hurt anything?"

"Wouldn't hurt a thing; help yourself. Now, the horses would be in front of you, and you would hold the reins like this, see?" Finn picked up the reins. "Yeah, there you go. I think you're a natural, Finn."

"You and Mrs. Elizabeth had two horses?"

The man looked at the blonde boy sitting on the wagon seat. "Yeah, we had two horses, a boy, and a girl. The girl was named Deezy, tall and black. I loved that horse; she was so sweet" Jon stopped and gestured to the grass field across from the barn. "Back then, the field was a pasture, and to come home and to see Deezy in that field of green grass in the waning sun, was just quite a picture. The boy horse, Andiamo, we called him, was tan, in color, with a blonde mane. He wasn't as tall as Deezy, but he was stout, a little hardheaded too, but Deezy, Deezy, she could make that boy mind. I tell ya, that horse loved his lady, and wouldn't go anywhere without her."

"You miss them, don't you?"

"Me, miss a couple of old nags? Oh, I don't know. I'm kind of missing a lot of stuff today. It's strange like I'm losing something that I haven't lost yet. It's probably old age or just the full moon tonight." Jon flicked his hand like pushing off the emotion plaguing his mind.

"Mrs. Elizabeth said this was the vineyard wagon. Do you have a grape vineyard up here? Can I see it?" Jon felt like the boy had given him an unexpected present. "You know, that's not a bad idea. Want to go for a little drive?"

Robert Gunn arrived on the mountain in the early afternoon. As he drove up the old familiar roads of his youth, he was pensive and curious about what Elizabeth's message meant. He had not been up to the mountain in some while because his work, as a Minister, in Tryon kept him very busy. In addition to the weekly meeting of the church, he had undertaken a rural project addressing Counseling, Mental health, and Health Education / Nutrition for those suffering from HIV/AIDS and cancer. When he started the clinic, people came from other churches and protested his work, saying that it was ungodly and that he was protecting Satan's children. It hurt his heart. How could people say that helping those in need was a sin against God? Sickness, illness, and disease could happen to any breathing, living bit of flesh. The human body was as fragile as fresh-cut flowers. Some say that breast cancer is because women committed sin against God and their bodies by having an abortion. He felt so horrible as his patients would push through these protesters just to receive help at his church facility. Christians with posters proclaiming that AIDS was God's judgment on Homosexuals. But AIDS was also a heterosexual disease that could be transmitted intravenously through blood transfusions or the reuse of needles. Anyone of the protesters could be infected just as easily as any of the patients coming to seek help at the clinic. Bobby hung his head in embarrassment at the use of God to condemn the sick. To use illness as a metaphor for living a dirty, immoral life. Even though Bobby was a church minister, he often detested "God's Children."

This afternoon off from work was something he needed for himself, and he hoped everything was okay with Jon and Elizabeth.

He pulled into the drive, passed the Sawmill, and looked over the sea of grass, which had always been a favorite view of his. The cabin came into view, and he could see Elizabeth sitting on the church pew and smoking her thin cigarette. He smiled when he saw her. They had always been close. Like they were brother and sister or two similar souls that had walked life's path together. Elizabeth had met him soon after meeting Jon. As Jon's adopted brother, Bobby could explain Jon's oddities and insecurities to Elizabeth. Bobby had been enchanted by the life Elizabeth had lived overseas, and her style, education, and beauty were things he always admired. She had always reached out to him when she doubted something. He kept her going in a different way than Jon, gave her a different perspective and different way of processing her emotions, seeing an issue but then being able to see it as a piece of art, an opportunity, whether it was in the form of visual art, music, or performance.

He needed today; he needed the feeling of home. His soul needed healing again. He desired the dry pan humor of his brother, Jon, and he needed to wash dishes with Elizabeth, whispering, standing side by side in their small place and opening his heart to her.

He needed healing because he had lost his person so many decades ago. His other heart form. His confidant, his person to whisper to in the small places. His heart healer. Ruby was everything and a man who had healed a thousand wounds in Bobby's heart. Ruby was alive one minute and in the next was entirely gone. Not because he wanted to, not because he had to. But some other man's hate, fueled by alcohol, fear, lies, and self-righteousness, took Ruby's life. He devalued Ruby's hopes and dreams and discarded his humanity, living, and loving soul. He took all of Bobby's hope and goals and, in that demonic rage, changed the trajectory of all the lives that loved and knew Rueben Fry.

Bobby parked his car next to Elizabeth's and opened the door to find her standing anxiously waiting to throw her arms around him. He got out of the car and Elizabeth stood on her tiptoes to wrap her arms around the big man's frame. Her face was beaming with a smile and Bobby smiled back at her looking into her blue eyes. She immediately burst into conversation explaining how happy she was to see him to have him back here at home where he was supposed to be. Bobby slowly and deliberately took in the beauty of his brother's wife and a woman so dear to his own heart that he considered her as his sister.

"I've missed you too." Bobby reached out his long arm and pulled Elizabeth in again for another hug. He popped the trunk. "I've got some things for you. I stopped by the French bakery and got some goodies. Thought I may stay the night out in the old apartment, just for old time's sake." Bobby reached into the trunk and filled Elizabeth's arms with tiny treasures. He filled his arms too.

"Oh, this is all so special, Bobby. Let's take this to the porch, and I will brew some tea for us." Bobby closed the trunk and then stopped to take a moment to look around at the place of his youth. His mind flashed back through the history of the meadow and the mountain, and he felt insignificant yet very much a part of the land. Breathing in deeply and surveying the grass sea and the large canopy of the trees. He remembered building the small outbuildings, with Jon, on the slope of the mountain and the wide boards they had cut in the sawmill. The sound of the fountain filled his ears, and his heart swelled with the warmth of being at home.

"Not much has changed; that's really nice, you know," He looked up to find Elizabeth bringing out a kettle of tea and two mugs.

"It's such a gift to have you here, Bobby. Your schedule has gotten so busy with the church and the new clinic that we don't get to see you much." Bobby reached over and touched Elizabeth's hands. "I get your notes in the mail, which lifts my spirits. Thank you for being a constant in my life, Elizabeth. You know, it's not that Tryon is a big city by any means, but when you start doing something that goes against the thinking of some people, they come from all distances to protest and to be hateful. I get worn out sometimes."

Elizabeth frowned. "We've seen the photos in the paper. We really can't believe the things we've seen. Jon gets so fired up that he's ready to storm down there and clear them all out. I tell him that's the last thing you need, but he's very protective of his brother, as you know."

Bobby smiled. "Yeah, I know; he once broke me out of jail with a bulldozer. Where is he anyway?" Bobby turned in the wooden chair and looked around the property.

"Well, I told, in my phone message, that we have a boy staying with us from down in the flatland. He's a darling," Elizabeth shook her head and looked down at her hands folded in her lap. She sat a little in her chair as if she was becoming anxious about what she would say next. "I know it's strange we have someone else's child living with us here, and before you think I stole him, let me explain."

"Elizabeth, we were orphans, I get it."

"How can it be, Bobby? How can a father and a Mother not see what they have in this child right in front of their eyes?" Bobby bit his lip. He and every orphan had thought about it nearly every day. "His Dad's sick, Bobby." She paused for a moment. "To hear Finn, that's the boy's name, to hear Finn describe his Dad's illness, it sounds like he is HIV positive. I don't know how far along he is, but his Dad is spending months, if not years, at a time in Bethesda, Maryland, at the NIH. He is in the AIDS units." "And, let me guess, Finn doesn't know about AIDS. He thinks it is some rare disease that has infected his father."

Elizabeth nodded. "Finn describes exactly what is wrong with his Dad, and it's like he has memorized a page out of the paper describing the nature of the disease, but he doesn't know its name. He may know what AIDS is, but he hasn't put it together; that is what his Dad suffers from."

Bobby took his cup of tea from the table, lifted the tea bag from it, and set it on the saucer. "I assume Finn's parents have removed the television from the house and any newspapers or magazines."

Elizabeth looked at him like he was a mind reader. "Yes, yeah, you're right. When he first came, we felt bad because we didn't have a tv and assumed kids would want to watch cartoons or something. Jon was even about to go down to Cohen's and buy one, but Finn said that he didn't have a tv at home and didn't need one. Said that he would much rather be outdoors during the day, and every night he's been having these deep, I mean deep, conversations with Jon about stuff that no kid his age should ever be thinking about. It's been a little too much for me. I don't really understand it. How did you know that his family wouldn't have a tv?"

Bobby tasted the tea, added a wedge of lemon and tasted it again, and then set the warm mug back on the saucer. "I often see it at the clinic and in the homes I visit. The stigma of AIDS is as bad as the disease. I have patients that deny they have AIDS; I even have AIDS patients that curse other AIDS patients accusing them of perpetuating the disease. The language is horrible but no worse than what the protestors say in front of the clinic. And yes, I have patients who do not want their children to know, so they remove the televisions and newspapers, start homeschooling their children, and stop taking vacations or interacting with anyone that may give their children an idea of what the disease is."

Elizabeth shook her head. "What kind of life that must be."

Bobby nodded. "What's it going to do to those kids' lives, truth not having a high value?"

Jon and Finn had made their way to the other side of the mountain. A road that Finn had yet to be down and a place that Jon called the French Valley. Finn didn't know why he called it that, but every time he said it, Jon looked like he was looking through an old window at a different time in his past. The way he said it and the way he looked when he said it made Finn suspect of ever asking him the origin of the name. Jon parked the red and silver Dodge in front of two stone columns with limestone finials on top. They were overgrown, with wheat grass, blackberry vines, and the occasional wildflower, but Finn could see that once it was an entrance that had a significant presence in time passed. "This is the vineyard?" Finn sat in the seat and slid as close to the dash as possible, looking at the road that had to be there, even though it was severely overgrown.

"Yeah, this is it. As you can tell, I haven't been here in a long time." Finn wondered how they could push through the briars and the tall grass. Jon slid the 4wd lever forward. There was a slight sound of gears grinding, and when Jon put the truck in drive again, it seemed to lunge forward as if it was ready and wanting to go. Finn had never known or even heard of a man that would ruin his brand-new truck by deliberately plunging it into a briar-infested field. Jon looked over at Finn, greatly anticipating the off-road plunge. "You want to drive?"

Finn didn't skip a beat. "On the way out, maybe," he said with a twist of his wrist and a finger pointing over his shoulder. The truck pushed quickly through the overgrown vegetation, and Finn cringed, hearing the thorns scratching over the truck's paint. They crested a small hill, and in a flat meadow below them, one could see the remnants of thirty-year old vineyard rows in dark lines across the overgrown field. In some areas, small pine trees and cedars sprung up in the rows between the grapes. Apple trees lined one side of the vineyard, and at the end was a small gazebo that seemed to still be intact but poorly covered with vines. The lower side of the vineyard seemed to fall away as if it were a cascading waterfall into the French Valley, and then the endless sea of mountain peaks cresting up and down. They got out of the truck in a patch of sweet grass. "Finn, there's a sling blade and a machete in the truck's bed; how about getting 'em for me." Finn crawled into the truck's bed and quickly found the requested tools. Armed, the two moved forward. "Watch out for the guide wires. They hold up the end posts and come out past them."

Jon swung the sling blade and moved away some tall grass and briars. He looked back, traded Finn for the machete, and hacked through some briars until the old wooden vineyard post stood clean and proud in the sunlight. Jon leaned forward and, with his finger, smoothed the edges of a brass plate that had been stamped and nailed into the post as an identifying marker. "That's what I thought," Jon said.

"What's that? What does it say?" Finn said, stepping forward and trying to see the word on the post marker himself.

"It says Eliot as in George Eliot. I marked every post with the name of some great writer." Jon turned to the next grapevine post. It, too, was covered in vegetation.

"What's that got to do with grapes?" Finn asked.

Jon looked over at Finn and smiled. "You know, you are the first to ever ask me that question. What do writers have to do with grapes? Profound, you never stop amazing me, Finn." The old man swung the machete and cleared the thick vines from the wooden post until it, too, came into view of the sun. The brass plate had tarnished, but the letters could still be seen. Melville came into view.

"Like Moby Dick?" Finn looked up at Jon.

"Yeah, like Moby Dick. In my mind, a great writer or a great book will lead you to other great writers and great books. One author can lead you to ten other good authors, and those authors will lead you to more. Before you know it, you are standing in front of a vineyard of literature, and each grape represents a good book.

Each cluster of grapes represents an author who turned you on to those books, and each vineyard row represents a different category or topic. I guess that's why I did it, though I've never really thought about my reasoning until now."

"I get it," Finn said. "It's like a library in a way. Rows after rows of books on particular subjects and the shelves stacked with author after author and book after book. It's your library garden, so to speak. I wish libraries were outdoors like this." Finn was enjoying himself, and the vineyard was enchanting with its rows of grapes representing knowledge and the setting spectacular with its views. "So, did you and Mrs. Elizabeth come here to eat grapes and read a lot." Jon smiled. "Oh yeah, we used to spend a lot of time here. We built this vineyard as a surprise for her. It continued for months, and I was sure she was on to us. Bobby, Ruby, and I hauled all this topsoil in here and laid everything out. Bobby is the one who first pitched the idea, he had always made wine out of the apples and pears that grew up here on the mountain, but he wanted some real grapes to produce finer wines. He did all the research on what we should plant and how we should plant them."

They made their way around the vineyard, exposing post after post and many authors' names. Sometimes they discussed the books the others had written, or Jon told Finn something interesting about the author's life. "George Eliot was actually a woman." Finn kept taking mental notes of the authors and what he wanted to read. They came up to the Gazebo, which was covered in heavy wisteria vines, but Finn was surprised to see that the structure had not been crushed by the vines, but actually, the wisteria vines had bent and formed around the frame. Finn walked up closer and touched it. "Its metal? The Gazebo is built out of metal?"

"Yeah, another one of Bobby's ideas. I was going to build it out of wood, and Bobby said we would be rebuilding it every other year because it is on this side of the mountain and collects more moisture over here. Which was good for the grapes but could have been better for wood structures. So, he drew out what he wanted, and we hired this metal smith to build it."

The structure was built from solid steel bars, which were two inches thick and ten feet long. The bars were clustered together, forming tight columns with panels in between the columns. The roof was a beautiful structure of arched metal brackets supporting the above copper roof. The gazebo floor was made of dark blue and green soapstone slabs, with white veins stretching like lightning on a dark night. The metal had been painted with a thick forest green paint, and the bark from the wisteria vines contrasted the fine, smooth textures with the coarseness of nature surrounding it. The soapstone was dirty and covered in thin layers of debris and dust.

"Needs to be cleaned up good," Jon said. Finn stood inside the structure, slowly pirouetting, taking the whole vineyard in. The two sat down side-by-side on the gazebo's wide, bullnose steps. "Say, can you keep a secret?"" Jon said. Finn turned to look at the old man. "Well, Betts and I are celebrating our fiftieth wedding anniversary this year. I've been stumbling around with what to get her." He stopped and looked over at Finn. "You know, since you've been up here with us, uh," the man looked up and out across the French Valley like he was searching in the distance for the right words to say, " well, having you around each day makes all other gifts seem puny to me. Elizabeth is so happy now. Before, she had me worried a bit. The best gift for Elizabeth would include you." Finn looked at him and, for a moment, thought he was going to cry. He quickly stretched out his leg, pulled his pocketknife, and started skinning an old wisteria vine. "I was thinking that maybe you and I could fix up this vineyard for her, like a surprise." Finn lifted his eyes and looked at Jon. "I'd love that!" "Good, good, me too." Finn stood up and held his hands up like he was about to decree something. "It's got to be a secret, though, like the first time you, Bobby, and Ruby built it. I want to be here to see her face. She's going to love it. We could even pull the wagon down her, too, for her to see it all again."

Jon kept smiling at the boy. "A secret? Okay, that sounds great! We will start in the morning. We will bring down the equipment and start cutting the brush down. I like it."

"This is going to be the best surprise," Finn said excitedly.

"We better get back around the hill." Finn nodded, and they both got up and left the gazebo. The sun was starting to develop in the French Valley, and the streaks of pink and purple were growing large across the sky. Finn looked over the meadow, and it reflected the pink light in the clouds and on every blade of grass.

"Oh, Bobby's, here!" Jon exclaimed.

"Who's that?" Finn asked. "That's my brother Bobby. We were adopted at the same time and brought up here to live. You'll really like him." Finn climbed out of the truck and followed Jon onto the side porch of the cabin. The lanterns were lit, and several candles were burning on the table and corn barrel. At the table sat a black man, and when he saw Jon, he rose up from the table and completed an imposing stature over the whole patio. Finn had never been so close to a person with dark skin. No one lived very near to the wheat hill house, and the closest people that did were white. No black people attended his church or any camp meetings, drawing in thousands of people. How could this be Jon's brother? How could they have been adopted at the same time? He watched the two men embrace, and then Mrs. Elizabeth hugged the black man, and they kissed on the lips. How was that right? Finn stepped forward with his hand outstretched, looking directly into the man's eyes; he said, "My name is Finn; it's nice to meet you." The man looked a little taken aback. Bobby had a guitar in one hand and stretched out his other to receive Finn's.

"Indeed, it's nice to meet you." Bobby smiled, and Finn politely excused himself. Returning he found a dish of small pickles, crackers, slices of cheese, cured meats, Blackberries, Raspberries, and peeled tangerines. Finn could smell lemon and lavender. Mrs. Elizabeth had put on a sweater and wrapped her hands around a cup of tea.

Jon picked from the plate and sipped a small glass of wine. "All this came from the French market in town? Betts, did you hear that? We've got to get down there and check that out. He sat in his chair with his elbows on the table, leaning ever closer to his Brother. "So, you're staying, right, going to stay up here for a few days? I cleaned up the apartment and stocked some wood by the stove. I doubt you'll need it, but just in case, you'll have it." Jon was jabbering with excitement.

"Oh, I wish I could, Jon. I'm going to stay tonight and then head back in the morning. Just so much going on with the church and the clinic right now."

"Jon," Elizabeth said. "Look at all Bobby brought us from his patients." Elizabeth opened a large box on her lap. Several pieces of art were inside, and as she explained each, she handed them over to Jon to inspect. "This painting is done by cutting thin pieces of veneer wood and then gluing them onto the hard canvas surface." She held the piece up in the lantern light, and you could see how the artist had taken different kinds of wood and trimmed them to form a sailboat heeled over at sea in front of a lighthouse. "That's amazing," Jon remarked. She then pulled out an oil painting and passed it over for Jon to inspect. "And these, Jonny, these are my favorite." She pulled out a set of four dinner plates from the box that had been hand thrown. They were light and thin, done obviously, by a professional potter, and expertly glazed in white and with thin blue lines. "Dear God."

"Bobby's patients are making all of this art, Jon." Jon looked over at his brother, and the large man just smiled. "Really, that's wonderful; how did it all come about, Bobby?"

"The live in associates have time. You know, it's strange how people view it differently. For some, time stopped when they were diagnosed like their life was sidelined or put on hold. They wonder when they will be cured or regain strength enough to return to work or just to their lives. For others, it seems that time is just slipping away, like they are hanging onto a cliff with just a limited amount of strength. So, we started reaching out to the community college in Asheville and got volunteers to come in and start teaching art classes and donating materials. We've got wood shops, painting classes, and pottery classes. These dishes were made by a fifteen-year-old who contracted AIDS through a blood transfusion."

"Fifteen?" Jon responded.

"Yeah, it is a sad case. He looks like he is in his forties; the disease has wasted him away. He's on medication that I think will keep him alive, but it also makes him terribly sick. It's hard to see; he's a great kid with so much potential."

"And he made these plates?" Jon laid the plate down on the table and began tracing the glaze's blue lines with his fingers. He ran his fingers around the underside of the leaf edge, trying to feel the hands of the diseased boy who made it. "Amazing," Jon said. "I want more. I want to help this kid. I want him to know how much I appreciate his art."

Bobby smiled. "It's been a great program, the associates' spirits have been rejuvenated, and they can spend time making gifts for their friends and family members. We plan to do an art auction at one of the restaurants in town. I will be sure to let you know when. Maybe we can all go together."

"Do you have a restaurant in mind?" Elizabeth asked.

"We have yet to get that far along. I also want to give the associates some time to build a good inventory of artwork." " Associates, Bobby?" "Yes, we are all in this together. Everyone in the clinic contributes; there are no staff or patients. That's the principle we operate from. Everyone gives what they can. Treatment is not for better or for worse. It is always for the better. Positive attitude, the truth of information. Even the worst of days can be better."

"Bobby Gunn, you are a beautiful soul." Elizabeth hugged his shoulders. "The Lake Lanier Tea House would be a great location for the art show. The wood walls, the lighting, the patio for a live band."

Bobby's eyes lit up. "Great idea, just like old times! Let's see what we can do with that."

Elizabeth stood up and ran her hand over Bobby's shoulders, "Just like old times." She pointed down to his guitar. "Play me something while I make us some dinner."

Bobby picked up the acoustic guitar and began to play. Finn sat in silence and listened to the music. He was slowly putting the pieces together that Bobby was a church pastor but also ran a clinic that helped sick people. People with AIDS. The only time that he had ever heard AIDS spoken of was at church meetings when a preacher would stand in the pulpit and talk about how God was judging homosexuals by killing them with a deadly disease. But the preachers didn't call them associates or speak of their humanity like Bobby did. The preachers in the camp meetings called them Faggots, Homos, Sodomites, Unclean People, and Reprobates that had chosen to go against God's way and chose an unnatural sexual life. Who was right? In Finn's mind, he questioned how a church pastor could be kind to these people whom God was righteously killing off?

And yet here in front of him was art, things not created in straight lines, like the vineyard rows or the columns of the Gazebo, but art created in circular, flowing shapes, the shapes of God. How could these diseased, forsaken people be making things in the images of God while he was judging them for their sins? How could Bobby, this "Man of God," work with these sinners to enhance their lives. Shouldn't he be like all the preachers Finn knew, curse them, and call them names? Finn watched as Bobby's fingers moved up and down the guitar strings. His playing was smooth, like water moving over the pools of water to the pond. Bobby would look over and smile at Finn, and Finn would smile back. His gut feeling about Bobby was changing. He could see how much he meant to Jon and Elizabeth. Finn had become happy here on the mountain. All that he had learned seemed to make sense to him. Most of all, Jon and Elizabeth respected him. They had treated him like he was human and not diseased. He had genuinely fallen in love with Jon and Elizabeth, and in his heart, he knew he could trust Bobby too.

Jon locked eyes with Finn from across the wooded table and raised his head toward the pond behind the house. Finn did not need to ask what he was saying. Knowing by now it was time to feed the fish. He got up, turned on the flood light, moved the candle from the corn barrel, and removed the lid. He went to the pond and began cascading the corn into the air, waiting for the fish children to dine. Bobby came and stood bedside Finn at the pond's edge. Finn looked at Bobby and said, "How long have they been doing this; how long have they been here?"

"Oh, they were here when we first came up here, not much older than you. So that's quite a while. We used to come down here and catch them for dinner. It wasn't until later on that we started throwing corn out there every now and then."

"What's the biggest fish you ever saw there, Mr. Bobby."

Bobby smiled at Finn. "You can call me Bobby; you don't have to be formal with me."

"Sorry, it's a habit," Finn said.

"The biggest fish I ever saw in this pond was . . ." Bobby held his hands apart.

"Whoa, that's like two feet! I haven't caught one that big yet."

Bobby laughed. "Yeah, Jon used to be really good at holding his breath, and he would dive down trying to find the bottom of the pond, you know, he would start out on the sides and hold his hands against the rocks while he kicked his feet just swimming straight down the sides of the pond. He would always say that as he got deeper, he would feel a cold rush of water coming up from the bottom of the pond like this was just a small pond on the surface, and there was a whole lake, or river, in the ground beneath it. That's the only way we ever figured so many fish could survive like that or get so big."

Bobby squatted down beside Finn, and Finn steadied himself with one hand on Bobby's broad shoulder and held a fishing rod in the other hand. "So, like, there's a whole lake or river under this pond?" Finn let his mind wonder about all the hidden caverns and places the fish would explore. "We've caught fish, and they run into those other places."

"What's your favorite part of the mountain, Bobby?"

"Oh, I've got a lot of favorite parts, but I'd say one of my favorites is the staircase that leads up to Skyuka's Rest. There is something about it that just puts me in touch with nature. It's like I'm walking hand in hand again."

"Hand in Hand with who?" Finn asked.

Bobby was looking into the pond now like he was dreaming of faraway summer days. "Say, what now?"

"I asked, whose hand you held when walking up the staircase."

Bobby looked over, smiled at Finn, and then looked back into the past. "God's hands, My God's sweet hands."

"Dinner is ready, you two." Mrs. Elizabeth set a large bowl and a basket of French bread on the table. The bowl was filled with Fettuccine, sautéed red onion, and garlic, cubed butternut squash roasted in truffle oil and sea salt, and garnished with arugula, lemon, and feta cheese. On the table beside the warm French loaf was a small plate of Spanish Olive oil and crumbles of Parmesan cheese. There was a clay pitcher of cold water. Jon still nursed his white wine. Bobby and Finn had stepped inside to wash their hands, and upon returning to the table, they caught Mrs. Elizabeth and Jon sharing a very long kiss in the light of lanterns. Her hand stretched across his chest, and his hand lifted, holding her arm. Setting down to eat, Elizabeth straightened in her chair, held her hands out, and declared that she would say the blessing. She prayed in the glowing light, and all three men had their eyes open and watched her like a Madonna. A thanksgiving of what she felt like she had dove to the bottom of the pond on a summer day, and there clung to the edges of the granite rock and let the cool, hidden waters of the earth flood over her. She finished praying and looked up. "What? What? What are you all looking at? You are all acting weird. Did you have your eyes closed while I was praying? Jon, did you?"

"Jon the Baptist!" Finn declared in laughter.

Mrs. Elizabeth took her cloth napkin and started swinging it toward Jon. "Jon, the Baptist, Jon, the delinquent, sneaky Baptist!" They all were laughing now. "Okay, stop this foolishness." Mrs. Elizabeth sat back in her chair and put her hand over her chest. "Whew, you fellows know how to get a Lady going."

Jon said, "I think you've taken leave of your senses, Betts. Like you have been drinking bug juice or something."

She swung the napkin at her kidding husband one more time. " You better watch yourself, Mister Man! Okay, let's eat before it all goes cold." They filled their plates with the savory pasta, and Bobby poured the water out of the earthen pitcher.

Finn looked at the large man. "Do you not drink wine?"

Everyone at the table stopped and gave a slight smile. Bobby wiped his mouth. "I've never been much of a drinker. However, I have always been interested in making wine and brewing beer. Just for some reason not much of a consumer. I just like the science of it. But, to answer your question or the question I think you are getting at. I don't have a moral issue with drinking, and I am not bothered by people who drink alcohol. I've just never really acquired a taste for it. I find flavors in other types of beverages. Cherry Coke, being one." Here, the big man laughed at his own explanation. "You know, many preachers have an issue with alcohol. Some even say it is a sin. I'm not in a big hurry to condemn it. However, I will say that alcohol has a way of showing what is truly on the inside of someone's heart."

"What do you mean?" Finn asked.

"Well, Finn, some people are happy, others are sad. Some people are stressed others are laid back. Some people are mad, and others are not mad. Some people are healthy, and some people are not. Some people are miserable, yet they pretend that everything is perfect in their lives." "Some people are in love, and others pretend to be in love," Finn said.

"Indeed, indeed. Many, many people are not in love, but they pretend to be in love. Some people believe they know God but are terrified that they don't even know if he truly exists." Bobby turned towards Finn and put his large hand on the table corner. "Alcohol is a drug that numbs the mind. If a person is sad, it compounds that sadness and turns it loose into sobs and tears. If a person is truly happy inside, they can't help but laugh, sing, and even dance. If a person is scared inside, then that comes out. Alcohol is meant to be used in balance, mindful of one's own heart and others' hearts."

Jon and Elizabeth were quiet; only the fountain spoke in the night air. Finn pondered what the large man had said. He took a drink of water and said, "Are you afraid? Is that why you've never acquired a taste for alcohol and only made it for others?" "Say?" Finn said. He reached his hand across the table and touched the dark skin of the man's hand, and held it.

Bobby was quiet for some time. "Yes, I am scared," he said. "I'm terrified over something that happened thirty-five years ago.

I'm sure that is confusing to you and all of you, but it is as real as two minutes ago for me. The slightest thought about what happened, how it happened, paralyzes me, debilitates me, and makes me gasp for air like I am drowning. The thought of your life's partner being here one moment and completely and utterly gone the next was enough to make me consider ending my own life and is every bit that powerful still to this day. That force, whatever that is, whether it is God or the course of nature, but whatever that power is, to take life, good life, loved life, and snuff it out, scares me to no end. That people, people as terrible and as horrible as the ones who took Ruby, murdered Ruby, could just do that and then walk away, go back home, to South Carolina, back to their churches, and not give another moment of thought to all they just stole from so many people, not just the one they murdered . . ."

The porch was quiet. Only the tree frogs and fountain could be heard. It was like everyone had lost their appetite, considering how each of them was scared in some way in their own lives but didn't admit it, didn't like to even think about it. Elizabeth set down her glass, reached across the table, and took Bobby's hand. "Why haven't you ever told us that, Bobby? It's been so many years since Ruby has been gone. I feel bad that we've never asked you about that. It just seemed, well, back then, it just seemed that everything we did, whether together or apart, just reminded us, reminded you that Ruby was gone. When you left the mountain and moved into town, we just thought . . . well, I feel horrible now, but, Oh gosh, I just . . . we just felt like we were making you sad. Like, seeing Jon and me and our lives was hard on you. We didn't know how to talk to you about it. Geez, I guess we still don't know how to talk to you about it, even after all this time." Tears were flowing down the beautiful old lady's cheeks now. Finn sat quietly, listening, trying to piece together the three grown-up's past.

"Jon and I have been so lucky in love, lucky in health, and happiness, it's hard to know, it's hard to speak with certainty, or to know how to console. I mean, we lost Ruby too, and then a year later, it was like we lost you too."

Bobby looked over at Elizabeth and smiled. He turned loose her hand and reached over and touched Jon's knee, and Jon extended his hand and grasped the hand of his brother. "The truth was, back in those days, at least for me. Seeing you and Jon, being happy and doing together, and being together, and traveling together, was beautiful to me; it was consoling. It was a glimmer of hope that life, at least some part of life, was still intact. It was evident that God was still in control, so to speak. That I could take it one day at a time. The hard part came, the change came, when I felt like I was holding the two of you back."

"Holding us back, Bobby?" Elizabeth asked.

"Yes, I felt like I was a weight, like an anchor around your necks. Not saying that in a mean way. I'm trying to say that in my bereaved state, I felt that every time we got together, a happy thought brought a sad thought to mind. In my state at that time, I felt like I needed to remove myself so that you two, your love, could go on and grow unimpeded."

"But, Bobby, you are our love; you and Ruby were the biggest part of our love. I mean, we knew that there would be hard times or hard years, hard moments in life, but we were family, and we'd get through it. We were willing to bear those hard times with you."

Bobby was quiet. He nodded and placed his large hand across his chest. "I know, Elizabeth, it was my wrong, my bad; my way of thinking was just as sick, as grieved, and as insane as my heart was. Instead of embracing and relying on you, I thought I needed to bear it alone so that you could go and be happy. It was the worst thing I could ever have done. I allowed my heart to be abandoned when I should have opened my broken self to you and let your love heal me.

"I'm sorry, Bobby," Jon said. "We were just kids, we were all just kids, Betts had lost her parents, but that was somewhat different; it was expected, and we had each other, but Ruby, we just didn't know; we were all grieving." Bobby nodded, and Jon reached for him. "I hope you will forgive yourself, and I hope you will forgive us."

With dinner finished, Elizabeth cleaned the kitchen with Bobby. They were quiet at first. She felt they both knew and understood the other's thoughts. "I told you," Elizabeth said, looking up into Bobby's eyes. "There's something special about him. I don't know if he's that intuitive, he's just had that much grief in his young life, or if he's just desperate for someone to tell him the truth." She paused and started drying the dishes. Bobby moved over to the booth table in the kitchen. She whispered, "He asked us the other night if we thought Skyuka was scared when they bound him and led him up the staircase to the rest. Jon still hasn't told him that they murdered him up there. I don't know, I don't know how you tell a kid like that the real truth. I guess that's why his parents haven't. I think he keeps asking questions about being scared because he's scared. He thinks this 'rare blood disease' just fell out of the sky into his father's body. The child thinks that one day the same will happen to him. Undoubtedly, whenever he gets a fever, he thinks his life is over and will waste away. He is living in fear, thinking he will never have a family or a wife. Do these people not see what they're doing to this child?

"And what about us, me and Jon? Aren't we culprits? We sit here and listen to his worries, but we can't say anything. We can't just tell him that his father has AIDS and that they've been lying to him; he's not our child. He's not even our grandchild. We do not have any business telling him what his parents should and should not do. When his father first got sick, Bobby he told us that he was taken to the hospital for two days while people did all types of testing and blood work on him. He told us how he felt scared because he had seen how sick his father was, and then his father was gone for so long. And yet no one, no one, has ever told Finn that he was fine. No one has ever sat down, held his hand, and told him the truth that he is not diseased. How long will that child have to carry his father's illness with him through life?"

Elizabeth looked at Bobby, then opened the cigarette case. She looked around for something to light it with. She never smoked in the house, but tonight was different. The whole day had been extra; maybe it was the full moon. This month, instead of affecting all of nature, it affected all of them. At some point in the night, they'd all turn to wolves and howl at the moon.

Bobby sat longways in the booth, the only way the giant man could. He didn't say anything, just listened. "It's not your place to talk to him about his Dad's illness or his parent's behavior. What about school or church? Does he have any extended family that he spends time with?"

Elizabeth shook her head. "He mentions this couple from Greer that it seems has been on the periphery of his life. But he doesn't talk like they are his family. It's more like a couple he has stayed with, and they've just been nice to him. And that's all anyone has to do is just show a little kindness to him, and he never forgets it. He talks about them as if they're saints. Sometimes I wonder if they were going to adopt him at some point. There's just that cloudiness around it. Bobby, it is so sad. He was supposed to be up here only for a couple of days, his parents were going to call and come up and get him, but it's been weeks we are nearly through summer. They've never called. Don't get me wrong, I don't want them to. I'm so happy he is here, and I can tell he is happy. He adores Jon and the mountain, and Bobby, he just comes up to me, gives me these long hugs, and lays his head on my shoulder. I can't get enough of it." Bobby had been listening and taking in everything Elizabeth desperately needed to get off her chest.

"Sister, I know it's hard, and I'm not taking the side of his parents. What they've done is wrong. However, you and I don't know. We are still determining what they've gone through. Giving Finn up may have been the most devastating moment of their lives. We just don't know, and we can't judge. The only thing we can do is embrace this beautiful gift and be in this moment with Finn. If he wants to play, then play. If he wants to read, then read, but most of all, talk. Talk to him about life. Be an example of balance and security. Let him ask questions and lead the conversations. Truth, Betts, truth is the universal language that every heart speaks. Just be there and be truthful with him. With this mountain and your love, he is almost free. Those things he is scared of are still on his mind, but this is a respite from the horrible world he has to live in now. Elizabeth, every time he looks at you and Jon, he is telling himself that one day he will grow up, and when he does, things will be different. Elizabeth nodded. "You're right. Give me a hug Dear One. You always know what to say. And I don't say that lightly. I know you've earned the wisdom." Stepping outside onto the porch, they found Jon and Finn sitting on the church pew, playing guitar next to each other. "I'm going to turn in," Bobby said. Jon stood and hugged his brother, and Finn stood as Bobby extended his hand.

Finn hugged the man instead and said, "I'm sorry." "What you sorry for, Finn?" "I'm sorry that you lost Ruby."

Bobby paused and turned his head. "Ruby is always with me, maybe not in body, but all around me, the full moon, the air I breathe, the words I hear. There was enough love to last me an entire lifetime. That's what true love is; it's forever, and death can't take it away. It doesn't force two people apart. Physically, yes, but spiritually no. It was a real pleasure meeting you, Finn. I hope we can get to know each other better, maybe do some more fishing." The man's large hand fell on the boy's curly hair, and Finn smiled.

Bobby stepped inside the sawmill apartment, as he had for so many years. He removed his shoes before walking upstairs. An action did so many times with Ruby and Jon. He began to climb the stairs leading to the small apartment. His hand grasped the wooden handrail, the handrail that Ruby had made, sanded by hand, and stained and installed. Bobby made it to the small landing that made the last turn up to the apartment, and he paused. Like each step had been another ten-pound weight on his heart. He touched the handrail, closed his eyes, and felt the shape of Ruby's hands in the wood. He stopped again at the top of the stairs and looked over the apartment just as it had been so long ago when all three of them lived there. He saw the couch, the wood stove, the long walnut table, and the soapstone sink. He went over to the sink, touched the smooth, soft stone, and thought about all the times he had stood there, washing dishes, as Ruby played the guitar in front of the wood stove. He looked over there now and could almost see him there. He got into the same bed they had shared and turned out the light, but the full moon lit the room. He lay there, his memories taking him back to everything they had shared. He began to cry. Old tears because his heart and soul were so weary after so many years of being physically apart from his soul mate. He turned into the pillow and spoke Ruby's name and cried.

"Good night Finn," Elizabeth leaned over and kissed him. The couple climbed the staircase to the loft bedroom and spoke softly, in French, as they dressed for bed and turned out the lights. "Why don't we talk about what we are scared of, Jon?"

Jon slid close beside Elizabeth in bed, his body lining up against hers, their hands folding into one another's. "It is something adults don't talk about, I guess."

"But are you scared of anything, Jon? You never seem scared, but I know when you came home from the war, you went into the garden, and we went into the garden for a long while. That had me scared to see you not being able to come inside our home. We never really talked about the details of that time. I know it's over, but. Well, I felt helpless." Jon was quiet, staring into the moonlit bedroom. "Say?" Elizabeth said. Jon leaned his head close to hers and kissed her temple. "Can you?" Elizabeth turned toward him, laid her hand on his chest, and then raised it to his neck.

"I've always been scared that you would leave me again one day. You know, one day, you'd come to your senses and pack up all your stuff and disappear or worse, say you never wanted to see me again or that all the time you had spent with me was a waste. For many years, the last mile coming home was always the longest." The tears began to run down the wrinkled face. "You have no idea how my heart leaps when I see you on the porch waiting for me, Mon Cherie." Jon reached and held the wrist of her warm hand on his body.

"Pourquoi, Jon? I promised you at the Salt Pond that I would never leave you." "I promised you." She wiped the tears from his face and kissed him. "I will never leave you. You are my Beloved, my Special Man."

"But what about children? I couldn't bring myself to have kids, and I know you wanted them, Betts. I regret it, obviously. But, even now, with Finn here, I'm so scared that you will start to hate me. To hate me for what we could have had, what we should have had. I robbed you of being a Mother. You've got to hate me in some way, Betts. Contempt, regret, I don't know how I could live if you hated me, Betts." He could see Elizabeth's face in the moonlit night. She was shaking her head, no. She touched his face, pulled him closer, and started to kiss him.

She placed her hand back on his chest, over his beating heart, and said, "Fear not. I am with you, I love you, those things are old and in the past, and every day I have is wonderful because you are in it."

Jon wiped his eyes, raised her hand to his lips, and kissed it. Whispering, he said. "What about you? What's this about the night season? Are you scared, Darling?" He could see her, her hair framing her face, looking in the moonlight like the young girl he fell in love with. She was facing her own fear.

"How can I know?" she said.

"How can you know what, Betts?" She was deep in her own thoughts, and he could see silent tears pop out from her eyes and roll over her cheeks. Jon kissed her hand again. "I'm here." The tears slipped faster, and she removed her hand and wiped them.

"I'm scared of leaving the life that I love. Fifty years together. I've loved every detail of our lives, Jon. Life has been so precious but never so precious as now. I'm not afraid of dying, you see. I just don't want to give this up." She wiped her eyes. "It is a beautiful sunset, but I don't want the day to end. Promise me it won't end." She was quiet now, not crying anymore but resolved. She lifted and looked at him. "Can we be Doves? I mean, promise me that in the next life, we will be Doves, two birds huddled together for life, in the eave of the old Sawmill, like we were when we first married? We fly out together and share the same fence post looking over the grass field. If any trouble comes, we fly away together, fly away from pain."

"Birds, Betts? You want us to be Doves?"

"Yes, Doves, Jon. We've had so much in this life. It seems foolish to ask, but can we return as two doves together in the next? Just a pair of Doves, in the sun or in the rain, just promise me we will be together, that this perfect love will always remain. Flying together, feeding, and sleeping together, like we always have. When I think about that perfect love, it casts out all my fears. I'm not scared then, Jonny; just promise me we'll be doves."

CHAPTER 11

"Fear Not I am with You"

Finn awoke, dressed, and found Jon making breakfast in a blue and white ruffled apron. "What, never seen an old man in a dress before?"

Finn laughed, leaned his head forward, and touched the space on either side of his nose with his thumb and index finger. "Maybe, you should just stick to coffee and drawing in the mornings; just saying."

"Oh, I'm about to make you the best breakfast of your scrawny life, kid. Look right here." Jon lowered the front oven door of the wood cook stove, and Finn saw a cast iron pan of homemade biscuits cooking in the smoke of the oven. "I'm a man of many talents, son." He snapped his fingers. "Why don't you just take a seat and keep me company." Finn did, and Jon delivered a small glass and filled it with juice. "How did you sleep, Finn?"

"Like a fat baby, full of warm milk." Jon smiled. "I didn't know you could cook."

"Of course, I can cook; who do you think taught Elizabeth to cook?"

Finn shook his head in disbelief. Elizabeth walked into the kitchen in her thin robe and silk pajamas, and silk slippers.

"Something smells wonderful!" She stopped at the booth, leaned over, and kissed the top of Finn's head. Then she walked over and kissed Jon on the cheek, which he presented, and tugged at his apron. "Blue has always been a great color on you; it brings out your eyes. Brings out his eyes, Finn," she said as she turned to look at him. Finn watched how they interacted as if love was a perfect gift that they passed back and forth to each other.

"Listen, Special Woman, how about a day of luxury? I've got a plan."

Elizabeth smiled and looked at Finn with exaggerated eyes. "A day of luxury; he's got a plan; this sounds exciting!" Finn immediately jumped up, placed a dish towel over his arm, and began to escort Mrs. Elizabeth outside on the porch and set her at the table. "Vous voulez du cafe ou du the?" "Finn, your french is getting so good! Cafe au lait, si'l vous plait." He then returned with a coffee and a chilled carafe of milk. "Tu veux du sucre et un peu de lait?" Finn placed the mug on the table and filled it with coffee. " Finn, where have you been picking all this up?" " I've just been listening when you two talk." "Jon, do you hear him? We've got to be careful." "You've got to be careful. Your mind's filthy, Woman." " Well, aren't you lucky?" He placed a cloth napkin and silverware in front of her and set two other settings. A small vase with yellow flowers was delivered to the table, and Finn, enjoying himself, started bowing every time he arrived and departed from the outdoor dining room. And suddenly, they were ready, and Jon stepped out onto the porch in the ruffled apron, placed the large cast iron skillet in the middle of the table, and lifted the lid. Inside there were homemade biscuits. Each was filled with pieces of red pepper, onions that had been sautéed in truffle oil, a slice of white cheddar cheese, fresh basil, and lavender-infused honey. Elizabeth was served, and they all sat down to enjoy breakfast together.

"The best breakfast I think I've ever had. Especially shared with my two favorite people." She reached out and touched both of their hands.

"I really like your pancakes," Finn said. "Don't get me wrong, these biscuits are delicious, but there's something about your pancakes. I mean, some have blueberries, others chocolate. I've never had chocolate in pancakes for breakfast. I'm not even sure that's legal in the flatland."

"I'm not sure you're much of a flatlander anymore, Finn," Elizabeth said.

Jon piped up. "I don't know. I need to get a little more work out of you before you can pass the test." Finn smiled at the old man.

"So, what about this day of luxury, this plan you were talking about, Mr. Joines," Elizabeth said. "What does that all entail?"

"Well, I woke up early this morning and just felt like we should do something special. Breakfast, some private time, and then a picnic for lunch, and then maybe, well, just perhaps dinner at the Lake Lanier Tea House. Something special for the love of my life.

"Oh, Jon, that sounds so wonderful! I'm so excited." Elizabeth covered her mouth. "What a wonderful way to spend a day." She was beaming.

"Good, I'm glad," Jon said. She finished her biscuit and wiped her mouth.

Finn started removing the dishes from the table. When he came back, Jon slid an arm around his waist. "Finn and I have a few chores, and we may be gone for a couple of hours. I thought this would be some nice time for yourself, and then we will come back and get you and go up to the upper pond for a picnic. Does that sound good to you?"

Elizabeth was still smiling. "That sounds wonderful. I can't wait for you to get back." Jon got up from the table and stood behind

Elizabeth, massaging her neck. He leaned down and whispered something in her ear, and her head turned into him, and she stole a kiss. She laid her hand on his and said, "I am a very lucky woman."

Jon and Finn rode in the truck, towing a tractor with a large mower out to the vineyard. "What did you think of Bobby?" Jon said.

"I really like him. I didn't mean to make everyone so sad last night."

Jon looked over at Finn. "Not your fault; let it go."

"How am I supposed to just let that go? I feel I'm not built to let things go when I have hurt someone."

Jon looked over again. "Listen, what I meant when I said it's not your fault is that adults often hurt inside. Like when you play football, your ribs and muscles are sore the next day. Well, adults tend to hurt like that from internal injuries, things that happened years and years ago, maybe in their childhood. I would call them soul bruises, things that never got the proper attention, explanation, or the right amount of love to heal and the proper time to forgive over and forget. Adults tend to stack soul bruises up inside and keep count of them, going back to them each and every day, reliving the pain until they find a way to face the pain, to be truthful about it. Some would say that every adult, no matter how old, has a child within, a child that needs comfort and healing. Forgiveness, we all need forgiveness. Forgiveness of others and forgiveness of ourselves is the only way to heal and become stronger and not afraid. That's what Bobby was saying about alcohol. It has a way of bringing all that hurt to the surface in a person. Some use alcohol to dull the pain."

"Do I have soul bruises?"

"Yeah, yeah, you do, Finn. You are a special guy, you have a tender spirit, and you've already been through a lot in your life to be so young. My fear, Finn, is that you will have a lot of soul bruises in your life. But I want you to listen to me. If you learn how to heal yourself up, forgive yourself, forgive others, take care of yourself like that, then you will be able to help a lot of people in this world."

"Does Bobby have a lot of soul bruises?"

"Yeah, Bobby does. But Bobby also had Ruby, who helped heal those hurt places in him. Ruby's love has sustained him his whole life. He is a good example of how someone can forgive others and use that forgiveness for good and help others."

They pulled into the vineyard between the stone columns and stopped in the small meadow. Jon unchained the machine and backed it off the trailer. "Finn, I want you to stay clear of the tractor while I cut some of this tall grass and briars - you never know when a rock or root could be thrown out from the mower and hurt you."

Finn looked at Jon, nodded his head, and then said. "Can't I just ride on the tractor with you?"

"Yeah . . . I'd like that." Finn climbed beside Jon and stood between him and the tractor's fender. Finn placed his small arm around the shoulders of the man and balanced himself with a hand on the fender, and together they rode up and down the rows in the vineyard while Finn daydreamed of the old days Jon and Elizabeth had spent in the vineyard. He could see the basic structure of the vineyard, how beautiful it once was, and how lovely it could be again.

There was still much that needed to be done, the saplings and small pine trees that needed to be removed from around the vineyard post, but they had made significant progress. Jon unhooked the trailer from the truck, and they left it in the vineyard meadow and started back up the gravel road to the cabin.

"I thought we could catch some fish and take them to the restaurant tonight, let the chef prepare them."

"A chef? Is he the Bantam Chef? Finn looked at Jon, thinking he may be joking.

"Yeah, a chef; this is a place you need to clean up for; they've got a chef who studied in France; you think I'm joshing you?"

"You might be. You pull my leg a lot."

The old man furrowed his brow. "Come on now."

Jon pulled the truck into the driveway beside the sawmill and sea of grass. "I'll check on Elizabeth and pack some lunch for us. Do you want to take the gear and go up the staircase to the pond? Start fishing?"

"I can go up by myself and start fishing?"

Jon looked at Finn and smiled. "Yeah, that's what I had in mind. Betts and I will be up directly."

Elizabeth had already prepared lunch and had it sitting in the wicker basket on the kitchen booth. Jon could hear her upstairs, and he slipped off his boots and walked up the stairs to their bedroom. Elizabeth was retrieving one of the hat boxes. She put it on the bed and lay down beside it. She looked up and smiled. "Hello, Special Man."

Jon smiled at his wife of fifty years, and yet he saw the same teenage girl he had fallen in love with on that enchanted evening so many years ago. "Special Woman." He walked around the bed and looked at his wife's long frame, hair, neck, buttoned blouse, and slacks with a rope belt. He wanted to touch her softly, kiss her, undress her slowly, and make love with her just as he had done so many times in the past.

Elizabeth opened the box and pulled out love letters they had exchanged many years ago. Elizabeth read one of the letters and smiled to herself. "Have I ever told you that I'm in love with you?" He lay down beside her and rubbed her back. Jon looked into her eyes and shook his head. "Seriously, I had no idea. Think it will last?"

Elizabeth smiled. "I mean it, Jonny; I love you. You've always made me feel safe. I think you make everyone feel safe. Everyone comes running to you when they when they need fixing."

Jon smiled and looked into her eyes. He touched her face and put one of the curls of hair behind her ear. "Every day, Betts, I wake up early not to start my day, but I get out of bed and stand there, and I count to ten just to make sure it's not a dream. How did this happen? I found my soulmate so long ago. I've never run out of conversation with you. You have taught me so much about love. You showed me so much about love. Especially when we lived outside in the garden. You showed me the love of a mother. You saw me hurting, devastated, and guilty in my mind, and you didn't try to change me. You just moved into that garden of grief and took my hand. You married care, and I married help. I have never, ever known another human being like you. You are my everything, Betts. I love you."

Elizabeth looked into his eyes and touched the small, exposed part of his chest between the collars of his shirt. "I was just reading the letter you wrote me about the field of Queen Anne's Lace. When you were convalescing, in that French valley, during the war. You described love as a field of Queen Anne's Lace where two lovers play, and that one field connects to another, and another, and that if something happened to you, then for me to chase love, to never give up but to chase love into the next field and you'd be there waiting, love would always be there waiting for me."

"I came home, and we built the upper pond together, with our love, and in the meadow made love, and the Queen Anne's Lace, just came and miraculously took it over." Jon reached out his hand and took Elizabeth's. He looked into her eyes but did not see fear or sadness. He saw only comfort.

"Amazing isn't it," Elizabeth said.

Jon nodded. " Our love made those flowers grow. Finn's up there now, making his own memories."

"Our handsome son?"

"Yeah, The Skyuka Child."

Elizabeth lifted herself up from the bed. "I'm ready; I've got everything packed. I just want to bring some of these letters and the rug, lay beside you, and play in our lover's field. One more time Jonny, forever, and always just once more."

Carrying the picnic basket, they crossed the moss-covered stone on the wooden walkways, and at the limestone staircase, Elizabeth removed her slippers. Barefoot, she stepped before Jon and slowly climbed the rock steps. She reached out and touched the bark of the ancient trees as she went. Jon watched her bare feet embracing the smooth stones, and he thought of a full moon night when they were young, and Elizabeth climbed the staircase in the dappled moonlight and a loose robe, her night dusky hair hung between them. She led him to the field, laid him down on a bed of leaves, and undressed him like she was a nymph and he naive Hylas.

She did not tire, but it was as if the earth was lifting her steps, cheering her on. Rising up to call her blessed, goddess of the wood and mountain. The water flowed out of the standpipe beside the stone steps, and she paused to enjoy it. She leaned over and touched some of the low-growing ferns around the steps as if they were cooing infants and her, their grandmother. She kept going, and Jon followed, and they stepped into the sunlight from the tree canopy, and the field, soft and tender as any bed, greeted them with butterflies and bird notes. When she stopped, he knew this was the spot she had chosen. He unrolled their favorite rug and laid the picnic basket on it. Elizabeth was looking across the pond to where Finn was standing and fishing. Jon, too, looked over at him, and they exchanged waves. Over the many weeks that Finn had lived with them on the mountain, he had learned to fish and tie flies to his line's leader. He now lined the interior of his woven basket with green fern and herbs from the field, and there he would lay the fish he caught like trophies to be forever remembered. They could see him casting the fly back and forth between the ten and two positions, pausing at each point to let the line fully extend in the sunlight and the fish basket behind him in the grass under the canopy of ancient trees.

Elizabeth opened the picnic basket and took out a stack of handwritten letters from her and Jon wrapped in a piece of brown lace made on the Island of Burano from a trip they took to Venice. She untied them and laid them on the rug around the basket. "We've never counted all these it's hard to know how many there are in all." They valued handwritten letters and constantly wrote to each other even when living side by side in the small cabin. If priceless treasure can be as simple as a written word on a scrap of paper. Then these notes were the greatest treasure in the world to them. As they would open the letters and unwrap the Burano lace, they would often suggest a letter, like a favorite poem using its descriptive name or phrase.

Lying on his side, Jon watched Elizabeth lay out the pieces of treasure, and she touched each one as if taking a roll call in her mind. She was in her own place, which she loved and knew as home, with Jon close by. With the tangible expression of their love in front of her, like Aesop, she counted her gold. Jon watched her lips move as she read. In his own heaven, with his greatest treasure. "What is it? Which one are you reading?"

Elizabeth looked up and showed him the postcard she was reading. It was a French postcard with a picture of a fern leaf and different Monarch butterflies, with handwritten descriptions. The sending address was Rue de Bellevue A, 7, Rue Vincent, Paris. Jon nodded his head in recognition. Elizabeth began to read to him.

Jon,
less than a week, and even though we just saw each other, it seems like months.

I thought you might see the reference to this postcard... with butterflies... when I hike and see the butterflies, there is a calmness and a feeling of safety.
You are my butterfly as well.
There is a beauty, a comfort, a secure feeling of our love for each other.
I love you with all my heart. I can't wait to be in your arms!
Love, Your Elizabeth.

Jon looked at Elizabeth and smiled. "That was wonderful; Paris was so wonderful. I've always wanted to spend Christmas there. Shopping, dining, walking the streets in the snow." Elizabeth did not look up at him. She laid the postcard down on the rug and picked up another. Typically, they read one of his letters to her and then read one of her letters to him, but today she was intent on reading her letters to him as if on this particular day, set aside for her, she wanted him to know how much he had meant to her and how much she loved him in return. She picked up a small gray envelope. The postage stamp had white roses laid on a handwritten letter. There was a large rectangle postman's stamp on the front that said in block letters POSTAGE DUE. She opened it and slid out a thin, petite sheet of handmade paper inked with blue and burgundy inks sequenced in shapes that reminded Jon of Peacock plumes. Elizabeth turned the form over and began to read.

Sunday, August 21st, 1948

My Dearest Love,
How do I love thee? Let me count the ways.
I love thee to the depths of the seas you dive and the heights of the cirrus clouds we see in the sky.

I love thee to the dawning of each morning and the winding down of every night.
I love thee to each day we see, holding hands and the days we are apart, waiting to hold hands.
I love thee with the breath, smiles, and tears of all my life!
And if so, be I shall love thee in the next life.
Me

Jon picked up the brown Burano lace and swirled it around his finger. Elizabeth handed him the small, delicate, handmade paper. He could see her thumbprint had bled through the paper as she had inked it. The thumbprint was now part of the words in the letter as if certifying their authenticity. Jon put the paper to his lips and took a deep breath. It smelled like Elizabeth. The letters had lived so long in the hat box, above the armoire, and had been touched so many times by Elizabeth over the decades that they had taken on the smell of her. To Jon, feeling the letter was like touching the hands of Elizabeth. Smelling the letter was like smelling the beautiful body of his beloved. He handed it back to her. "It's precious, Betts." She smiled to herself again, and Jon admired the light pink of her lips, her eyes, and the curls of hair that framed her face. He remembered how often they had made love, in this field, by the pond, and how they had spent entire days here wrapped up in each other's limbs only to go home and spend the night sharing a bottle of wine, lighting candles, sleeping intertwined through the night.

"Oh, this is the one I was looking for." Elizabeth opened an envelope that was dark in color and written in bronze ink. It had been mailed from San Juan, Puerto Rico. "I wrote this after you sent me the letter describing the Sparrows." Jon smiled at her. He recognized the card. It had a base color of brown, but there were bright and vibrant flowers on the front, in pink, red, and yellow-gold. Elizabeth opened it, only to turn her head and look over her shoulder across the pond to where Finn was fishing. Satisfied he was there, she turned her attention back to the card.

Tuesday, August 16th, 1945

My passionate man,
I saw this poem today, and it made me think about how fast we fell in love…

> *"No sooner met, but they looked.*
> *No sooner looked, but they loved.*
> *No sooner loved, but they sighed.*
> *No sooner sighed, but they asked*
> *one another the reason.*
> *No sooner knew the reason,*
> *but they sought the remedy.*
> *And in these degrees have they made*
> *a pair of stairs to marriage."*
> *- WILLIAM SHAKESPEARE*

Love, Betts

This had always been a favorite card of Jon's. It was the first time she had ever expressed the desire to marry Jon like she was walking into her destiny with absolute confidence and certainty. Fulfilling what her godmother had promised her so many years ago, that her love would be perfect, one not soiled with hardships, disappointments, or war. Had it all come true?

"I love you, Jonny," Elizabeth said.

Jon whispered, "Je t'aime."

Finn walked up from behind Elizabeth, looking like an experienced outdoorsman, his fly rod in hand and the fish basket slung behind his back. "My handsome Son," Elizabeth said, extending her arm to touch the boy.

"I like when you call me Skyuka Child," Finn responded.

"Skyuka was a fisherman; how about you?" Jon motioned to the fish basket with his head. Finn laid the wicker basket in front of them and displayed several trout he had caught. All lined up beside each other, bedded on herbs and fern.

"Good job!" Elizabeth exclaimed.

Jon nodded his head. "Not bad, not bad at all."

Finn set the basket and his pole in the shade and then washed his hands at the water's edge. When he returned to the blanket, he knelt down and looked over the letters spread around the picnic basket. "What's all this?"

"These are the letters and postcards we've sent to each other throughout the years." Elizabeth turned her head slightly as she explained the significance of the letters to Finn. "Some of these letters are fifty years old. They tell the story of our love through World War II when Jon was in France, and I volunteered as a Nurse at the Red Cross. These letters crisscrossed the Atlantic Ocean and sometimes found their way through small villages. They are precious to us. They're almost a novel of our lives."

Elizabeth saw his interest in the letters. "You can read some, Finn; it's okay." Finn looked into her eyes and then wiped his hands on his shirt. He picked up a thick envelope and, opening it, began to read the letter to himself as Jon and Elizabeth exchanged smiles.

Finn smiled and picked up another. "You talk a lot about the sea," he said.

" The sea was a big part of our lives back then," Elizabeth said. "We traveled by ship a lot. We spent weeks on the ocean; it was poetic in many ways. We also talked a lot about the moon and stars because we promised each other early on that at every full moon, we would stay up and watch it cross the sky at night, no matter where we were or even together. It was this bond between us, a way for us to reach each other, no matter where we were in the World."

"How often would you write?"

Jon said, "During times we were apart, we would write nearly every day. So homesick for each other. Back then, it would take months for a letter to reach you, and when they did come, they often came several at a time. So, you would have to pay attention to the postmarks and dates to read everything in order. Things were not really relevant anymore, so you'd get a little bit of what was going on, but most letters were written about things that would transcend time, describe places that you hoped you would go back to together, or small things that brought back a memory you shared together. That makes these letters more novel than just a journal of days passed. No matter how our lives went, these letters always brought us back to each other."

Seated in the back of Elizabeth's car, Finn admired the sunset over the lake on the way to Lake Lanier Tea House. Dogwood trees and pine trees overhung the winding road. Large houses were built on the left side of the road, and summer lake camps were built directly over the lake's water. He could see antique boats, water skiers, and the silhouettes of two mountains on the far horizon. They pulled up at the Tea House, and a man with a large build about the same age as Jon met them at the car. "Theo, it's great to see you; how's Alice?" Finn stepped out of the car, opened Mrs. Elizabeth's door, and offered her his hand. She took it and smiled at him as she exited the vehicle. Finn could smell her sweet fragrance, and he loved the feeling of her soft hand in his. He gave her his arm, dressed like a gentleman in his navy suit jacket and khaki pants.

Finn escorted Elizabeth around the car to where Jon was talking to the man. " Elizabeth, my dear, how are you doing? It's been too long." Theo leaned forward, kissed Elizabeth on the cheek, and then turned to Finn.

Finn stepped forward, looked Theo in the eyes, and extended his hand. "I'm Finn Kindhart; it's a pleasure to meet you."

Theo chuckled and took Finn's hand. "Pleasure is all mine, young man."

Elizabeth said, "Theo served with Jon in World War II; they were in France together and have been close friends ever since." Finn looked at the men standing beside each other and tried to imagine the two as young soldiers with canteens, carbines, and bandoliers of ammunition.

Theo slapped Jon on the shoulder. "Jon single-handedly won the war. I still cannot believe the things I saw this man do. He did not fight like a young man; he fought with his mind." Jon lifted his hand, and Theo stopped his story. "Bobby is already here, he is by the bar with Clarence, and he brought his guitar, so he is going to play something very nice for us. I miss the days when Bobby, Ruby, and Lang would play jazz all night. How I wish for those days again. Come now, my friends, come it is such a joy to have you here at the Tea House tonight. A supreme joy to my old heart. Friends, come in." Theo opened the door to his restaurant.

The inside of the Tea House glowed with the warmth of the stained wood floors, walls, and overhead beams. The dining room was filled with white tablecloths, and candles flickered on each table. Waiters in white coats and black ties were whisking past with silver trays above their shoulders. All the waiters seemed to know Jon and Elizabeth. Finn had never seen a setting like this. He was only ten miles from the Wheat Hill House, yet it felt like a lifetime away.

"Bobby!" Elizabeth reached for the tall man, pulled his head down, and kissed his lips. Finn hugged Bobby around the waist, and Jon shook his hand. They were shown to a table near the wall, and

Bobby sat across from Finn, and Elizabeth sat across from Jon. Finn reached over and touched the logs of the restaurant wall, and it was like when he had scrambled up the bank to find Jon kneeling in front of the wild azalea. A feeling of history and nature surged through his fingers like the wood and building were alive with nostalgia. Finn touched the tablecloth and found it thick in his fingers. It had been ironed flat and starched. The candles flickered across everyone's faces, and Theo appeared at the table with a bottle of champagne and opened it, letting the cork pop loudly into a white cloth. He poured three glasses, and a waiter set a champagne flute full of sparkling water in front of Finn and poured fruit syrup, which spiraled and cascaded throughout the glass. A toast was proposed to great memories, friendship, the stone terrace with its music and dancing, and most of all to the beauty of Elizabeth. The glasses clinked together, and everyone, including all the waiters and Theo, drank the toast.

During the meal, Jon and Elizabeth shared memories of all the times they had come to the Tea House and spent the day boating and sunbathing off the dock.

Towards the end of the evening, when all the guests were starting to leave, Theo came over to the table and placed his hand on Jon's shoulders. "If you, my dear friends, are feeling up to it. Clarence has made an extraordinary dessert in honor of your wonderful visit. If I may suggest, let's retire to the terrace for dessert, port, espresso, and laughter with the entire restaurant family. Everyone is insisting you cannot say no. Everyone wants to spend time with you, dear ones."

Jon and Elizabeth looked across the table at each other. "We would love to," Jon said, touching Theo's arm.

"Theo, this place, means so much to me, and you do too, and Alice and all the waitstaff. I miss when everyone would come up to the mountain and spend the day."

Theo nodded to Elizabeth. "The full moon parties, the pond parties. Say. Do you remember the pond party when we dressed up the standpipe like a totem pole and made the fire beneath it, and all the kids were there riding around on the horses in the firelight? I remember looking up the treetops, and there were millions and millions of fireflies in the canopy." He raised his hands as if remembering all the glowing lights of the fireflies. He looked into Elizabeth's eyes. Do you remember that night, my dear?"

Elizabeth was smiling, almost tearing up. "Yes, yes." She stood up and hugged Theo. The terrace was made of random shapes of flagstone. The wrought iron tables were lit by delicate lights strung from the boughs of the trees. A fire was started in an outdoor chimney, and as the waitstaff was done cleaning, they all joined in the laughter and conversation on the terrace. Bottles of wine were opened, Bobby began playing his guitar, and the instrument's sound filled the outdoor patio.

The Chef appeared on the terrace with two servers carrying silver trays of dense chocolate cake. Ice cream was scooped on top, cold and hard. Elizabeth instructed Finn to dig his spoon into the center of the small cake. When he did, there was revealed a molten pool of dark chocolate. Finn's eye grew very large, and Elizabeth smiled, patting the boy's thin knee. Bobby finished a song, and everyone clapped.

"Say, Bobby," Theo said, "remember when you and Ruby, and Isidore Langlois, played here? People would come from all over on those nights. We stayed up all night, just listening to the music and serving people drinks and food. Those were the glory days of the Tea House. People would spend all day, all weekend even, but mostly they came just to hear you all sing and play."

Bobby smiled at the memory. "Oh, indeed, indeed, Theo. Lang was trying to get us to move out to New Orleans, and I guess we were about ready too. That was certainly a dream of ours, playing in New Orleans. Ruby was very hopeful of that." Bobby paused, and for a second, he seemed somewhere else. "Thank you, Theo, for letting us have those good times."

"My friend, thank you. You gave so much for love. People do not die for love anymore." Theo looked over at Jon. "Jean-Paul. . . Jean-Paul died for love." Jon nodded his head.

Bobby continued playing, and Clarence, the chef, came over and asked Elizabeth to dance in front of the fireplace; then Jon danced with Elizabeth, and she stole kisses from him and rested her head on his shoulder.

As the night ended, everyone said their goodbyes and hugged each other. Some of the waiters kissed Elizabeth's cheek or hand and bowed in their leaving as if departing from a queen. She beamed as she held tightly to Jon's arm, walking to the car.

The ride home up the mountain was quiet. Finn rode in the back seat and listened to Elizabeth and Jon share favorite moments of the evening and of times gone by. The grass in the meadow moved like dark waves in the moonlight. Finn put his arm around Elizabeth as they went inside the house. She kissed his cheek in the great room by the day bed where Finn slept. "I love you," she said. "I love you too. I wanted to dance with you, but." "But what?" "Well, I don't know how to dance. It's not allowed." "Dancing not allowed? I'd say, Skyuka spent many nights dancing right here where we stand now. Dancing is an expression of joy that can't be put into words. Speaking of words. Do you know what ensemble means in French?" "Ensemble?" "Oui, ensemble. It means together. And dance is danser." Finn rolled the words in his mouth, "Danser ensemble." "Very good. Say it again." "Danser ensemble." "How do you feel about dancing now, since we've given it a new name? "It's unspeakable joy expressed together." Elizabeth nodded her head yes. "Everyone has that little voice in their head that says they are not good enough, they will embarrass themselves, or do not deserve joy. Finn, that little voice does not tell the truth. The truth is that you were born perfect, and you deserve unspeakable joy, and your expression of that joy will be manifested perfectly."

She cupped his chin in her hand. "Tomorrow, let's go to the French Valley for sunset. We will have a dance together," she said.

Finn smiled back at her. "Okay, ensemble." "Child, we will always be together."

She climbed the stairs slowly, and Finn watched her ascend into the bedroom. Jon came into the great room, still in his black suit, the collar of his white shirt opened, and his necktie loose. "Good night, Sport. I hope you had fun tonight." He touched Finn on the shoulder.

"It was great; I loved it."

Lying beneath the covers, Finn felt comfortable in what he had come to regard as his home. It had been a long time since he had seen his family or his real mother. No one had called to check on him or to say hello, but that was normal. He was used to that. He wondered how he could ever tell his family that he knew what dancing was or that other languages could change the feeling and, therefore, the meaning of an action in one's heart.

He thought of Bobby, marveling at his hands, so large, the dark skin, the light color of his palms. His gentle eyes, the deliberate and gracious voice. It felt good to be Bobby's friend.

The couple climbed into bed, and Jon leaned over to turn off the light. He could see Elizabeth was tired. She reached for him, and he grasped her hand on his chest. "I love you, Jonny. Today was just wonderful. You make me so happy."

Jon smiled into the darkness and leaned over, and kissed her forehead. "I love you, Betts," he whispered. "You make every day so special. You are my special woman."

Elizabeth fell asleep with her hand in the center of Jon's chest. He lay there thinking about the grief of Bobby, the loss of Ruby, and the loss of Jean-Paul, who died for love so many years ago in France. These things still troubled him as they had for so long. He closed his eyes and hoped a reason for the pain would be explained turn his sleep. The night was cool, and the sounds of the mountain serenaded him as they had every night for so long.

Jon dreamed of the cabin at the end of the sea of grass, nestled amongst the boulders of the mountain and the small pond. The ancient Cherokees' trees stretching out their limbs, like arms and hands, beckoning him to come closer to them, our gods, our god—people, our caretakers, our lovers. Jon dreamed of the pond and his fish children swimming in tight schools. He plunged into the cool water and pulled himself deeper and deeper into the cold depths, into the rushing cold water, from the rushing cold water place. He could hear the fountain pouring into the pool, and under the water, he could listen to it amplified and thunderous like a cascading waterfall that would never stop, but then suddenly, it did. Jon was in the cold water, but it was silent.

The absence of noise caused Jon to wake from his dream. He lay in bed listening to the silence, trying to understand the quiet. What had changed? He had lived here nearly all his life. He only knew it with the noise that nature made, but now something was different; what was it? He got up from the bed, his heart beating rapidly; he couldn't catch his breath. Something was terribly wrong because there was no sound. Was life as he knew it over? Did an asteroid, again, strike the earth and stop the fountain? That was it. That was it! Jon got to the bottom of the stairs, turned the corner into the kitchen, and flung open the door. To his horror, the fountain had stopped silent as stone. Jon could see from the porch that his fish children were floating on their sides in the small pond. The birds were no longer singing, and green summer leaves were turning loose from the trees and falling down upon the brown dead moss covering the rocks. The boards of the walkways were popping loose and curling upward. But most shocking was that the fountain that had always flowed through droughts, and famines, and wars, and death had stopped. Abruptly, the noise of life was no longer there. In his heart, he knew the greatest reason for his living was gone.

Jon suddenly felt a spear of ice had been plunged into the center of his chest and was beginning to twist. Writhing in pain from the twisting and the freezing cold and the absence of all balance in the world, he screamed out in pain and sat up in bed, forcing himself from the nightmare. He fell back onto the bed, but the cold plunged into his chest. Jon reached up and felt Elizabeth's ice-cold hand. His heart raced, and he panicked, spinning his body quickly in the bed. "Betts, Betts!" He got to his knees in the bed, still holding the cold, lifeless hand. He reached out and turned on the bedside lamp.

To his horror, Elizabeth's pale skin had purple and blue lines running from her neck to her beautiful cheeks, and her lips were blue. Jon shook her and tore back the covers, shouting her name. She did not respond. He squeezed her cheeks, opened her mouth, and stuck his finger inside her mouth to clear anything blocking her windpipe. He lunged across the bed, grabbed the phone beside the bed, and dialed 911. He placed the receiver on the bed and pulled the pillows out from behind her head as the phone began to ring. He knelt at her side, pinched her nose, breathed into her lungs, and then plunged his locked palms into her abdomen, begging her to live. The phone connected, and a stale voice could be heard asking about his emergency. With his old military precision, Jon gave his address and the need for an ambulance. Then Female, her age, blood type, weight, no allergies, nondrinker, non-responsive, cardiac failure. He repeated it over and over and over. He finally let the phone fall to the bed. He stuck his forefingers under her chin and felt a feeble pulse. He continued CPR, shouting for Elizabeth to come back to him. Calling her name as if she was lost on the mountain.

The purple from her face was retreating, the color was coming back, but her eyes were not responding. Jon pleaded for Elizabeth to return back to him, back to the living, back to their own heaven. Finn yelled up the stairs that he would clear a path for the EMTs. Jon finally heard the sirens of the ambulances. It seemed as if several vehicles were turning by the Sawmill now. Jon was on top of Elizabeth, counting out loud, continuing to breathe into her mouth and press forcefully onto her abdomen. The EMTs came into the room, and immediately Jon moved out of the way. They lifted Elizabeth from the bed to the floor using the bed sheet that they ripped from its place. Blood started streaming from the corner of his precious wife's nose, and he fell to his knees to plead with the only hope he had left of saving his wife. The EMTs opened duffle bags of equipment, and one prepared a shot of Epinephrine. Jon could hear his wife's ribs cracking under the downward pressure of the fire Captain performing CPR on Elizabeth. The sound was sickening. In the commotion, items were knocked off the bedroom tables, and furniture was pushed out of the way. They removed Elizabeth's clothes, exposing her breasts and preparing to shock her with a defibrillator.

Jon was on his knees, rocking back and forth, holding his head in his hands and crying. Pleading with God, begging God to take him and not Elizabeth. Pleading, begging, willing to make any deal, especially his life for hers. God was not there. He clawed at the carpet and began to rip the fibers of the fabric up with his fingers. Digging in his fingers again, pleading to God for an audience, but God was not there. He plunged his fingers again, ripping into the carpet, lifting it from the floor where it had been glued down, and his fingernails began to pop off the end of his fingers and bleed. An

EMT came over to calm him, grabbing Jon's hands, but with his hands lifted near his head, Jon grabbed his hair and ripped chunks of it from his scalp. The EMT knelt down and hugged Jon's arms surrounding the man with his body to bind him. Jon rocked back and forth, pleading with God, any God, to save his precious wife. He was going into shock, his hands curling inward, his fingers becoming stiff, unable to stretch out his arms. The fear and shock had taken over, but his mind was still keen, pleading for a life trade. He watched the EMTs on the other side of the bed. The local Fire Chief came up the stairs and stood before him. He saw the lead EMT sit back and let out a long sigh. Jon knew the worst had happened that Betts was forever gone. The night season was done, and the day's setting sun had set. The EMT stood. His white shirt had come untucked from his dark pants while attempting to save Elizabeth's life. He removed his plastic gloves, slowly turned, and walked over to Jon, kneeling on the floor, his fingernails popped up and bleeding. The Captain knelt beside him and put a hand on Jon's shoulder. "We've done all we can. Maybe if you had lived closer to town… but she was too weak by the time we got here. I'm sorry, Sir, but your wife has passed away; she's dead, and there's nothing else we can do."

Jon nodded his head up and down like a beaten prisoner of war. He understood what the Captain had said, but he was in such shock that his tongue had turned thick. A ragged "Okay" escaped Jon's lips.

"If this gentleman lets you go, you promise not to hurt yourself? Not to rip any more hair out? If he lets you go, I need you to just breathe, and I'm here; I will breathe with you. Look at me." Jon turned his head, like a stiff clock marking time, and rotated around and looked into the eyes of the lead EMT, a good forty years his junior. They locked eyes. "Okay, let him go. Let's breathe together now." Jon breathed, focusing on the young man's mouth and the air that passed through his lips. He tried to match it. Still, on his knees, every breath felt like he was breathing out all the life he had ever known. Every nutrient that had ever sustained him. He could see Elizabeth's legs stretched out past the end of the bed in an unnatural way. The EMT brought his eyes back to his. He nodded his head. Jon nodded and crawled on his knees and disfigured hands to Elizabeth's side. He began to sob. His tears poured out of his eyes onto the body of his dead wife. He leaned over Elizabeth. "We can be doves, we can be doves, Baby. I promise you, Elizabeth. We will be doves, we will be doves together, baby, we will be doves." He kissed her blue lips and moved the curly hair from her face. As he spoke to her, promising his eternal love, a thin red line of blood broke past her lips and trickled down the side of her face. The room was emptying out now. Jon was whispering into Elizabeth's ear, promising her over and over they could be doves in the afterlife when he felt a small, warm hand reach around his shoulder and lie over his franticly beating heart. He turned his weeping, red eyes and tear-wet face to see Finn standing over him with tears in his eyes. "Fear not; I am with you." Jon grabbed the boy's arm and hugged it, and Finn knelt and cast his body over Jon's.

CHAPTER 12

"I have loved thee with an Everlasting Love"

Facing the cruel truth that Elizabeth was gone caused Jon to find the courage to help move her body to the EMTs' transfer board, ensuring every bit of her skin was covered except her face. He carefully supervised the securing of her body to the board so it could not move. Then he placed himself at her feet and counted to three, and everyone lifted his wife's body, and with the precision found in a professional soldier, he stated, "Prepare to move." And they moved in unison down the narrow staircase with Jon in the lead. Often, they reached out for the maple handrail or touched the walls to steady themselves over the carpeted stairs. Finn watched from the great room.

    Once on the side porch, Jon asked for a "Secondary hold." And the group stopped, laying the board across the patio table. Jon wanted to give Elizabeth's body one last moment to take in the patio's air, the fountain's sound, and all their days and nights spent in their favorite place. After a few minutes, Jon led the paramedics on and entombed his wife in the Ambulance that would take her away forever. Bobby was here now and walked over and embraced him. Jon stood by as they closed the doors of the Ambulance. As it pulled away, he followed it for a few steps. Then he stopped, knowing it was the last time Elizabeth's body would ever travel over the gravel driveway, past the wooden sheds, the weeping trees, and hanging sap boards, past the old sawmill and its outbuildings, and along the sea of lamenting grass. Jon watched it until it could no longer be seen, the Ambulance lights blinking but not giving off sound anymore, raising a small cloud of dust.

A man, even though he may be old, if he is still strong, can be useful in war, but he had not been able to save the most precious person in his life. He could think and plan ahead, take care of himself and his brothers, live alone on a mountain, and move the earth to his will, but he could not protect his own wife. Why?

Bobby walked over to Jon, stood beside him, and wrapped his arms around him, but Jon did not want to be held. He was dying inside, like what had just happened had cut his remaining time of life in half, and rightfully so. Didn't he just lose his life? Jon turned slowly to walk back inside. He reached the porch step but found the one step too high for his weak body to conquer, so he grabbed the porch rail, his body swung low, and he sat on the smooth planks of the porch, his legs too weak to stretch out in front of him. He leaned over and felt as if he was hollow, inflated only by air, and could be simply folded up to save space or dissolved like a puddle into the earth.

Finn saw Jon as he swung onto the steps and leaned over. He saw the lanterns hanging above him near the porch ceiling, and for a moment, they appeared to be hourglasses that had been broken and all the time-sand drained out. Jon seemed to be that same kind of broken vessel. A hollow sphere that only had meaning when someone cared to fill it and wrap the union in a bit of wax cloth, and rotate it, watching and waiting for the moment when fulfillment would near its end and then suddenly turn over to actually find that life was full each day, and a new beginning. Now, the binding cloth, the turner, the watcher, the waiter, and the admirer were gone. What is an hourglass if no one is there to tend to it? Is it just an empty soul full of wasted time? How much value does stopped time have? What if the time in your soul clock stops, but all the other watches in the world don't notice? What if they continue? What if they do see but say that it is only broken and will be mended, surely to be filled again in time, serving its intended purpose just as before. What if all the other clocks keep ticking and only pause to say, "Shame, but everything happens for a reason, don't despair." Would this make the stopped clock feel better, or would the etching of the sand on its atrium walls be finally seen for the scars they really are? How thin the glass looks when it is not flowing? Jon felt this hollow, and Bobby knew it. He walked over and rubbed his brother's shoulders and held his hands and wept with him, on his knees, in the dirt, weeping, bringing the sackcloth to match Jon's ashes. After some time, the two men found comfort in this shared burden, and they hugged each other and stood up.

"Will you try and rest in the shelter, Jon?" Bobby asked, but Jon had no intention of sitting on the porch in his usual spot because he felt so cold inside himself. He shuffled across the porch, almost too weak to move his feet, as if the death of Elizabeth had suddenly brought on extreme old age.

Inside, he stopped briefly at the flannel shirts hanging in the kitchen, picked up Elizabeth's favorite, and smelled her scent. He entered the great room, and it seemed that all the furniture he had known and walked by, at least twice a day, for so many decades was all standing at attention against the walls and holding their breath. His heart was ripping apart inside him. He did not feel strong enough to climb the stairs but thought of reaching the daybed where Finn had slept. He set this as his goal like a runner in a distance race, looking at the mark though his legs were weak and faltering beneath him. Realizing how precious the flannel shirts hanging in the kitchen were, knowing that Elizabeth was the last to wear them. He didn't want them moved now. He wanted to take time to go back and notice every little thing that Elizabeth had displayed for him, but right now, he was too weak, and lost, and so cold.

Jon was desperately tired, but there was no way he could sleep with the drum of reality beating so loudly in his mind. He sat down on the daybed, removed his shoes, crawled under the covers and thick comforter with all his clothes on, and stretched them entirely over his head. In this cocoon, he searched for solace, but he found it empty as the hourglass and not opaque enough to hide him from his fear. He entered a translucent, dream state, a place where his aching soul connected to the aching soul of Elizabeth. Her soul, not ready to give up the heaven she knew for the afterlife she was being ushered into, was everywhere, thrashing about, kicking up the wind, causing birds to misbehave, and most of all, weeping throughout Jon's mind. She held the hourglass that was his heart in her hands now, gazing into it to find that his life was in danger of draining out, separating her eternally from him, and she was on the wrong side of the fragile glass wall of life to stop it. Jon, now in the fetal position, hiding under the blankets, teeth chattering from the heart shock, prayed to his newly minted Angel, begging her for help, begging her to not leave him behind and alone, begging for her to always know that he loved her and most of all to take him with her. Jon realizing that his paradise could never be paradise again without her.

Bobby sat down with Finn on the church pew of the side porch. He leaned back and breathed in deeply, trying to process the events of the night and day with this small boy sitting next to him; tears dried on his face, and his blue eyes turned red. Bobby sat for a long while, being in the moment. "How are you feeling, Finn? I know it's been a tough day for you, a tough day for all of us." Bobby ran his hands down his faded blue jeans and breathed in deeply again. Looking out across the backyard and the wooden walkways that ran over the moss-covered stone. "I talked to the EMTs, and they said that you were very brave and directed them through the house. One said you brought them glasses of water; they didn't even realize how thirsty they had become. They were very impressed by you. I'm very proud of you too, Finn. You're a good man."

Finn sat looking out across the backyard and to the shadows the dark canopy of the trees cast over the boulders and barrier of the forests. His hands were folded on his lap, in front of the knot in the white cotton rope belt laced through the loops of his blue jeans. He sat there for a long while before answering. He continued looking forward and said, "There's this machine at the Hardware store in Inman that you can bring bags of pecans to. You know, the ones you gather up out of the yard? They have those smooth shells that are brown with black smudges mixed in, you know, the ones? The shells end in those sharp points on each end." Finn raised his hand as if touching the point of the pecan shell with the tip of his finger. "You bring all those pretty pecans into the store, and they pour them into this machine, and the machine starts up, and the nuts start shaking and moving, and this big heavy plate drops down, over and over, on the thin, hard shells, and cracks them open. A little dust fills the room, and bits of shells fall all around the machine to the floor, but when the nuts come out the other side, the shells are all cracked and damaged, and broken up. It's supposed to be better, somehow, like it's easier to pull the shells apart, discard the brown and black pieces and the pointy ends, and just get to the heart of it faster and quicker. We go there and crack up the nuts, but every time I see those beautiful shells come out the other side of that machine, it breaks my heart in some way. You see the tender, heart-meat of the nuts, just laying, all broken up in what they've always known as their lives, their protection. Some greedy Mother is pleased, thinks it was a good deal, sacks up the broken nuts, and drives home to pull them further apart over the next few days. Pulls out the heart and chews on it, discards the rest. Throws it in the garden or in the trash. That's how I feel right now, Bobby. I feel like one of those pecans that grew and fell under the tree and laid there gazing up in wonderment at all the beauty around it, but now, now, I feel like I've been run through that machine. I feel like I've been bashed up, and my heart is exposed. Still beating, still feeling, and hurting." He looked over at Bobby, listening to the words flowing from the child's heart as if it was a story he had never heard. Finn said, "If I could choose, I'd choose just to lay there, to lay under the tree, you know? I'd lay there and just decay in my beautiful shell, looking up into the tree's canopy and the blue sky. I may give myself, my inner self, to something or some cause one day, but I'd be fine to just lay there until that came along. What I'm saying, I think, is that I'm not a person that needs the machine. I'm not a person who needed the machine to show me that I had a heart and could love with it. I already knew that Bobby; I didn't need some machine to mangle me up like this." Small tears were forming in his eyes. The memory of the machine was obviously something that had imprinted on Finn's mind.

Bobby reached his arm around Finn and drew him to his side. The boy tucked his head into the man's chest and placed a small hand on his stomach, like holding on to a tree. "I get it, Finn. I didn't need the machine either; life's not fair. We didn't ask to be broken or damaged or hearts exposed like this; we didn't get a choice. It was just the hand we were dealt, and that's not a good feeling."

"It's a scary feeling to me," Finn said.

Bobby pulled the boy tighter to him and then let him go. "We will get through this; we've got each other. I'm glad you're here. You are here for a reason; at least, I feel that in my heart."

Finn nodded. "I wish I could have had her longer, Bobby. I've only known her for this summer. It would be different if I had longer with her."

Bobby had felt that way at the loss of Ruby, and he felt it now with the loss of Elizabeth. "I know Finn, I know how you're feeling, but Elizabeth was, is, something special. I have known her for fifty years, and guess what? It's still not enough. She has probably been the best and closest friend I've had since losing Ruby, and like you, I didn't deserve this. I didn't need this hurt to realize and appreciate what I had. I already knew it; every day, in my heart, I knew it and thanked God for it." He was opening up to Finn now. This small boy was sharing his heart's burden, not talking, not trying to explain it away or say that God had a plan for the pain, but just hearing him and being there.

The two left the porch and went inside. Bobby entered the great room with a cup of tea and placed it beside the daybed on a small table. Jon heard them, removed the comforter from over his head, and sat on the daybed. "Thank you, Bobby. Here sit down with me." Finn sat on the steps leading up to the bedroom.

"We will need to make some plans about the funeral and all and what you want." Jon could only nod. "I called McFarland, and they said they knew you. You had done some favor for them in the past, and they wanted me to express their condolences. We have a tentative meeting with them at eleven tomorrow if that's who you want to go with." Jon nodded his head. "I thought, and I'm just saying things, you stop me when you want, but I thought we could do a receiving of friends there and then the service at my church, and then burial—"

Jon shook his head. "We don't have all that many friends alive anymore, Bobby. I mean, we aren't young anymore. Two- three events seem a bit much. Elizabeth would agree. I think we just do a receiving of friends at your church and then just a small service at the same time." Jon looked down at his hands and then back up. "Maybe just some refreshments afterward."

Bobby liked that it would be simple and quick, and none of them had the strength to draw something out over several days. "Flowers or donations?"

"Flowers, she would definitely want flowers, and then we can give them away after the service; we can give money in her name too. Money seems worthless."

Bobby nodded. Elizabeth had been in love with flowers her whole life. When they first saw her on the gravel road to the Oak Hall Hotel, her bicycle basket was full of flowers she had picked for some guest's table. She always had flowers around, and it seemed fitting that she would be surrounded by flowers at this moment.

"Do you want me to call Finn's parents and have them come and pick him up?" Bobby looked over at Finn, sitting quietly on the stairs and looking earnestly at Jon. Worry covered his face over Jon's well-being, and he hated to say what he knew he had to.

Jon looked up at Bobby as if he had just hurt him maliciously. "No, that has not crossed my mind. Do you want to go home, Finn? Are you feeling okay?" Jon stretched out his arms and motioned for the boy to come over to him and sit on the daybed. Finn got up and moved quickly and sat down beside the old man. He hugged Jon. "I don't want you to go back home, Finn, but at the same time, I understand that Elizabeth dying, and you being here and seeing that is unsettling. I would understand if you wanted to leave and return home."

Finn shook his head. "I want to stay here if you want me to." He was looking into Jon's eyes now. "I want to stay because I feel close to Mrs. Elizabeth here, and I want her to feel close to me. I want her to know I'm here, thinking of and loving her. I want you to know those same things." The boy had folded his hands but was now forcing the palms apart and showing the underside of the clasped fingers out in front of him. The action clearly showed how bound up his own heart was in grief. Jon nodded at him like he understood. "She's like the eagle now," Finn said, "the eagle that came and watched over Skyuka when he was hurting on the rock. She's our eagle; if we are here, she will always be above us, between us and the sun, protecting and watching us. You know?" He paused, raising his clutched fist to his cheeks, wanting to be strong and fighting the oncoming tears. "And we made a promise to her to finish restoring the vineyard, as a gift, we have to do that, we promised! Well, we didn't promise her because it was a surprise, but we, in a way, did promise because we said we would, didn't we? We said that we would do it, and she would be proud, and she still will be proud because she will see us doing it, and she will circle high above us, and she will know, forever, right, that we love her, right?" Tears were coming to Jon's eyes again. He was nodding. He put his hands on the boy's shoulders. "Yes, yes, Finn, we will do that, we will do that together, and she will see us each day, and she will see how broken our hearts are because she's gone, but she will also see how much love we have for her and that she will never be forgotten but will live on and on."

Bobby looked on and saw the two contemplating the perception of their shrine. He recognized the impulse because he had felt that way when Ruby was murdered. To take all Ruby's music, recordings, and pictures and promote him still as an artist, a voice able to be heard and admired from the grave. He knew this was a natural response to grief, like a non-swimmer fallen through a frozen pond fights the shock and peril by pushing it away and, in doing so, can gasp a breath and find a why for living until a helping hand or a stable branch is extended, from a sounder place. "Jon, I'm going to go out to the apartment and make some of these phone calls, then I will come back and make something for us to eat."

"I'm not hungry," Jon said. "I can't even think about eating anything. I don't have the strength."

Bobby saw for the first time Jon thinking of only himself; the grief was so great that his survival instinct had kicked in, and he wasn't considering Finn or Bobby. "Well, I will come back up and make something for Finn and me, maybe some beans and toast, something simple." He got up before anything else could be said, stopped at his brother's side, and placed a hand on his shoulder. "I will put some new sheets on the bed when I get back so you can try and get some rest tonight. I know that is going to be hard." Bobby stopped at the doorway to the kitchen. "Want to take a walk, Finn?" The boy looked at Jon, who was frozen, looking up the staircase to his future like a desperate miner in front of the daunting Golden Stairs of the Chilkoot Pass.

When Bobby and Finn left the cabin, Jon left the daybed. He did not stand up because where he was now was sacred and holy. Kneeling, he crawled on all fours to the staircase, and with bowed head and closed eyes, he leaned over and kissed the carpeted stairs, and mumbling as if reciting prayers in the blue mosque, he slowly began to climb each stair on his knees. The moment's weight was so great he could not open his eyes. Like he had sustained trauma to the head and was suspended between two countries he loved that were at war, the here and the now. He reached the top of the stairs and the bedroom, and he opened his eyes to see the bed torn apart, the lamp still on, and footprints in the carpet made from the heavy-soled shoes of the medics. He noticed the place where the carpet had been lifted and its fibers torn out. He stretched his hands out to feel the area, and for the first time, he saw the bandages around his fingers where the nails had been torn off. In shock, he hadn't realized the first responders had bandaged his bleeding hands and head. He picked up the individual carpet strands and remembered pleading with the absent God to spare Elizabeth's life and take him instead. He would gladly do that now. He cleaned up the tiny fibers, smoothed out the carpet, and placed the debris in the small waste basket; that was his mess, not anyone else's.

He was standing now and looking at the bed that had been abused. The mattress shifted the pillows thrown aside. The sheet that had been on the bed was poorly folded in half and had been placed on one side of the bed. Jon walked slowly, step by step, to the place where the emergency personnel had desperately tried to save Bett's life. He noticed a blood stain, on the carpet, at the corner of the bedpost. He knelt down, horrified about what to do. It was her blood. This was part of Elizabeth, and it was all he had of her body for now. He touched the edges of the stain, bowing in front of it, wondering how to do what he knew he had to do.

He walked into the bathroom and ran the water hot. He soaked a towel, and twisted it, the water soaking his bandages. He returned and dabbed at the stain, the blood turning pink in the towel's fibers. He returned to the sink and rinsed Elizabeth's blood from the towel, watching it mix with the water and disappear down the drain. It felt like a stabbing in his chest to dispose of her remains this way. He was in a stupor and heated the towel again in the water and returned to the spot, soaking it, washing it, letting it go, into the unknown, time stealing her away still, now, after she was dead.

Jon looked at the bed, and knowing that he would have to change the sheets and make the bed, he wondered how he could save whatever was left of her there. He picked up her pillow and smelt it, breathing in her fragrance, and under the pillow, he found a piece of her hair, long and curly. He picked it up and searched the bed for more. He pulled the bed away from the wall, and more of her hair was on the floor. He gathered them all up until they formed a small lock of hair. He wondered where to place them to keep them safe and secure. His secure places had always been in the old sawmill, but he wanted something here in their place. What were her safe places? Jon turned and looked up at the hat boxes along the top of the armoire. His heart leaped, knowing that was it, that was the place where Betts kept her most sacred treasures. He pulled the hat boxes down, set them on the bed, and opened the lids.

* * *

Bobby and Finn walked side by side down the long gravel driveway, past the outbuildings, and along the grass sea, rolling in the wind. "Do you think he will be okay?" Finn said.

"He's got a long road in front of him; only time will tell."

Finn looked up at Bobby. "What do you mean, time will tell and all?"

Bobby was quiet for a moment, then he said, "People fall in love in one of two ways. Either they fall in love at first sight, or they fall in love at last sight."

"I've heard of people falling in love at first sight, but what do you mean about the last sight?"

"Well, for Jon and Me, we fell in love with our other person from the moment we first saw them. We didn't even know their names. It was just this rush of a feeling, and we knew. Other people's love is not that way. They may like or admire the person and be attracted to them, but it's never all-encompassing until that person walks out the door, fed up with mediocre love. Then the other person realizes what he's taken for granted, what they are going to be without. From then on, it's like getting hit by a train. This train of love and emotion. Realizing what they once had and will never have again. You see, when you tell someone to get out of your life, you are never guaranteed to ever having them again in your life; it's permanent. No one has the right to play with someone else's life or emotions or disrespect them. If you do, and that person decides to leave, you may never get the chance to go back and apologize. You may learn your lesson and even change, but you may never get the opportunity to show that person you deserve a second chance."

"So, what's the best love?"

"The best love is love at first sight," Bobby said. "That's how Jon and Elizabeth fell in love. First-sight love, maintained with kindness and mindfulness, may very well last a lifetime."

"But the love at last sight kind of love?"

Bobby looked over. "That love doesn't start until it's all gone, over and done with. It is a shame; it's also the most common."

"Bobby, do women fall in love at first sight and at last sight, like men?"

Bobby chuckled and sighed. They nearly reached the sawmill. "I don't know, Finn. I know they fall in love at first sight, but I've never heard a woman speaking about falling in love at last sight. Women are smarter, wiser, and more intuitive than us men. They are more evolved than men, emotionally stronger, and foresighted. Their love has more tensile strength. Whereas a man carries all his strength in his arms and shoulders, a woman carries her strength deep within her soul. Does that make sense?"

Finn interlocked his fingers and held them up. "Tensile strength?"

"Yeah, yeah, just like that. Some Women are woven together with moral fibers, which makes them strong and wise. Now they may and often do fall in love with foolish men, which can cost them a lot, but the difference is they don't ever regret having taken a chance on love."

"Did Ruby fall in love with you like that? Did she fall in love with you at first sight?"

Bobby turned and looked at Finn. He hadn't realized that the boy did not know that Ruby was a man. That Bobby and Rueben had been a loving pair. Even now, Bobby felt pain after so long because people had forgotten who Rueben was. Like a name in a journal or history book, time had lost the essence of who Rueben Briscoe Fry really was. Bobby wondered if he would have to once again defend his love orientation all alone to this white child who was already fragile, having been systemically infused by bias his whole life. Bobby's soul was weary and tired of all he had been fighting, non-violently protesting, his entire life. He looked into the white child's blue eyes. "Ruby and I never had a choice about love. It was something God intended from the very start. It was a perfect and pure love from first sight." He reached out and hugged the child to his side. "Would you chop some kindling for the stove? I will be down in a few minutes."

* * *

Jon reached for the hat boxes and set each on the bed. He slowly opened them and laid the lids behind each box so they wouldn't be mismatched from how Elizabeth had last left them. Acutely aware that everything he was touching now was something that Elizabeth had last touched, and with each item he held, he did so in a way as to feel her hands, and his ears were open to her voice. He removed photos that had been in the boxes for so long that they had begun to stick together. He removed old dinner menus from places they had eaten on their travels abroad. He withdrew a journal of her godmother Gertrude Bell and held it, pondering the strange markings, and he remembered back to when he had first read Gertrude Bell's translation of Hafiz's poetry before he had even known Elizabeth. One box contained their personal letters wrapped in the brown piece of Burano lace, and as he picked it up, he noticed a new letter, one he had never seen before and one that had been placed on top of the bound stack of letters. A brown envelope with Jon written in the center and Me under it. Jon stepped back and knelt on the carpet, turning the crisp brown envelope over and over in his bandaged hands. He sat on the carpet and put the envelope to his lips, and he could smell Elizabeth's fragrance on the letter. He knew what this was, and he was scared his heart racing. He slid a folded sheet out of the envelope and held the thin paper between his fingers. He opened the letter and read with a shaking hand over his mouth.

Jonny,
If you are reading this letter, it means the sun has set for me, and I know you will have been weeping because I know how much you love me. I want you to know that I did not have a choice in leaving, but it was something that I knew was coming. Something I could not explain but that I could feel inside, like a debt that was coming due, something unavoidable and costing more than I wished to pay. An obligation not from God or nature but from time. Like it had been measured out in grains of sand, in a glass, slipping down the sides, into eternity, or another place, and I had few remaining.
Jon, I will be waiting for you, my love, in our field of Queen Anne's lace in that garden where all lovers play. I will be watching, I will have the rug spread, and my arms will be open and waiting for you, my face smiling, my eyes free of tears.

So, when from your window, where the sparrows once played, you see your own night season coming, have no fear because I will be there, my love, but until then, as you once told me, chase love, my Special Man, choose to always chase love, and know I have loved thee with an everlasting love.
Me

* * *

Jon reread the letter over and over. He could see places on the paper where Elizabeth's tears had fallen, and pooled and mingled with the ink of the pen. He knew this must have been the hardest letter for her to write and he wondered when exactly she wrote it. He closed the letter and leaned back against the love seat and raised his head and cried big sobbing tears. His heart was aching so much for the lovely and beautiful wife he had known and loved each day and every night for so long.

Jon heard Bobby and Finn come back into the cabin and he knew he needed to get up and wipe his tears, make the bed and probably shower. He stopped briefly and looked into the mirror. He looked like a man who was lost, homeless, his compass broken, a man who had fallen in love with the moon for one night, only for it to disappear and searching franticly, finds only the sun, sneering with light. He got out a new set of sheets. He knew he would have to throw away the old ones that had wrapped Elizabeth's body and were stained with her blood. He placed them in a plastic trash bag and though it hurt to do so, he knew he had to let that go, it was one thing, a small thing, he had so much more, he didn't need that.

He walked into the bathroom, and it hit him again. Elizabeth was everywhere, her toothbrush, towel, and makeup. In the shower were her shampoo and the bar of soap they had shared. Jon decided to leave everything as it was, as a shrine, grasping again at anything that would prolong her presence in his life. He showered and shaved, started brushing his teeth, and saw the toothpaste where she always squeezed the tube in the middle. Jon would run the tube on the counter, push the paste to the top, and squeeze it up from the bottom. She was obviously the last person to use the toothpaste, and Jon again was confronted with what to do. He decided to squeeze the toothpaste like Betts and prolong the shape she had created. At that moment, he thought that divorce from a partner was infinitely different than losing a partner to death. Your marriage may be done, but the attachment or the tether to that person remains. Their absence was not death; they were still living, still squeezing tubes of toothpaste, just not the one they shared with you. Death was final, a shut door and an unexpected, slammed door in Jon's case.

Jon walked from the bedroom down the stairs and into the kitchen. Bobby was there, and Jon noticed that he had brought a set of kitchen utensils from the apartment and a set of glasses. At that moment, Jon realized that his brother knew what was happening in his mind. Bobby knew that everything, every dish, every plate, every photo, even the trash in the bin, was all turning sacred in Jon's mind because it was precisely how Elizabeth had left it. She was the last to touch it, her fingerprints were all over this house, and he did not want them disturbed. Jon realized he was not alone; he was not the only person in the world, in Polk County, or even in the cabin that had lost the love of his life.

Finn sat in the kitchen booth, quietly watching Bobby cook. He wore one of the flannel shirts that hung in the kitchen, one of those that Elizabeth would grab at night. They were nothing special, something that no one would have ordinarily missed or would not have discarded when they became old, but Jon noticed it now, that it had been moved. He walked to the boy, reached out, and touched his shoulders, his hands feeling the fabric. Finn looked up at Jon. "I'm wearing it because it makes me feel close to her."

"I know, son. I know."

"Cup of tea, brother?" Jon embraced the steaming cup with weak hands. "We've got an appointment in the morning." Jon nodded. "Also, I spoke with Theo and Alice. They want to stop by, bring some food, and visit with you for a bit before we go. You think you'll be up for that?"

Jon nodded and walked out onto the side porch. It had begun to rain. He pulled out the chair and sat down at the small table. He watched the rain pelt the granite stones and then splash back on the smooth deck boards of the porch. He could hear the fountain pouring into the small pools, and he remembered his nightmare where the fountain had stopped, and the silence was deafening. He heard it now, and he felt like it should stop. Since his life had stopped in grief, nature and the world should also stop to grieve. It was a sharp pain that it didn't. "And flow it did, not taking heed of its own bounty or my need," Jon whispered the verse while losing faith in his God that surrounded him because it suddenly felt cruel.

Bobby walked out to the porch and sat down. "Jon, what kind of service do you want? Do you want me—"

Jon raised his hand. "I just want you to say a couple of things about Elizabeth," he said in a raspy voice, "and play a couple of Ruby's songs for her. Then I want to say a couple of things, and maybe, I thought, I'd share a couple of our letters, that's it, that's all she'd want."

"Okay, Jon, simple, that's how she would like it. Well, it's been a long day. I'm going to turn in." Bobby put his hand on Jon's shoulder. "I want you to know that I will be here for you today, tomorrow, the day after that, and the day after that, catch my drift?

You are not alone and do not have to face this road alone." Jon reached up and touched the large hand on his shoulder. He shook his head yes.

The rain picked up and it thundered on the tin roof of the cabin. Jon came in from the porch and saw Finn had turned in. He sat on the floor and leaned against the daybed, his back to the sleeping boy. Jon needed the presence of Finn. He needed to borrow courage from the boy to walk up the stairs and to spend his first night alone in the bed he had shared with Elizabeth for so many years, sleeping beside her, holding her hand through the night. Their bedroom was lit by a small lamp. Jon sat there for a long time looking up the stairs as if waiting to see Elizabeth pass in front of the bed, hoping to see her shadow move on the wall as she reached for one of the hat boxes or looked through the armoire for something she had misplaced.

His mind could quickly drop into another world that allowed her to be here. He could feel that world's tug on his mind. Insanity does have multiple gates; what would it hurt to enter there if it eased his heart's pain tonight? Wasn't that the purpose of life to avoid pain? He shook off the idea. He needed to pull himself together and practice stoicism. He remembered the small green book of meditations of Marcus Aurelius. Jon slowly got to his feet and walked up to the bedroom. He looked in as if it might have all been a dream and Elizabeth would be there, sitting in front of her mirror, combing her hair, but she wasn't. It was true; the nightmare was absolute. Jon walked to his side of the bed and pulled back the covers. He had changed the sheets but still used the pillowcases they had used the night before. Turning off the light, he got into bed with all his clothes on because he was cold, freezing, like the cold hand of Elizabeth was still inside him, her fingers wrapped around his heart. He edged closer to her part of the bed and pulled her pillow to him longways. When he closed his eyes, he could still smell her and feel her presence close to him. He begged her again to take him with him, and he heard her voice saying that he needed to be there for Finn. He needed to watch and care for Finn, her Skyuka Child. He promised he would, but made the point that the boy did have parents, it wasn't his job, he could just come with her and skip the responsibility, he could skip the pain, if she would just let him go with her, they could be together again. He heard her voice say that she was always going to be there, always. Jon thought of how they had spent hours, probably months or years, of their lives on the side porch. Him writing or reading, and Betts just inside the kitchen door, creating or making something for them to share. He imagined himself there now that peaceful place where Betts was always near, always close, always stopping and coming out to rub his shoulders and place kisses on the top of his head.

* * *

Elizabeth and Jon were lying on the rug in the meadow before the gazebo in the vineyard. Books were strewn around the picnic basket, and Elizabeth's laughter echoed around him. She leaned over him, and the sun silhouetted her brown hair, and she was kissing him softly, stealing kisses, laying her hand in the center of his chest, her fingers running inside his shirt buttons and over his chest. Jon did not want to leave, but he could hear the cold rain pelting the tin roof as the sunny dream faded, replaced by the coldness of his fragile new reality. He lifted the covers and swung his legs over the side of the bed. He was still wearing all his clothes from last night. His mind was like an empty hallway lined with lockers as far as one could see. He could stop and open any locker and be filled with a treasure trove of memories, but he couldn't take the pain of memory right now. He wanted the lockers there, and he wanted everything in the lockers, and at some time, he would open them, each one of them, but now, today, he needed strength, and he wasn't sure that in old memories was where to find it.

He looked at the table by the bed and opened its small drawer for no reason. Inside, he found a small note Elizabeth had written and left it to surprise him. "Find me, kiss me, Make love to me." Jon smiled, knowing that his dream had been real and she actually did spend all night with him. He thought if it was possible to be with her each night in his dreams, then maybe, just maybe, it would be possible to do this, to keep doing this, to keep living. He looked back into the drawer and saw his favorite book of Wordsworth's poetry. There was a Chapstick and a book of matches, and there was a small silver charm that Jon remembered Elizabeth buying from a street vendor in Barcelona. It had been raining, and they were walking through the square, and Jon remembered looking at his feet crossing the wet cobblestones only for Elizabeth to pull away from him. He looked at her walking through the misting rain in her long, navy blue, hooded cape. He followed her to the vendor's table, and she was holding the silver baby's charm with the silver ball inside. The vendor said it was for a baby, and Elizabeth nodded. She handed him a handful of coins, and it disappeared into the palm of her gloved hand. They turned without talking, and Jon imagined how Elizabeth must have grasped the charm in the palm of her hand when she hoped for a child with the man she loved and adored above all.

He knew she held to the charm for strength and hope. He picked up the charm, studied it, and placed it in the palm of his hand for strength and remembrance of Elizabeth's unattainable dreams, and he promised to put her first today and every day from then forth. How much of Elizabeth's life had he squandered? How wonderful would it be to have children at this moment, children of theirs, children that would undoubtedly have had the same hands, smile, and voice as Betts? Wouldn't life have meaning, then? Couldn't he find a why for living then? A reason to start and end each day? Someone, to call on the phone and grandchildren's birthdays and recitals to go to?

Elizabeth had looked ahead and had seen the future and seen that the promise of the future outweighed the fear of the moment. She was stronger and wiser than him, and he should have listened. He should have given his fears over to her because she could have managed them, taken care of them, and made his worst fears bloom into something life-giving and beautiful. They had a beautiful life, one that was full of dreams coming true. But for him to have faced his fears would have meant crossing the line of allowing something he knew to be beautiful to be ruined and then hope, hope without ceasing, that it could be just as beautiful or more beautiful than it ever had been.

Jon pocketed the charm, thinking of Elizabeth, and her courage, walking through the rain over the cobblestone streets, in the navy-blue cape, with the talisman of hope in her hand. He made the bed, put Elizabeth's pillow back in its place, briefly looked around the room, and walked downstairs. He could hear voices in the kitchen, and he knew he had to go in there, but he didn't want to face the conversations he would have. He was relieved to find only Bobby and Finn in the kitchen. Bobby stood over the stove poaching eggs, and Finn wore the blue and white ruffled apron. It brought a smile to Jon's face. "Good morning," he said.

"Morning," Bobby replied. He lifted the coffee pot from the stove, grabbed a mug, twisted a lemon with one hand, added cream and brown sugar, and then filled the mug nearly to the brim with dark, rich coffee. The coffee though steaming in the mug, did little to warm his soul. He looked at Finn and realized he was making biscuits in the oven.

Bobby brought a small plate to the table. "I know you may not feel like eating, but I need you to try. You are already losing weight, and I know Betts would be getting worried, can't have that, so I need you to eat." Jon nodded, knowing that his brother was right.

"When did you say Theo and Alice were coming?" Jon said.

Bobby looked over from the stove, making plates for Finn and himself. "Oh, they should be along anytime. I imagine this rain is slowing them down a bit. Hasn't stopped all night." Jon looked outside. He could see water pooling across the stone in great puddles; only the walkway treads were exposed. Then a sound came, like feet on the porch, and Jon knew that Theo was there. He saw them pass in front of the window, and Bobby opened the door and let Theo and Alice in. Jon knew he should stand, but he felt old and weak. They exchanged hugs with Bobby and Finn. One of the waiters from the restaurant was with them, and he brought in tray after tray of food.

"Jon." Theo reached his arms out and embraced him. He looked into Jon's eyes. "Jon, I am sorry for your loss. It breaks our hearts."

Alice came over and hugged Jon. "We love you, and we love Elizabeth. She was a beautiful woman with such grace and kindness, Jon. We are heartbroken over her passing."

The words of Jon's old friends were genuine, and he found comfort in them being there. They talked and visited, and Jon found the strength to get up and show them into the great room and the display cases on the walls of Elizabeth's jewelry and the photos of her parents and Elizabeth's godmother. Alice pointed out a necklace she bought Elizabeth years ago for her birthday. It had been one of Elizabeth's favorites though Jon had not realized it had been a gift from Alice. "Jon, I wanted to ask you. Well, if it would be alright, would you mind if I wore that necklace of Elizabeth's to her funeral? That would help me feel close to her right now, to wear that necklace around my neck."

Jon was quiet. This necklace, everything, was precious to him. It had barely been twenty-four hours, and he had felt like he was losing so much of her. And yet he knew that this was a close friend of Elizabeth's, someone who had known and loved her. Alice said, "Jon, I bought that necklace for her." She put her hands on her hips. Jon didn't understand why she was acting this way. "I gave it to her; I should be able to ask for it back in memory of her." Jon didn't want problems. He hurt enough. He agreed to let Alice wear the blue stone pendant to the funeral.

He opened the delicate glass case and, with tender hands, lifted the necklace and placed it in her hands. Alice turned to the mirror, put the blue stone pendant around her neck, and laid her hand over it like it was returned to its rightful home. Jon looked at the necklace around her neck and forced a smile. At least he could see it being worn, and he would think of Elizabeth, and then after the service, Alice would return it.

Theo and Alice left with tearful goodbyes, and Jon turned to Bobby and Finn and looked at the trays of food, bread, and baklava. "We can't eat all this food," Jon said, shaking his head.

"I know, Jon, I know. I will make some small plates for us and take the rest to the clinic for the patients. I want you to meet some of them anyways, Jon."

Jon, Bobby, and Finn arrived at the McFarland Funeral home and were welcomed inside. After a small tour of the facility, they were set inside a small office. Against one wall were displayed various urns. Jon looked at them and knew only two would work for what he wanted for Elizabeth's ashes, and they were simple wooden boxes. A small-statured man took them to see a casket they would rent for Elizabeth's body to lie in during the service. Bobby had written a short obituary notice for Elizabeth and gave it to Jon to proofread and make any changes, but none were needed. Jon approved it and handed it to the small man. Having been so close to Elizabeth, Bobby knew precisely what to say.

Jon asked where Elizabeth's body was now, and the man replied that it was at St. Luke's Hospital, and with his permission, they would pick it up and bring it to the funeral home. Once prepared, it would be transported to the church and back to the funeral home, where the body would be cremated. Jon nodded very weakly; he turned in his chair, his jacket seeming to hang from old bones. Jon looked directly into the man's eyes. "Listen, ever since Elizabeth has been in my presence, she has been treated like a Lady. What I mean is, when you are driving her around, I want you to make sure you miss the potholes."

* * *

Jon wore his only black suit the morning of the funeral, the same one he wore the night he first met Elizabeth in the garden. Bobby, too was in a black suit and tie, and Finn was dressed in a new navy-blue suit. They were quiet on the drive down the mountain in Bobby's car and arrived at the church early. Though it was not raining, it was still cloudy, and they were thankful for their long shirt sleeves and jackets in the absence of sun. Bobby pastored the church on a small hill near Main St. It was set parallel to the road and a sidewalk lined with mature Sycamore trees.

Inside, Finn walked to the front of the church and turned around at the altar, looking back over the rows of wooden pews with their soft, thin cushions. Jon rested a hand on his shoulder. "You, okay?" Jon asked.

The boy nodded. "I'm hanging in there; how about you?"

"We can do this together. I want you to stand beside me in the receiving line, okay, can you do that? Do you want to do that?"

Finn nodded again. "I can."

Bobby had two men from his staff bring long folding tables into the back of the church, and Jon turned to greet them. They covered the tables with white cloths, and Jon told them again how much he appreciated their help. Jon opened the hat boxes he had brought with him, and as Finn stood beside him, he slowly lifted out treasure after treasure. "What is all this stuff?" Finn asked.

"It's our letters from all the years. It's like our whole lives. It's the best way to explain how wonderful Elizabeth was and how much she meant to me." Jon pulled out the letters tied by the piece of brown Burano lace.

"I've seen those before. Mrs. Elizabeth had them up by the pond. She was reading them to you." Jon smiled at the boy's interest. "Yeah, yeah, we wrote so many letters to each other from all over the world. We valued them in some way, I guess, some way that's been lost to time now. We cherished them like small worlds, feelings without inhibitions."

"What does inhibitions mean?"

"Inhibitions are things that would make you feel self-conscious and shy. It's like when you open up your feelings to someone but don't know how that person will respond to what you said; you feel vulnerable. You see, that's what love is, its vulnerability. It's opening up the most hidden parts of yourself without hesitation or reservation to someone. True love is having a partner you can open up to be vulnerable with, and that person doesn't ridicule you, make fun of you, or judge you. That person takes your vulnerability and treasures it as a priceless gift."

Finn watched Jon set out the letters He and Elizabeth had shared detailing their love without inhibition. "Why are you choosing to be vulnerable now? Why are you laying out all these precious letters for anyone to read and all these pictures of your lives for anyone to see?"

Jon stopped and looked at the boy and then motioned for him to sit down in a chair beside him. The florist was coming in with bouquets of fresh flowers and bundles of long-stemmed flowers wrapped in paper. Jon leaned his elbows on his knees, his suit coat pulled tight across his shoulders. "Finn, some people will go through their entire lives without ever falling in love or knowing what love is. That's kind of sad." Finn agreed. "Other people will rush to failure. What I mean is they will find someone that they like but think they can change in the future, and so they will marry, but you can't really change someone, and if you do, you'll only succeed in changing them into someone that doesn't want to be with you anymore."

Jon paused, letting the thought soak in. "Control is not love. Trying to change someone to your own will is not love, and it only breeds contempt, which is another word for hate." Finn moved forward on his elbows, now matching Jon's eyes, looking over and speaking softly. "How will I know when I've fallen in love, true love?"

Jon smiled. "That's easy. Love, true love, feels like standing under the fountain on a hot summer day and letting the water pour over your head, closing your eyes, raising your arms, and just letting it cover you and soak you within and without, and parting your lips and letting it flow inside you, love is an all-encompassing flow, that you will very certainly know, and once known, never be able to live without."

The small boy leaned back in the chair, ran his hand over his white-blonde curls, and said, "So, I'm good then. I will definitely know." He raised his index finger as a sign of being crystal clear, and the sight of it made Jon laugh, which lightened the mood. "Well, can I help you? I mean, I will be really careful."

"Yeah, absolutely. Why don't you ask those ladies for the cut flowers, and you can lay them out around the photos and letters across the table. Finn laid the flowers along the letters and around the photos of the lovers' lives. People began arriving at the church, and Jon came, put his arm around Finn's shoulders, and said, "It's time." Elizabeth's coffin was rolled into the church and placed before the altar. Jon, Finn, and Bobby all took a moment with her. A floral spray was placed on the wooden coffin, and Bouquets of flowers were poised beside it. People began to come forward and shake their hands and recall their memories of Elizabeth. Few asked Finn who he was, standing between Jon and Bobby.

One woman approached Jon and said, "Jon, I'm so sorry to hear about your wife." A short, round woman with a black skirt, shawl, and a small hat clasped Jon's hand in both of hers. "I'm Margot Bagsby. Pleasant was my father."

"Yeah, Pleasant's daughter, my gosh, how are you?" The lady smiled.

"He used to talk about you and your brothers all the time. You know Jon, I own the real estate company in town, and you know most people, after they lose a spouse, want to sell their house and place and, well, get a change of scenery." The woman reached into her purse and presented Jon with her business card. She leaned closer to Jon. "When it's time now, and you get all her stuff out of the house, call me."

Jon couldn't believe what the woman was saying to him. How in the world could someone be this way? Jon turned and looked toward Bobby. Bobby had heard everything and reached his arms to bring the lady towards him and out of Jon's way. "And I sell cruises, too. That's what you really need, a three-day cruise to Grand Bahama; you'll come back as good as new, well, you know what I mean." Jon was shaking his head, and Bobby reached out and waved a hand in the woman's face to get her attention.

Most of the people who came through the line were very kind, saying softly how they had loved Elizabeth and were sorry for Jon's loss. One man came through with glasses and tussled hair. From the looks of him, it appeared that it had started raining again.

He shook Jon's hand quickly, then pulled off his glasses and wiped them on a cloth he carried in his pocket. He looked at Jon. "How did she die? Your wife, how did she die? Was it ahh, heart attack, brain aneurysm?" Jon looked at the man, confused, and then over to Bobby. "I read the obituary in the paper; it says you live on Panther Mountain. I drove up there to your cabin; there weren't any other places around. Do you own that whole mountain? Are you rich or something?" Jon cocked his head and looked at the man. "Do I know you?"

The man looked back at his glasses, put them on his face, and looked around. "No, I don't think so. I just thought the story was interesting, and it didn't say how she died, so I thought I would come to ask you. How did she die?"

Jon looked at this sick man and spoke. "In my arms." He put a hand on the man's shoulder and pushed him towards Bobby, and Bobby walked him outside.

Jon and Finn finished shaking hands with the people who came, and then they sat in the front row while the service started, and Bobby played Elizabeth's favorite songs. They all listened. When Bobby finished playing, he stood behind the pulpit and recounted his life, knowing Elizabeth and what she meant. He then introduced Jon, and Jon touched Finn on the knee, stood up, and walked forward. Jon did not walk to the podium but stood beside Elizabeth as she lay in front of the church surrounded by flowers. He looked at the filled church. "Thank you all for coming today. Elizabeth and I were going to celebrate our fiftieth wedding anniversary in a few weeks. People have often asked me when Elizabeth and I first met, and my response has been the same all these years. It was one enchanted evening. For me, life with Elizabeth was simply one enchanted evening after enchanted evening. Ah, well, I'm not much for speaking to crowds, but when it comes to Betts, well, then, I will always have something to say. It's just that today, I thought the best way to say everything, a good fifty years' worth, would be to just read you some of the letters that we've written to each other." He took one letter from the stack and laid the others on a small table beside him. "This is a letter Elizabeth wrote me about a couple of months after we met. It's dated June 18, 1943. It starts with a quote from Robert Frost.

"Love is...Love is an irresistible desire to be irresistibly desired."

My dear beloved Jon,
How I have longed to be so completely in love with a man. A man with such passion, such commitment, such intimacy, such desire for me.
How I have longed to share quiet moments, share laughs, dreams for the future, and the heart to live in the moment of each day with a man.
Without a doubt, you are the man that I have longed for. Jon—you are my love, my one true love. I look no farther. I will love you always.
Yours, Betts

Jon slid the letter back into the envelope and set it down. He picked up another and said, "Not too long after Betts and I met, she moved up to the mountain." He shrugged his shoulders. "It just seemed right. Love doesn't follow a specific timeline; it just flows. It's like a river; it doesn't care what's in front of it. If it can't flow over, it will flow under; if it can't flow around, then it will move it. If it can't move it, then it will simply flow through it. Love is this mindset that two people just understand that says we will be together for the rest of our lives, and that has to start right now because every second of life that I have left on this earth just became too valuable to waste." Jon lifted both hands in the air. She moved up to the mountain, and we lived atop the Sawmill, which I think most of you have seen. She made it our home, there's one letter where I talk about that, and I would like to read it to you. It's dated October 22, 1943.

> *My Dear Elizabeth,*
> *The time I have shared with you has been the sweetest of my days.*
> *I have recently started living. I didn't know you were the key.*
> *You unlocked the door of happiness; you filled that room with love.*
> *You spread the curtains so we could see our future.*
> *You're making a home for my heart, and I shall give you my undying love.*
> *Love, Jon*

The following letter is the one that I proposed to Elizabeth. At that time, we were spending a lot of time at sea. I was going to Europe to fight in the war, and Elizabeth joined the Red Cross and was stationed in Puerto Rico. Letters wouldn't reach us for months, so when we got the latest news, it was no longer relevant. Unable to speak, we agreed to always look up to the moon and stars at night as a way of connecting. We also made a pact to spend every full moon together in that way. So, many of our letters began to talk about the moon, stars, and, naturally, the ocean. This one is dated December 17, 1943.

My Elizabeth,
If I were the tides of the ocean
Then you would be my goddess, the Moon.
You could move me with words unspoken
The soft light, the touch of you.
You turn your gaze to me nightly
I adore you from my world beneath
You whisper, "How many days will you love me?"
I reply, "Shall we count the grains of sand beneath the sea?"
Love, Jon

He looked out occasionally at the congregation, but he mainly was having a moment with Elizabeth, reading their letters with her, again, one last time. "The final letter that I'd like to read is one I wrote to her nearly fifty years ago, and it really says it all. For me, Elizabeth was so many things. She was the first woman to ever show me a mother's love. She had a way about her that she could sum up things I struggled with all my life in one phrase. In that way, she healed thousands of wounds for me. I think this letter was inspired by the overwhelming love that she showed me. It is dated February 3, 1944.

My Elizabeth,
Because of you
I have it all.
I have all hope
I have all courage
I have all confidence
I have all strength
You are the definition of Love
The meaning of Companion.
The true meaning of friend.

Everything is defined by you.
Love, Jon

Jon stopped reading and dropped his head for a moment. He then looked at the congregation. "I am sorry for your loss. Elizabeth was so many things to many people; she was everything to me. I feel fortunate to have had her as my wife for so long. Thank you all for coming."

Bobby told the congregation about the photos and letters displayed on the tables in the back of the church and thanked everyone for coming. Finn stood beside Jon as people came to shake his hand and pay him condolences. Many people took time to read the letters and look at the photos. Theo and Alice came to speak with Jon. Jon could see the blue stone necklace around Alice's neck. His mind went back to when he'd remembered Elizabeth wearing it. Alice lowered her eyes. "Jon, I know I told you I just wanted to wear this necklace during the service, but now, now." Alice seemed to choke up, holding the bluestone between her fingers. "Now, Jon, I just can't imagine not wearing it. I can't imagine taking it off. It makes me feel close to her."

Was it not enough that he'd just lost his wife? Now people were also stealing away all of her precious things. She didn't ask if she could have it. She claimed it. She was stealing it. Jon said nothing to her. His friends Theo and Alice were still here alive. It was Jon that would bear the pain of the loss of Elizabeth and now the loss of all the tangible items of her life. The toothpaste would run out in their bathroom. The bar of soap would slowly disappear in their shower. All these things that Elizabeth had last touched would disappear, and Jon was helpless to stop it.

Everyone was leaving, and the church soon emptied. The rain was beginning to fall harder. Jon stayed with Elizabeth, sitting in a chair and sometimes standing beside her. He was tired, and he felt lonely, but for her, he could stay there forever. He didn't want to think of what would happen to Elizabeth's beautiful body. The body he had always loved and cherished. The funeral home had asked him what outfit he wanted her to wear when she was cremated. He had taken the question seriously and laid out her favorite, most comfortable things. Standing over her body, he reached into the casket, pushed her hair back behind her ear one last time, and whispered, "The road from here on will be so lonely."

* * *

Bobby asked Finn to come with him to his office and pack the letters and photos to be taken back home. Finn walked with the big man from the church to a new building addition. Large glass windows ran across one side and overlooked a parking lot, where multiple tents had been set up, and cars were pulling up and letting people out. Other people were helping people out of the vehicles using umbrellas, and some pushing wheelchairs. Finn asked what it was about.

"That's people coming to the clinic we run here at the church," Finn remembered the conversation Bobby had at dinner with Jon and Elizabeth and the pottery plate that Jon loved and had run his fingers over and over.

"Are they coming to make art?"

Bobby stopped for a minute to look out the window. Finn saw frail people taken from the cars and helped into the wheelchairs. Fragile people with jaundice faces. "Some are," Bobby said. "Others are coming for lunch or to get some food. We have a food pantry here at the church where people who need food can come and take whatever they like."

"But they have to pay something, right, for the groceries? My church would make them pay something."

Bobby shook his head. "No, no, everything is free, and they can take as much as they want."

"But, Bobby, don't people take advantage of you and the free food."

Bobby pursed his lips and shook his head again. "No, Finn, these people do not take advantage of the church, me, or anyone. They are hurting and in need. Salvation is free to anyone who can forgive themselves. That is the cost, Finn. Why would we ever ask them to pay more?"

Finn had never heard that reasoning before. He had always heard preachers say that you must ask God to forgive your sins and your past and beg for salvation. That God then would wash you in the blood and change your life, but Bobby was saying that salvation was something that was already within each of us. That forgiveness was also within us. That ultimately, God was already within us and that by taking these small steps of truth, we could have faith that the trajectory of our lives was our own to change.

"Finn, these patients are suffering from physical ailments and illness. They are not suffering because of sin. Anyone can become sick or ill or be born with illness or deformities. This was not a choice for them; it was the hand they had dealt in life. These people that you see are rising to that challenge. They are finding a reason to live each day. They are being courageous, taking control of what they can in life. These people have taught me so much about God and love." Bobby turned and opened French doors which led into his office. The space was not overly large; wood bookcases filled most of the walls. There was a desk and two chairs in front of it. Finn started looking at the photos and books on the shelves. A guitar on a stand with a leather guitar strap said RUBY in bold letters.

Behind the guitar on the wall were many photos, and hanging in the middle of the pictures was a wooden dulcimer that looked very old and had been patched with thin strips of wood and tack nails from a horseshoe.

Finn began to slowly look at all the photos. He saw Jon and Elizabeth and Bobby and another man. In another image, he saw the other man, shirtless, washing his torso in the fountain outside the cabin, and the man was laughing with water cascading over his face. He saw another photo of Bobby and the man playing at the Lake Lanier Tea House, and in this photo, the other man was holding the guitar in front of Finn, and the leather strap that said Ruby ran across his chest. Finn realized at that moment that Ruby was not a woman but a man. He looked at Bobby and then back to the photos. There was another photo of Ruby, in a sailor's uniform, sitting in front of an American flag. A newspaper article framed behind glass showed Rueben Briscoe Fry, an American sailor, rescuing people during the attack on Pearl Harbor. How could this be? Ruby was not a woman but a man. Bobby and Ruby were not just siblings of Jon from the orphanage but also in love. True love, first sight love, the eternal, everlasting kind of love. Bobby, the man that Finn had come to admire, the man that had taught him so much about God and Love, was a homosexual man. A gay man who was a pastor, a gay man who was a doer of good deeds, a gay man who knew God. Finn tried to understand how this would be possible, and then he remembered a verse he had learned standing at the kitchen table in the wheat hill house. "Neither height nor depth, nor anything else in creation, will be able to separate us from the love of God that is in us." And now Finn understood whose hands Bobby had held when he walked up the stone staircase to Skyuka's Rest. The hands of Bobby's God, his sweet God. Now Finn knew truly in his own heart what it meant that all who love are of God.

CHAPTER 13

"And the Child grew and became Strong in Spirit"

Jon stayed with Elizabeth until the funeral home came to take her body away from the church. He had stood with her, not letting her be alone, and as they closed the casket, he watched his wife disappear beneath the wood cover and flowers. He walked slowly behind the men that rolled her out of the church, and he stood in the cold rain as she was placed in the back of the hearse, the rain mixing with his tears. He whispered to her to calm his heart. As he whispered, the tall sycamores seemed to weep too. Jon watched the car pull away, and he walked out into the middle of the street and looked down the alley the Sycamores made until he could see her no more. Bobby walked out to him in an overcoat and holding an umbrella. "Jon, Jon, it's done now, brother. It's done. Jon, can you hear me? You don't have to face the road alone, Jon. Come on, let's get you inside and dried off."

Jon allowed himself to be led over the cobblestones and up the limestone stairs into the church. Bobby had a towel for Jon to dry off with, but he could not feel its comfort, just like he could not feel the misery of the rain. Bobby took the towel and wiped the rain from Jon's suit. "Listen, Jon, I know you don't feel like it, but I want you to come and meet some of the people in the clinic. We've got hot chocolate and some snacks down there, and Finn is already in my office; we can stop by and get him. Anyway, listen, before you say no, the car is parked over there, and we've got to go there anyway."

Jon didn't have a choice. He nodded to Bobby and followed him to the office, like a dog so old he has forgotten the leash is no longer around his neck, and what would he do with freedom anyways. Jon saw Finn looking at old photos and went to stand by him. He had not been in Bobby's office since the renovation and didn't realize how much of a shrine Bobby had turned it into. Looking at the photo of Ruby's smiling face under the cascading water of the fountain lifted Jon's spirit. He remembered that day when they had all been covered in black topsoil. They had gotten the truck stuck in the soft soil and had toiled all day trying to dig it out. They had gotten back to the sawmill so filthy that they couldn't go inside, so each had taken turns washing in the flowing water of the fountain behind the cabin. Elizabeth came out and snapped photos of each of the brothers splashing, soaping, and feeling alive in the abundance of water.

"Isn't that something? I haven't seen these photos in years. I remember that day like it was yesterday." Jon was talking to himself. He could see an arm in one of the photos, and he knew immediately that it was Elizabeth's arm reaching out to him when he was in the fountain. "She was asking me to turn towards her, reaching for me like that. I reached out and grabbed her and kissed her, and she just dove in with me, clothes and all, kissing me, drenched we were, and she was holding the camera high and out of the water. God, I love her." He touched the glass that covered the photo as if touching the pause button on old times. "How that fountain flows."

Jon was losing himself, now, in the old memories. After his brothers went back to the sawmill, he and Elizabeth soaked in their clothes, left the camera on the table of the side porch, stripped each other's clothes off, and kissing each other, wet with the water and the taste of each other, they made it to the stairs but no farther before they worshipped each other, fell into each other and, in the warmth of desire, they lusted and satisfied each other. They slept only to rise too late for dinner, made love again in bed, and read their letters out loud, lying upon each other's naked breasts.

The large hand of Bobby on Jon's shoulder brought him back. Jon's mind wanted to stay, but his body was in a colder, newer reality. The grains of time were not pouring into another vessel. From here on, they slipped as slowly as the sap on the boards of the outbuildings. "Hot chocolate and snacks downstairs, and you can meet some of our volunteers and their folks." Bobby insisted, and Jon slowly nodded his head. They closed the office and walked down the stairs to a large open room that was well-organized with comfortable chairs and sofas. It did not feel like a clinic but more of a communal lounge where people sat with each other talking, drinking coffee, and eating. The room was well-lit and painted bright colors, and the volunteers there were smiling.

When Bobby entered the room, the whole place lit up. People waved to him and blew him kisses. Some people asked him to play his guitar for them, and seemingly everyone wanted to steal him away for a private conversation. With each person, Bobby introduced Jon and Finn. Telling the people stories of how he and Jon grew up and how kind Finn was, who had been spending the summer with Jon and his late wife, Elizabeth. At first, Jon was taken aback by this, as if Bobby was trying to open the unhealed wound for more of the world to see, but soon Jon started hearing the condolences of the patients. These people, who were obviously suffering from illnesses, many wasting away, looked at Jon in his eyes and said, "I am sorry for your loss." Many covered their hearts as if just the thought of

Jon, this stranger, having lost his wife, was piercing their weak souls. Many said. "I know exactly how you feel. I lost my wife, I lost my daughter, I lost my son, I lost my true love." Jon was astounded and found himself sitting down to hear each person's story. He was in tears holding the hand of a mother that had just lost her fifteen-year-old son, a talented potter, to AIDS. An illness contracted by transfusion. Jon told her that he had some of her son's plates and that every time he held them, it was like shaking hands with her son. He said in that way, he felt like he had known Jared and that even now, he sincerely wanted to visit his grave.

Each person Jon met in the room had a story that was more devastating than his own, and yet each person at the end of their telling looked Jon in the eyes and said, "If you ever need me or want to talk about your wife, I will be here for you." The sick, the helpless, and the dying, those with tough outer shells cracked by the machine and their meaty hearts exposed, had found profound healing and strength within themselves. Talking with the patients of the clinic revitalized Jon. It had given him strength again to smile.

He and Finn left the clinic in Bobby's car, and once outside of town, they crossed the last fertile plain and began the steep climb up the mountain. Jon and Bobby talked about the different patients he had met and their stories. Jon sincerely told his brother what it had meant for him to hear their stories and that he wanted to visit again, maybe each week. "Volunteer Jon, you've always given money to the clinic but volunteer. Teach a glass on native plants and the local history. I can't imagine a better teacher than you. Please, please, do this for yourself and for others. The patients would love it."

Finn looked over from the backseat and saw the waterfall pouring off the side of the mountain. Inside, he thought of how that water had passed through the upper pond, down beside the stone staircase, into the small pond, amongst the fish children, slipped over the moss green dam and down, down, over the side of things and falling, falling, like a person in first sight love, to unspeakable, breakable, unsurvivable depths, and once there, exploding apart into the ether, for no one to see but only for the lover to know how deep and exhilarating was the plunge. The rain had stopped, like the tears that had marked their faces. The car reached the grass field, but Bobby kept going. They passed the fork leading into the French Valley and the vineyard. Still, they kept going up around the long curve of the mountain's spine, past where you could stop by the upper pond and up, and up until they reached the parking spot by Skyuka's Rest. They all needed this. They all needed to look over the waves of peaks, down the Blue Ridge mountains, and back to the high peaks of Attalulla, and out across the flatland, imagining the sea at the end of the horizon, and seeing for themselves that not all was changed, that some bit of the firmament remained. They all took different places around the rest, all sitting there, trying to breathe, trying to make sense of life without Elizabeth, their mother, Sister, and Wife, for the first time not with them.

"What happened to Skyuka?" Finn said. "You know after the Elder Fire sent the Eagle to protect him and proved that he was pure of heart?" Bobby and Jon turned and looked at each other, hoping the other would answer and answer well. Finn noticed the men's hesitation and read into their quietness as if the story had not been entirely told. "After they untied him from this rock and set him free. What happened?" The men were still quiet for a while, but Finn needed an answer. "Say?"

Jon turned on the small boulder he was sitting on in the dusk of the setting sun. "Son, this is hard to say, and I'm not sure I feel up to telling the whole story, so I will tell you what I can, but we may have to talk about it later." Jon paused and took a deep breath. "Finn, Skyuka, never left this rock."

Finn shook his head. "No, you said the Eagle came and tore the buzzards apart. The Eagle protected him for two days, you said."

"Yeah, you're right. The Eagle did come and protected him. The problem is that the people that accused him refused to see the truth or to accept the proof sent from the Cherokee's God, the Elder Fire. They had made up in their minds that Skyuka was bad, and not even their God, the Elder Fire, could change that. They decided that if the buzzards weren't going to rip him apart in some sort of justification, they would have to. They brought up large knives, things they used to butcher meat in the great hunting grounds. They started to cut into him, and the great Eagle, the spirit of the Elder Fire, fell out of the sky and tore the knives out of their hands. They took up others. They started again to cut into the chest of Skyuka, and the Eagle again fell out of the ether, between them and the sun, and took the eyes of the man who was set to cut into the Chief of Peace. Still, instead of listening to the truth and their hearts and their God who had manifested himself as this majestic bird, they hardened their hearts and stopped their ears and ran upon the man and began to thrash him with clubs and rocks, and this time when the god spirit came to save Skyuka a great marksman of the tribe took his bow and shot the Eagle through with an arrow. They willingly killed their God to have their own way, to justify their own truth. In the fray, the people murdered Skyuka, their Chief of Peace and the spirit of God, and in the end, the great Eagle lay as bloody as the man.

Some say they took what was left of Skyuka and separated him to the four corners of the Cherokee Nation. Others say they took his body and hung it from a great sycamore tree near the town, so all the white settlers would know that they were not to be blamed for what Skyuka did, alone." Finn laid his hands on the stone, then suddenly lay down and placed his cheek on it.

The sun was fading now, and Jon stood up, but Finn was still prostrate on the stone with his face against the rock. Bobby went over and rubbed the back of the small boy who clearly had been devastated by the events of the day and now had the reality of this story revealed at the very spot it happened, no less. Scooping Finn up from the stone and cradling him to his chest, the small boy reached his arms around the giant man, and Bobby placed him in the back seat. On the ride back down the mountain, Finn laid his head against the window and watched as the ancient trees passed by.

When they reached the cabin, Jon walked inside and straight upstairs to the bedroom. Removed his clothes and went to bed even though it was only late afternoon. He was not sleeping but again entered a semi-dream state where he called out to Elizabeth, and soon, within a few minutes of him calling, she talked back to him, and Jon entered the first gate of insanity because it calmed his heart.

Finn crawled under the covers of the daybed and, once there, cried into the pillow. He could not understand why bad things happened to good people. This went against all that he had heard. That God would judge humanity alone. He remembered the Bible verse he had learned standing at the wheat hill house table "I have been young, and now am old: yet have I not seen the righteous forsaken, nor his seed begging bread." But, God did leave the righteous forsaken, and at times in the wheat hill house, they had not had any food. And his father was dying. The voice from the phone had told him many times, "Your father has five minutes to live to live; you need to tell him that you love him." His father would die just as Skyuka and Mrs. Elizabeth died.

A boy's life should be a time when his hourglass is being topped off with the most precious of grains. Grains that will last and sustain him until the very end of his life, but when Finn was discerning his own vessel, he was already seeing the wax cloth joining the two spheres unravel and peel back from its edges. Those edges of the adhesive fabric were collecting grains of sand that were no longer in Finn's sphere but only trophies through a glass. Distraught about the goodness of his life being taken away, Finn mumbled through the tears into the pillow. "Precious memories, how they linger. How they ever flood my soul." He stretched his hand over the comforter, longing for the warm touch of Mrs. Elizabeth's hands.

Bobby gathered the last things from the car, walked inside the cabin, and set Elizabeth's hat boxes, a vase of flowers, and a bundle of fresh cut flowers wrapped in brown paper on the kitchen booth. He returned to the car, removed a small duffle bag with casual clothes, returned to the cabin bathroom, and changed out of the suit he had been wearing. He was mindful of Jon and Finn sleeping. Still, he knew, from experience, that they were not sleeping, only that their bodies had become so laden with the burden of grief that they could no longer carry it but now could only lie prostrate before it and let it run like water, over, under, around, and most painful of all, through them. Bobby placed the hat boxes on a small table in the great room beside the glass cabinets filled with Elizabeth's things. He took the small vase of flowers and placed it on the elephant-leg piano. He slid the piano bench out from under the piano and sat down. The soft melody of "Precious Memories" filled the room. Bobby began to hum the verses of the hymn as he played, tears flowing down his cheeks. Finn got up, sat beside his giant friend, and reached his hand out timidly and placed it as light as a goldfinch upon Bobby's hand and connected to the arcing notes of the divine melody that he knew by heart.

The song ended, but Bobby and Finn did not look at each other. "I hadn't intended to play," Bobby said. "I looked at this beautiful piano, with its dark walnut wood, and I thought of how many times we had all gathered around it and sang late into the night. Me and

Elizabeth sitting beside each other, laughing and playing. Ruby, standing above us with some sheet music in his hand or an old gospel hymnal. Singing, laughing, filling this room with his songs."

Finn leaned forward and started turning the framed pictures on the piano towards him. He had lived in the cabin for a while now but had always been with Jon or Elizabeth and had never taken the time to look at all the beautiful things that filled the great room. "Looking at these pictures. You all look so happy," Finn said. Elizabeth was in photo after photo, surrounded by Jon, Ruby, and Bobby, like an adored princess. There were instruments in the photos, an old truck with PMI written on the door. There were pictures of them all lounging on Skyuka's Rest. And photos of the gazebo in the vineyard, all in bloom with Wisteria.

Bobby reached forward and touched one photo of Ruby, in a tuxedo, sitting in a wooden chair, with the old wood dulcimer on his lap and the guitar, with the leather strap at his side. "Betts always had a camera around. Took pictures of just about anything. She would plan these whole days of us doing nothing but traveling around the mountain, dressing up, dressing down, taking pictures of us." He looked over at Finn. "We would never complain. It's like you said the other day. We knew what we had, and we loved it."

Finn smiled at the thought but suddenly turned serious. "How did Ruby die?" He paused. "I'm sorry. I'm not trying to be mean or make you hurt. It's just that everyone talks about Ruby and him passing away, but no one talks about how he passed away." Bobby ran his hand over his head and closed his eyes. As if the pain was still like blunt trauma.

"Finn, I will do my best to explain this to you. I feel a little weak right now, so if we get to a spot and I can't say anymore, I want you to know that we will finish another time. I'm just emotionally exhausted; we all are." Finn nodded. "Okay, well, as with most things, a series of events led up to Ruby being murdered, and if I tell you all the events, I think it will make better sense. Finn, do you know who the Ku Klux Klan is, the white supremacists?"

Finn looked down at his hands. He remembered the small gas station down from the wheat hill house and the black and white photos he had seen on the wall behind the pot belly stove. Of men in white hoods lined up for photos. He remembered the sign hanging in the middle of the store that said, "Colored and Mexicans enter one at a time." He remembered a tall man who owned a painting business in the area and had stopped there for a can of beer, and Finn heard him say to another man, "I'd rather my daughter be dead than ever find her with a black man." Finn had watched the man leave the store, and he had turned with the can of beer in one hand and held his hand out flat out in front of him towards the man he had been talking to in some sort of salute. Finn nodded his head. "I know who they are."

"There was this Klan leader named Bob Jones from the other part of the state; I think it was Greensboro. He had come down to South Carolina, right across the border, towards Greenville, and he had held a KKK rally there at some church called Tabernacle. People had come from all over the area to hear him speak. One guy who went to hear Bob Jones speak was a man named John King Fysher. He was a delivery truck driver. His parents had named him after a famous gunslinger from Texas. Anyways, you've never been able to buy alcohol in South Carolina on Sunday, so John King Fysher and some of his buddies, from the rally, came across the border to Tryon to buy alcohol since Tryon is the closes city to where they lived. Ruby and I had played for the Tryon Garden Club the night before. We always played music for those parties. Well, the party had run late into the night, and when we packed up our things, I had forgotten Ruby's dulcimer on the house's porch. It's not a fancy instrument, but it's one he had since childhood in the orphanage. It's hanging in my office; I will show it to you some time. It's got a lot of sentimental value."

"I think I saw it. It's been repaired on the side." Finn held up his hand, showing the curve in the wood that had been fixed with thin strips of wood and small tacks.

"That's the one. Well, it was my fault. I left it at the house, and Ruby had woken up early the following day, and it bothered him so much that we had misplaced it that he drove our car back down the mountain to the house where we had played and was looking through the garden and around the house for it. We had played there many times, and the owners were this couple we had become good friends with, so Ruby didn't give a second thought to going back and looking around early in the morning like that. He left before I'd even woken up. He just left a note on the kitchen table saying that we forgot the dulcimer and was going back to find it, and he'd be back soon, and we'd make breakfast.

I woke up in some kind of panic that morning. Something I couldn't explain. Just my heart racing, nervous. I got up and looked through the apartment for Ruby and found the note. I read it and tried to figure out how long he'd been gone. I walked over to the window and looked down the road to see if I could see him coming back, you know, back up the hill. I tried to calm myself down, Finn, but I couldn't. It's hard to explain; I knew something horrible was happening. It was dread like someone was pulling my skin inside out. I tried to shake it off, brew some coffee, and start the breakfast, but I kept going back and back to the window, hoping to see him there. He wasn't there. I can still feel how I felt like there were icicles, real sharp ones running through my veins, and I couldn't catch my breath. I was brewing chicory coffee Isidore had given us from New Orleans; it has this distinct smell. To this day, that smell takes me back to panic.

Finally, I just ran down the stairs, got in the ole sawmill truck, and started down the mountain to town. Around every curve, I prayed that Ruby would be there. That I'd see the car making its way back up and Ruby smiling, asking where I was going on a Sunday. Or that he'd just been broken down and be waiting for me, but he wasn't."

Bobby stopped, took several quick breaths, and closed his eyes tight to keep back tears. Seeing the pain in Bobby's eyes, Finn reached out his hand and placed it on Bobby's leg. Bobby reached down and scooped up the small hand and held it tightly. "Ruby had parked in the service entrance of the garden and walked up through the garden to the house where he thought the dulcimer might have been left. He knocked on the door and windows, but the ladies living there must have been asleep upstairs. He found the dulcimer sitting on the porch where I had left it. John King Fysher and his friends had been drinking after the rally all night. They had bought liquor from the store, had come over, parked off of Harris Street, and were still drinking. They saw Ruby walking through the woods around the house and then back to the car with something in his hands. Drunk and full of hate from the rally, they thought Ruby was a thief, stealing from the white women's house. They drove their station wagon up behind Ruby's car, blocking him in, and began to taunt him. Then they drug him out of the car and beat him. Ruby was calling out, but no one could hear him. They put him in the station wagon, and in their drunken rage, they took the gravel road out of town that goes back into a bootleg hollow called Dark Corners. They tied Ruby to the back of the car and drug him up the road there. They stopped beside the river where the Boy Scout camp is now and hung him from a tall Sycamore tree."

Bobby was looking down now, his fingers spread out above the piano's ivory keys but not touching them. Finn was still as a mouse in horror over the story. "They killed him, but that wasn't enough.

One of them figured that since it was Sunday morning and all were supposed to be in church, they should do something spiritual. So, as Ruby hung from the Sycamore, they cut saplings, and they stretched out Ruby's arms like he was on the cross, and John King Fysher took his sheath knife and lashed it to a sapling and pierced the side of Ruby, like the Roman Centurion pierced the side of Christ, to see if water had mixed with the blood. They took a photo of themselves in their white hoods with Ruby's body hanging on display."

    Bobby stopped and looked over at Finn, whose eyes were full of tears. "I got to town in the old truck, and there was still no Ruby in sight. I was driving faster and faster, and I went to the house, but when I got to the car, I saw the door open and the dulcimer lying in front of the car door. I can't explain it, but I knew. I knew what had happened and started off down the dirt road toward Dark Corners. I was blowing the horn of that truck, trying to get people to wake up. I passed them, Finn, I passed those men in that station wagon, and I looked down into their faces from the truck, and Jon King Fysher was driving, and he looked at me with a beer in one hand and spit out the window on the ground and just kept staring at me. I raced up that road, Finn, blowing the horn for help from somebody, and when I got there when I got up there, I saw Ruby hanging, hanging with his arms stretched out."

    Bobby broke down and wept. The big man's frame heaved up and down. Finn stood and hugged the man around his ample shoulders. "I got there, and I pulled that truck right up under him, got up on the hood, and lifted him up, but he was all gone, Finn. Dragging him down the road had torn chunks out of his body and head. I took the rope off his neck, and he fell onto me, and I held him rocking back and forth, pleading with God to not take him, to save him, to save his life. I was screaming out Finn uncontrollably. His blood was running red down the yellow paint of that truck and pooling on the ground. It was all over me. I was screaming for someone to help, someone to come.

"Then I heard the police cars coming. They reached us, and I was hollering for help, and they came up with their guns drawn on me, telling me to let the body go. I tried to explain, and the sheriff clubbed me across the face. John King Fysher had stopped by the sheriff's office on his way out of town and told them that they'd seen two colored men fighting up the road and were afraid one would get killed. Said to them it almost looked like, like some lover's quarrel. They put me in jail for the murder of Ruby. Can you believe that, Finn, they put me in jail for the murder of Ruby? To tell you the truth, I sat there in that jail and felt like I was guilty of his murder. If they had come into that jail and said that I had to die for the death of Ruby, I would have said okay, please kill me." Finn turned his head slightly, questioning what Bobby had just said. "I felt like I was to blame. You see, I left that dulcimer out on the chair that night. If I hadn't, well, if I hadn't, Ruby would have never been there. Or maybe if I had been there with Ruby, then it would have been a fair fight, at least. They may have tried to hurt us, but they wouldn't have been able to kill us. It was my fault in some ways, Finn; it has to be still."

Finn stood before Bobby with one hand on his knee and the other on his shoulders, looking into his teary eyes. "No, Bobby, you went as fast as you could to help him, you blew the horn, and you went to save Ruby. It's not your fault."

Bobby bit his lip and shook his head, and his eyes squeezed tight and pushed out tears. "When you can't save the ones you love, it's your own fault. It has to be my fault, Finn."

Finn shook his head and sat down on the piano bench silently. Darkness had fallen and only the kitchen light and one small lamp illuminated the great room and the photos on the piano. Finn looked into the face of Ruby. Impossible to imagine that beautiful spirit being abused by another human. "They spread him out like Jesus? Lifted his arms and pierced his side?" Finn said into the darkness.

Bobby closed his eyes in weariness and nodded his head. "But Ruby was not violent a man. "No, no, He was sweet," Bobby said.

"So why?" Finn looked into Bobby's brown eyes.

"Why what, Finn?"

"When the Cherokee thought Skyuka was wrong, and they laid him out on the rock for the Elder Fire to judge, and their God in the form of the Eagle came to protect him, proving that he was innocent, why did the people not accept the truth in front of them? Why did they kill the Eagle to follow lies? Why did the mob kill Christ when he was healing the sick and spreading love and peace? Why did John King Fysher kill Ruby? Bobby, why do we hurt so much if God loves us?"

Bobby, looked down at his hands. "Finn, you've been up here on the mountain all summer long enough to know it. When you close your eyes, how do you see it?" Finn exhaled deeply and stretched his hands over the piano's black keys. He closed his eyes. "I see the fish children when it's time for corn. Their long bodies glide around the edges of the pond at sunset. I see the wooden walkways over the moss-covered stone. I notice that they rest on ledge stones but are not anchored into them. They just exist together. I feel the smooth stones of the staircase on my bare feet. The green ferns hang over the edges of the corners. I look up into the canopy of the ancient trees and the birds singing and playing there. I see the branches swaying, waving, and reaching for me to touch my hands. The trunks are so strong and round, and the sunlight spills between them. They love me, and I love them. I've named some of them, and some names I can't pronounce, and I wonder what they've named me, but it doesn't matter because we speak a universal language. I climb up the staircase and reach the upper meadow. I wonder if the Cherokee lived here too, or was this a garden, a place for bees. It must have been sacred because all the baby deer come here with their mothers and are never scared. This is where that flower blooms. Mrs. Elizabeth called it her field of love. I hear her now saying for me to chase love. This is heaven, isn't it, Bobby? Is this Eden? Finn's hands moved across the piano and connected with the wood. "Finn, remember the story of Eden in the Bible with Adam and Eve?" Finn opened his eyes and looked over. He nodded. "Rember there were two trees?" "Yes, there was the Tree of Life, and then there was the Tree of Knowledge. The fallen Angel lived in the Tree of Knowledge." "Yeah, and what did that fallen angel tell Adam and Eve?" "He lied to them. Said that God didn't want them to eat the fruit because they would have the knowledge and be just like God."

"You're right. Man ate the fruit, and the fruit became a part of him. When we believe in a lie, that lie becomes part of us. It becomes that voice inside our head that says we are not good enough. When Adam and Eve were first married, they lived in Heaven. They walked with God just as you talked about walking among the trees. When they accepted the lie that they were not good enough, what did they do?" "They hid and made clothes of fig leaves. They saw themselves as being naked." "They never felt naked before, in front of God?" "They never realized it until then." "You mean they were never embarrassed? They never judge themselves or each other before?" "No, they lived without, what's the word. Jon told me at the funeral. Inhibitions. Bobby, Adam, and Eve lived without inhibitions. They told each other everything and didn't judge or blame." Bobby closed the lid of the piano. "Finn, why do you think the Cherokee's killed their God to murder Skyuka? Why did they kill Christ? Why did John King Fysher kill Ruby?" Finn looked knowingly into Bobby's eyes. "Because they separated from God and believed lies." Bobby nodded his head. "When people judge themselves as not enough, they begin to judge others." "Finn, when you are out here in nature, do you feel unworthy or not enough?" "No, Bobby. I feel at home. I feel like I belong here and am in awe of everything around me." "Even if there's a broken limb or damaged tree?" "It is what is Bobby. It all belongs. "Is it perfect, Finn? Is nature all the trees, the fountain, the fish-children, is it all perfect?" "Absolutely!" "Is man perfect?" "No, my church says that man is supposed to be in power over all nature, but people are not perfect." Bobby shook his head. "So, Man is an imperfect leader of all that is perfect? Does that make sense to you? Finn crossed his arms and laid his head on the piano, thinking. "Finn, what if people were born perfect? What if we live perfectly? What if the greatest lie ever told was that we are not good enough? Finn set thinking. "What if Jesus didn't rise from the dead and is not returning? " "But, Bobby, how can you say that? You're a Pastor of a church." "Finn, that's my calling because, most often, the ones who think they have salvation are the ones who need to be saved. Finn, you asked why do we hurt so much? Why is life so hard? Maybe this World was not made for us? Maybe it was made for those baby deer in the meadow and the bees that fly from the white flowers. Maybe Elizabeth is telling us that this moment in life may be the only Heaven. You know? How would people live if they didn't have a future? Would they kill each other?" Finn lifted his head and turned to Bobby. "No, If there is no future, then heaven or hell is right now." "Yes, Heaven is the result of good choices. Hell, is the result of lies. You see, all religions in the World have a mix of truth and untruth. All knowledge has truth and untruth. That's why the Tree of Knowledge is also called the Tree of Good and Evil. The benefit of knowledge or practicing a religious form is that you absorb the good and discard the untruth. To do this, your mind and heart must be at peace. False religion is made by those who trust only in lies. They see God as someone to punish. If God judges them, then they will judge others. Finn, up here on the mountain, when you see the great birds, are they carrying instruments to measure the wind?" Finn adamantly shook his head. "No, Bobby, they just soar." "Exactly, that is Heaven. To not think but to feel. The emotions you feel when walking in nature are genuine.

What you feel about Mrs. Elizabeth and the baby deer in the meadow is true. The Cherokee always had their Chief of Peace until they believed in lies." "But why did they kill him, Skyuka? Why did they kill Christ?" "Finn, Adam, and Eve fell in love with each other in Heaven, in Eden. When they left Paradise and stopped walking with God, they began to live in hell. They raised their children in a land with thorns, a land with pain. That hurt has never left us. It is our legacy heritage. Since then, humankind has desperately been searching for a way to get back to Eden and walk with God. That's why when you describe walking among the trees, you feel the way you do. To be in awe, to feel like you belong, to feel loved. But the truth is met with untruth. Good is faced with Evil. Throughout history, the great Chiefs of Peace have sometimes been murdered for telling the truth. Shams-i Tabrizi, Martin Luther, Scientists throughout the ages. Even my friend Dr. King was killed in 1968. Evil sometimes kills the good, the Chiefs of Peace, but time has never stopped seeing them born."

Finn was seeing it now. It was making sense. He had lived with Shane and heard the names he called people he didn't like or understand from the pulpit. He could see it very clearly. "That's why Skyuka was killed? That's why they also killed the Elder Fire, Jesus, and Ruby?" Bobby nodded, and Finn leaned closer, laid his head on Bobby's chest, and touched the piano. "What can I do, Bobby? Do I pray for wisdom?"

Bobby lifted the boy's head from his shoulder. "Finn, look at me. You've got wisdom. It's right here inside of you already." Bobby tapped Finn's chest. "Wisdom is inside of you just like God is inside of you. You have God inside of you because you can forgive yourself and others. Remember that. Sometimes, it may be hard to find, and you may even go months or years without it, but you remember what I'm saying. If you can do that, you have the power to heal yourself and give others the courage to heal themselves.

"Finn, the language that all hearts speak is truth. The heart knows goodness no matter how it is communicated. Search for understanding, and, most of all, listen to your heart. Then you will always have truth to stand on. When this happens, you can listen to what people say, even if you disagree. You can take the truth and leave the rest. The lies they believe in are the story the voice in their mind has told them. It will not affect you, and your truth will probably not change them, but that's not your responsibility. You don't have to prove them wrong, and you don't have to create drama. With this simple philosophy, you show others the wide and welcoming path to their own Eden.

Finn listened to all that Bobby was telling him. It made sense. It resonated inside him more than anything he had ever heard at church or home. He knew his heart was hearing the truth even though it was completely different from anything he had heard from his church or home.

Bobby opened the piano and played a few more notes of the hymn, and Finn stretched out his hands and touched the keys. He laid his head on Bobby's shoulder just as he had laid his head against Mrs. Elizabeth's shoulder the first night he came to the mountain as they picnicked upon the rest. "Finn, there's a way that the Cherokee, who lived in this great plateau, said goodbye to their loved ones. It was a way of healing themselves and letting the departed soul be at peace. Would you like to take part in that with me?" Finn said nothing. "Say?" Finn lifted his head and nodded, unable to speak. "Okay, maybe put some warm clothes on, and we will get started." When Finn stepped out onto the side porch, Bobby had a bundle of the cut flowers from the funeral, a small bottle of lamp oil, and a box of matches. He had taken down two of the lanterns from the porch eaves, and they lifted the globes and lit the wicks. Bobby gave Finn a small smile. "When the Cherokee did mourn Skyuka, and the loss of the Eagle spirit, they came to this very spot of the plateau, to the fountain that had always flowed, and they spread blankets and rugs across the backs of these moss-covered stones. You see, they also respected Mother Nature's grieving of her son. They went up the staircase, hand in hand, to the greatest and oldest trees and picked up the large dry leaves of last season. Then they returned, and stepping onto the blankets, they came to the edge of this small pond. They filled the dry leaves with flowers and poured oil into the center of the leaves and lit the oil with the fire of the Great Elder and they released each in the small pools beneath the fountain and watched them spiral through the pools to the small pond and slip silently over the granite dam, forever free. While watching, they sat on blankets over the covered moss stone and communicated with the deceased spirits. Sometimes in grief, our spirit is willing to let go, but our minds cannot without regret. This tradition of giving thanks, setting their intentions for the future, is a way to give one last gift to the departed and receive the gift of healing and forgiveness." Bobby looked into the eyes of Finn. "Is this something that you would like to do with me?"

"Very much."

"Okay, then." They removed their shoes and socks, took the rug Jon and Betts had used for so many years and laid it over the moss-covered stone near the pond's edge. Then, each taking a lantern, they walked to the stone staircase, and holding hands, they slowly climbed each step, occasionally stopping to reach out to touch the ancient trees. They reached the oldest tree, stopped, set down the glowing lanterns, and looked for the giant leaves with broad flat bases and curled tips. They picked each one and rolled it over and over in the lantern light, and occasionally Bobby would lift the leaf to his lips and whisper prayers.

Finn gathered leaves, and as he did, small tears appeared on his checks, and he went to wipe them, but Bobby stopped his hand and touched the tears on the boy's face and, with his finger, used the tears to write on each leaf. "Tears write words only the dead can read. Say it here, like this." Finn held the giant leaf with both hands, leaned his head over it, and let his tears and words to Mrs. Elizabeth, fall into it.

With arms full of leaves, they walked slowly back down the staircase, in the lantern light, under the canopy of the ancient trees to the moss-covered stones. They took the fresh cut flowers and laid the petals and blossoms inside the old, dried leaves, and then Bobby mixed the lamp oil with his own tears, set the oil in the leaves alight, and placed them into the swirling pools of the fountain. When the pools were filled with small, glowing, floral boats, they extinguished their own lanterns, sat on the rug, and watched the boats slip one by one, turning and swirling through the small eddies like grains of sand, slipping through time, into the small pond. The glow illuminated the tree canopy above the pond, and Finn and the giant man sat side by side on the rugged stone, just like the ancient Cherokee had done thousands of years ago.

Finn closed his eyes to communicate with Elizabeth. He could see her face, smiling but covered in soft tears. He could see her reaching her hands out to both of them. She was saying with her own tears words only they could understand and hear. "Thank you, my loves, you've given me the best year of my life here, the final year, the happiest year; I wouldn't have changed a thing."

The first boat slipped over the granite damn, but they did not mourn it. They were healing. She was healing. Another boat slipped away, and another, and the water of the pond made a noise. More boats moved and swelled faster, and frothing deep from within the pond could be felt and heard. And the glowing light of the dried, leaf boats illuminated the deep water, and from the depths, the fish children began to sing and beat their tails against the water as marchers on a giant drum. The fish children were praising the great mother, the giver of life, and corn, and love, and they were saluting her now as nature inside them commanded. The water began to boil, and they began to escort the passing lady with acrobatics and diving. The boats twisted and turned and slipped one by one until only a few remained, and the calm returned to the water's surface. Still, all the children, hundreds, could be seen in attention, facing in one direction, saluting the barges passing, and as the last two were nearing the dam, Finn and Bobby stood with tears running down their faces holding each other's hands. They wished the sister and mother farewell and felt healed, though weak, and Elizabeth felt comforted and whole, and Bobby felt closer to those now waiting beyond for him, and the Skyuka child grew and became strong in spirit.

CHAPTER 14

"Speak to the Earth, and it Shall Teach Thee"

"Jonny, will you still love me when we get old?" Elizabeth looked at Jon, her straw hat blocking the sun, and Jon, lying on his back, looked up into his wife's face, framed by her curly brown hair.

"Reckon, I'll love you to pieces."

"To pieces?"

Jon nodded. "Yeah, most likely to pieces. Wrinkled, sundried, cracked pieces, I imagine. Probably, drop my false teeth into your wrinkles and have to call the volunteer fire department to fish them out."

Elizabeth slapped his chest. "You are horrible, you ruin—I am not going to have wrinkles so deep that you'll lose your teeth in them."

Jon rolled over quickly, took Elizabeth in his arms, and ran his hands up her sides and under her arms. He loved feeling her body. He was in love with every part of her. Her skin, her voice, her laugh, her words, her mind. He had never been able to get enough of her, and he knew that he never would. "Listen, Special woman." He stole a kiss from her lips. "I'm going to love you to pieces every day and, more importantly, every night until the day I die."

"Don't say that, Jonny."

"Don't say what? That I'm going to love you every day until I die?"

"Don't say die, Jonny. I don't want to think about that. I want us to be doves, Jonny. Just promise we won't die, but we will be doves."

Doves, Doves, a dove, was standing outside the window of Jon's bedroom. It woke him from his beautiful dream, but he didn't want to wake up. He hugged the pillow and turned it long ways beside him, and in this dream state, he could smell Elizabeth and still feel her in his arms. "Stay with me, Betts, come on, just stay." He was begging her now before opening his eyes. "Promise me, tonight, you will come back, promise?"

"I promise, Jonny." She faded from his mind, and he forced his eyes open, and still hugging the pillow, he looked over at the window, and there was one lone dove pecking the glass. Was it true? Was she really a dove now, waiting for him to join her? Sitting outside his hourglass, patient as sap, speaking softly, whispering lovely things to him, cooing in her own way.

It was early, and the rest of the house was still quiet. Jon walked into the bathroom to shower, and again he was faced with Elizabeth's shampoo and soap sitting where she had left them. The tube of toothpaste as she had smashed it. He opened the towel closet, and her perfumes and lotions were on the shelves. When would he have to do the inevitable? When would he have to wash the towels, sweep the floor, and clean the shower and sink? When would he have to face that he would be responsible for washing the small details of Elizabeth's life away? Not today, he thought. Maybe a year from now, but not today.

Jon changed his clothes, made the bed, and put Elizabeth's pillow beside his but left them under the covers, hoping to keep the scent contained as long as he could. He went downstairs, and Finn was still asleep on the daybed. He made a small fire in the kitchen stove and began to brew some coffee. He opened the door to the side porch and stepped outside. He noticed the rug was rolled and left on the church pew. It struck him as odd. Someone had used it since he and Betts. Someone had thought they could just open it up and use it, and that was okay, acceptable. Jon picked it up, brushed the moss off its fabrics, took it back inside, and put it away. He even thought of putting a note on it to say not to use it, but maybe that was too extreme.

He made his coffee, but instead of drinking it like he always did, he made it like Elizabeth's. Cream, cinnamon, and a spoon full of honey. He took it back to the table on the porch and sipped it, and he could taste her lips. It made him smile. He opened a thin book of poetry and began to read. It seemed like each phrase was a scripture that spoke directly to his heart. He reread each line out loud. Each word impacted his mind like a mallet to a taunt skin drum. It was like the dark spot in his chest was causing him to be more sensitive and more intuitive to small things. He underlined the words soaking them into his mind like ink bleeding into a dry page. He instantly wanted to rewrite the poems in his own words and probably would.

Finn came out with sleep in his eyes, and he stood behind. Jon gave him a slight hug. "Who is this you're reading?"

"Andre Breton, a French poet born in Normandy and then conscripted into the first war." Jon flipped the book over. "He was a surrealist. He had this style of writing known as Mad Love."

"What's surrealist mean?" Finn asked, sitting down at the table and picking up the book of poetry that Jon had laid down.

"Surrealism was the movement in art and literature that sought to use the creative power of the unconscious mind. Almost like creating something in a dream state. A reality where things are completely different and strange but work together to sustain something, like time or love."

"Art, like paintings?"

Jon scratched the bridge of his nose. How could he explain this to Finn without revealing his emotional state? Jon realized that subconsciously he had picked up the book of Breton this morning and that he was allowing himself to enter into a dream state each night where his subconscious found comfort in things he didn't understand. "Yeah, an artist like Dali, Frida Kahlo, Picasso, Maggritte. Actually, now that I say that, I think one of my favorite surrealist pieces of art may be one by Maggritte. It's called 'The Lovers,' or in French, 'Les Amants.' It's these two people kissing with cotton towels over their heads. It's like the lovers were parted by something thin, as thin as glass, yet they can feel the pressure of each other's lips through the cloth, but they can't feel the actual touch of the lips. It's infuriating."

"Where did you learn French?"

Jon looked into the eyes of the boy. He hadn't expected that question and wanted to express his feelings. He tried to search out his own peculiarity. "When we first came up here, the three of us, we were adopted by this man who owned the whole mountain and the sawmill. He, uh, well, he just disappeared after a while. Don't know where too, but he was a bad drunk. We looked for weeks but never found him. We had been running everything up here ourselves for a while, so we just continued. Finally, we decided that to make the mill better and better suited for us to live in, we needed to redesign it. We bought this machine built in Germany, with all these German manuals. When we set it up, we were missing parts, and I couldn't understand the manuals, so I went to the Tryon library and got a book on German. After reading it for a few weeks, I understood the manual and put the machine together. After that, I kept studying the language and started reading in German. Learning a new language was like giving myself a new world. I could read everything that German authors wrote. So, I kept going. I went back to the library and got a book on French. Started studying it. Little did I know that I would use French and German throughout the war. Languages have just always been easy for me. Then, I read Plutarch's Lives, I started learning Latin, and then the romance languages were so similar that they were all the same. I'm not perfect, mind you, in any language. I fumble through them. Betts always made fun of my French. I'm not even proficient in English, but languages have certainly enriched my life, and during the war, they certainly kept me alive at times. You might not be able to outrun your enemies, but you can often outwork them, outthink them. I learned much about strategy from Napoleon, Clausewitz, and Sun Tzu."

"Like the grape vineyard and literature? The rows led to grapes, and the grapes to clusters? One author leading you to another?"

Jon smiled at the boy, almost forgetting his grief for a moment. "Yeah, if literature was a grape vineyard for me, then different languages were like an airplane, in a sense. It allowed me to expand my view of the world and its people."

Finn looked at Jon across the table and folded his hands. "I wonder if I can ever speak another language?"

"You already do, Finn; you speak a language straight from your heart. "Jon's subconscious was trying to open a door of conversation where he could speak of his grief, but realizing this, he refrained. "Listen, umm, I was thinking we could go down to the vineyard and start cleaning things up. Around the gazebo, what do you think? Do you feel up to it?

Finn smiled at Jon. "Yeah, I will just eat something quick, and then I'm ready."

Driving with Finn across the French Valley to the vineyard, it felt strange to be doing this work now that Elizabeth was gone.

They could not help her out of the truck and walk with her hand in hand through the vineyard rows, looking at the brass plates on the posts and sitting beneath the gazebo to picnic, watching the sun fade into the French Valley. They could not light the torches around the vineyard at dusk and see the fire reflected in her eyes as she beheld their love gift to her in its nighttime splendor. But she would know the intentions of their hearts.

On the drive, Jon was quiet. He seemed to be smaller, and he was thinner, and he seemed to sit lower in the seat. As if the grief was not only taking his reserves but reducing the man's stature. He remembered when he and Elizabeth would bring the wagon and the horses over to the vineyard, and Elizabeth would lay her head against his shoulder. Sometimes she would read aloud to him during the ride over and back. She would call out to the horses, Andiamo and Deezy, telling them how wonderful and beautiful they were, and their ears would perk up and turn to hear her voice. She sometimes traced the veins in his hand that she loved. All this brought him closer to her. He fell deeper and deeper in love with her the more she touched him. Her hand on his leg. Her hand rubbing the tops of his hands. Her touches called his soul to her embrace like small and lovely whispers. She never confused Jon's emotions with touching; she never flicked his ears or pinched him. A man as hard as a stone, yet she alone had the power to change him. With her voice, with the softest touch, she whispered him to her sweetly like forgiveness that spreads as quietly as a tear. She calmed his heart and quelled his fears. ""Lover of mine,"" he could hear her whisper.

Jon nearly passed the stone columns, having been in his own memories. "We're here," he said. And wondered why he'd said it. For a moment, Jon wondered what he was doing. What was it worth now without Elizabeth here, without children of their own to pass it on to. He looked at Finn, who was eager to work and was grasping in his own small way for something to hold on to. Something that would keep him from having to leave the mountain. "Finn, I want us to do some pruning around the gazebo, and once we get that done, we will pump up some water from the cistern and clean the soapstone floor. How does that sound?" Finn nodded. "Good. Let's grab the pruners and get started.."

Jon took two pairs of Felco pruners from his truck and handed one to Finn. They walked over to the gazebo where the vines had intertwined with the steel and hung down all around. John showed Finn how to make a proper cut, flipping the pruners in his hand and keeping the blade close to the central leader of the plant without cutting the branch collar. "If the limb becomes damaged or diseased, the branch collar will close and not allow the infection to enter the rest of the plant. Likewise, if the limb is damaged, it will close off nutrients, and the limb will die, but the damage will not affect the heart of the plant. When the dead limb falls off, a dormant bud around the branch collar's edge will produce new life. It's rejuvenation, reincarnation, in some way."

Finn began to look around the large vine. "Do trunks ever die when they get old?" He pointed to a thick stalk of the brown and decaying plant.

"Yes, this is what is considered a multi-stemmed plant. It has multiple trunks, kind of like a rose bush. A plant mostly flowers from the younger trunks, but it is the older trunks where it gets most of its sustaining nutrients. Sometimes these old trunks die, and the crown of the plant, in that case, works like the branch collar. It closes it off and heals itself."

Finn looked at the old-growth stock of the plant and then back to Jon. "But before the old stalks die, there are new ones that spring up and take its place?"

Jon nodded. "Yeah, yeah, that's the course of nature. Things change, damage happens, or old age, but the plant can continue. There can be flowers and new growth, even beauty again. Time never stops producing new central leaders." Nature was teaching him a lesson today, caring for Jon just as Elizabeth used to soothe his old wounds. But he wasn't ready to hear that lesson. He wasn't ready to heal that quickly. It didn't seem fair to see the truth that quickly and embrace it, there needed to be a long period of mourning, but it seemed as if his own branch collar was trying to close off the damaged part of him and heal, but he wasn't ready to do that.

He wanted to come to the vineyard each day and toil. Not with the soil or the plants but toil with his heart and mind. He wanted to be bruised by the memories and regret the moments that would never come. He wanted to fight the healing because healing didn't seem right, maybe years from now, but not today. What seemed right now, what seemed natural at this moment, was to destroy the plant. To cut the plant and the branches all the way down to the crown. To leave the gazebo and the cold green steel unwrapped, alone on the hill as a martyr who died for love. To see the plant, which had grown and survived for nearly fifty years, all but uprooted. Cut back so hard that one good frost may entirely kill it. Devastate the plant like Jon had been devastated and see if it would survive. Would it be possible to ever regrow and reach out and feel, once again, the cold green steel of the world, and embrace it, to wrap his hopes and dreams around it again and see it bloom in season? Could something as beautiful as his life with Elizabeth and as beautiful as this old vine be destroyed entirely and still come back to create something beautiful, something worth living for? Or had the best days of his life passed, never to return again?

"Are you okay?" Finn said. "Can you hear me? I think you've got to flip your pruners. Like you showed me."

Jon felt Finn touch his arm, snapped back, and looked at the boy's face. "Oh, I'm sorry. I've been getting lost in old memories. Especially here, I guess. Hey, there's one other thing. You see these buds on the new vines. You see how they point in a direction? This one goes that way, this one the other way, you see it?"

Finn stood closer. "Yes."

"Well, whatever direction you want the plant to grow in, you cut right after that bud, so the plant will grow in that direction." He snipped the vine.

"Doesn't that hurt the plant?"

"No, a sudden loss like that and the bud produces a branch collar. It's almost immediate. Amazingly, nature protects itself like that. It's like a mother knowing her child cannot survive. It's like nature says there will be a better season and time."

Jon was looking around the Gazebo for other branches to prune when Finn stopped and sat down on the soapstone steps. "Do we have branch collars?"

Jon wanted to ignore the question but knew the boy would only ask again. He sat down with Finn, looking out towards the French Valley. "Yeah, yeah, I guess we do, Finn, but humans heal differently; we all deal with pain and grief differently. There is a branch collar, so to speak. It feels a little cruel in a way. Because for us, for you and me, going through the loss of Betts, well, it seems like life should come to a complete halt, and if it moves forward at all, it should do so in small steps or a different way. Some way conscientious of what we've lost, but the problem is, the hurtful thing is that it doesn't happen. Time doesn't stop. Clocks keep going. The sun keeps rising and setting. Hell, the full moon will be here again before too long." Jon threw a piece of the pruning on the ground before him.

"How do humans heal differently? If we all have these branch collars that protect us, the core, from more pain?"

Jon thought for a while, and Finn kept looking at him, and then he started using a stick to trace the white veins of the blue stone. "Finn, you see those tall green trees up there on the ridge? The ones that look kind of soft at the top?" Finn nodded his head. "Those are pine trees; we've got three types up here on the mountain. We've got Loblolly Pines, Virginia Pines, and White Pines. The Loblolly pine is widespread. It grows fast and straight. As it gets taller, its lower branches don't get as much sunlight, so its branch collars close them off, and they die. When those branches die, they fall off, the branch collar heals over, and the tree grows much faster and straighter. We use that wood for many things because it's straight without too many blemishes.

"The Virginia pine is just like the Loblolly, but when the branch dies, it holds on to it for some reason. For years, the dead branch just hangs there as part of the tree. The branch collar never heals up; therefore, the wood is knotty, hard in some places, and very soft in others. We usually grind the tree up for pulp wood or mulch. We can't really use the timber for anything because it's kind of ruined from hanging on to the old stuff.

"The third pine is the white pine. A young tree doesn't grow very tall, but it's beautiful. It grows in a pyramidal shape." Jon held his hands up. "So, the branches are always in the sun and never die. The tree is short-lived, shallow-rooted, with a thin trunk. They are ornamental, and because they grow so fast, they are very fragile. If they do experience any disease or damage, they tend to just die. If they survive, what branches they lose becomes a huge hole everyone sees. They live with a wound that never heals, making them susceptible to other injuries."

Still tracing the white veins of the soapstone, Finn said, "What kind of tree are you?"

Jon looked over at Finn, the boy in love with the mountain, and Elizabeth, and the soft stone, with the shapes inside it. Jon wished that Elizabeth could be there to see their handsome son, their Skyuka child. He breathed in deeply and exhaled. "Hmm, never thought I'd be confused about that before. I feel like, lately, I've kind of lost my identity, I suppose. I feel like a tree, not any specific tree, but one that had grown thick and old, beside a river in a green pasture. And year after year, it became more familiar with the river, with its surroundings. Branches wide, and in the sun, and close to other trees, but far enough away to be admired by everyone who could see me. "Then, in one summer night's storm, the river rose, and the earth around me began to move, and I stood calm because I had known the banks of the river to swell before. I had seen the soft silt break free only to return in another way, but I was cleaved off from the land that night. My roots washed out, and over I fell with my bow breaking and my limbs tangled with debris. My beautiful life and the pasture flooded away. That's the kind of tree I feel I've become. I've lost the name I was once called by and now just referred to as another gone." Jon was filled with anguish, and it was pouring out of him like sweat. Like he was inside a whirlwind with no air to breathe.

"What kind of tree am I?" Finn said.

Jon looked over at the boy and laughed. "You're not a tree yet. You're just a nut." Finn laughed, and it made Jon laugh and lose his seriousness. "A mostly good nut." He reached out his hand and rolled Finn's curly hair around. "What do you say about us going to town for lunch today. Get away and see some new scenery. I've got to stop by Cohen's anyways. Sound good?"

* * *

The bell on the glass door of the Bantam Chef rang as Jon and Finn entered. Penny's face popped above the counter, and as soon as she saw them, her eyes widened, and she stared like a celebrity had just walked inside the restaurant. She didn't say anything, just stood there silently, smiling.

Finn looked at Jon for guidance with the menu. "What's the Amish haystack?"

"I'm pretty sure that's a bad rendition of a taco salad."

Finn raised his eyebrows. "What should I get then?"

"I like the seven-decker club," Jon said.

"But it's got mayonnaise on it."

Jon looked at Finn. "It's required in some states."

Finn approached the counter, "Hi, my name is Finn. How are you?

"What can I get you, handsome?"

"I would like to have the patty melt, please, with chips."

Jon ordered the special with unsweetened tea. Penny rang up the purchase, and Jon paid, and they went and sat down in a booth, and Finn went to get some napkins.

"Jon Joines?" Jon turned in the booth to see the same short, broad woman at Elizabeth's funeral. "How you doing, Jon? It's Margot Bagsby, the realtor. How have you been?"

Jon was a little taken aback. "We are, well, we've been sad; it's been tough without Elizabeth."

"Oh my gosh, you still sad about that? Listen, it's like I always tell my customers who've lost a spouse. You've got to let the dead bury the dead. I told you, quick cruise to Grand Bahama, and you will have it all worked out." Jon shook his head in disbelief, and Finn slid around the woman back into the booth. "Listen, Jon, I know exactly how you feel. I got divorced from my first husband, and I loved him, I did, but he just wasn't going anywhere. I understand how you feel, but you need a change of scenery, and I can sell that house, subdivide that mountain, and find you a new place, maybe a condo. Listen, you've got to do this for yourself. God has a plan, and we must trust that everything happens for a reason." Jon was hoping it would end. She was talking so loudly that everyone could hear his business.

She was about to leave when she turned around, nearly knocking Finn over in the booth. "Listen, all those letters that you had at that funeral. You've got to burn them. That relationship is over, and you got to get rid of everything and move on. Do yourself a favor and just burn all those letters and things. You will be better off, I know. I see it all the time." She patted Jon on the arm, noticed Finn for the first time, and reached out to pat his head, but Finn dodged the hand. Jon and Finn sat across from each other, looking at the table. They had gone out to lunch to try and get away, yet grief was following them everywhere they went.

Penny brought two trays to the table and set them down. "I'm sorry about what that lady said. That was cringe-worthy. Everyone loved Elizabeth and admired all she did in the community. And, just to make one thing very clear. What you said about love and the letters you read and let everyone read, well, it was beautiful. I don't know that I've ever seen something as sincere or romantic as what I did there. Of course, in the movies, but never real as that. It was powerful, and you should keep those letters for you and for him someday." She gestured to Finn.

"Thank you, thank you for saying that, really, truly. This is Finn."

Penny smiled. "Yeah, I know; Bobby has been talking about this handsome young man lately." She reached over and rubbed Finn's back. Enjoy your lunch."

They made several stops in town, one being Cohen Hardware, where Jon was greeted by old friends who expressed their condolences and love for Elizabeth. The store owner had whistles lined up behind the counter, and he took one and blew it for Finn replicating the sound of an old train. They drove out of town as the sun set, across the last fertile plain and then up the mountain. The waterfall was gold in the setting sun. The only sound was the truck's diesel engine changing gears as they climbed.

"Will we work at the vineyard tomorrow?" Finn said.

Jon gave no answer. He turned onto the gravel road, thinking of the first time Elizabeth had come up to the mountain and how they set on opposite sides of the truck, with windows down, desperately wanting to be close to one another yet trying to be reserved. Jon had taken every road and showed her every flower, and waterfall he could, waiting for the right moment to kiss her. He was drifting now into the dream state, looking away and down to nothing. The truck began to veer.

"Hey, hey, Jon." Jon snapped out of the daydream and took control of the wheel. He slid up in the seat and adjusted his seat belt like that was the problem. "Will we work at the vineyard tomorrow?"

Jon leaned forward and turned the headlights on. "I suppose we could early in the morning, but I was thinking of visiting the clinic and possibly volunteering or at least visiting with some of the people we met last week." He looked at Finn. "What do you think about that?" Finn didn't say anything. He just looked back at the road and nodded.

They reached the Sawmill and turned beside the sea of grass. Jon noticed the kitchen light had been left on. Finn ran ahead and lit the porch lanterns, and saying nothing to Jon, he opened the corn barrel and plunged his hands into the kernels. He walked quickly to the pond's edge, threw the handfuls of corn into the air, and watched them fall like drumbeats across the face of the small pond, and the fish children fed, dashing, leaping, and crashing into the water again and again.

Jon chopped vegetables, sautéed onions in butter, and then slowly added garlic, pepper, and vegetable broth and let it boil until the potato skins were soft and being torn by the rolling over against the cast iron pot. He served it in the blue and white bowls made by the deceased potter and topped the soup with chives and Parmigiano – Reggiano cheese. He toasted pieces of a French baguette and then thought of red wine. He looked behind the small curtain and found a bottle of Barolo, and then in the back of the cabinet, he saw the small bottle of Bourbon. He remembered telling himself he wasn't going to drink, but this was just a glass of wine with dinner, nothing more, and anyways, it had been a decent day; he could enjoy this.

Finn entered the kitchen, washed his hands, and poured himself tea. They took their bowls and small plates and sat on the porch. Both not saying anything, just sitting under the light of the lanterns. Finn got up to wash his bowl when they were finished. " I got it, kid. You probably want to dive into your book anyways. What is it Hemingway, The Old Man, and the Sea?" " That's the one, you sure? I don't mind helping." "Yeah, take the night off, Sport."

Jon sat alone on the porch with his glass of wine and pulled out his notepad. He began to sketch the small silver charm, the baby rattle that he had found in the drawer, that Elizabeth had grasped in her hand, for hope, over the cobble street stones, wearing the blue cape. He drew the charm and the outlines of Elizabeth's gloved hand holding it. Jon set the drawing on the table. He reached for the glass of wine, but it was empty, he looked at the kitchen as if he could just ask Elizabeth to bring the bottle, but she was not there. He could not remember when the house was this quiet, with only the sound of the fountain.

He returned inside, pulled the cork from the bottle, and filled the small glass again. He went back to the drawing, now sketching the light shadow under the hand on the cobblestone. He knew it was getting near bedtime, but he was not sleepy and didn't want to embrace the insanity dream state. He wanted to be with Betts more than anything, but it was getting harder to be in that moment and not be able to touch her, to feel her, to see her breathing beside him, to feel her touch him, her lips on his neck, his cheek, his lips. He finished the second glass of wine and was still not sleepy. He did not want to just lay in bed and stare at the empty room, the hat boxes on top of the armoire. He sketched more of the shadow. He wrote the name Elizabeth under the drawing. He got up and stood beside the table in the lantern light. He was still not tired. He thought of walking up the gravel drive beside the field or even up the staircase to the upper pond, but neither seemed right without Elizabeth.

In the kitchen, he got out a highball glass, set it on the counter, and stared at it. He reached under the cabinet, behind the curtain, without looking, and pulled out the bottle of bourbon and poured some into the glass. He put the bottle away, took the glass to the porch, sat down, and drank it. He fumbled through the pages of sketches and poems, but each one stabbed at him, now reminding him again and again of something he lost and could never regain. He liked the way the bourbon was strong and biting. It felt like what he needed to control the pain inside him, so he went back again, reached behind the curtain blindly, pulled the bottle of amber spirits out, and poured it into the glass again. Pull by pull, he drank it and could feel his head swimming. The red wine mixed with the liquor. He didn't mean to go this far; he'd just wanted to skip the memories and sleep. He blew out the lanterns, left the dishes in the sink, and closed the door to the porch. He did not feel like seeing the toothbrush or Elizabeth's towels. He removed his clothes and climbed into bed, but instead of calling out to Elizabeth, she was already there, not saying anything to him, just looking at him. "If you don't like it, Elizabeth, then just come back here to me, and change it. The truth is that you're not here. Come back or take me with you. I just can't do this. I don't want to do this, Elizabeth." Jon's eyes filled with tears.

He woke early in the morning before the sun came up. His mouth was dry, but his mind was clear as cold water. He could taste the alcohol on his breath, and it seemed to be seeping from his pores.

He looked at himself in the bathroom mirror, surprised to see a much older, hollow man who appeared beaten or guilty of something he could not take back and was helpless to change. He stared at himself, disgusted, and eventually faced the pain of the toothbrush, the toothpaste, the towel closet, all the evidence that Elizabeth had been there, close enough to touch but never would be again. He brushed his teeth, showered, and then brushed his teeth again.

He went quietly downstairs and drank three small glasses of water from the hand pump. He made coffee, but it was too strong. He sat at the booth, but this morning he had no desire to read or draw outside. He thought of the alcohol he had drank and wondered why. Something got his attention outside the window on the porch rail. It was the dove. He stared at it, not believing it was there alone, just as he was alone. He got up and opened the door to the porch slowly. The dove was still there. He stepped out onto the porch, and it stayed. He walked slowly over to the corn barrel and, reaching in, sight unseen, grasped a handful of corn. He set it on the lid of the barrel and then, looking around, found the brass ashtray of Betts, picked it up, and ground the corn to meal. Finished, he scooped it up in his hand and spread it on the porch rail. The dove turned her head and looked at him, studying him. It walked over slowly and ate the meal. Jon stayed there with his arms crossed, watching the dove.

Finn came onto the porch and nestled up against Jon's side, reaching his arm around him and giving him a small hug. "What is it?" Finn asked.

"It's a dove, a love bird."

"A love bird?" Finn asked.

Jon shook his head yes. "Greek mythology always showed the dove as a symbol of Aphrodite. Because doves are always in pairs. Two birds, preening over each other, chatting with each other." Finn looked at the bird. It was content and happy to be there, cooing. "Where's the other one? Where's the mate?" Finn asked.

Jon looked at the bird. "Oh, I'm sure he's here." The bird flew away, and Jon and Finn sat at the table and ate a breakfast of toast with jam and honey. The sun was coming up, and Jon was reading. Finn had brought the thin copy of The Old Man and the Sea out and set it on the table. Jon caught Finn's eye and nodded. "One of my favorites. Did you see what was written on the flyleaf?"

Finn thumbed back to the single page meant to protect the printed copy. It was handwritten and addressed to Jon. He read aloud, "Who knew the world's most interesting man rarely says a word and owns a whole mountain. Thank you for the days of fishing. Ernest Hemingway." Finn looked up at Jon. "You know him?"

"I knew him. He used to come to Tryon and stay in the old Swayback cabin. Anyways, he and his entourage wanted to do some fishing. I thought he was a bag of air, but soon we started talking about literature and authors. He was thrilled to learn I had read Rilke in German and French. I showed him some of the streams in the French Valley. Ones, you have to hike into and out of. He gave Elizabeth these Spanish wine flasks, the ones you hold straight up in the air and squirt in your mouth, like this. Anyway, I always laid herbs and ferns under my trout, like I showed you, and he asked me about that. I told him about Jean-Paul, my friend, a boy who died in the war. I told him how we cleaned the mud off his body and we laid him in a crate that we found. It was cold and snowing, and we couldn't take the thought of our friend lying there freezing, even though he was dead, so we broke evergreen branches out of the trees and lined the casket." Jon paused and breathed deeply. "For some reason, when I came home, I started doing that for the fish; I have no idea why. Just something about it. Anyways, he gave us that book and those wine bags after that. Promised he would come back but never did.

"You know, one of his best books was Green Hills of Africa. That book seemed real, like the man I knew then."

Finn closed the book. "Do you think you will ever get married again?"

Jon was startled to hear the question. He took a deep breath and shook his head. "Finn, to tell you the truth, the thought of that right now is repulsive. It makes me feel physically sick. I know people often get married again, which is not bad, but I can't even imagine that. I don't know how to even think about that."

Finn looked down. "I'm sorry. I didn't mean to make you feel sick."

"It's not your fault Finn. It's an understandable question. I'm sorry, myself. I feel a little off. I'm supposed to pick up Elizabeth's ashes today. I didn't know how to tell you that yesterday. You know, her remains will be in a box. I'm sorry, I just want to prepare you for that. I'm trying to prepare myself. Umm, that's why I thought we could work a little in the vineyard and then pick those up and then stop by the Clinic and talk with some of the patients and see Bobby if he's there.

"Cremation?"

Jon looked over his reading glasses at Finn. "Do you know what that is?"

"Yes, Sir, but my Preacher says it's a sin against the body. Not that you'll lose your salvation but that, well, like God might not talk to you anymore or that you might look funny after the resurrection."

Jon leaned back in the chair and looked across the yard. "Finn, some people believe that heaven and hell are experiences we go through here on Earth." He paused and let the thought sink in. "They are not places our souls go in the afterlife according to whether we've been good or bad. Saved or lost, so to speak. Heaven would be the reward we got here on Earth for living moral lives, mindful lives, compassionate lives, being hardworking, and making thoughtful choices. The idea is this type of life would lead to happiness. Not wealth or monetary riches but inward peace, a good night's sleep.

Hell would be the opposite. If someone didn't live a moral life and continually made bad choices based on untruths, they would live in hell. No peace, even if they did have great riches. "My point is that many Christians are so focused on attaining heaven in the afterlife that they miss heaven here on Earth. They miss their children's questions, bedtime stories, or meeting their neighbors who may be from a different country or race. They may never see Paris in the snow. I'm saying, Finn, that I'm not sure if it matters so much what happens to our bodies when we die as it matters to our souls while we are alive."

Finn looked at Jon. "But the Bible says, 'The dead in Christ shall rise first.'"

"Don't they?" Jon pushed back from the table. "Listen, Finn, I'm a little off today; I've got a headache. I don't want to be mean, but I need a break from this conversation. Let's, uh, get ready and head over to the vineyard and get on with the day." Finn finished his toast. This was the first time he had seen Jon react to him in this way, making him feel uncomfortable, like he was walking on eggshells. Like Jon could send him home anytime. It made Finn nervous. What did Jon mean by? "Don't they?" He took his dish to the kitchen, cleaned it, and put it away. He looked at the flannel shirts hanging there, and since Jon was not in the room, he stopped. Buried his face into it and breathed and then kissed them. He gathered up his things for the day and decided to bring the thin book with him.

* * *

They stopped by the Sawmill and picked up buckets and scrub brushes. When they reached the Gazebo, Jon cleared the cut vines from the gazebo floor and piled them nearby. He then took a push broom and swept the years of debris and dirt from the soapstone floor. "Hey, Sport, how about taking a bucket and pumping some water up from the cistern. Oh, make sure there's no wasp nest in that pump first."

Finn walked around the Gazebo to where an old hand pump stood in the ground. He knelt before it and looked inside to see if the wasp had built a nest, then hung the bucket from the spout and began pumping. After a few tries, water began to flow slowly, with small splashes and then coming in a rush that sloshed over the edges of the bucket onto his boots. Finn struggled to carry the bucket of water to the Gazebo, and once there, Jon dumped it onto the floor without a word. Finn returned to the pump and brought back another bucket. The water began to reveal how beautiful the stone was. Its blue-green colors and white veins seemed to blend seamlessly with the old color and structure of the Gazebo.

Finn noticed something on the stone's surface before the metal columns. He knelt down and brushed the debris off a bronze plate. Words were engraved into the plate with some kind of rough tool but still done well. The boy got on all fours and read out loud, "My woman whose eyes full of tears."

Jon came and looked over his shoulder. "You found them. There should be six. I had forgotten about them until a dream I had last night. I wanted to come down and find them. Should be one at each column base." Finn went and started looking at each column, removing the vines. "I think the poem actually goes this way, clockwise around."

Finn scooted back across the floor to where Jon was standing. He read out loud again. "Whose eyes are compass needle are violet panoply." Finn moved again. "My woman whose eyes are savanna." Again, to the next column. "My woman whose eyes are water to drink in prison." He moved to the next column. "My woman whose eyes are wood under the axe forever." At the last column, facing west, he read, "Whose eyes are level of water level of air earth and fire." Finn looked at Jon standing in the center of the Gazebo with a broom and an empty bucket. "Did you write that?"

Jon shook his head. "No. But it means more to me today than it did back then.

"Who wrote it?"

"Breton, that French fellow." Jon started cleaning the floor again.

"Did you put them in the floor?" Jon kept working. "Yeah, I did, but not when we first built it. A few years later. Betts and I had a well; how do you say it? A tete-a-tete in our marriage. I made those brass plates and inset them in the stone after that. I guess it was a way of communicating when words were not enough. You know the saying. Actions speak louder than words. Back then, we used to spend a lot of time here. We would pile up branches all around the vineyard, and in the early frost, we would light them in bonfires to try and heat up the air temperature around the vines to keep them from freezing on cold nights. We would stay up all night, keeping those fires going. Sometimes we would invite all our friends up and make it a party. Elizabeth and I would sleep here under the Gazebo and read and make love." "And the poem?" Jon looked over. "Oh, the poem was one of my favorites. Memorized it while sailing across the North Atlantic one winter. I just loved the last lines. "My woman whose eyes are savanna. Whose eyes are water to drink in prison. Whose eyes are wood under the axe forever. Whose eyes are the level of water, level of air, Earth and Fire. All that said precisely what Elizabeth was to me. So, I stamped it on those plates, inset them in the stone, and then just sat back and waited to see how long it would take her to find them there. It was a different way of writing a letter to her now that I look back on it.

"And when she saw them, what did she do?"

Jon smiled. "When Betts was overjoyed by something, she couldn't talk. She would just cry these silent, warm tears and smile through the tears. She saw those plates right away and started going from column to column, tapping her lips, like she always did when she was thinking, and then she turned and ran to me and jumped in my arms, and those tears, well, they ran all down my face and my neck." Jon had now moved to the gazebo's steps and was looking out at the morning clouds hovering in French Valley. "I remember it all like it was yesterday."

They continued cleaning the floor and then the outside of the structure. When they got done, the stone floor was alive again, showing its original luster and beauty. They packed up their tools and headed down the mountain to town.

When they arrived at the funeral home, the same man who had helped plan the funeral asked them to wait for a moment, and then he returned with a wooden box and a small brown paper bag. The paper bag contained a small box with the jewelry that Elizabeth had worn during the funeral. He handed the box to Jon and the small bag to Finn. Jon took the box calmly, but inside, he was shocked. It was hard to believe that this was all that was left of the body that he had known for so long. Jon thanked the man and his staff, and slowly they walked back to the truck. He struggled to open the door, not wanting to take chances with the box of ashes. He set the box in the middle of the bench seat, and as they drove, they both kept a hand near the box to make sure it stayed secure.

They drove to the clinic and parked. Jon looked at Finn and then at the box of Elizabeth's ashes between them. "We can't leave her here," he said. Finn shook his head. Jon got out of the truck and tilted the back of the bench seat forward. He took out a jacket stored there and wrapped the box of ashes in it.

People sat outside at picnic tables, and some walked with volunteers around the parking lot for exercise. They went up the stairs to Bobby's office and found Bobby sitting at his desk. Jon knocked softly even though the door was open. Bobby was happy to see them. Jon walked over to the chairs where Ruby's guitar sat, and he opened the jacket he was carrying so delicately in his arms and revealed the wooden box. He sat down in the chair and began to cry soft tears. Bobby looked at Finn and then got up slowly from his desk, knelt beside Jon, and placed a hand on the box and a hand on Jon's back, and both men cried together. Finn came, placed his small arms around them, and hugged them.

"You bring them so much," Jon said. "You bring them the most precious being in the world, and this is what they give you back. How can you fit all that she was and all that she still is in a box?" The three separated, and Bobby handed them tissues to wipe their eyes.

"It is hard to understand," Bobby said solemnly. He made room on a small table beside the guitar and in front of the dulcimer and the photos that hung on the wall for Elizabeth's ashes to rest. Finn knelt in front of the table. He was listening, casting a line between the ten and two positions, pausing at the end to let the fly clear the leader, waiting, for a bite of hope, waiting for the next tug of the heart, waiting for the next steppingstone, the sturdy branch, the next lesson that would tell him this happened for a reason.

"Have you eaten today, Jon?" Bobby asked his brother.

"We had toast this morning."

Bobby leaned his head back. "Theo had a freezer go down at the Tea House. He donated all the food to the clinic, and Clarence is in the kitchen downstairs, making up all kinds of stuff. We had volunteers call all of our patients and their families so everyone could enjoy the feast. Why don't you go down there and see Clarence? You know he'd love to see you, Jon. Elizabeth's ashes can stay here until you are ready for them." Bobby extended his hand and placed it on Jon's knee. "This is a safe place for her. She's here with Ruby." Bobby lifted his gaze to a small shelf beside the photo of Ruby in the fountain water. A small pottery urn of blue and white rested there. Jon looked over his shoulder and pursed his lips. He nodded and got up.

Finn occupied the seat where Jon had been sitting. In his hand was The Old Man and the Sea. Finn asked if he could stay with Bobby and come down later, and Jon left the office to find Clarence.

Bobby smiled. "Did Jon tell you to read that?"

"No, I saw it in the barn, and I liked the cover because I like to fish." Bobby chuckled. Finn slid to the edge of his seat. "Bobby, do you think there is hope for Jon?"

"What do you mean, Finn?"

"I mean, like in this story. The old man has lost his wife, and he becomes unlucky. He doesn't have food, he can't sleep, and all he has is the boy. Then he goes way out to sea, away from everybody, away from any sight of land, and he battles the giant fish, but then the sharks come and take it away, and all that's left is the skeleton. But in the end, the woman looks at the skeleton and says it's beautiful. It makes you think there is still hope for the old man to be happy again and lucky again. The boy may be able to stay with him and fish with him. Or at least the old man would bring limes on the boat or at least buy a good killing lance made from a truck spring to kill the sharks that come in the future."

Bobby reached out and touched Finn on the leg. Tears began to streak Finn's face. Bobby reached for Finn, and Finn stood and came over to Bobby, who wrapped him in his arms. The boy cried, and Bobby did not move but simply comforted him. He handed Finn a tissue. The boy pulled back, wiped his tears, and blew his nose.

Bobby put his large hand on Finn's chest. "You are quite a wonderful young man, Finn. Why don't we talk for a minute?" Finn sat back down on the edge of the seat. "Finn, when people become shocked with grief like this, like with Elizabeth passing away suddenly, there is a tendency for those close to her to live, for a while, in disbelief. It's a coping mechanism. It's like when a body goes into shock because the pain is too great. What I'm trying to say, Finn, is that Jon is in some sort of shock. He is desperately trying to hold onto Elizabeth and, at the same time, make her memory last. He's also desperate for everyone to know her and to grieve her passing like he is. In a way, his mind begs everyone to comfort his soul while his body is determined to build some monument to Elizabeth.

"The truth that you need to prepare yourself for is that you will have to go back home soon. Jon is going to crash. He will have to face reality, and when that happens, just as you have expressed, he will go through a long period of not being lucky. Just like the old man in the story lived in a certain fantasy about the day's events or the baseball scores. Jon will go through phases of not wanting to face the truth because it's too painful. Finn, Jon will have to see himself through this period. He will have to go, just like the old man did, and battle his greatest enemy, his fear that life will no longer have meaning without his wife. But Finn, like the old man, Jon, can do this. I'm not saying that life will be the same, but he can again have hope and find happiness each day once he is ready to face the pain and call it brother, just like the old man did with that great fish."

"When will I have to go home?"

Bobby leaned back in his chair. "I don't know, Finn. I know Jon loves you, and I know you love Jon, but it will happen at some point, and I don't want you to be crushed again, not on top of all that has already happened. Have you heard anything from your parents?" Finn shook his. "Okay, let's just take it one day at a time."

*　*　*

While Jon chatted with his old friend Clarence, eating a plate of roasted chicken and vegetables, Penny entered the clinic's kitchen. She saw Jon sitting at the counter and froze but then smiled. "Hi," she said.

With a mouth full of food, Jon nodded, covering his mouth with a napkin. "Hello, nice to see you again. You know, Penny, I don't know your last name."

"It's Burgess."

"Burgess . . . Would Wayne Burgess, from Mill Springs, be your brother?"

Penny smiled at Jon and leaned on the counter. "Yes, Wayne and I grew up there on the farm."

Jon set down his fork. "Well, I've known Wayne for years. He and Bobby have been friends for a long time. How's he doing?"

Penny looked as if the question was surprising. "Wayne passed away."

"But, uh, oh, I'm sorry for your loss. I didn't know. I mean, Bobby, never—Did he, did he die here?" Jon said, pointing to the counter.

Penny straightened. "No, he was healthy. Um, he was fixing a leak in the chimney of our parents' old farmhouse and fell off the roof. The funny thing is, it wasn't that high. I mean, it wasn't a large drop. He just landed in some way and was instantly gone."

Jon was embarrassed not to have known. "I'm so sorry, Penny. Were your parents there?" "Oh, gosh, no, they've been gone a long time. Wayne had kept the house and fixed it up. He was thinking of living there since he always had."

Jon looked down at his hands and then back to her. "I'm really sorry, Penny. I didn't know. I thought the world of Wayne. He came up to the mountain and helped me move equipment around all the time years ago. Pretty much any day it was raining too much to work, Wayne would come up to the cabin and spend the day with us. He was a great guy. I used to fish with your father in his pond behind the old farmhouse. I don't know how I didn't ever meet you then."

"Oh, I left that farm as a teenager and never really went back."

"So when did you start volunteering here, at the clinic?"

Penny crossed her arms and looked at the floor. "Well, after Wayne passed away, I found myself coming over here just to see Bobby and talk. You know he's great about that, just listening. He was pretty broken up too. I mean, even after they weren't seeing each other anymore, they were still close and always played music together and spent time with each other. Bobby told me about the remembrance ceremony they do here at the clinic every year. Everyone who lost someone during the year can stand up and talk about their loved one. Well, I came. I felt awkward at first, but then all these people started getting up and talking about the brothers and sisters and family members they had lost that year, and I suddenly realized that I wasn't alone. All these other people had experienced the same loss as me. Since then, I just keep coming back because it reminds me that I'm not alone in this life. I see that all these people have lost someone, and yet they keep coming here, some even struggling to survive themselves, and they have a smile on their faces; they want to know how they can help me. I've never seen that before, Jon. I've never found that type of community before. I feel like this is my church in a way, these people."

Jon had forgotten about his meal. He listened to what Penny said about not being alone; others have lost loved ones. "You should come and read some of your letters at the remembrance ceremony," Penny said. "It's on Saturday morning."

"I will, Penny. I will."

* * *

On the quiet ride home, Jon thought of the remembrance ceremony he had promised to attend. He wondered what he should say and how to say it. He didn't really feel like touching the old letters again, at least not right now. It was just too much. However, he still had a longing to write to Elizabeth. He wondered how he could write to her now. Would he write to her and then read the letters to the dove? Would he leave the letters for the dove to find? He thought about the Cherokee way of writing on the great leaves in tears because the dead can read words written in tears. The ancients, the trees, the breeze, the past moons, that language, tear language, like the truth was universal, both the living and the dead could read and understand it. He thought of the tears, smudged, on the letter that Elizabeth had left for him in the hat box, giving the care of the letters, their life story, over to him. Her tears, he understood. His tears she, too, could understand. He would write to her, and undoubtedly because he wept and his heart wept while writing, Elizabeth would read the letters and know, truly know, what he was saying to her.

By the time they reached the cabin and exhaustion had overtaken Jon. He retreated almost immediately upstairs with Elizabeth's box of ashes. He set the box on the nightstand beside his bed. He opened the drawer, pulled out the yellow book of Wordsworth's poetry, found the small note Elizabeth had written him, and laid it on the box. He noticed something sticking out of the small book and opened it. Small note after small note rained from the pages. Elizabeth had filled his favorite book of poetry with precious small things to feed his soul, like the corn falling from the sky that fed his fish children. Jon picked up the scraps of paper one by one and read them. Elizabeth had written words to reassure Jon that she was there. Jon laid them one by one upon the box of ashes. Then he lay in the bed on his side and touched the box, desperately wanting to feel her by his side.

Jon awoke later, with his hand stretched out towards the box of Elizabeth's ashes, and he realized that in his dream, he had done as Elizabeth asked him to in the note. He had found her, kissed her, and made love to her. He sat up slowly, still groggy from sleep, turned on the bedside lamp, and looked at the clock. Downstairs the great room was dark, but there was a light coming from the kitchen, and he realized it was the light from the lanterns outside.

The stove was still warm, and restarting the coals of the fire, he reheated a plate of food for himself. He did not feel like eating, but it was something to help fill the void. He poured a glass of wine. He picked at the food, sipped the wine under the lantern, and listened to the waterfall. He went back through the notepad until he found the sketch of the Cherokee washing their clothes in the small pools of water in front of the fountain. He wondered if he could change the drawing. He flipped to a new page and started to draw but stopped. Just as it was in his life, shouldn't he make a distinction here in his journal? Instead of drawing on this page, he made a line and then, above the line, wrote the word "After," Elizabeth's passing had created a clear division in his own life. He then turned the page and began to draw the new sketch of the Cherokee kneeling by the pools of water in front of the fountain, but instead of clothes in their hands, they were holding the broad, dried leaves of ancient and sacred trees. Catching each other's tears with the leaves, they set them adrift in the pools. Jon needed to know that what he felt was the same as people had felt here, in this meadow, for thousands of years. That it was possible to have lived and loved and experienced beauty and joy and pain and to still find comfort in the course of nature. Even though his life felt utterly out of control, something deep within him, something ancient, something wise and peaceful, was leading him even though his own compass rose was gone. Under the sketch of the Cherokee weeping into the leaf and setting it at peace, he wrote a line he remembered from the little yellow book. "Some natural sorrow, loss, or pain that has been, and may be again?" Jon closed the notepad.

    He rested his forehead on the table and looked at the smooth planks of the porch floor. He was tired, bone tired, but he knew he couldn't sleep. He would try reading, but he knew he would get lost in every other word that reminded him of some old memory of Elizabeth. He finished the wine in the bottle. It still wasn't enough. He thought of the bottle of bourbon, something more robust, something that would help him rest. He got up quietly, not wanting to wake Finn, reached for a clean glass, moved the curtain aside from the cabinet, found the bourbon, and poured some into the glass. He left it this time on the counter. He saw the flannel shirts hanging in the kitchen, and he went over and buried his face in them and took in deep long breaths of Elizabeth's scent, and he wondered how long it would last.

* * *

"My woman, whose eyes are Savanna. My woman whose eyes are water to drink in prison. My woman whose eyes are wood under the axe forever. Whose eyes are level of water level of air, earth, and fire." Jon was lying on the rug in the Gazebo with Elizabeth covered in blankets while the large bonfires kept the vines warm. He was over her body, softly kissing her closed eyes, cheeks, ears, and down her neck, quoting the poem's lines over and over.

    Then Elizabeth kissed his face and placed his hand on her breast. "My man, whose hands are Savanna. My man whose hands are water I drink from in prison. My man whose hands are wood under the axe forever. Whose hands are level of water level of air earth and fire."

"Jonny, Jonny!" Jon could feel her under the blanket with him, but then under his hands, she suddenly started turning to dust; the night wind had begun blowing up from the valley floor, and her body was separating and blowing away in small fine particles. She called to him, and Jon jumped up and desperately tried to collect the dust Elizabeth had become, desperately, frantically, trying to collect all of her that was slipping between his fingers and put her back together.

With Elizabeth's pillow beside him, Jon woke up in a panic, sweating. He instinctively looked under the cover for her ashes blowing away, but when he found none, he realized it had been a dream. He turned and saw the box with Elizabeth still there, and one of the notes said, "Hello, my Darlin." He reached over and kissed the note with parched lips. His head was aching, and he felt sick. His tongue felt thick, and he was very thirsty. He knew now why he was thinking of water in his prison in the dream. He had gone to bed again, having not showered or brushed his teeth. Even though he was sweating under the blankets and his stomach was unsettled, he was cold in his extremities. His fingertips and toes felt icy, and the sweat across his brow was cold.

He went into the shower and again faced the shampoo, and conditioner Betts had always used. He didn't want them moved; how could he? He stood in hot water, trying to get warm but couldn't. He touched the shampoo bottle as if he was touching Elizabeth again under the covers beneath the Gazebo. He closed his eyes and was there again, but his throbbing head was beating back the sweet memory. He dressed and went downstairs. Finn had made a fire in the cook stove and started brewing the coffee as he had seen Jon do each day.

When Jon came into the kitchen, he saw the bottle of bourbon still on the counter, and instead of putting it under the counter in shame or disgust, he placed it inside the spring box to keep it cool. He walked out to the porch where Finn was sitting and started a new book called Flight Deck by Robb White.

"Good morning; how are you?" Finn asked.

Jon sat down. "I'm fine. I just need some toast this morning."

Finn got up and brought him a coffee mug. "You want cream and sugar?"

"No."

Jon felt the presence of the dove before he ever saw it. He knew instantly that she was there. But he didn't really want to turn and look at her because inside, he felt ashamed of having drunk so much to sleep and now knowing that anyone could smell it on him. The dove climbed the railing to the porch and stopped beside him, softly cooing. Like she was trying to whisper Jon to her, trying to heal his wounds.

Jon got up, walked over to the corn barrel, used the brass ashtray again, ground the kernels into meal, and laid them out on the barrel lid. The dove, not minding his presence, came over and fed while Jon and Finn both stood there in her presence.

"Where's the other one?" Finn said.

Jon looked at the dove. "He's close." His eyes were full of tears.

The dove turned and, having fed, flew away. "I wish she would stay here all day," Finn said.

"I'm sure she will be watching us from somewhere above." Jon put his hand on Finn's shoulder. "Hey, sport, let's go to the vineyard and start clearing some rows. I've kind of got in my mind to get the place cleaned up and then talk to Bobby about having everybody up from the clinic. All the patients and their families. Maybe have their next remembrance ceremony up here in the vineyard."

Jon packed a jug of water and saltine crackers. He needed something to quiet his stomach. When they stopped by the sawmill, Bobby's car was parked there as he had been staying in the apartment most of the time since Elizabeth had passed away. Jon loaded two chainsaws and gas cans into the truck and was on their way.

At the gazebo, Jon prepared the saws on the truck's tailgate. "I figured we start over here on the upside so as to carry all the debris downhill. Does that make sense? Come here. I want to show you something." The two walked over to a row of grapes. They passed the wood post with the brass plate, but it was blocked by several Red Cedars and could barely be seen. "Finn, grape vines are kind of particular. I mean that it takes multiple years for a vine to produce fruit. Here, look at this." They got down on their knees.

"You see, Finn, a plant's crown is right at the dirt level. The crown is where the plant grows both upwards and downwards. For all of the plant you see above the ground, a percentage grows beneath it to sustain them. Remember when we were pruning the vines on the gazebo, and I told you that the new growth produces the most blossoms? Well, look here. You see these little legs coming out and around the plant's crown and into the ground. That's the new growth of the vine. They are very, very important. So, when we trim around a grapevine base, you have to do it by hand. If one of those is damaged, it puts the whole vine in harm's way and can set it back. It will survive, but there's no guarantee that it will ever be the same as it was. It may take a while to come back, you know to bear fruit again." Finn nodded in acknowledgment. "Okay, good. I want you to take your pruners and work down the row, just trimming out the little saplings and any grass that's grown up or near the crown of the plant. While you're doing that, I will start cutting down some of these Cedars with the chainsaw. Alright? Are we clear?"

Finn nodded. "Clear."

Jon walked back to the truck and got the chainsaw. He cranked it and walked back up to the row where Finn was making his way, trimming around the base of each vine. As Jon walked, he remembered bringing Elizabeth to the vineyard for the first time in the wagon. Andiamo and Deezy turning in between the stone columns with the limestone finials, and Elizabeth in wonderment at what they stood for and where they came from. She reached out and touched the finial as they passed. As they crossed the small hill and looked down upon the beautiful vineyard and the gazebo and the apple trees and the falling away of the land into French Valley, she gasped at its beauty.

Jon plunged the saw into the first cedar, and the tree fell. He moved for the second. In his mind, he could see Elizabeth holding her hand over her mouth, reaching out to him in disbelief at what she saw. It was like she had been instantly transported across the globe back to all the places she loved in France, Italy, and Spain. French Valley, indeed was now part of their home. The second tree fell, and Jon, in his dream of Elizabeth seeing the vineyard, turned to look and see the name of the author on the post. A scream pierced his dream of Elizabeth, and then it registered that as he stood and turned, he had let the saw dip and then heard the scream. Jon turned quickly and saw blood gushing from the upper thigh of Finn. His heart raced, and he threw down the saw, pulled off his belt, wrapped it like a tourniquet around the leg of the boy, and cinched it tight. Finn was lying facedown on the ground, no longer screaming but holding pressure on the leg with his hand. Jon was nearly paralyzed with fear wondering how severe the injury was. Finn's pant leg was ripped apart, and blood was everywhere.

"Finn, I need to see the wound. I need to know if I need to cauterize it. We are a long way from help, son. You've got to trust me." Finn nodded. "Okay, when I say so, we are going to lift your hand, I will look at the wound, and then we will put this rag on it and hold pressure. Okay, one, two, three." Finn raised his hand, and Jon ripped the pant leg and looked at the wound, and then the rag was slammed back down under Finn's hand over the cut. "Strong Work." Jon patted Finn on the back. "It's a flesh wound. Nasty, but you are going to be okay. You're going to need stitches, but Bobby can do that. He was a medic during the war. Keep pressure on it. I will pull the truck up here and get you inside."

Jon started blowing the truck's horn when they got near the Sawmill. Bobby opened the apartment window, and Jon told him to get his kit and come to the cabin. Jon picked Finn out of the truck, took him inside, and laid him down on the daybed.

When Bobby got to the cabin, he was out of breath but immediately positioned Finn with the wound above his head. "What kind of wound, Jon? Tell me what happened."

"Flesh wound, upper thigh, about five inches long, needs stitches. I was running the chainsaw, and he came up behind."

Bobby shook his head. He laid his hand on Finn's chest. "I know it hurts, but you are going to be fine. This is part of growing up. Now, I'm going to remove your jeans around the wound with scissors." He laid his hand over the boy's hand. When that was done, he said, "I'm going to clean the wound and put some bandages over it. Then you can change your pants, and we will go to the hospital for some stitches. You will be okay; I promise you trust your Uncle Bobby now." Finn nodded and let the giant man do his work. Carefully and methodically, Bobby cleaned and bandaged the wound. "Okay, this is some Tylenol to help with the pain and swelling. I know you don't want to move it, but it's okay too. It looks worse than it is. I'm going to have a word with Jon, then I will be back."

Bobby led John out to the porch. "He's going to be okay, Jon, but he needs stitches."

"Can't you do that here?"

"Jon, this isn't France, this isn't the battlefield, and that's not one of your soldiers in there. That is a boy. A boy whose parents don't even know he's been hurt. And no, I don't have any numbing agent or medication, and that wound will infect. God Damn it, Jon, you know that better than anyone. Again, this is not the battlefield." Bobby paused for a long moment. "I know you love Finn, Jon. I love the boy too, but it's time for him to go home." Jon started to protest. Bobby raised his hand. "He's not your son, Jon. He is someone else's child and has been cut in the leg with a chainsaw. He has to go to St. Luke's for stitches and then home."

Jon started to explain how it happened, but Bobby raised his hand again. "I know it was an accident, Jon. If you can't take him to the hospital and home, then I will. Do you understand me, Jon? The child is someone else's."

Jon nodded. "Okay, I understand."

Jon sat on the church pew of the porch and looked over the backyard and the wooden walkways to the staircase. For a split second, he wanted to run across those walkways up the stairs to the rest and lay his own life down for the buzzards to eat. He wanted to run away from the pain of losing Elizabeth, of losing the small things, of hurting Finn, hurting the ones he loved. It was like a thousand small cuts. He wondered how he would tell Finn.

He got up, poured a glass of water, and took it into the great room, where Finn was putting on a new pair of pants and hopping on one leg to keep his balance. Jon set the glass down and steadied the boy's arm. "Difficult, huh?" Finn said nothing in response. He sat down on the bed slowly. Jon sat down on the edge of the daybed beside Finn, breathed deeply, and exhaled.

"I'm going home, right? You're sending me home?"

"Look, Finn, I'm sorry, I shouldn't have had you working in that row, and I should've told you not to come near me when the saw was running. It's my fault, and I'm sorry. I was trying to read the name on the post." Jon squeezed his lips together and shook his head. "Bobby's right, regardless. You've been hurt. I'm going to take you up to St. Luke's for stitches and then home. Your parents are doubtless worried."

Finn made it easy for him. He reached over and touched Jon's shoulder. "I want you to know that this has been the best summer of my life. I love Mrs. Elizabeth, I love you, I love the mountain, and this day bed, and feeding the fish." He was trying not to cry. "I love the books, and your notepad, the smell of brewing coffee on the stove, and my rope belt. Thank you for being kind to me. Thank you for answering my questions." Finn was crying now. He leaned over and hugged Jon, and Jon hugged him.

Jon gathered up Finn's things and placed them in the red bag. Finn asked Jon if he could take the new book he was reading with him, and Jon said yes and suggested others he may want to read. Bobby waited on the porch to tell Finn goodbye. He gave Finn a small envelope and told him to open it when he got home. He also told Finn that his phone number was on the card and if he ever needed him to call.

Finn, crying, climbed into the truck with the red bag, and Jon put the boy's small axe in the bed. As they drove away from the cabin, the sea of grass waved in the sunlight. Finn looked at the small outbuildings and the rough-cut boards with sap that never moved. He looked into the eaves of the Saw Mill and saw the Dove watching them leave. They turned, and Finn looked back to the cabin in the corner of the meadow, and he wondered if he would ever return.

The hospital stitched up Finn's leg and covered it with bandages. They gave him a prescription to fight the infection, and Jon stopped at the local drugstore and had it filled. He came back to the truck and climbed inside. He looked at Finn sitting on the far side of the bench seat. "Ever had a dipped cone?"

Finn shook his head. "Nope, what is it?"

"Reckon, you'll find out."

They pulled into the parking lot of the Bantam Chef and got out. Finn was walking slowly, and they went to the counter and ordered the ice cream dipped in chocolate. They sat on a picnic table with their backs against it, looking at the road. Finn said, "Why did Bobby and Ruby choose to be . . . you know?"

Jon had heard the question a thousand times. "To be gay?" Finn nodded his head. "Finn, let me ask you something. Did you choose to be a boy? Did you get a card you filled out before birth that let you choose to be white, brown, or live in America rather than being born in the Mediterranean, or Bombay, India?" Finn shook his head no. "Did you check a box that said you wanted to be attracted to girls rather than boys? Something that said you wanted to be born healthy without any disabilities? Finn shook his head no. "I didn't either. Finn, those aren't choices we get to make in life. You don't get to choose to be a boy or a girl, or white or black, or to have hair or no hair. You don't get to choose to be straight or gay or short or tall. Finn, the only choices we get to make in life are whether or not we will be ignorant and prejudiced. Bobby and Ruby did not have a choice over their sexuality, just as you and I didn't. They did not have a choice of skin color or to be orphans. But the choice that they did make was one of truth and compassion. That's why Bobby is helping the people in the clinic. He chose truth and compassion over prejudice. That's why there is a library in nearly every city. Read everything you can, Finn; truth will always reveal itself."

"Why did you and Bobby close down the Saw Mill?"

No one had ever asked Jon that. He thought for a moment. "Well, after Ruby died, things changed in a big way. Bobby was heartbroken; we all were, but Bobby especially. He had always kept the books for the Saw Mill, but after Ruby died, he really couldn't do much. He stayed in their apartment for about a year and then left. He started traveling all the time and was gone for many years. We really drifted apart; it was sad. I started taking the equipment we used around the Saw Mill and began to do odd grading jobs for people. It was just easier. I could do those things myself. We could've kept the mill going if we had increased our market share, but we never did. We were just young and had all we needed to get by. And we each had a little bit of money we found." Finn was finishing his ice cream cone. "What's Market Share?" Jon looked over again. "Market share is a practice that for every dollar you keep or give away, you spend a dollar to increase your footprint in the market that earned you the dollar. Does that make sense? Let me say it this way. For instance, your church gives money each month to missionaries, right?" Finn shook his head. "One hundred and thirty missionary families, yes." Jon nodded. "Okay, well, I imagine that if they support foreign missionaries, they also give an amount of money to the needy in the church and the surrounding community. That way, if the church members and the community stay financially healthy, they can always support the foreign missionaries abroad. Everyone will benefit. It's like Bobby's clinic. They spent money to add a new addition, a kitchen, and a food pantry. Anyone in need in the community can come and take what they need, no questions asked. The community grows, stays healthy, and reinvests back into the community; that way, the clinic's ministry is sustained. Same way in business or your personal life. If we would have grown the market share of the Saw Mill way back then, maybe purchased a retail lot in town, well, by now, fifty years later, we would have building supply stores in three states." Jon turned towards Finn. "No one does anything big alone, Finn. Not even God."

They took the last turn and started up the paved road to the wheat hill house. Finn could feel a sickness in his gut. He had been gone for the summer, and no one had called to check on or find him, not even his real mother. Finn hoped that no one would be home and he could slip into his bedroom and try to stay hidden. He even thought about when Jon left, just running away and living in the wheat fields and peach trees surrounding the area. When they got to Finn's house, Jon pulled into the driveway lined with red stones and parked. He asked Finn to open the glove box and hand him the envelope inside. Jon opened the envelope, pulled out $150, and gave it to Finn. "This is for work, up there on the vineyard. Helping me and all."

Finn looked at him. "You don't have to pay me."

Jon gave a nod. "Go on, you earned it, Sport. But listen, you don't tell anybody about this money. Okay? That's not wrong; it's yours. I want you to take it and hide it, and if you get hungry or need something, you go down to that store and get it. I want you to take care of yourself. Okay, Finn?" Finn nodded. Jon slid the rest of the money into his back pocket.

Like two strangers visiting, they got out of the truck, Finn with his bag and Jon holding the boy's small axe. He gave it to Finn and took the bag, and Finn used the axe handle like a cane for his wounded leg. They stood on the front porch, and Finn waited with Jon, not going into his home. Jon realizing that Finn didn't feel comfortable enough to open the door and go inside, pulled back the screen door and knocked on the wooden door of the home. After several minutes Marlene pulled the wooden door open. She didn't say anything, only looked at Jon and then at Finn.

"Mrs. Kindhart? I'm Jon Joines." Her face did not change. "We've been keeping Finn up on the mountain." Her face still did not move. "There's been an accident, uh, we were cutting some trees, and Finn came up behind me, and the saw cut his leg. It's a minor wound, but he had to have stitches." Marlene looked at Finn and nodded her head slowly. Jon felt strange; the woman was peculiar. "The doctor said that the leg would be stiff for several days, and he won't be able to bend over or walk very quickly. Here's a prescription to fight infection. Stitches are supposed to come out in about two weeks. I can pick him up and take him to get those taken out if you like. I'd be happy to do that." There was a long pause where Jon thought the woman would say something. Jon pulled out the envelope from his back pocket. He handed it to Marlene. "I know this isn't much, but I wanted you to have it. It's Sixteen hundred and fifty dollars. I just wanted you to have it in case Finn needs food, clothes, or shoes. He's got some with him, but I don't know. I just want to make sure he has what he needs."

Marlene took the cash as if she was owed the money, and a large smile crossed her face like a dead clown in a case. She remembered now what Reggie had said about God may want Finn to go up to the mountain, and then he would bless them. Like Abraham, laying his son on the altar to be slain. God had rewarded their faith. God had given them enough money to pay two months' mortgage payments. He had met their needs. She opened the door wider and smiled at Jon. Finn did not smile, did not go to Marlene, or embrace her. "I'm sorry about the accident, Mam. It was entirely my fault. I know he is in pain and needs to rest."

"Oh, don't worry about that. Come on, Finn, come here." She stretched out one arm to the boy. "What kind of boy doesn't want to hug his mother?" She looked up at Jon and shook her head. Finn stepped forward, turned, and stuck his hand out to shake Jon's hand as if the contract for his labor was done.

Jon discarded the hand and pulled Finn to him, and hugged him. He whispered in his ear. "Remember what I said. Remember, Elizabeth loves you, and I love you. Okay, Sport?" "Will the Eagle be watching me?" Jon looked deep into the boy's eyes. "The Eagle and the Dove, Son." Finn wiped some tears from his face and reluctantly stepped into the house. Marlene hugged him and made a point to kiss his cheek in front of Jon. "He's going to be fine. If you ever need him again, just stop by and get him."

Jon felt sick like he had just made another horrible decision that hurt the people he loved most. "He's a good boy, a good little man. You take care of him. You be good to him, Mam." Finn disappeared into the house, and Marlene closed the door. Jon turned and glanced at the view of Panther Mountain before he got back into his truck and drove back towards the North Carolina line and Tryon. He found himself looking over several times, but seeing the empty seat was like another empty space opening up in his heart. He wondered why Bobby had never even mentioned Wayne Buregess's death to him or Elizabeth. Not only had Bobby mourned the loss of Ruby, but he had also mourned the loss of another man he had loved. Even though the relationship may not have been the same or worked out, he still loved Wayne, and they had remained close, playing music together and being friends. How strong must his brother's soul be now to have endured so much loss? How could a man become so accustomed to losing those he loved and still keep finding a why for living? How could he lose someone so close to him and not even mention it to his brother?

Jon feeling his own bereavement and appreciative of all Bobby had done to comfort him, came into town to see if Bobby was at the church. He wanted to be there for him with the loss of Wayne. He was still cloudy from the bourbon the night before. If he hadn't drunk so much to sleep, then Finn probably wouldn't have gotten hurt. Had Bobby found the bottle in the spring box? Did he blame Jon for hurting Finn? He pulled into the church parking lot but did not see Bobby's car, and there were no lights on in his office. He saw Penny carrying something on her way to her car. He thought to say something to her momentarily, but he knew she would ask about Finn, and he drove out of the lot toward home.

He thought about Penny. He wanted to talk to her. She was easy to talk to, and talking to a woman somehow comforted him. That didn't seem right. He had been touched by Elizabeth every day for fifty years. He could close his eyes and still feel her hands, but that was just it. His soul and mind could talk to her all night in his dreams, but his body ached for the touch of its healer and caretaker. He started talking with Betts like she was in the truck. He could feel her that close and near. He could continue conversing with her and still hear her audible voice, laughter, and tears echoing in his mind and heart. Like his heart was a stone chamber, and her voice echoed through it.

"That's just it, Betts, you are not here. I want to feel your touch on my skin, your kiss on my lips, your hand in my hair. Just take me with you; I'm ready to go." She was quiet. In his mind, he knew he had hurt her feelings thinking about Penny. The thought made him feel awful and small, knowing that he had crossed a line and was faced with his worst fear that Betts would leave him. Even from beyond, she was the dearest thing in his life. "Then do something about it, Betts. Either come back here or take me with you. Please, Betts, just take me with you. I can't do this. I don't want to do this."

He heard Elizabeth's voice telling him that he must stay. He had to take care of Finn and Bobby. Jon wiped tears from his eyes and drove on under the ancient trees of the mountain road. He turned down the driveway, and the sea of grass waved in the moonlight. For the first time in his life, the corner of the meadow where the cabin stood was utterly dark and alone. He walked into the house and saw the flannel shirts hanging near the phone and the booth with no one. He looked down at his clothes and saw the chain oil from the chain saw and wood dust from the cedar. He wondered too if Finn's blood, his Skyuka child's blood, was on his jeans just like the blood of Elizabeth was on the carpet. He knew he needed to go upstairs and shower, but he also knew that anywhere he went in the house, he would have to face the reality that Elizabeth's things were there, but she would never be there again herself. Never again would he come home to a well-lit, warm house unless he planned ahead and left it that way. Elizabeth would never be on the porch, enjoying her afternoon cigarette, waiting for him to wrap her arms around him in the driveway and say, "I missed you all day." He looked at the stove and the countertop and stood there with his arms bracing himself in the doorway. His mind listed all the ways his life would never be as lovely or the same again. He lifted his head and saw the jar of sea salt flakes they had always used. Almost hidden behind it was a note.

> *Jonny,*
> *My gift is salt and memories*
> *A present that needs no explanation.*
> *The first may dissolve in water*
> *But the second will never dissolve away.*
> *Place it on your lips*
> *Mold it with your tongue*
> *Let it take you back*
> *To the high-water mark*
> *Where the sea left us, to dry in the sun.*
> *All my salty memories were made with you.*
> *Me*

Jon placed the note to his lips. He hadn't seen it for years and wondered how long she had it there. Closing his eyes and placing the paper on his forehead, he returned to the island and the afternoon they had spent collecting sea salt. The Tunisian wind blew strands of hair across her face. How they held hands on the trail back to the village town. He remembered Elizabeth saying she wanted a son because she wanted more of him. She placed the salt on his tongue and then kissed his lips, smiling with her eyes beside the wine-blue sea. "It's just more of you, Jonny, and more of me."

CHAPTER 15

"My Flesh and my Heart may Fail"

Finn, sat in the yellow bedroom like a deer hoping to not be seen. When he heard his father's car go by the window, he sighed with relief. It would still be strange, but he knew he could make it through the night. He heard his father come in the back door. He could hear Marlene greet him, probably giving him a hug, and then she told him God had provided for the mortgage, just in time. Finn heard the relief in his father's voice. He could hear his father walking to his room, but the footfalls became more of a run. His father went into the bathroom right beside Finn's room. His father stayed there a long while. Finn wondered if he was okay.

 A knock came to Finn's door and he watched his father open it, his thin lips framing a big smile of sharp teeth. Finn was surprised at how much older his father's appearance had become in the short period he had been gone. He looked seventy years old. Finn stood up slowly, the leg much stiffer now and embraced his father. He loved the feel of being in his arms, even though now, Finn could feel only bones beneath his father's skin. Finn, breathed in the sweet smell of his aftershave.

 "I tell you what. I really missed you, Finn. There was at least a dozen times I had to stop myself from just driving up there and getting you." His father showed genuine excitement to see him, and Finn was happy to see his father but, in a way, he wished it was just for a visit, like when he went to see his real mother on the weekends.

"Why didn't you? I thought it was only going to be a couple of days, but it was long time. I mean, I'm not complaining, I had fun, but I did miss you, Dad."

"Well, you see. Now, that's just it Finn. Every time I got so homesick to see you, I thought about you being up there on that mountain fishing and enjoying yourself. How were the nights up there, pretty chilly?"

Finn immediately thought back to the lantern lite nights he would sit outside and talk with Jon and Mrs. Elizabeth. How they would wear the old flannel shirts that hung in the kitchen. "It could be a little chilly. But you would've liked it because of the cabin and the wood cook stove. Then outside, a fountain just comes gushing out of the mountain, and the fish children in the pond feed on corn. Daddy, you'd love it." His Father looked at him and tilted his head. His pants were baggy, and he had made several new holes in his belt. His work boots were beginning to look like oversized clown shoes on the end of his legs.

"Fish children, Finn? What's that all about?"

"Well, Jon, you know the man, well he, well he didn't . . . but, anyways, there's this pond, not a giant pond, but a smaller pond that comes up close to the back of the house and well there is all these trout." Finn held up his fingers to show the length of the fish. "It's full of them, and I get to go out there and feed them corn from this big barrel, and they all—"

"Supper's ready," Marlene called out.

"Finn, this all sounds really wonderful, and I want to hear all about it, but right now, we've got to eat and get ready for church tonight, but I promise, I want to hear all about it." Finn nodded. When Finn came home to the wheat hill house, his Father didn't know about his leg because Marlene had not mentioned it; the financial blessing of God was so great, but Finn, being so happy to see his Father, did not think about the pain.

The Wednesday night church service was moving quicker than most. Pastor Shane started his sermon directly after the youth choir sang. "Tonight, Church Family, I want to speak about the garden of God's presence. I'm going to read right here from the book of Mathew. After the last supper, Jesus asked the best of his men, his disciples, to go with him to the Garden of Gethsemane and pray awhile. Jesus, being both the Son of Man and the Son of God, was feeling weak. His heart was troubled, and his flesh was troubled. He asked the fellowship, the brotherhood, to watch and wait with him. Knowing, now, knowing that his hour had come. It wasn't a week earlier he rode into Jerusalem on a donkey, and folks were laying their coats and palm leaves down worshipping the son of God, and now, Jesus is desperately pleading with his father to let this cup pass from him. You see, that was the son of man side of Christ, that was the flesh failing. Now the son of God side of him said. What did he say? Let's look here in verse thirty-nine. "Nevertheless, not as I will, but as thou wilt." Now, say Amen right there! You see the difference, don't ya? The God-man, and the flesh man? The flesh man went running back to his buddies and said. Hey! Wake up, Judas is coming going to betray me, and they are going to kill me. Can't you stay awake with me? 'The spirit is willing, but the flesh is weak.' He said it right there, didn't he? How many of you can say that? The spirit is willing, my spirit is willing, but my flesh is weak."

Shane lifted his arm and pointed around the auditorium. He leaned back now, arm's length from the pulpit. "Jesus begged his father over and over and over until he sweated drops of blood. Now, let me tell you what scientists say, Doctor's tell me when I ask them about this particular passage. That sweating blood is a condition that only happened a few times in history, Jesus being one of them, that a person being under such mental and physical anguish actually drops blood out of their body. I want you to think about that now. I want you to think about the son of God, the son of man, kneeling in that Garden pleading with his father to let him live. Can you see him there weeping as if it were blood drops from his head? See him there with his hands in his head, desperately calling out to God to not let this happen, and yet, when he doesn't hear from God, he finally says. 'Not my will, but thine.' Church family, now tell me, tell me tonight, can you imagine the Son of God, Jesus's pure white blood, being dropped on the thorny ground of Gethsemane? The holy blood of Christ. Do you know why? I say do you know why Jesus was weeping blood, church family? Jesus was weeping, crying out because he wanted his beloved. Jesus wanted his beloved in the Garden with him."

Shane closed his Bible; it had been a quick sermon. "'Thy will be done not mine.' Jesus got victory over his flesh. Like an onward Christian soldier, he had faith, blind faith in what God the father was doing in his life, and he gave it all. He gave all he had. Do you know why? So that one day he and his beloved would be in the Garden together. We wouldn't be here tonight if Jesus hadn't given his all and won the victory over his flesh. We wouldn't have this truth, this word of God, right here to rely on. We wouldn't have ever made it into the Garden with God. Not my will but thine, not my will but thine."

There was a quick invitational. There was only one person who went to the altar to pray, and that was Reggie. He had slipped out from the fifth pew and quietly went to the front of the church to pray. Finn watched him and then watched him return. Shane usually dismissed the congregation with a word of prayer, but tonight he said that the church needed to address two matters of church business.

This was very odd because church business was usually held once a month and after a Sunday night service.

Jay Parham read the minutes and called the congregation in order. Preacher Shane addressed the church and said that one of the deacons, David Childs, would speak to the church. As David Childs got up, his wife stood and marched herself and their children out of the church. David walked up the stairs of the altar, the hole in the bottom of his shoe showing for everyone to see. He shook Pastor Shane's hand and then faced the waiting congregation. "I just want to thank Preacher Skelton and you, the people of Beau Pre Baptist Church. I have been a deacon here for thirteen years. It has been one of the greatest honors of my life to serve God and this church. However, one of the requirements of a deacon is to have his house in order, and as Preacher Skelton has preached many times, that means being able to financially pay your bills. And that is where I have failed, God, my church family, and my own family. My wife Deborah got breast cancer three years ago, and we just haven't been able to gain victory over that disease. I missed so much work, with her in the hospital and sick, trying to care for the kids and our elderly parents. Well, I lost my job, at the plastics plant a while back. Now, we looked at that as maybe a blessing because then I could be home all day to help out and then be able to work through the night restocking at the BI-LO, but they don't have the same insurance as the plant, and Brother Walker, who owns the grocery, doesn't pay overtime, it's just straight hours. I didn't realize that, but anyways. I guess I'm rambling on.

"I can't be a Deacon anymore because we have to file bankruptcy; we tried selling our house. We did sell our car and started driving my parents, but it's just not enough, and this is the only thing that, well, we don't want to mind you with our troubles, but it's come to that. I'm sorry, Church Family. I know I've failed you, Preacher Skelton, and my wife and kids. I just, I just, I do have faith that God has this under control. I do have faith, but I have to resign." David Childs shook Preacher Shane's hand again, walking down the altar and out of the church.

Preacher Shane stood behind the pulpit again and addressed the congregation. "I appreciate David Childs. He is a fine man, and I know that God has a plan for him and his family and will meet their needs in his own time." The door of the church closed behind David Childs. "The next item of business, church, is my least favorite and an item that comes up every year. It deals with my compensation from the church and my annual raise. So, having said that, I will excuse myself and turn over the church and this meeting to Deacon Marty West, who will lead you in a vote." With this, Shane picked up his Bible and the overcoat he used to cover his sweat-drenched suit and left the service with his wife Norma in the new Mercedes that the church had bought them.

Marty West humbly and somewhat awkwardly took possession of the pulpit and the church's business meeting. It was apparent that Marty had been coached in what to say. He looked over at Jaime behind the piano several times. "So, as you can see here in this verse of the Bible that men of God are not just ordinary people but worthy of double honor. That is why we would like to put forward to the church that in addition to the annual income of Preacher Skelton of $55,000 this year, the Lord has led us to propose giving the preacher an additional love offering of $25,000. We would like to start that love offering tonight by taking a collection and peoples' pledges for this coming year. Any balance would be paid out of the church budget." There was a quiet that fell over the congregation. One elderly man stood up. Finn did not know him because the man rarely ever said a word. "Why?" he said. "Why would a man who puts his pants on just the same way I do make double my money?"

Marty West stammered. Jaime, sensing that Marty was losing the solidarity of the congregation, quietly slipped out from behind the piano, maneuvered over to the pulpit, and stood behind him. Another man stood up. "Shouldn't this extra money, if there was extra money in the church, be split equally between the church needy?"

Marty turned and looked for Jaime. Jaime stepped to the pulpit, and Marty returned to his seat with the congregation. Jaime flashed a giant smile across the assembly, and Finn thought that one day, Jaime would undoubtedly hear the call to preach like his father. "Church family, church family. Now, folks, what we are trying to do and have not fully explained here is that my Daddy, Preacher Skelton, nine times out of ten, merely signs his name on the back of any checks he is given from the church and simply returns them to the offering plate. Time after time. I can't tell how much this man has suffered for this church's and ministry's sake. If sister Wanda, our bookkeeper, were here tonight, she would tell you herself." Jaime kept his hands raised, and the smile never dropped from his face. "So, Dear Ones, hear me now, I want to set that record straight that what we are trying to do here is make him actually take some money for himself. To show our appreciation. And yes, the Bible says that Men of God deserve double honor. Now, let us vote on this as a church family. We just need two audible votes from members to pass this. Can I get a motion?"

Someone from the crowd said. "Motion." Someone else seconded the motion. Paul Gilbert stood up and testified that Preacher Skelton had been such an example to them and wanted to give Twenty-five dollars to the love offering. Curtis Brown stood and pledged Seventy-five dollars. He said they didn't have much, but they wanted him to know they appreciated him. Others stood, and the evening continued with people telling how they had given when it hurt, and God had always blessed them. Jaime Skelton interjected, referencing the disciples with Jesus in the Garden of Gethsemane, who couldn't stay awake to watch and pray. He said. "God gets gone when the right people do wrong. You want to keep God here. You want to keep your children safe. Then you got to take care of God's man."

Fin thought it was strange for them to take up a love offering for a special gift to Preacher Skelton when David Child's family was hurting so badly. None of it made sense. Those who were hurting just caused themselves more hurt to give a gift to Preacher Skelton even though he lived in a big house on Edith Drive and drove a new Mercedes and pickup truck. He had cows and a fat dog, a dog he loved, and cows he punched in the face. A large yard full of onions and property to sell.

Finn's father stood up in his suit of clothes that hung from his shoulders like drapes. His Bible was tucked under his arm like a badge of honor, and he raised his thin arm to get Jaime's Skelton's attention. "Brother Jaime, I know you can't outgive God. He's been good to us. I want to give Sixteen hundred and fifty dollars to the Pastor.

"Oh, my goodness, Brother Kindhart. Oh, my, now, that is powerful! That is quite a love offering, Brother Kindhart. Isn't that a tremendous testimony of faith, church family? God will certainly recognize you." Reggie stood a little straighter for a second. But then Jaime acknowledged the next donor, and Reggie was left standing, unchanged, only favored in God's eyes for a few seconds and now needing to sit down next to his wife and children and face the reality of having returned all of God's gift back to him. Marlene did not return her hand to his knee when he sat back down beside her. Finn heard the plastic squish of his father's diaper compact against the wood of the church pew. Reggie held the checkbook on his lap as he wrote out the check.

The drive home was quiet. Marlene sat on her side of the car, her purse and Bible in her lap. She was devastated again. She could leave. She could wait until Reggie left the next day, and she could tell the kids that she was going to pay the mortgage, but in fact, she could take the money, still in the kitchen drawer, and just leave. But that was God's money now. And without it, she wouldn't get far. She no longer had any money herself. Money left from her divorce slowly went away each month the mortgage was due, and Reggie hadn't been paid yet. Every month when they needed groceries or wanted to have hamburgers or something special, there was also a bill that needed to be paid. Little by little, the security she sought to add to had slipped away like she had. She was married to a desperate, terminally ill man with two kids who hated her. Kids who set different silverware on the table for her that did not match the silverware of the three of them.

Reggie was still passionate and sweet to her. He was a dreamer who was certain better days were ahead. Healing was ahead, but the truth was that his flesh and heart may have to fail for that to happen. That would actually be the best thing. It would be painful. It would be challenging, but then she could believe that God did have a plan in it all because she could do the hard work to restore her own life. Her own sense of self-worth.

Marlene stayed in the car's darkness when everyone got out at the wheat hill house. Marlene sat looking out the window. "Honey, I have some other money." Reggie got back in the car, and they sat alone in the dark.

Marlene just raised her head once but didn't turn toward him. If he had other money, why hadn't he told her before this, so she wouldn't be sick every day with worry? "If I gave a gift to someone and they always handed it back asking for something greater, I'd feel unappreciated. I'd eventually not give to that person but start to ignore them or distance myself from them. Is this the part where I'm supposed to blindly trust God that he will meet our needs again? Where I'm supposed to blindly trust my husband? Just as Preacher Skelton has preached so often, God has endowed you with the wisdom to lead and provide for our family? If I'd had just left that money in the kitchen drawer until after the church service. You would still have given thirty percent to tithes and twenty percent to missions, but that still would have left half of the money for us. That still would have paid at least one month's mortgage payment."

"God just laid it on my heart to give that money to the love offering," Reggie said. "You know that's how God tests our faith, Sweetheart. Being his servants and all. Whether or not we are truly willing to trust him. To take our worries to God and just leave them there."

She lifted her head again but still didn't look at him. "So, where's this extra money you have? Please tell me you won't borrow from Kersey Greene again. He makes you pay everything back double, Reggie. We can't keep...."

Reggie laid his hand on her arm. "No, I have some money for times like this."

Marlene turned and looked at him, her arms folded across her body. "Where is this money, Reggie, that you have for times like these?"

"It's hidden, honey. I put it away so it wouldn't be easy to get to."

"Where, Reggie? I am your wife, and when you . . ." She paused and sighed. "I should know these things."

"It's buried in the ground, but I have it. I promise I will pay the mortgage tomorrow and bring money for groceries."

"How much are you going to give me for groceries?" "Two-hundred dollars, Reggie, would get us groceries and pay the late bills." Reggie turned back toward the steering wheel and gripped it with both hands looking forward.

Reggie nodded. He reached over, and she allowed him to touch her hand. "Listen, Sweetheart, I just need you to trust me. I will work hard, finish this motor I'm working on, and get paid. That will be $1,200, and then I know where this other motor is that I can buy and sell immediately. That will bring in $6,000. Okay? You see? When I get this done, how about you and I go back up to Johnson city for a couple of nights, sometime when the kids are with Pansy. Just you and I and some special time away. Okay? I promise we will do that."

Marlene allowed herself to be pulled over to Reggie, and they kissed. Reggie got out and walked around to open the car door for Marlene. He helped her out of the vehicle, and they walked inside.

Marlene went into the bathroom and locked the door. She leaned her back against it and cried. Was Reggie lying to her? She didn't want to think about that. What else was he lying to her about if he was lying about the money he had hidden in the ground? What if this blood disease was AIDS, and the doctors were telling the truth to them? What if this really was the disease God had brought on gay men, and that was why Reggie disappeared so often for days at a time. It was too much. She couldn't take the idea of him lying to her. She couldn't take the idea of him being with another man and then coming home and kissing her. She needed a plan to protect herself. She needed someone to talk to and confide in, but there was no one. She could call her brothers in Statesville, and they would be there in a matter of hours. But she had alienated herself from her family by telling them they were all lost sinners needing Jesus's salvation. What if Finn went back to the mountain and then returned? Would the old man again bring an envelope of money? Maybe she could drive up there weekly and pick up his pay. She crumbled to her knees, bowed to the floor, and laid her forehead on the Bible she always carried. She prayed to God silently, through her tears, for help.

Marlene came out of the bathroom, still carrying her Bible, and sat at the table with the rest of the family. Reggie was spreading peanut butter on saltines and began to pass them to everyone, sitting around the table like birds waiting to be fed. Finn had been thinking about when his father had stood and given all the money away that Jon had given them to ensure he had food. He thought about what Jon had told him about market share. Of every dollar someone kept or gave away, they needed to spend a dollar to ensure their own security. Finn was sure that still needed to be done. He thought about David Childs standing to speak to the church and ask their forgiveness for being unable to pay his bills. He thought about David Child's wife getting up and leaving the church before David spoke. He wondered what soul scars they were carrying. If he were back on the mountain with Jon and Betts, in the lantern light of the porch, he would ask them why? He couldn't do that here. He somehow knew that if he questioned his father's actions, it would hurt him. It would hurt him because his father couldn't defend them. He couldn't defend them because he didn't really have faith in them. Embarrassment would be the result of actions not based on truth. Why did he give the money away if he wasn't sure God would bless them or heal him of the rare blood disease? Why would he intentionally jeopardize his own well-being and the well-being of the family? Was it pride? Could pride make someone go against their own well-being? Did Reggie give that money away so he could feel a few moments of power when he was powerless? Could that be the true definition of sin? Finn watched his Dad say nothing, just feed his family the peanut butter and saltine crackers, the best meal of the week, in Finn's mind. Finn wanted to break the silence. Compared to the mountain and the evenings by the fountain that had never stopped, this life was a prison. The poem came back to Finn's mind. "My woman's eyes who are water for me to drink in prison." What would feed his soul now that he wasn't on the mountain in the lantern light, where he felt comfortable, questioning, learning, reading, and expressing himself?

Finn ate the cracker passed to him, and he thought about how Jesus, in his most desperate hour, went to a garden and wept drops of blood, and when not hearing the voice of God, he probably dug his fingers into the earth and pulled up roots. Just as Jon, in his deepest hour of need when he could not save Elizabeth, had dug his fingers into the carpet and, lifting it from the floor, ripped pieces from it. Jon had not wept drops of blood, but he did go into shock, his hands turning inward to his heart and his fingers like the stiff branches of the azaleas lining the wheat hill house. Was Jesus so desperate because of his own impending death, or was he devastated by the thought of being taken away from his love? Was Jesus the son of man and the son of God in love? Finn thought about how Jon would react in the same situation. Finn could never imagine Jon pulling up the carpet or going into shock if he was facing his own death. Jon reacted that way for only one reason: his love, his true soul, was being ripped away. It made sense now why Jesus was weeping drops of blood and pleading with God to let this cup pass from him. Jesus, the man, was in love.

Finn cleared the peanut butter from his mouth with a drink of water. He looked over to his father. "Do you think that Jesus, you know the Son of Man side of him, was ever in love? You know, with a person. Like married or ever thought about being married?"

Reggie and Marlene both looked at Finn. Marlene did not say anything but looked at Reggie. Reggie took the cloth napkin from the table and wiped his mouth. He leaned forward in his chair. "Finn, you already know the answer to that. I mean. For God so loved the World."

Finn looked at his father and was not afraid of him. "I know, I mean, I know that God loved the World that he sent Jesus to save it, but since Jesus was half God and half man, isn't it possible that he, well, that maybe he fell in love at some time? Marlene smirked and shook her head. Finn cast eyes towards Marlene and then looked back to make contact with Reggie. "I was just wondering because of how Preacher Skelton described him grieving in the garden of Gethsemane. It just seemed like maybe he was in love and would miss that person."

"Well, Finn, Jesus was in love with his ministry, with the people he had come to save. He wept and prayed like that because he loved that work and the people. You know, healing the sick and raising the dead, remember Lazarus?"

"So, Dad, you don't think that he ever fell in love, like at first sight, with someone, like wrote them letters, or planned things for them or wanted to have children with them?"

Marlene sat back from the table, tucked her chin down, and spread her hands straight out in front of her as if Jesus was standing over the table and his celibacy was being questioned. Reggie leaned back in his chair. "Finn, are you hearing yourself right now? Son, Jesus had one purpose in this World: to seek and to save the lost. He knew from the beginning when he was still in heaven sitting by the right side of God the father that he would enter this World so that one day he would be a pure, unblemished sacrifice for the lost. A white man laying down his life for humanity." Finn nodded. "Yes, Sir, but he had friends, right? I mean Lazarus, his sisters, and then all the disciples, the men he hung out with. I mean, he had people around him that he was close to. It's a question because I can't imagine a man weeping so desperately for his own life."

"Finn, Son, Jesus was not that way. He was not attracted like you are insinuating to women. You know, he was born of a virgin.

That means that he wasn't born from the seed of man. There were no evil or impure thoughts in his mind."

"But he was tempted in the desert by the devil for forty days," Finn said. "How do you tempt someone who wasn't born with anything to tempt? He was thirty-three years old. That's old enough to have been married and to have children." Marlene grabbed the large Bible and held it over her chest. "If he wasn't attracted to women, was he in love with a man? I mean, the Bible only talks about him being with men constantly?"

Reggie's face turned bright red. He slammed his fist down on the table. "You need to go to room Finn! Your mouth is going to get you spanked. I don't know where or when you started questioning God, but this is the devil. You need to go pray and ask God's forgiveness. Leave the plate; just go." Finn got up and left the table. He went to his room and closed the door. His leg was aching and stiff, and he slowly pulled off his church clothes and climbed into the bed.

The following day Reggie came into Finn's bedroom. Finn was changing the dressing on his wound. "Finn, you know better. I even told you to be careful working around that old man. He could've killed you or, worse, cut your privates off."

Finn looked up at his Dad. "I walked up behind him; it was my own fault." Finn wrapped the bandages with a compression cloth and pinned it. Then stood slowly to slip into his pants.

"Finn, I want to discuss what you said at the table. I know you will soon be a teenager, and I don't know how much trouble you will give us, but I want to stop this now. Jesus was born of God for a purpose. Impure thoughts did not affect him like they affect us. I mean, yes, he was challenged and tempted so he could relate to our experiences, but ultimately, he had the strength of God to see him through. You know. He traveled preaching and healing the sick and raising the dead because he was the son of God. If he wasn't the son of God, then we'd all be lost now. There wouldn't be a heaven waiting on us Christians. If he was not the son of God, there wouldn't be any hope of, or, the hope of miracles now."

"You mean it wouldn't be true? It all hinges on him being born of a virgin and being different than us?"

"Yes!" "Yes, Finn. God is greater and bigger than any of us can imagine. He was born perfect. We, humans, are not born perfect. We have to strive and work hard to be perfect. Jesus is everywhere and in everything."

"Is he in everyone's heart?"

"No. There's a lot of evil in this world. You know that. When God comes knocking on your heart's door, you can either let him in or deny him. People going to hell."

Finn didn't want to cause any trouble.

Reggie reached out and hugged Finn. "You have got to start back to school today, son, and I don't want any problems between you and Momalene." " Do I have to call her Momalene?" " Well, you know she wants you to call her Mother. You know she loves ya, son. Is that so hard?"

School was the same as always. Finn and his sister lined up beside the kitchen table, pledging allegiance to the United States Flag and the Christian Flag. After that, there was Bible verse memorization and then the study of different subjects. At lunch, Finn was wondering how the mountain would look in the other seasons. He turned the calendar to January and noticed the name Martin Luther King Jr. Bobby had said that Martin Luther King was a Chief of Peace who was killed. He looked at Marlene, reheating the beans over the electric stove. "Do you know who Martin Luther King was?"

Marlene looked over at Finn. "Yes, he was a black man, a very bad man. He cheated on his wife and caused a lot of problems. He even smoked cigarettes."

Finn imagined that Martin Luther King was a lot like Bobby. When he thought of Marlene, he thought of Cruella de Vil. One moment fawning good, the next being genuinely evil. "Did the Ku Klux Klan kill him?" She shook her head and stirred the beans. "I don't know, I suppose they did. Ask your father; he knows all about them."

"My Dad knows all about them?"

Marlene looked over. "Well yeah, they support the churches."

The words beat like a gong in Finn's ears. He immediately left the table, went to his room, and closed the door. He thought of how John King Fysher had murdered Ruby. Had his own father been at those kinds of rallies? Bob Jones had come from Greensboro, where his father and real Mother were both born and raised. Finn felt like he had been hit over the head. How could this be? How could his father, the man he loved, be like them. How could his father talk about God and salvation and have considered the KKK's work good? Finn heard Marlene call him to say the beans were ready, and he knew he only had seconds to get to the table before trouble would erupt. He returned to the table, ate the warm beans with the cold ketchup, and returned to schoolwork.

Finn was setting the silverware for the table before dinner that night when his father entered the house and sat in the rocking chair before the wood stove. "Reggie," Marlene said, "Finn was asking about that black preacher who caused all that trouble. He saw that the government had given him a holiday on the calendar. I don't even want to say his name." She shook her head. "Disgraceful."

"Martin Luther King?"

"Yes, did the Ku Klux Klan Kill him?"

Reggie looked over at Marlene and then at Finn. "I guess I don't really know. I know that's what happens when you go against God."

"Do you like the Klu Klux Klan?" Finn asked.

"Well, son, you know that's for each person to decide, but I think they had some good ideas."

Finn dropped the silverware on the table. "Dad, they kill black people."

"Well, well, hold on. You don't know that. They keep the races in line. God doesn't want the races to mix. That's why he separated them at Babel, and that's why God commanded the sons of Ham into Africa and to serve all other races. Finn, the KKK was just enforcing God's word. There's no arguing that. You've just got all these liberals that are trying to deny God. The KKK has supported local independent Baptist churches more than any other social organization. Without them, most cities wouldn't have a place to worship. Pastors couldn't afford to preach their own gospel without them. Most of them are Good Christians."

Finn pictured Ruby's body being dragged behind a car and then hung from the tree in the effigy of Christ. "For God so loved the World, Dad. The world means all. All who love are of God."

Reggie raised his hand in confirmation. "Yes, Finn. You're right. God loves the colored people as much as anyone else. And he saves them just like he does white people. I mean, that's why we have missionaries going to tell these people about the gospel of Christ and Jesus's love. Finn, I love negro spirituals. God saves them, he just doesn't want them mixing. And if the war of states' rights had turned out differently, then we wouldn't be so dependent on other countries. We probably wouldn't have had the Cold War. We wouldn't have to pay so much in taxes either. That's my point. God intended for us to have this help. That's what happens when you don't read your Bible. If the government just did as the Bible says."

Finn's mind was tumbling now. He couldn't believe what his father was saying. He would see if he could only meet Bobby and know the story of Ruby. "Have you read any of Martin Luther King's books? Do you know anything about him?"

"I know enough. I know they gave him that doctorate degree. I know he has ties to the communist government and Marx. I know he smoked, drank, and ran around on his wife in motel rooms. I know they killed him 'cause he was a seditionist. Have I read any of his books? No, don't need to. Finn, the only book a man ever needs to read is this Bible. If you want an adventure story, it's got adventure. If you want history, it's got history. You want to know how the World was made; it will tell you the creation story. This is God's inherent, pure word, penned down by King James in 1611."

"But Dad, that was after Columbus discovered the Americas. A lot was going on in the World by then. The Blue Ridge is a billion years old. 1611 was a short time ago in the scope of things."

Reggie's face flashed red. "Your little mouth! Your mouth is going to get you in trouble! I don't think you need to eat tonight. No, sir, not with that sass. You can go to your room."

Reggie entered the bedroom and sat in the darkness on Finn's bed. "Finn, I'm not sure what the change is in you. I guess it has to do with you being too old to be a boy yet still too young to be a man." His father reached out and laid his hand on Finn's shoulder. "Listen, I've got to leave in the morning for Charleston. I will not be back until the weekend so you will be with your mother. I just want everything to go easy while I'm gone. You know, you can't get up with me. Phones don't always work at the Knight's Inn. Mamalene is frustrated with that. Finn reached and grabbed his dad's hand. "Me too Dad. Things are always better with you here."

"You know, Finn, the FBI was looking into that man. He changed his name so that Christians would follow him. He caused a lot of trouble. I'm not saying that all black people are bad, but, you know, Finn, they just don't think like us. You can't tell me that there is not something different. Now I have known some good ones, some that really loved God, and I worshipped with them, but you know they had truly given their hearts to God. They didn't act black. Not like these ones you see around here."

Finn thought of Bobby, of how he had walked and talked and grieved with Bobby. How they had gone up the staircase holding hands and collected the old leaves from the ancient tree and came down and filled them with flowers and tears and set them glowing in the pools of the fountain and, in their own way, said goodbye to Mrs. Elizabeth. "They didn't choose to be black, Dad. Just like we did not choose to be white. Just like you did not choose to be sick." Finn remembered a phrase from a poem he had read in a book on the mountain. "A being breathing thoughtful breath, a traveler between life and death. I think we are all the same, Dad. God didn't divide the races at Babel by confusing the languages of mankind so we could be different. He divided us so we could choose."

"Choose what Finn?"

"Choose to learn the universal language of all mankind."

"God calling you son? Is that what all this has been about?

I wouldn't mind that, son. No, Sir, I wouldn't mind that at all." Reggie closed the door and left.

Finn woke up with a lot of pain in his leg. As he changed the bandage, he saw the skin around the wound turning white. He could not really bend his leg and walked stiffly to the kitchen table to salute the flag and to repeat from memory the first chapters of First Corinthians. Finn was having trouble sitting in his blue jeans on the wooden chair at the table and continually tried to straighten the leg and relieve the building pressure in the thigh. Marlene's index finger again went into the milk jug. She appeared to taste it and deemed it good. Finn's cereal bowl was filled and consumed. The school day started.

"Finn, I noticed." "You noticed what?" "I noticed you purposefully did not take your schoolbooks with you on your trip." She looked down at her hands that were clasped around her Bible like she was deciding how to handle the misdemeanor.

"I was only supposed to be gone for maybe two days," Finn said. "Dad said he was going to come and pick me up."

Marlene looked disappointed. "You could have called Finn. You know... that we care very deeply for you, and you could have called, and we would have brought your schoolbooks up to you. You didn't do that because you did not want to take responsibility for your work. You chose to not do what was right."

Finn shook his head. He knew where this was going and that no matter what he said, it would end badly. He stood up from the table, at least having the table space between him and Marlene.

"Where do you think you're going? I am talking to you."

"I'm sorry, it's just my leg where I got cut by the chainsaw. It's just really hurting today. The skin around the stitches is getting really soft. It's uncomfortable with these jeans and sitting at the table. Maybe if I was allowed to wear my pajama pants outside my bedroom for just today?"

Marlene slammed the Bible down on the wood table, and her lips began to curl. "You are lying through your teeth. You should be ashamed of yourself. She was moving now around the table, picking up the Bible.

Finn moved slowly around the table, raising his hands in protest. "No, no, I can show you. I can't move that well."

"I have never seen a more ungrateful child! You are not only trying to get out of your schoolwork, but you are trying to get out of your chores!" She came closer, her eyes flashing wide

Finn kept retreating, dragging the leg. He stepped into the narrow space behind the wood stove. "I can still do my chores."

Marlene picked up the wooden paddle that hung nearby. "You just don't care about how much I love you. Why would you do that to me?" She was starting to cry, but her anger flashed again. "You go away and don't care enough about your schoolwork to take it with you. You don't care about your family enough to call and check on them or invite them to your mountain vacation." Finn shook his head. He raised his hands in front of him, trying to find a way to make sense to her. "This rebellion has to stop, Finn. Bend over." Finn shook his head. "I can't bend over. The doctors said. It will tear my stitches."

"You are a liar!" She grabbed at Finn, and he pushed her hands away. She had to turn and set her Bible down. "The Bible says to spare the rod is to spoil the child."

Finn didn't mind the spanking, but the leg was painful today. He turned, offering his backside but did not bend over. He had his hands raised as if trying to draw her attention. He began to speak to her. "Do you think that rod was not a rod but a tool for measurement like a yardstick?"

"What?"

Finn turned back around. "Spare the rod" means do not spare a child's education or structure. It doesn't mean physically beating a child."

"Do not tell me what the Bible says, Liar." She picked up the Bible and shook it before Finn's face. "This is the word of God, and when it says rod, it means the rod of correction so children will not get spoilt. It is God's commandment. You've got sin in your heart, and I will get it out." She spun Finn's backside toward her in the small, confined space. "Now bend over!"

"You're just choosing to be ignorant." As soon as the words left Finn's mouth, Marlene swung the wooden paddle with all her might into Finn's kidney. A warm light washed over him, and his mind went numb. She shoved the boy violently over and began beating his backside with the paddle, but because Finn's leg was tight, he fell forward onto his face between the wood stove and washing machine. The stitches in his leg split apart, and blood started to soak his jeans. Marlene, enraged, swung the paddle wildly, hitting the wood stove and the washing machine, trying to reach Finn, crumpled in the narrow space.

The only part of Finn she could reach with the paddle was his right foot, and she began to beat it, shouting, "This is going to hurt you worse than it is going to hurt me!" She stopped as Finn screamed. He felt blood in his sock and crawled away from her out of the narrow space. He tried to stand but couldn't put weight on his injured foot. He limped to his bedroom, holding on to the wall for support, and slammed the door. He wedged the axe handle under the doorknob and stumbled to the chair where he kept the bandages for his leg. He looked at the white sock that was now filled with blood. The foot was tingling like something he had never felt before. He slowly pulled the sock off the foot, and four toes were turned at odd angles. Three toenails popped up and bleeding, and the foot turned purple. He painfully pressed the toenails back down and tried to straighten the toes. He used the bandages and a small roll of tape to wrap the foot. He put a clean sock on, slid the damaged foot inside his boot, and cinched the laces tight. He pulled his pants down and saw blood had filled the bandage on his left thigh. The stitches had torn through the infected skin. After cleaning the wound, he applied an antiseptic from a Boy Scout first aid kit. He couldn't close the stitches with a butterfly band-aid. He covered the wound again with bandages and tape and tried to elevate the throbbing foot.

He didn't know how long he would have before Marlene would demand he return to the kitchen table to start school again. His father would return after Finn went to his real mother's house for the weekend. He would have to hold out in the room until his real mother arrived. Then he would push passed Marlene out the door and take her fury and punishment another day. If he did not open the door to Marlene and she realized that the door was blocked, then she really could lose her mind. Things could go very badly for him and his sister. There was no phone in his room. No way to get in touch with his real mother. He could try crawling out the window and hiding in the wheat field until his mother arrived. While contemplating, he heard the family car go past his bedroom window. He opened the blinds to see Marlene turning out of the driveway and heading toward town.

Now was his time. He grabbed Jon's cash and threw a fresh pair of jeans and socks into the red fireman's bag. He put on a hat, removed the axe from under the door handle, and leaned on it as a crutch. It would go with him now. He would carry the axe with him for protection. He opened the door, and his sister was standing there. "Mom's coming from work to take you to the doctor. She's on her way."

Finn stared at her. "Are you certain?"

"Yes, Marlene called her and then handed the phone to me. She's coming to get us, Finn, I promise." She turned and went into her room. Finn hobbled on the axe outside and stood behind the trunk of the old pecan tree. From here, he could see who pulled into the driveway, and if Marlene did, he could stay hidden behind the tree and then slip away into the wheat field. He stood, leaning against the axe, until he heard the distinct sound of his real Mother's car pull into the driveway. He saw his sister come out of the house's front door, and then he started moving to the car. His Mother did not see him approach, and he slid into the back seat of the Ford Tempo, the red bag and the axe beside him.

His Mother turned to look at him. "You've grown up, Finn. My goodness!" Finn reached forward and kissed her hand. Finn's sister got in the car's front seat, and they started driving down the road.

"Marlene called and said there had been an accident. Your Daddy promised me he would get you insurance, but he still hasn't. Thank God I have a job. We'll go to the Emergency Care by the Chapman's house." She looked into the rear-view mirror at Finn. "Do all your mishaps happen with Lewis Chapman?" Finn didn't understand the question. He was in so much pain. He felt like he had just escaped from prison, knowing that he would be returned to it in two days.

Finn sat on a bed in the emergency clinic with his foot newly cleaned. The Doctor came in and said, "So, this is the little Dare Devil." He leaned over and looked again at the foot. "Well, you certainly did a number on your foot, son. I'd bet you've got four toes broken. The foot seems okay, just a lot of swelling and bruising. You're definitely going to lose three toenails. They may never grow back correctly. Now, I'm just going to numb the toes of the foot so I can remove the nails. There will be multiple shots, and then we will wait a while. So, we will numb you up and remove the toenails so you can be on your way. The toes have seemed to realign pretty well on their own. Probably from you taping them up. That was impressive, by the way.

"Can you look at these stitches?" Finn asked the Doctor.

The Doctor looked over his glasses at the blood-stained pants. "They said you had another injury, but I thought that was taken care of." Finn pulled down his pants, and the Doctor inspected the chainsaw wound. "Son, didn't they give a prescription? Doesn't your mother—"

"I don't live with my mother. I live with my father."

The Doctor looked into Finn's eyes. "I see. That's infected. I can remove the stitches and properly bandage them up. The skin is too damaged to try and restitch it. You will always have a scar there, but you will be fine with proper antibiotics. It might be good for you to spend a few days with your mother." Finn nodded. "Okay, son, we'll have you on your way home in a couple of hours."

"Couple of hours?" Finn was tired.

"Yes, it takes a while to get the shots and for them to numb you fully." Finn leaned down and snatched the toenails from his foot like breaking twigs from a dried tree. Small amounts of blood oozed from the fresh wounds. The Doctor dumbfounded, looked at Finn and then back to the foot. "Okay. I will get the nurse to patch you up, and you'll be on your way."

Finn laid back on the bed. He was looking forward to being at his real mother's home. In exchange for mowing her grass and washing her car, he got all weekend to sleep, rest, eat, and not be harassed. That kindness from the stranger he called his real mother kept him from committing suicide. Once the Nurse finished, the doctor came back in one more time. "Well, there you go, Mario Andretti. Next time keep that go-cart on the track where it belongs! When you run them into your dad's truck like that, the fun is over quickly, right?"

On the way home, Finn's Mother looked at him again in the rear-view mirror. "Finn, I didn't know you had a go-cart."

Finn looked up at her in the mirror. "I do, but it doesn't have a motor. It doesn't have wheels, and the steering wheel is frozen with rust. It has always set on top of Dad's scrap pile of metal, but he calls it my go-cart. Says he will fix it one day."

CHAPTER 16

"He satisfies the longing soul."

Jon woke each morning to the reality of being alone. He found himself wandering through the cabin in the evenings, not touching anything but just staring at items where Elizabeth had left them. Her purse was still sitting on the corner of the chest of drawers. He wasn't eating and drank every night now, just to try to sleep, and he still had conversations with Betts. Sometimes he thought he could hear her in the house or outside. He would call for her sometimes to ask if she remembered something.

One morning in the kitchen, he heard her whistle from up the staircase by the fountain. He quickly went to the porch door, looked over the wooden walkways, and then went outside to the porch rail, his heart leaping and his ears straining. For a split second, he thought it was all a horrible dream, and she was up the staircase whistling to the trees. The sweet laughter echoed through the forest and off the granite walls of the meadow, off the stone walls of Jon's heart. After realizing it could not be true, Jon closed his eyes in shame, regretfully returned to the lonely house, and closed the door behind him.

Getting out of his truck, he slid on a thin jacket. As he closed the door, he noticed the yellowing leaves of the sycamores lining the clinic parking lot in the reflection of the glass. Fall was showing up early this year. He saw his own image. He was very thin, having lost nearly forty-five pounds in the month following Elizabeth's death. Now, seeing the old man, the frail man, he had become in the absence of the sun, he wondered if he like the trees, could just sleep, sleep through the pain until the sun would come out and warm his soul again. He placed his hand against the truck door and breathed a deep breath. He never thought he would ever be going to a remembrance ceremony to be comforted by others also grieving.

He crossed the parking lot to the basement door of the clinic with a note in his pocket that he was considering reading. He was greeted by several people standing behind a desk. They welcomed him. "I'm Jon. How are you?" They wrote the name on a tag, and Jon stuck it on his jacket. Jon sat in a room with forty or so people of all different races and ages and a few children. When his eyes met someone else's, he nodded and smiled, understanding the familiar pain that had brought them all here.

Then two small Hispanic girls pushed into the row he was sitting in. Not more than three or four years old, they hugged his legs, climbed beside him, and nestled under his arms. Jon did not know where their parents were, but because the babies had attached themselves to him, he placed his arms around them and felt love from them like a tincture for his soul. Their parents came into the row and apologized, but Jon smiled and waved bye to the sweet children.

Jon saw Bobby in the hallway, looking busy. A minute later, he stopped and hugged Jon and then went to a small podium. He turned on a microphone and adjusted it. Reached behind him and lifted a guitar over his chest. He placed the leather guitar strap that said RUBY over his head. Without saying anything, Bobby began to play. He played several songs. Song's people knew and started humming and whispering the lyrics. The music set the tone for remembering.

Jon watched Bobby play, and he could see his brother losing himself in the lyrics and old memories. He remembered all the nights he and Elizabeth would sit at the Tea House and watch Bobby and Ruby play and sing. He thought back to when he found out about the murder of Ruby and that Bobby was being held in the local jail charged with murder. Jon shook his head and closed his eyes. The pain of losing someone he loved as much as Ruby was still just as painful today as it was thirty-five years ago.

Bobby set the guitar down behind him. Making eye contact with the people sitting in the room, he smiled. "I'm very thankful that many have attended our remembrance ceremony today. Every person here represents someone in our community that we have lost this past year." He paused and took a deep breath. "I am sorry for your loss. I think back to all the ones who have come to the clinic and the church. Death is part of the living experience. When you boil it down, it is part of growing up. Dealing with grief and mourning the loss of loved ones are parts of that living experience. We come together today as a family, a beloved community. Listening, caring, and sharing our burdens with each other. We are as weak as our weakest brother or sister here in our grief. And we are as strong as our strongest sister or brother here. Together our community can and will rise. I urge you to share your stories and memories today with all of us. Speak from your heart. Give to the community, and the community will give back. I promise you . . . no one here today has to leave empty-handed or feeling alone."

Jon was proud of Bobby. He admired his strength. He had been through more loss than anyone he knew, yet he learned from it and then returned to give all of himself to others again. How had he done it? How had Bobby managed to find peace in the chaos of loss and grief?

The first person to stand was the mother of Jared, the fifteen-year-old potter. She spoke about Jared being born. She thought she couldn't carry a baby full term and that every day and night, she prayed to God that the child would survive. Even how the last two months, she was on complete bed rest. Every breath was uneasy until he was lying in her arms one day. She spoke of the joy that he gave to her life. Even after he contracted AIDS from a blood transfusion, he kept positive. Always encouraging his mother. She spoke of his pottery and how he had found so much healing in creating works of art that would outlast his existence in his last years of life. One day when she was feeling deficient, Jared came to her and said that even the clay must go through the burning fire to become everlasting and beautiful. He wiped her tears with his hands and molded them into the bowl he was creating. She held the bowl up for everyone to see. "He made this for me, and he said that when I ever felt alone, just to pick it up and hold it, I would feel his hands. Even though he is gone, he lives on in the things he created. I believe eternal life is measured by how much love we leave behind. My son will live on forever." She said if she could help anyone who was going through grief and the loss of someone they loved, then she was there to help.

The following person to speak reached inside his collared shirt and pulled out a necklace with a diamond ring and a gold band. He held it up and said they were his wife's wedding and engagement rings. They had fallen in love while in Graduate school. He spoke of his wife as a strong woman who could do anything. He talked about how sweet she was to him and how they all wanted to have a child. He started to cry, and Bobby came forward and handed him a box of tissues. The man said that his wife had been doing very well through labor and that their baby was born, and she held it, but then alarms started going off, and he didn't understand why. He was told to leave the room, and the doctor and nurses came in, but they couldn't save her. His wife, a strong woman, had died from internal bleeding. He stopped there and walked to the front row, and from a small carrier, he picked up a beautiful baby girl wrapped in pink. He held her up for everyone to see. He said that he had lost the most precious thing in the world to him, his wife, but that she had given him the most adorable baby girl he had ever seen. He looked at the crowd and asked if he could help anyone here today. "I'm for you."

Some said they were thankful for the clinic and the counseling that they had received from the community. Others took turns telling their own stories of loss and grief. Jon listened to these stories but didn't know how he would fit in. His life was unique in that he had known the love of his life and had lived in paradise for fifty years only to lose her, but he felt that he did need to say something. Not that it would help others, but that it would at least release some of the pressure that had built up within himself. He stood and walked forward.

From behind the podium, he saw the two small girls that had snuggled against him. He saw Bobby standing beside Penny in the back of the room. He reached inside his jacket pocket and removed his notebook. "Good morning. I didn't know what to expect from this remembrance ceremony. While driving here, I wondered how many, if any, would be here. An hour ago, I had no idea so many people in my town had lost a husband, wife, or child. My heart breaks for you. I'm very sorry for your loss." Jon looked down for a moment and then back up.

"I feel a little embarrassed. You see, I met my wife over fifty years ago. From the first moment I saw her in the post office here in town, I couldn't take my eyes off her. I remember walking outside on the street and trying to find her in the crowd just to glimpse her again. I was like a deer panting for water. I got fifty years of living life nearly every day with my soulmate, never taking it for granted. Now you see why I feel a little awkward. I realize now that so many of you got just a few years, days, or even minutes. I'm trying to say that an hour ago, I was so hurt and even mad over losing my wife but hearing your stories has made me realize how lucky we were to have each other for so long." He looked at the small notebook and opened it.

"My wife's name was Elizabeth. We actually met a few streets over at a garden party. That night, I made a pretty big fool of myself trying to saber a bottle of champagne but catching my necktie instead, and... anyways, it was a fiasco, but Elizabeth followed me into the garden. I remember it like it was yesterday. The music in the lantern lite garden. She called me Jonny." He smiled and looked towards the back of the room. "A night so enchanting birds couldn't sleep. Elizabeth and I wrote hundreds of letters to each other during our lifetime. I still write to her now. I know that may seem strange, but it's like inertia, I suppose. Love inertia. I guess that's a thing. We've lived our whole lives together on the mountain, and these granite walls surround the meadow. Sometimes, her voice echoes through the trees and off the granite walls. Betts had this beautiful whistle. My favorite is waking up and hearing her on the porch watering the plants. I can't really describe how beautiful it was to wake up to hear her whistle and the spill of water from the pots. I still hear that some mornings. It crushes my heart, but I just lay there soaking it in, and I love it." Jon closed his eyes for a moment. Standing in front of everyone, he could hear Elizabeth's soft and loving language. He could see her hand reaching out for him. He opened his eyes and focused on the notebook. "I wrote this for her, and I hope it means something to you."

> *"You precede me; that's okay*
> *Your laughter still echoes in the low ceilings, the ventricles*
> *In the stone chambers, these atriums*
> *In the causeways, those veins of my heart, your home*
> *You and I are nowhere alone."*

Jon closed the notebook and returned it to his jacket pocket. He placed his hands on the podium. "In French, we would say... Plus lentement, si'l vous plait. It means more slowly if you please. In losing Betts, I've realized there is another reality where life can be slowed down. Where you not only feel emotion but can see it with a different eye. If we are made of light, then our love must be the spectrum of light. In this moment of grief, we are closer to the alternative reality than the reality we usually live in. Why? Because right now, we have had to face our greatest fear whether we want to or not, we are in it now. Cruelly, life without our beloved continues, and realizing that our love, the spectrum of light, is infinite and flows to us, through us, and from us to all matter and will do so eternally. We are light, we are the spectrum of love, and we are the infinite. While we are experiencing this great loss. Our loved ones and all the beloved that have ever been may be giving us the greatest gift of our existence. To slow down, to heal, to see, and most of all to believe in the spectrum of love."

Jon sat down and listened to others' stories of overwhelming loss. He never knew such tragedies happened to others around him. Bobby closed the ceremony by speaking of the beloved community, of sharing each other's burdens.

Jon stopped by the table where he had been given a name badge, seeing Penny packing things in boxes. "Your poem was lovely, Jon, how your heart has turned to stone and is empty, but Elizabeth's voice and laughter still echo there. It was very sweet. I will talk to Bobby, but we may want to put that in our newsletter if you wouldn't mind."

Surprised, Jon reached inside his jacket, removed the paper from the notebook, and handed it to her. "Thank you."

She looked at it like someone had given her an etching from Picasso. "Well, umm, I will copy it and give it back."

"No, you'll do more with it than me. You should have it. I will just repeat it to myself anyways. Can I help you with these boxes you leaving so soon?

"Sure, that would be great. Last summer, my ac unit was overflowing in the attic, so now that's it cold, I'm going to try and go home and call someone to look at it. I don't know if anyone can come out today, but it will get cold tonight. Especially on the lake."

Jon collected a couple of the boxes, and they started for the door. "You live on the lake?"

"Yeah, Wayne left me the cottage when he passed away."

"Oh, the Bach, I know exactly where that is. I mean, we used to spend entire weekends there." They walked to Penny's car and loaded the boxes into the trunk. "Well, you have the wood-burning fireplace in the cottage, right?" Jon asked.

"Yeah, but I haven't gotten any wood delivered, and I haven't got it inspected either. I guess that doesn't make me a very good homeowner, but I just stay busy with the restaurant and now this." She bit her lip and smiled. Then turned to get in her car.

Jon stood at the driver's side door. "Penny, I'm not an HVAC repairman, but I'm pretty good at fixing things and know the house. Would you want me to stop by and look at it?"

Penny thought for a second. "Are you sure you wouldn't mind, Jon?"

"Not at all. I'll see you in a bit."

Jon walked to his truck. Nervous, he looked up as Penny's car passed. "It's something I'd do for anyone." The voice in his head became audible. He'd always fixed things for people. It was simple for him and seemed so difficult and daunting for others. Why was he nervous, though? This was not a date. He was not cheating on Elizabeth; he was just simply going to fix a heater. Jon shook his head to clear his mind and fished out his keys. Early winter rain pelted the glass, and the wipers moved the sycamores' fallen leaves.

Jon parked and walked to the Bach, a cottage boat house on stilts over the water. The front door was open, and he could hear Penny inside. He knocked. "Hello?" " Hey, I'm in here." Still in her jacket, Penny was in the kitchen unpacking the boxes. "Just wanted you to know I'm here. Winds picking up blows right through this place." Jon looked around the boat cottage. It had been years since he had been here, yet it looked the same. Photos were all over the walls, and Wayne's wooden skis stood by the sliding door in the corner of the living room. "I've always loved that art deco fireplace, hanging like that," Jon said.

Penny turned around. "Yeah, I've kept everything pretty much the same, just cleaner." Jon smiled. "I may need to turn the breaker off to the attic unit before going there. That still downstairs?"

"Yeah, this way." Penny opened the door beside the refrigerator and turned on the light. They descended the stairs, and when she opened the door to the boat house, the smell of lake water filled the air. An antique ski boat was hanging in the boathouse above the water.

"Oh, my, God. You've got CHIEF! I haven't seen this boat in thirty years." Jon ran his hand along the rich mahogany of the vessel, its chrome gleaming in the light of the boat house. He turned and looked back at Penny. "This boat is legendary on this lake." He turned around and touched the boat as if greeting an old friend. "I've spent so many wonderful days on this boat. Water skiing, sunset cruises, late-night cruises. Hell, I've even spent the night on this boat a few times and watched the sunrise."

Penny stood by the door with her arms crossed. She smiled and looked down at her feet. "Yeah, Ole CHIEF. That's the last renovation project that Wayne did. He restored her brand new. I haven't had the heart to set her in the water without him. I thought I'd ask Bobby to come over and do it with me, you know, for old time's sake but, well, I just haven't gotten to it. It's bittersweet, you know?

Jon nodded. "Seeing it brings back a lot of great memories, Penny. It would for Bobby, no doubt." He touched it once again. "He used to get us all drunk on apple and plum wine and then haul us around. God, those were the days. Theo, Alice, Ruby." Jon shook his head and removed his hand. It's nice to see it survived all these years." He reached above the workbench and turned the breaker off to the heating unit. He picked up a flashlight and checked to see if it was working. "Okay, let's take a look."

He followed Penny to the top floor and opened the attic staircase. "Are you sure there is nothing I can do to help?" Penny asked.

"Oh, no, I will take a look and then be right back." Jon went up the ladder and into the attic. He made his way over to the unit and could see the overflow pan was full of water. The exhaust tube was plugged with insulation from the attic. He removed the debris, and the water from the pan began to drain. He leaned over his shoulder. "Hey, Penny? Turn the breaker back on and try it now." Jon waited a few minutes, and the unit cycled and started running. Everything seemed to be okay. Jon came back down and lifted the stairs to the ceiling. Penny was standing there still in her jacket and smiling.

"It was simple. Just a piece of insulation from the attic had gotten into the pan and plugged up the exhaust tube. That's why it overflowed. Should be fine now."

"Really, just like that, you fixed it?" "Things don't stay broken in my presence very long." "Really? Can I show you my heart?" Penny looked down, blushing.

"Probably one of those summer thunderstorms, wind rushing up, disrupting things. You know." "Well, can I pay you something, Jon?"

Jon shook his head. "No, course not. It's my pleasure." As they walked down the stairs, Jon stopped and looked at the photos on the wall. He saw one of Wayne, Bobby, Ruby, Elizabeth, and himself. They were all on CHIEF facing each other and had turned to look toward whoever had taken the photo. Jon felt the picture. "Like yesterday." Seeing Elizabeth in her swimsuit and the old straw hat, Jon shook his head and smiled. "My, my."

The house was still cold, and Penny felt the floor vent to see if the air was warm. "Guess I will be on my way." Jon said.

"Thank you." She came forward and extended her arms to give Jon a hug. Jon let her hug him. "Penny, the house needs to warm up. I was going to stop by the French market and pick up some things for the cabin. I know they have sandwiches and soups there. Would you like to go and get a bite to eat while the house warms up? I'm going by there anyways."

After a slight pause, Penny said, "Yeah, that place is cute. Umm, well, it is cold in here. I don't want to impose. Sure, no yeah, sure, I would like that. Just let me get my keys."

"Uhh, I don't mind driving, Penny. I mean, it's just at the bottom of the hill. You mind riding in a truck?" He looked into her eyes.

She smiled. "Okay." They climbed into the Dodge, and Penny said, "This truck is huge. What do you do in here?"

Jon laughed. "My taxes, mostly in this area. Lawn darts and croquet storage is under the seat." She smiled. Jon had never noticed the distance between the truck driver's and passenger's sides, but it felt cavernous tonight. Strange, like he was dating his best friend's sister. He would listen to her love problems as she twisted the combinations of his own heart. The truck ambled around the lake in the setting sun. "You know, Penny, it was nice to be back at the boat cottage again. We used to spend a lot of time there." He looked over at Penny, and she met his eyes. "A lot of great memories." Jon laughed and then shook his head. "You know, the great thing about that place is you can jump off any story into the lake. Oh, my gosh. We used to play these drinking games, and for every answer you got wrong, you had to just run out and jump into the lake. So much fun." Penny was nodding her head. "Yep, Wayne was something else. There was nothing he loved more than people being there and having fun. I really admired his view of life. You know, just living in the now. He was just always there. Always positive."

A bell on the door rang as they went inside the French market. They ordered, and Jon filled a small basket with sundries. He rejoined Penny at a table, and they waited for their meals. Penny looked into his basket. She nodded her approval. "I tried this olive oil; it's so good."

Jon smiled. "Betts, and I went to Andalusia. I used to tell everybody that we drank the olive oil and sipped the wine." He looked over at Penny. "It was a wonderful trip. I will never forget the Straits of Gibraltar and looking over into Morocco. You know they say you can travel three hundred miles into Africa and still be on the coast of Africa. Amazing."

"I love to travel too," Penny said. "It's something how when you are young you plan out your life, you know, in your mind, of how you think it's all going to go. Then slowly, you see it won't work out as planned."

Jon laughed and agreed. "So, why didn't we ever see you back then?" The food was set down in front of them, and Jon got up to grab napkins and silverware.

"I left home the day after I graduated," Penny said. I got in my Opel and took off. I was halfway to New York, thinking I was going to Miami." She shook her head and laughed. "I was headed for the beach and sunshine. Then I wound up in New York with a suitcase full of bikinis. Those were great times. I met these great people who took me in and then saw the ballet one night. I knew that was what I wanted to do. I started learning to dance and then was given a job." Jon leaned closer and snapped his fingers. "Yeah, that was it. Wayne went to New York and spent the whole summer in the city."

Penny took another bite and nodded her head. "Yeah, yeah, you're right. He loved the big city. He just couldn't get enough of it. He would spend all day in the museums and then all night seeing Broadway shows. We had so much fun. Nothing was better in my life than that summer with Wayne in the city. I lived in an apartment with four other girls; he just moved right in. He was everywhere. He was cooking dinners, or doing the girl's nails, or fixing their cars, or beating up their boyfriends. You know, I mean, Wayne was the absolute best." She set her sandwich down and looked at Jon. Jon looked over at her. Jon touched her hand. " I know he was."

The bell on the door rang again, and Tom Cohen and his wife walked in. "Well, hey Jon, Penny, how you doing?" Tom said. They exchanged small talk, and then Jon and Penny returned to their conversation while the Cohens ordered their meals. "So, if you were dancing ballet in New York City and loving living in the city, how did you get back here, to the small-town USA?"

Penny suddenly took a deep breath and turned her head. "Well, that's a big story." Jon hoped the question had not created pain for her somehow, but he was genuinely enjoying the conversation. "Oh, gosh, well. So, Wayne came up to New York and was living with us girls in this small place, and of course, we were all just having the times of our lives. Well, Wayne, being Wayne, just had to work out. You know, he was training for an Iron Man. So, he borrowed the neighbor's dumbbells and was lifting and exercising in the apartment one day, and I was being goofy and dancing around him and making fun of him. Then in the tight space, I tripped over the coffee table, and Wayne went the other way and dropped the dumbbell on my foot. Broke my foot. Oh my gosh. I can still see Wayne's face. He was racing downstairs with me in his arms, hailing a cab to take me to the hospital. It was so bad. It hurt so bad, but I, a ballerina, could no longer point my toes when dancing." Jon looked down at his plate. "It was the end of my ballet career. Wayne felt so horrible. I felt horrible. It was devastating in a way. I didn't realize, the young me didn't realize, that I had put all my eggs in that basket. What was I going to do? Wayne said that he was going to send me money every week. That he would pay my salary for the rest of my life since he ruined my career. I couldn't be mad at him."

Jon looked into Penny's eyes. "So, what did you do?"

She nodded and rocked back and forth with her lips pursed. "Well, you know, I kept dancing in New York, just not on that stage." They locked eyes.

"Well, I'm sure you were one of the finest dancers in New York."

"Oh, I was damn good." They both smiled. "And then, life just goes on, and that got old. Don't get me wrong. I loved it! I made tons of cash and met the best people, but Wayne kept sending me photos of the lake and Pearson's Falls and saying how we could live together. One day I just bought a bus ticket. I told myself I was going back for a visit, but inside I knew I was done with New York. The bus let me off by the Bantam Chef, where they used to let the soldiers off. I was walking by the place, and Samson asked me if I was looking for a job. I've been working there ever since. Now I run the place. Hell, I have for fifteen years."

"What about wages?"

Penny paused. "Oh, Jon." She reached over and touched his arm. Jon felt a surge of electricity pass through him. "It is unbelievable how much people tip you for a dip cone. And you know, I lived in the boat cottage, and Wayne never let me pay for anything. He always had a car for me to use. It was just cash, and I had no debt. I've always worked through the summer months and then traveled when we closed in the winter. It's been great, actually. I miss dancing, but you know, I'm old now, that was years ago. Who knows how long dance would've lasted and, well, the thing that hits me most is that if Wayne wouldn't have dropped that weight on my foot, then, well, then I wouldn't have had all that time with him." She was quiet for a while. "Really, that made all the difference. I had every day with him. It was beautiful."

As Jon and Penny finished their meals, Tom Cohen and his wife walked out. Jon looked up and smiled, noticing his longtime friend looking at him and Penny strangely. He waved to Tom, and he seemed to snap him out of his stare, and with a huge grin, he waved back. Jon looked back at Penny, and they shared an awkward smile.

"Do you drink, Jon? I noticed that you just got some tea. There's so much wine in this store."

"Yes, yeah, I love wine. Bobby got me into that. I don't really know why. It's an interesting taste, but now that I think of it, it has to do with all the history. You know? I mean, when you read a book, even something ancient like Plato or the diaries of Lucretius, they speak of wine, and then you can go and find that very wine they drank. It's a connection. It's like being in Calabria, seeing those deep valleys and steep mountains, knowing the sea is just beyond them. You can pull off the autostrada and still see old Sicilian carts full of artichokes on the streets. You can buy bread and cheese and the same wine from the same vineyard of a thousand years ago and then wander into some Olive Grove and spend all afternoon just thinking of how life was, in the very same way, the very same place, a thousand years ago."

"You've done that?"

Jon nodded. "Oh, yeah. One of my favorite ways to spend an afternoon."

"Did you live there?"

"For a while, not long enough. One of my favorite areas is Sicily. You know you can sit in the old coliseum in Taormina and watch the sunset and watch it fall right into the volcano they call Etna. And then, when the sun goes down completely, you can see the volcano's rim glowing, like it swallowed the sun. It's beautiful. I used to eat pizza at this place called Mama Rosa's. It's this hole in the wall. I ate there almost every night. Pizza and an Arugula salad. I'd walk home past these alcoves; each alcove had a statue. I'd see something moving behind the statues and then realize it was kids making out. Kissing and carrying on. Great memories." Jon sat back and put his arm over the back of the chair.

"That sounds really wonderful."

"Bobby had always been interested in making alcohol. I don't know why because I can count how often I've seen him drink. Anyways, when we all returned from the war, he wanted to start a vineyard. He picked a spot on the mountain and designed the whole thing. Told us what we were going to plant. He got me into it first because he said it would surprise Elizabeth, and you see, I started really taking an interest in it by then. I started reading books about vineyards and the history of vineyards and then trying the different grapes. I was really into horticulture; growing plants and trees became my hobby after the war. So, that's how I got interested in it." Jon shook his head. "I feel foolish. You asked me a yes or no question, and I just rambled on about Italy and half my life story. Sorry."

Penny smiled at him. "Don't be. I've been to many places but have never been to Italy. I've always wanted to go. Your description sounds amazing. I want to go there and see the sunset on that volcano. Etna, you called it?" Jon smiled and nodded. "So, you have a vineyard of your own?"

"We all have a vineyard. Well, I guess Bobby and I have it now. Finn and I were fixing it up as a surprise for Elizabeth for our anniversary. You should come up and see it sometime. Anytime you want. The sunset is really great from there too. It looks over French Valley. We can invite Bobby, or you can bring some of your friends. Anyone's welcome."

Penny moved to get her jacket. "I'd love that, Jon. Just let me know when." They got up, and Jon cleared the table and then waved to the waitstaff in the market. He held the door for Penny, and they walked out into the rain to the truck. As Jon drove her home, they did not say anything. The slow curves around the lake. The rain pelted against the glass, the wipers slowly moving back and forth. They pulled up in front of the cottage. They both got out, and Jon walked Penny to the door. She paused momentarily, opening the door, and they both stepped inside a warm house.

"Looks like the heat is working! You did it."

Jon smiled. "Oh, it's a simple thing. Most problems can be fixed by just stopping and taking time to look at things."

"Well, thank you, and thank you for dinner."

Jon turned to leave. "My pleasure. "You know, if you ever need anything done around here or help with CHIEF. You know I'm around. I'd love to help." Penny opened her arms to give Jon a hug. Jon felt strange. He wasn't a big hugger, and he had never really been close to anyone other than Betts. He embraced Penny, and even though his arms felt strange, embracing a different frame, he found comfort in her hands on his shoulders. He pulled away. "Have a good night Penny. Hey, listen. I will bring you some wood for the fireplace, and if you want to come up and see the vineyard, just let me know." Jon turned to walk out the door, thinking the conversation was over.

"How about Thursday? I have that day off from the restaurant. I have tomorrow off, but I promised Sophie I would watch her kids. So, Thursday? I can drive up, and we could do sunset at your vineyard?"

"Yeah, yeah, sounds good. I will be around the cabin or the sawmill. I'll see you then."

Penny smiled. "Okay."

The door closed, and Jon walked to the truck and climbed inside. Everything about the ride home was familiar, yet one detail made it completely different. He thought of Penny and how nice it was to speak with her, but it felt strange, like learning to walk with a cane. If he could just be going home to Elizabeth now. If he knew that when he got home, she would be there. A cup of warm tea in her hand. When she saw him, she would set it down and come and place her arms around his neck and kiss him. She would look at him with those blue eyes that smiled in their own way. She would kiss him and tell him how much she had missed. She would rub his shoulders, and in time she would rub his hands. Penny was a nice lady, but Jon wasn't interested in her in that way. He liked speaking with her. He enjoyed having time alone with her, but in general, he always enjoyed the company of women more than he did men. They were just smarter and more in touch with reality. But he didn't want her, not in that way. He was in love with Elizabeth. It would always be Elizabeth who he loved. Jon felt confused, but he couldn't understand why. He wasn't trying to have a relationship with Penny. He wasn't trying to replace Elizabeth. He wondered if his being around Penny made Elizabeth upset. What if Penny did come up to the vineyard for sunset? Would that be wrong? What if Elizabeth saw them there or the dove saw them riding together up the driveway past the Sawmill and in front of the sea of grass together. How would Elizabeth take that? Would she be hurt? Is she hurt? Is she needing or finding a man to speak to her there, on the other side?

Jon turned into the driveway. He could see the wind moving the long strands of grass in the moonlight. He looked up into the eaves of the Sawmill. He thought of pulling over and standing under the eaves where the dove slept just to be near her but drove on to the cabin.

He lit a fire in the stove and saw the note he had found earlier with the salt. He moved it to the front of the shelf, where he could see it each day. "Why did you leave this note here, Betts? Am I desirable? To you? Are you telling me we will be united again like back then? I thought all was lost, and I came for you. Betts, come for me. Just come get me right now. I'd be done with this place." He thought of the dove in the eaves alone and him here alone. "A damn bird. I'm losing it. I know Betts; it's not a damn bird. I just mean." He gave up and filled the highball glass halfway with bourbon. How strange it had been to wrap his arms around another woman. Her shape was unfamiliar to his arms. He leaned against the cabinet and put the bourbon to his lips, and an image of his waiting rifle flashed across his mind. The kitchen was exactly as Betts had left it, yet the room seemed empty and void. He thought of sitting at the booth, but it seemed claustrophobic. The great room seemed overwhelming with all the memories he didn't want to face. He looked at the flannel shirts and thought of walking over and smelling them one more time.

" For what? Remind me that she will never be back?" Stalling, he drank. He sank down, lowering himself to the kitchen floor, his back against the cabinets. He reached for the bottle of bourbon again and filled the glass half full. He drank another large gulp, and the bourbon ran out burning the micro cuts of his shaved face. He slumped farther down, only his head off the floor. He couldn't feel the heat of the stove from here. He could only hear the sound of the water bubbling up and out of the spring box.

Jon struggled with the awkward shame of inviting Penny up to the mountain. "I'm not lying to myself. I can't love again and don't want to."

The bourbon numbed his tongue. " I hate this shit. This feeling can't be true. That'd make me a worthless son of a bitch if it were. If I'm lying to myself, I'd lie to her too. I will never love again. I'm taken."

As his brain spun, he wondered what it would have been like if he had lost Elizabeth when he was young, say thirty. "I couldn't do it." Jon slurred his speech and shook his head. He tried to focus on the feet of the old cast iron cook stove. "I couldn't do it. I couldn't live that long without you." Jon let his eyes close, his mind still swirling. "I'm old, at least. I could die tonight," he said aloud. His eyes opened and were transparent with the idea. "That would be great! I could just die tonight. Old men die, too, in their sleep. We were the same age. How about that?" Jon's eyes dipped closed again. His head nodded. "Okay, Captain. I stand before the mast. Then, I die tonight, good. I couldn't have done it." Jon's eyelids briefly opened, and he yelled into the empty void house. "I could have never lived so long without you, Betts!" He fell back, his head bumping into the cabinet. "That wouldn't have been any kind of life, no life. Life couldn't, wouldn't be, life without you. I love you. Betts, I said I love you." Jon had a moment of clarity where he thought he should stand up, put everything away, get upstairs, and brush his teeth. He knew Elizabeth would be there, ready to tuck him in and soothe his pains. He wanted that, but he didn't want the hurt of waking up and knowing it was just a dream. He thought about it, then closed his eyes and thought more about it. What had she said that time? When they had finished the cabin and were going to move in the next day, what was it? Something about returning back here, always coming back here. "There's a lot of love here, Jon."

* * *

Penny closed the door behind Jon and stood there for a second with her hand on the door. What was that? She wondered. Was that a date? No, It couldn't have been a date, but it was something to her. She didn't know what it was, but she felt it. It was like she had been to church or counseling or a moment with a Buddhist monk. In a few short hours, he had heard him pour his grief out in a poem. He had fixed her house and brought warmth into it. He had fed her body, but more substantially, he had fed her mind and soul. His quiet words had been like butter, and she like dry bread. Her soul felt alive, and at the same time, she didn't realize that she was so dead. When did that happen? How did that happen? She had dated men in the past. She had men in her life. No, no, that was it. She had dated boys in the past. Jon was a man. A man who was not chasing her. A man who did not expect her to follow him or expected her to admire him. Jon was something entirely different. Jon was a man who was on a path of his own. A path searching for learning and understanding, and happened to look over and see her on her own path of searching and learning. It was as if they had looked over, standing shoulder to shoulder as equals, and then he had said to her. "Oh, how wonderful you are here. A friend, a companion to journey with." She opened her purse, retrieved the slip of paper Jon had torn out of his notebook, and handed her. Balancing on one foot, she read the poem over and over. She could hear his voice speaking the words. She read the last lines out loud. "In the causeways, those veins of my heart, your home, you and I are nowhere alone." She looked at the handwriting, the handwriting of someone who had written thousands of letters in his lifetime.

She left the kitchen and turned out the light but took the poem. She climbed the stairs, where all the pictures were hanging from the years of fun they all had at the lake cottage. She stopped at one of CHIEF lying in the water and all of them on the boat. She saw Bobby, Wayne, and Ruby on the bow holding the line. Jon, Theo, Alice, and Elizabeth were in the stern, facing them in her wide hat and looking at the camera. Penny took the photo off the wall and let her fingers drift over the lines of the wooden boat. She touched the faces, Ruby, so tall and thin, and his black skin glowing like Lucius, the emperor of Rome. Wayne, with his smiling face, waved to the camera. Bobby at the helm with a guitar behind him. Theo, tall and Mediterranean, with a drink in his hand. Penny leaned back against the handrail of the staircase. She held the photo in both hands, the scrap of paper with the poem laid on the glass. She studied their gazes, trying to take in the mood of the day. She moved her thumbs around Jon's face. The handsome man with blonde hair and blue eyes smiled at the camera. Penny took her hands and covered all of the photo except for Jon's face. She looked deep into his eyes, searching for something. Something that had once been at the forefront of her mind, something that had been tried on and tried on like a nice-looking shoe that just didn't fit but was always in the closet reserved for future hopes. When did she lose it? When did she lose hope for love? When did the farmer's market on Saturday morning, and the yoga classes, and the flowers in the window boxes, and the beach chair with a new book, in the sun, on the deck above the water all become enough to make her okay with not feeling loved?

Jon had not touched her, barely even hugged her, yet that connection had taken her breath away. Even seeing him at his own wife's funeral and reading the letters of his love for Elizabeth had entranced her. She shook her head. This can't be right. This is not proper. She placed the photo back on the wall, and still with the poem grasped snuggly between two fingers, she went to her bedroom.

The sliding glass doors facing the lake and the skylights let the moonlight flood the room. She took a long shower. Her hair in a towel, she went over to the bed and pulled back the covers. The house was nice and warm. Jon had kept her from freezing tonight. She imagined him up on the mountain, by the stove. Reading or writing another poem. Maybe he was writing a memoir of his time in Italy. The poem was on the nightstand, and she read it again, seeing if the phrases were as she had memorized them. "You precede me, and that's okay." She opened the bedside table and removed the moleskin journal. She couldn't write about tonight because she didn't know what tonight was. She didn't want to write something that she would one day come back and read and feel foolish for. She stuck the poem in the pages and softly closed it like it was a living, breathing thing, going to sleep.

She turned out the lamp and pulled up the covers. The moonlight flooded into the darkened room. She looked up at the light from the darkness. Wasn't she too old for love? This couldn't be, not after so long, never experiencing it. This couldn't be because Jon was in no way searching for love; he was in love. All the letters, the outpouring of his heart in front of strangers. He was not seeing her in the way that she was seeing him. She closed her eyes but found that darkness too much to bear. That darkness of refusing love when it had appeared beside you unexpectedly alongside your own path. She looked toward the lake; the rain stopped, and the moon glowed as the clouds passed. Besides, how could she steal Jon away from Elizabeth? That would be horrible. That would be selfish. She couldn't live with herself if she just took the widower. Took his attention, his words, his mindful thoughts, his stories of Italy, his hands, his letters, his heart. If she met him in his vineyard and shared the air, Elizabeth's air. She already felt guilty. And yet she felt intoxicated on a rich, full-bodied wine. An entire life having been lived without ever falling in love. She closed her eyes and wondering became dreaming, and there she found the answer. He satisfied the longing soul.

CHAPTER 17

"But my God shall supply all your need"

"Preacher Skelton, this is Margot Bagsby." Shane cringed internally. He had almost made it out of the nursing home. "She helped me with my reverse mortgage. I never thought I could come here until Margot explained I could use my house to pay for it."

Shane stepped forward and shook the pink hand of Margot Bagsby. "A pleasure to meet you, but I really must run. See you all next week, Lord willing."

Margot looked at him with a blank expression. "Looks like God has been mighty good to you, Preacher."

"Indeed, he has. You're Margot, the investment counselor here?"

"I'm on my way out too, Preacher. I'll walk with you." She turned to the occupant of the wheelchair. "Pleasure doing business with you; take care, now." She took Shane's arm and guided him out to the main corridor.

"Tell me," Shane said, "what exactly are you doing here for these folks?"

"Oh, it's simple, really. You see, old people who can't pay for their treatment can do a reverse mortgage with the Firm."

"The Firm, Margot."

"The Firm is the corporation that owns these nursing homes. You know they are a big outfit. They have properties all over the east coast. Anyways, say you have some old person who can't afford care here, which, let me tell you ain't cheap. They give their home to the corporation in return for their care. And then when they pass away, the corporation owns the property outright."

Preacher Skelton held up his hand. "Now, Margot, what if that person only lives another month?"

Margot shrugged. "It's in the fine print. If you sign that piece of paper, you better have good representation. Now you see, that's where I come in. I help the client determine the fair value for their property and present good assets to the Firm for their consideration."

"Good assets?"

"Well, Sugar. The Firm can't just take any old property and give away all this service for nothing. You see, some people just don't die; they keep living forever. The Firm's shareholders need assurance they will earn healthy returns." Shane was following what she was saying.

"So, you get paid to bring properties to the Firm, and you get paid to sell them for the firm too?"

Margot smiled. "I tell ya, your mind is sharper than your suit." She reached out and touched the tie of Preacher Skelton. "My contract with the Firm allows me to manage the property in these western counties. I make a commission to bring them the good assets and then sell them. You know, it's all God's work in a way, Preacher. I think you understand. Some of these elderly folks and their children think their property is worth much more than the Firm is willing to give them. That's where I have to really get in the trenches and help them see that the Firm is taking a huge risk on them. They need to be thankful for how God has brought good Christian companies like this to help them and their families through struggles such as these. Take, for instance, a while back, we had this old white-headed lady here; what was her name now?" Margot looked down and snapped her fingers. "Oh, Ledbetter. Mrs. Ledbetter. Now she came in without much money and swore that we were taking advantage of her when the offer was made. Even her children got involved. Now, when that happens, I just sit back and wait and let them get the first few invoices in the mail. You know the Firm at first doesn't invoice you monthly. They wait and invoice you for the first quarter all at once. And that bill is staggering. So, I just wait. Well, then they usually call me and are ready to accept the offer." Shane did not mention the Ledbetter woman had taken him to court.

"So, what do you do here?" Margot asked. "Checking on people from your congregation?"

"Oh, no, I pastor down in Taylors, SC. I just come up here to do a weekly service for these people. It's a private ministry, I call it. I dabble in real estate a bit too. I've bought several properties from older people in the community, developed them, sold topsoil and timber off them, and then cut them up for lots."

"A developer, An entrepreneur, and a Pastor? My, what a powerful combination." She reached out and palmed the buttons on the double-breasted sports coat. "You know what, Shane? May I call you that, Sugar? Maybe we could work together on some of these endeavors. Actually, I know one right now that needs attention." She had Shane's focus. "I'm not sure what it's going to take. Do you have good funding?"

Shane slowly nodded. "Let's just say I have a good cash flow."

Margot squeezed her lips together. "If I only knew that money would do it. You see, that's where you being a man and a pastor who knows how to use words, could be useful."

"What you got in mind? Why don't you tell me?" He took her hand from his chest.

Margot looked behind her to see if anyone was in the hallway. "There is an old man named Jon Joines. He owns a whole mountain right outside of town. I don't know how many acres we are talking about, probably thousands. This mountain has got views for days, waterfalls, everything. It would be a developer's dream come true. You see, I think there may be an opportunity because the man's wife just died. He is pretty broken up about it." Shane did not tell Margot that he knew of Jon. He did not tell her that he had been responsible for the small boy being with him this summer. He had only just met this woman, and though it seemed they had a keen understanding of each other, he wanted to keep his cards close. If he was going to profit from this arrangement, then he needed advantages. Shane looked at her now and slowly nodded his head. "Any idea how much money would be needed, Margot?"

Margot stopped and began to whisper. "That's just it, Shane. I think the man is pretty well off. My father used to run the Old Post Office on Main St. and knew Jon and his brothers, well, his adopted brothers when they were young. My father used to tell me about a whole load of Confederate gold coins that went missing at the end of the Civil War. The legend tells about an old Jug Factory the Cherokee Indians had up on the mountain. Some people say the gold is hidden up there, but my father always had the suspicion that Jon Joines and his brothers found that gold."

"Uncirculated Confederate gold coins, you say?"

Margot nodded. "And the whole mountain. Timber, topsoil, three hundred and sixty-degree views. I mean, this is an unbelievable jackpot, but we need a strategy. I have seen him a couple of times since his old lady died, but he doesn't seem to connect with me. That's why I think maybe you should just ride up there and talk with him. Now, don't talk about anything having to do with that mountain. Talk to him about men's stuff, and then when he brings up his wife dying then, just comfort him. Then keep going back and just being friends. We are playing a long game. Can I count on you? I need to know that I can count on you, and this will be private."

Shane extended his hand. "Fifty, fifty?"

"We will deal with that later. We've already got a buyer with deep pockets." She pointed to the floor. "The Firm is in the real estate business, not the caregiving business."

* * *

"What did you say, Betts?"

"Jonny, I'm being serious."

Elizabeth was sitting on the back of the vineyard wagon. Deezy and Andiamo were wandering around in the grass of the meadow and in front of the cabin Elizabeth and Jon were moving into. "Betts, I just don't understand what you're saying. We built this together." Jon laid his tools down and removed his gloves. "I'm going to war, and you are crying, telling me what you want me to do when you die? You're the healthiest person I know. I'm sorry, but that is just a bit confusing to me." Jon had been installing the last of the porch rail. "We are moving in here tomorrow." He moved towards her, but she was blocked by Andiamo. The horse, having heard or felt the tears of his caregiver and had come and placed his head over her shoulder and then turned his whole body as if protecting her from the scary World. Jon, entirely blocked by the horse, saw Elizabeth's arm come up around the horse's neck. He laid the gloves on the new planks of the side porch and walked over behind Andiamo, and touched his flank. He could see the horse's reflexes in his velvet skin. He got closer, and Andiamo shifted, trying to move Jon out of the way and away from Betts. "Come on, Fella. I've learned my lesson." Andiamo pushed again, and Jon pushed him back. "You got to share." Jon wedged himself between the horse and Elizabeth and moved between her legs, dangling off the vineyard wagon. Elizabeth was sitting with her head down. He leaned over and tried to catch her blue eyes. "Hey, hey, Darlin." Jon touched the smooth chin of Elizabeth and raised her head. "I'm sorry. I've just been so focused on all this. Trying to make you proud of me. Are you?" Jon raised his arms and pulled Elizabeth close into his chest. "I'm here, Betts. I'm sorry."

Elizabeth pulled back. "Jon, nine times out of ten, I don't need you to try and fix things. Life has worries and scary things. I just need you to listen and let me talk them out. Not advice or a plan. Just hear and see me; yes, I'm proud of you. This is a beautiful home, and though we did it together, I know it is a gift from you to me and an expression of your love. And that's why I'm saying. If I were to die, then I know it may be impossible for you to ever love someone again." She started to cry. "But, but I hope that you can at least find someone that you can be happy with."

Jon shook his head. "Betts, we just accomplished this together for each other. We are both healthy and young. All I want is you every day."

She slid her fingers inside his buttoned shirt. "I know, I know, I just feel like I need to say this." Jon nodded his head and pulled her into his chest again. "And another thing. I want you to come back here to the mountain. I mean, I know that you may have to go away for a while, but I hope you will come back to the mountain because there is a lot of love here."

"Come back? A lot of love here? Darlin, help me understand what you're saying about that?" Jon picked up her hands and kissed them. He kissed them again, and then from her hands poured water, clear, pure water from which he drank. Jon woke up on the floor of the kitchen next to the spring box, his mouth open and his eyes watery. The highball glass was on his chest where Elizabeth had just touched him. The fire had gone out in the cook stove, and Jon could see his breath in the winter air of the cabin.

His thoughts were clear and cold. Like he had pulled himself down to the depths of the pond where the cold water rushes out and just clung there, letting it clear his mind. He set the glass down on the floor and pulled himself up. He didn't feel the cold of the room. He didn't mind having slept on the hardwood floor. It didn't even phase him. His mind was still focused on Elizabeth sitting on the vineyard wagon. She talking about what he should do after she died. He remembered that day now. Elizabeth had always been unworldly like that. Significant events causing her to sober in her happiness and tell people exactly what she wanted if circumstances were to change.

The flannel shirt caught in the stubble of his beard. He turned and slid into the emptiness of the kitchen booth. The cold alone tethered him to this quiet world as a dusting of snow covered the wooden walkways outside. Even a fire would not make him feel alive. He looked at the corner of the kitchen that had been his bed that night. He saw the highball glass on the floor and the bottle of bourbon on the counter. He remembered calling out to the Captain. Standing himself before the mast and condemning himself to die. "Shit, it didn't happen." Blinded, he stared through the window to a world awakening with light. "What's the matter, God? Can't kill me?" The residual bourbon swelling in his head. "Well, I'm sure you're not down casting stones just yet." He thought of drinking more, but something caught his eye.

The Dove had flown to the porch table. Jon opened the door and stepped outside. Taking in the Dove, the cold, and the snow. He eased to the corn barrel and, with the brass ashtray, crushed a handful to meal. He scooped it with both hands and brought his offering to the Dove. She came and, in between his fingers, ate the meal and, when finished, did not fly away but nestled in Jon's hand. Jon didn't know if he should talk or just be with Elizabeth in his mind. He remembered that on cold mornings birds needed water. He poured some into his palm, and the Dove, cooing there, drank water from her man's hands. Jon felt the soft touch of the Dove. "My woman, whose eyes are Savanna. My woman whose eyes are level of water, level of air, earth, and fire." The Dove having drunk, and fed, flew away.

Jon wiped tears from his eyes. Elizabeth had come to see him. To reassure him that no matter where he was, she would visit him in his dreams. She could still love him, even though he was lost now, forty-five pounds thinner now, a functioning drunk now, so cold inside that he couldn't feel the cold outside. So uncomfortable within that he no longer needed a bed to sleep on. The floor was as comfortable as his soul. If she could still love him as he was spiraling toward hell, then she deserved more of him. He was going to straighten up.

He walked back inside and immediately washed his hands and face. He turned and started a fire in the cookstove, then picked up the glass, washed it, and dried it. He put the empty bottle of bourbon in the waste bin. He stripped off his clothes and went upstairs to shower and shave. In the bedroom, he noticed Elizabeth's purse sitting on the corner of the dresser. He briefly touched it like a sleeping cat. He walked into the bathroom and turned on the shower. He couldn't throw the old shampoo and things away, but he could at least move them to the bathroom closet. He slowly did so, reverently. He was not ready to move the toothbrush; it could stay. He did open the vanity drawers and placed Elizabeth's hairbrush and makeup mirror inside. That was fine for now.

He lathered himself, trying to remove the smell of alcohol from his body. He brushed his teeth twice. He dressed like he was going to a meeting, yet ready to work the day outside. He gathered his dirty laundry, walked downstairs, and started the washing machine. He walked back out to the kitchen and made himself breakfast. He thought how nice it would be to have a newspaper. He wondered if he might go back into town today. Maybe spend some time in the stores and meet new people. He could tell them about Elizabeth. Wait, maybe he shouldn't. Maybe he should just work at the vineyard and then go into town. See if he could just be around other people. He thought about how to prevent himself from spiraling. He thought he should go into town for lunch more often. It would give him a chance to be around people, get a good meal, and then possibly have leftovers for dinner. He would also start taking walks up the staircase to the upper pond and to the rest, then back down the arcing road of the mountain. That would help keep him in shape. Snows would be coming more often, so he should chop wood and fill up the bin on the porch. He should also take Penny some firewood for the boat cottage. "She's doubtless cold." Though he thought of her warmth.

Jon finished his breakfast and the black coffee. It being good and bitter, in a way, that could help him pretend he didn't have a belly full of bourbon. In truth, he knew that he was probably still drunk. At least his emotions were vulnerable, but his mind felt very sharp. He could remember every part of last evening. The dinner with Penny, his thoughts on the drive home. He felt he could see himself lying on the floor, the taste of the brown liquor. He could feel the shape of Elizabeth in his arms folding into his chest, even if it was just a shadow of a dream. He wondered if she saw him standing before the mast at attention in his drunkenness. He closed his eyes, and his eyebrows lifted. "Jesus." He ran his hand over his blurry face. " I just want to be with you, Betts. Just give me wings."

He dried the dishes and put them away. He checked the fire in the stove and suffocated it with the damper. He approached the flannels but then decided not to. Maybe, he would start wearing those at night to feel close to Betts. He went to the coat closet and pulled out his jacket and winter hat. He wanted to work in the vineyard, and while the truck warmed up, he thought of what tools he needed from the sawmill. The sea of grass lay in one direction, reflecting the sunlight in its icy covering. In the sawmill, he put his tools in a canvas bag and noticed the vineyard wagon from his dream in the corner. Winding his way between the machinery to get there. He pulled back the tarp and ran his hands over the coarse wood. The paint flaking. "You're not so bad, are you, girl?" Jon lifted the canvas, looked at the back of the wagon where Elizabeth had sat, and told him that she hoped he would always come back here because there was a lot of love.

"What were you trying to tell me, Betts? I don't want to get this wrong." He wondered exactly what she meant. "I hope you'll come back here because there's a lot of love here, Jonny." He thought of Penny coming up soon to see the sunset. "Is that a clue? Someone coming to be with me here?" The thought of a new love taking Elizabeth's place turned his mouth to ash. He touched the seat of the wagon and then the guides for the reins. "It's okay. I'm going to fix you up good as new. We will make another trip together. Like old times, we will take Elizabeth out to the vineyard again." If he did all this work restoring the vineyard and the wagon, would it be enough to fill himself again? Could he fix this? Fix Elizabeth's anguish from being separated from him? Fix his anguish from being separated from her? Fix God's mistake?

He covered the wagon and picked up the tool bag. " God Damn, God! You impotent Son of Bitch; you can't even kill me."

He parked the truck by the vineyard's stone columns, walked down to the rows of grapes, and started unwinding the steel wire from around the cedar post that needed to be replaced. He looked over the valley. The speckled blanket of thawing snow reminded him of the first time he saw Queen Anne's lace in France from his window.

He heard a vehicle coming up the gravel road and wondered why Bobby would be coming this way. He looked at the stone columns and glimpsed a grey-blue pickup. He could hear the dual exhaust of the truck. It parked just past his own. Jon kept rolling the rusted wire with his leather gloves. A large man wearing blue jeans, a white button shirt, and a jean jacket exited the truck. The man's hair was combed straight back. Even from this distance, Jon could see the acne scars on the sides of his face and recognized him as the church pastor he had done work for a couple of years before. The man walked around Jon's truck and looked in the window. Then he stopped and looked over the vineyard shielding his eyes from the sun. Jon waited for his gaze to turn towards him, and when it did, he raised a gloved hand. The man acknowledged him and began to walk towards him.

Jon studied the large man's walk as he descended the hill towards him. An old habit. He detected he was off balance and that he favored one leg. Jon assumed the man had an injury or an old wound on one side, probably an ankle. He kept working.

"How are you, Jon? It's good to see you." Shane walked closer to Jon and stopped at one of the vineyard posts. Jon nodded.

"These muscadines?"

Jon looked up, squinting against the sun. "No, these are different cultivars primarily for wine."

"Ha, well, I imagine you use them for jams and jellies then."

Jon shook his head and placed the roll of wire on the top of one of the posts. "No, we make wine. This whole area is pretty good for it."

"Oh, come on now. You don't say? This is the Bible Belt. I don't know any good Christians drinking wine." Shane chuckled.

Jon shook his head, "Well, I've never cared much about being in that category." " About being a Christian?" "Yeah, I've never been a follower. Of any certain religious tradition." "Well, being a born-again believer in Jesus is not what we'd call Religion. We see it as gospel and don't consider our beliefs a tradition. We see it as worship of true faith." Jon moved the coil of wire with the toe of his boot and looked out to the valley. " Well, I see growing grapes and pressing them to wine as a tradition. I don't think it has anything to do with Religion. But, to each his own, right Preacher? The idol must go to the idolator."

Jon picked up his tools. "I feel like we might have gotten off on the wrong foot here. I thought you'd remember me. I'm the Pastor down in Taylors that you did the grading work for us a while back. You recall that?" Jon didn't say anything. He put the canvas tool bag under his arm and started walking back towards the truck. Shane stepped back out of the smaller and older man's way. "Say?"

Jon stopped in front of him, his shoulder still turned towards him. "Yeah, I remember."

A look of relief came over Shane's face. He smiled. "Good, good, well, you know you and your wife came down a couple of times. Seems like you both really loved the children, and they loved you. I remember you giving out dollar bills and candy to the kids. Your wife must have come to that dedication service with a whole purse full of candy." Jon couldn't help but smile at the memory of Elizabeth dumping candy bags into her purse, planning on giving it all to the children. "Well, that's why I came up here today, Jon. I hope you don't mind. A lady in town told me that your wife passed away. I can't imagine how you must feel, but I just wanted to come up here and let you know that I am thinking of you. You got my prayers and the prayers of the church." Shane reached out his hand and touched Jon on the shoulder. "I'm truly sorry for your loss. I didn't know her, but I could tell she was a wonderful woman."

The words touched Jon's heart. Anything said about Elizabeth was what Jon wanted and needed to hear. He was desperate for anything about her. A memory, a story, a prayer. Anything that could be done to keep her here. "Thank you."

The two men walked towards the parked trucks. "I sure enjoy this country up here. Once a week, I do a little service at the nursing home in town."

"Seems like a way to drive for that."

Shane raised his eyebrows. "Oh, It's the right thing to do. You know, at the end of the day, when it's all said and done, you've got to do the right thing. Say, uh, did that boy come up here this past summer, Finn?"

Jon stopped and looked at Shane. "Yeah, Finn was up here for a while."

"Here when your wife passed away?"

Jon nodded. He recalled the moment they said he couldn't touch Elizabeth. "Yeah, he was here when she died." Jon paused for a moment and sighed. "He opened all the doors to the house and turned all the lights on. Moved furniture out of the way so they could get to her quicker."

Shane looked down and shook his head. "Yeah, yeah. Now I tell ya. That Finn stayed with Norma and me for a while too. He's quite a young man. Norma just wanted to keep him. I tell ya, I wish we had a dozen grandsons like him. A fine boy."

"We had an accident here in the vineyard his last day up here. I was cutting some of these saplings with a chainsaw, and he walked up behind me. I let the saw swing beside me, not knowing he was there, and it caught his jeans and tore into his leg."

"Oh, now that's too bad. But you know, I recall seeing him on crutches a few weeks ago. Better now, certainly, better now."

Jon was surprised to hear about the crutches. He wondered if everything was okay. Finn had seemed to get around okay using the axe handle. "I left him with Marlene at their house."

"Yep, Sister Marlene. Good woman." Shane was nodding his head.

Jon searched Shane's eyes for clues. "She seemed odd to me."

"Well, well, uhh, Sister Marlene is uhh. What's the term for people like that? Misunderstood. I think. You know she means well, and her heart is in the right place, but sometimes her facial expressions and possibly her demeanor are taken incorrectly." Jon said nothing. "You know Finn's Dad; Reggie is a very sick man. I'm not sure why God is not choosing to heal him. You know, that may be why sister Marlene comes off as a little serious-minded. I'm sure her burden to bear is large and confusing."

Jon read between the lines. "Does Finn need anything? Is it possible for me to give you or your church some money, and then you give it to Finn's family to help cover some of their costs?"

Shane put a hand behind his head. "Well, now, Brother Joines, if the Lord indeed laid something on your heart, then I could do that. I could make sure it got to them."

Jon nodded. "Good." He started walking again.

Shane hustled to keep up. "I bet Finn sure did enjoy himself up here on this mountain." Shane tried to catch his breath after ascending the small hill. "I imagine a large number of young boys like Finn would gain so much from being up here away from their bad circumstances and home life."

Jon had never thought about that. If so many people in the community had lost loved ones that he hadn't known about, then certainly there were more children like Finn that needed help too. Jon got his wallet from the seat of the truck. "We love the Earth because we were once children growing up in it." Shane looked at Jon, pondering what he had just said. "Did you come up with that?" Jon shook his head. "No, I read it in a book. A book about wine." He cracked a slight smile.

"Can you see to this for me?" Jon handed the preacher five hundred dollars. "This is all I have with me. If you stop by next week when you are in Tryon, I will give you more. Now my main concern is Finn. If he needs anything, shoes, clothes, food, then get someone to buy it and give it to them. Don't just give them this cash. Do you have someone that can do that? I'm sure you have a ministry like that in your church."

With wide eyes, Shane turned the bills in their proper direction. "Oh, yes, sir. We sure do. I will get sister Wanda right on this." He pocketed the money. "I know what you're saying. Some people. Good people now. They love God but don't know how to budget."

Jon looked at the man. "You don't have a ministry for that in your church?"

"Of course we do, brother Joines, but I hate to say it, but it's a waste of time and money to try and help people with their money. Some God intended to have and others. Well, God does mighty things with the poor. I will be back by next week. Oh, and I am truly sorry about Elizabeth. You will be in our prayers." Jon watched as the truck roared up the road.

Jon thought about what Shane had said as he chopped firewood and kindling for the cookstove. He chopped more than he needed and loaded it into the pickup. There must be many young people who could use an escape from their home lives and would enjoy all the mountain had to offer, hikes and scenic views, fishing, canoeing, and kayaking in the French Valley. He envisioned Finn and himself working together, building cabins on the open land and planning hikes that talked about the history of the mountain. He thought of young people standing on the moss-covered stones without their shoes, standing under the waterfall that never ran dry, and climbing the stone staircase in the light of the full moon. It could be something that could go on and outlast his life. It could be something dedicated to Elizabeth, and there could be talks about her, explaining who she was and how she lived her life. It could be like a foundation that goes on and on and helps children. How would he do it? It was just him, and all their friends were slowly passing away. He was old too. Just as old as Elizabeth. He could die any day. He wanted to die and go and be doves. If someone was to come and say Friday is the day. Friday, you will end your life on Earth and join your wife on the other side of the hourglass; he would be overjoyed. He would sing and dance and shout with glee at the top of his lungs. He wondered what would happen to the mountain, the sawmill, the sea of grass, the ponds and the fish, Skyuka's Rest, the staircase, and the ancient trees after he died. He took off his leather gloves and leaned against the tailgate. He and Elizabeth had been so busy with their own lives and each other's love that they never stopped to think of what would happen to it all when they died. The great room was full of photos and memorabilia, the hat boxes, the flannel shirts, the spring box, the church pew, the lanterns, the books in the sawmill, the vineyard cart, and the doves.

The doves. Elizabeth had wanted them to live their next lives as doves, in the eaves of the sawmill, just like they had spent the first year of their marriage. Where would they be if there was no more sawmill? What kind of paradise would it be if he couldn't provide for Elizabeth then? What if he couldn't protect or save her in the next life? He prided himself on forethought, but he was entirely exposed in this. He had lost so much and realized he may lose it all. He could not die on Friday or next week or possibly for the next month, even six months. He had to devise a plan to preserve the mountain and the home of the doves. He closed the tailgate and headed into Town.

* * *

Shane was sitting behind the small upright piano at the nursing home with a hymnal in front of him when Margot Bagsby came by and set her purse on top of his brown leather Bible. He looked at her, frowning. It was a sin to place anything on top of a Bible.

"I wondered if I'd see you today," Margot said. "Any news?" She leaned her elbows on the piano and looked down at Shane.

"I went up there and looked around."

"And did you talk to the old man? I doubt he's even in his right mind."

Shane nodded. "He seems pretty sharp, but you are right. His wife is his tender spot and also that kid, that boy named Finn."

"Finn? Not sure I know him. Is that his grandson?"

"No, Finn was a boy staying up there with them on that mountain. Little tow-head. The boy's Daddy's got AIDs, probably a queer, though he's married. Reggie, ain't got a lick of sense. God might forgive sin, but he ain't going to help anyone that doesn't help themselves."

"Oh, is his Daddy part of that Clinic? The one at that Church with the Sycamores?"

"Nah, Nah." He shook his head. "I mean, he better not be. That place is full of the devil. From what I hear, that's a regular Sodom and Gomorrah."

Margot Bagsby shook her head. "Confounds me. I don't know why we must have that kind in our Town. I certainly know my Church is not supporting those people. They are reprobates."

Shane leaned forward. "Scripture says they've given their minds over." Shane shook his head no. "No, Reggie ain't up there. I don't think Finn even understands what kind of disease his father has. Reggie is just looking for a miracle that ain't going to happen. Jesus isn't interested in that. I mean, look at Lot's wife." Shane snapped his fingers. He stood up and pulled his Bible from under

THE BOOK OF SAY 339

Margot Bagsby's purse. He looked around to make sure no one was watching. He opened the Bible and showed Margot the cash Jon had given him. "The old man gave me this." Margot's eyes grew wide as she saw the bills stuck amongst the yellowed pages of the Bible.

"What's that?" Margot asked.

"Like I said. The old man's got soft spots. He gave me this to go and buy clothes and food for the boy."

Margot crossed her arms, looked down at her feet, and stepped closer to him, forcing Shane to sit back on the piano bench. "I want to make one thing clear here, Preacher. We are playing the long game, the slow game, but an assured game. We are investing in this. Investing our time and our brain power. We will build trust and a rapport with this old man. We are not distracted by a little cash. What we want is the whole mountain, lock, stock, and barrel for a song. Now listen to me. You will have your wife or someone in your Church take this money and buy that boy clothes, food, and school books. You going to make sure you get receipts for all of it. You going to get this person to sign the receipts or circle the dates and the amounts. Put them in a church envelope, and next time you go to that mountain, you give them to that old man. Tell him this is just a record of what you did with that cash." Margot Bagsby leaned over Shane and looked him in the eye. "Can you do that, Preacher? Who are you going to get to do that for you?"

Shane swallowed hard. "Sister Wanda. She'll do anything I ask. Need's her husband saved."

Margot Bagsby backed up from between the legs of the Preacher. She smiled and touched him. "Good, good." "You don't let me down now, Preacher Boy."

CHAPTER 18

"See how the flowers of the field grow"

Jon turned down the steepest part of the mountain grade, put the truck into a lower gear, and took his foot off the accelerator. Since Elizabeth had died, his emotions had been whipsawing back and forth. His feelings seemed filleted, open, raw, and sensitive. One moment he could be laughing at a memory, and the next, weeping at the same memory.

He felt like his soul was some source of gravity, pulling all things that were hurting, confused, and in need of help to him. He felt her loss had connected him to a higher deity or at least another plane of thought. It seemed as if he heard sounds differently and could see birds' expressions as they conquered the wind.

Tonight he would go to the high place of the mountain, the rest, and watch the sunset. He would talk with Elizabeth and ask what she wanted for the future of the mountain. If he did this, if he created a plan for the sustainability of the mountain, then he would be free. He would have completed everything that Elizabeth wanted. He would be free then. Free to embrace the end.

He reached the last fertile plain and headed into town. The truck seemed to drive itself. He hadn't told Penny that he was coming to drop off firewood. He didn't think he would even see her. It felt awkward, and he didn't want to bother her. He would even feel embarrassed if she saw him, but he had told her he would bring the firewood.

Penny's car was at the boat cottage, but he didn't knock on the door. He stacked the wood in the storage area by the door and placed a small bundle of kindling next to it that had been tied with string. He then considered leaving a note. He returned to the truck, removed his notebook, and tried to decide what to write. He felt all the words caught in his throat, so he sketched something instead. Something so Penny would know it was him that had been there. He wondered what to draw. He thought about CHIEF, the boat cottage. He considered drawing the vineyard where they were supposed to meet for sunset. Then he remembered the snow under the edges of the trees this morning in the French Valley. They had reminded him of the Queen Anne's lace he had first seen from his window in the chateau hospital in France. His pencil found the page and sketched the likeness of the flower. The strong stalk, the branches. The flowers were like a veil of lace draped across it. Under the sketch, he wrote. "See how the flowers of the field grow." He got out of the truck and placed the note in the twine of the bundle of kindling. He left and went into town.

Jon parked outside the florist shop on the corner. He went inside and saw a bundle of white star gazer Lilies. "May I have those?" Jon pointed to the bouquet.

"How many?" The florist asked.

"All you can spare, they're for my brother."

"Need a card?"

Jon shook his head. "No, ma'am, thank you." Jon took the bundle of flowers and walked across the street, up the small staircase, and through the cemetery's iron gates. He hadn't been here in a long time, but his feet knew where to go. He came to Ruby's grave and knelt down in front of it. He saw that other flowers had been brought, and he was surprised. He assumed that it must have been Bobby. He wondered briefly if Wayne was buried here too. "It's been a long time Ruby. I'm sorry I haven't been by." Jon was quiet for a long time. Not knowing whether to tell Ruby that Elizabeth had died or was it something that he already knew? Jon laid the stargazer Lilies in front of the granite stone. "Please take care of her, Ruby."

In his mind, he could hear the jubilant voice of Ruby. "Indeed, Jon. Indeed, we having ourselves a good time." Jon smiled. "I love you, Ruby. I love Elizabeth too. I'm confused. I don't know what to do. I want to be with you both more than anything, yet there's still so much here that must be done. It's like my soul wants to leave, yet my mind says I must finish well down here first. I got to finish well so I can enter well up there or out there, I don't know." He could see Ruby's face now, nodding and pondering Jon's dilemma. In his mind, he could hear Ruby's words. I didn't want to leave. I would've given up my hopes and dreams to stay. Hell, I would give my voice or my fingers to stay. Jon, you've got more time. Make use of it. Weren't you the one that said chase love?

Jon closed his eyes and shook his head. He could hear what Ruby was saying as clearly as a bird sings, but his heart didn't want to hear that. Jon touched the stone and then stood up. "I will be back soon. Take care of her for me." He turned and walked back through the cemetery. He saw the ABC store and went in and bought a bottle of bourbon. He knew he should buy some groceries but just wanted to get home now. He didn't intend to drink the liquor, but it would be good to have it just in case he acquired a taste for it. He drove home.

* * *

Penny chopped vegetables for the homemade soup and started to sauté them with onions and garlic over the stove. The drawing Jon had left for her on the firewood was now framed behind a small piece of glass and sitting on the kitchen counter. She had gone outside yesterday and noticed the firewood and the note and immediately came inside and built a fire in the green metal art deco fireplace and curled up in a blanket. She read the sketch like a novel. Taking in every line of the pencil, every bit of shadow and shading. The handwriting below and what it meant. She would set it down in the lamplight and pick up her mug of tea only to realize that she was looking over and still studying the figure. She wasn't sure what kind of flower it was, but she knew it was something that she would cherish. She had gone to the junk drawer and pulled out an old, framed photo. Removed its back and then placed Jon's sketch inside. She considered framing the poem he had written but liked the idea of it beside her bed in the moleskin journal.

She looked at the clock and wondered what time would be appropriate for her to arrive at Jon's cabin on the mountain. When the soup was ready, she filled a thermos and packed a bag with a baguette, butter, napkins, and two bowls with spoons. It was a chilly day, and she felt like this was fitting. She sat at the kitchen table and looked at the clock. She didn't know why she was acting this way. A strange way, a girlish way. Finally, she got up and left the cottage.

She was not someone who felt comfortable in the great outdoors, but she liked adventure, and the thought of driving up here to a rustic destination was exhilarating. She glanced in the rearview mirror and could only see the dust kicking up from the mountain road. She turned onto the gravel driveway and saw a thin trail of smoke rising from the cabin. Jon's truck was parked in front.

As she got out of the car, Jon walked out onto the side porch. "You made it, have any trouble?"

Penny smiled at Jon and reached into the back seat for the basket. "None at all. Those are pretty easy directions. All lefts from town, really."

Jon smiled. "Yeah, you're right. It's good to see you." Jon gave Penny a slight hug. He took the basket from her.

"I made us some vegetable soup; I hope that's alright."

Jon opened the door to the truck and set the basket inside. "Sounds wonderful. I don't get many home-cooked meals anymore. I guess that is something I took for granted. Climb in. I promised you a tour."

They drove down the gravel roads, and Jon explained how the mountain was thousands of years ago and then how he found it as a small boy. At the vineyard, they walked around, and Jon showed her the different kinds of grapes and the places they used to light bonfires to keep the fruit from freezing. He showed her the authors' names on the brass name plates and explained how Finn had made him realize why he had named each row in that way so long ago.

"You miss him, don't you?" Penny said.

"What, that boy? He's mostly good."

"Mostly good. What do you mean?"

"Well, if something is just perfect or the best ever, you wouldn't feel that comfortable around it, but if it's mostly good, then, well, that's alright. Finn is alright. To tell the truth. I love that boy with all my heart. I never knew loving a kid so much that wasn't your own was possible."

Penny smiled. "I guess that's how Grandparents feel."

"Do you have kids, Penny?"

Penny took a deep breath. "No, no, it wasn't in the cards. Just never found the right person, I guess."

They walked to the gazebo, and Penny was amazed. She reached out and touched the green metal structure. "This is so beautiful. I never imagined." She turned like a ballerina under the roof of the gazebo. She came and stood beside him and looked out over the valley to the peaks to the northwest. "Bobby told me about this place. The mountain and the vineyard and the place he calls the rest. Skyuka's Rest?" Jon nodded his head. "Bobby told me about all the people that lived here for thousands of years. Told me about the full moon nights, the rushing wind, and what that means." She looked over at Jon. He was smiling. "Is that true?"

"What's that about the wind? It's what they say. When you feel a mighty rush of wind up here, it's a tormented soul who finally found their way to true love. The wind is them rushing to embrace their lover."

Penny smiled and laughed. The cold air was making her eyes water. "Bobby told me stories of the people's lives here. He told me about Captain McGraw and the Confederate gold."

Jon turned his head with a serious look. "He told you about the legend?"

"Unh huh. Told me how you found it. He's selling some of the gold coins at the clinic auction next week. I made the flyers for it. Are you going? It's at the Tea House."

"You made flyers? Flyers with the gold coins on them?"

Penny nodded. "And of the artwork. There are door prizes too." Jon looked down, and Penny noticed he was troubled. "Did I say something wrong?" She came over and touched Jon's arm.

"No, it's fine. We just found that gold a long time ago. Damn, long time ago. We sold some when we fixed up the sawmill and when I built the cabin, but it was always a secret. We didn't want anybody knowing because we didn't want people coming up here looking for the gold and hurting themselves. I mean, I feel bad. I've got a lot of emotions right now, but I wish Bobby would have told me. I mean, we had all sold some of the gold before, but we used proxies, and we certainly didn't put it on flyers and send it out into the community."

"Oh, gosh. I wish I wouldn't have said anything."

"Hey, it's not your fault. I'm overreacting. We found that gold as kids. I imagine it is time to do something with it. It's fine, really. I just wish I would have heard it from Bobby first." They stood there a moment longer. "Come on, it's chilly. How about we take the truck up the mountain. I've got some other spots to show you, and we can eat in the truck up there."

They drove up by the upper pond, and Jon pulled over and showed her how they had built it and installed the standpipe. He told her how Bobby had pulled the old sawmill truck right into the bottom of the pond and then laid in the back of it playing his guitar while Jon and Elizabeth ran the tractors, moving the topsoil again across the dam. He told her about the fireflies that came out in the summer and illuminated the canopies of the ancient trees at night. He told her of the deer lying in the grass beside them and the butterflies that would light upon the rug while they picnicked there.

He drove on up to the rest. They got out and looked over the ridge, taking in the views. "I think you can see the edge of the lake from here," Penny said. "That's it, isn't it?" She moved closer to Jon and felt the warmth of his soul. She grasped his arm to steady herself.

When they got back into the truck, "You chilly?" "Oh, yeah." "Well, how about we go back to the cabin, and I will make fire, and we can have the soup," Jon said. "Get warmed up."

"That would be nice."

In the cabin, the fire was low in the stove, but Jon snapped some kindling in his hands and restarted it easily. He put the kettle on to boil. "Want some tea, Penny?"

Penny sat down at the edge of the booth. "Chamomile would be great."

"Honey?" Jon asked.

"Yes?"

"In the tea. Do you take honey in your tea?"

"Yeah." She noticed the rotary phone with the scrap pieces of paper of telephone numbers all stuck to the wall with tape.

"Like my Rolodex?"

Penny looked at Jon and laughed. "Well, if you do your taxes in your truck, it does stand to reason that this is how you would keep your address book."

Jon shook his head. "Not sure how that happened. Somehow it became a joke that we just kept up with. I used to draw these little sketches and leave them there for her to find. She's got a whole hat box full of them upstairs."

Penny, bringing the conversation back to her. "Speaking of sketches. I like the one that you left me."

Jon gave an embarrassed laugh. "Yeah? Could you tell what it was?"

"A flower?"

"Yeah, it was a Queen Anne's lace. That field by the upper pond is full of them. They have always been special to me."

"Well, it was lovely. I don't really know much about plants. I usually buy whatever is blooming at the Farmer's market, bring it home, and promptly kill it."

Jon laughed. "Horticulture has been my hobby for a long time. At one point, I had the whole yard area where the moss is full of pots and plants with lights at night. We practically lived out there in that space all summer long." The kettle began to boil, and Jon poured the tea into the cups. "That was right after the war."

They ate baguettes with whipped butter and sea salt flakes sprinkled over them. "This is really great, Penny."

"My mother's recipe. Wayne brought most of my parents' stuff over."

"I had no idea how much paperwork there is to do when someone dies," Jon said. "It must have taken me two weeks to get through all that. Elizabeth and I were married for nearly fifty years."

Penny nodded. "Yeah, that is a big thing. We immediately discovered how much that could upend any type of healing for our people at the clinic. I hate to say it this way, but if you love your family and your children, then you do all this for them in advance. It's the last thing someone who is grieving should have to do."

"Yeah, I had no idea. Now, I get it. I need to do that for myself."

They were quiet as they finished their meals. "Would you like a glass of wine?" Jon said. "I'm sorry. I should have offered it to you before."

"Sure, that sounds great."

Jon got up from the booth. "Okay, let me get a couple of glasses."

"We could share one." Jon looked over at Penny. "I mean, if you want?"

Jon nodded. "Yeah, yeah, that's fine." He opened the bottle of wine and filled the small stemware glass.

"Well, that's a tiny glass."

Jon laughed. "It's a trick I learned in Italy."

"Really, that does seem like a trick. There's not hardly enough wine in that glass for one person, much less two." Jon was smiling. "So, what's the trick?"

"Well, you share a bottle of wine at lunch, and you use these tiny glasses because, well, it's lunch, right, moderation. So, you think you're drinking less because of the tiny glass. You keep refilling your glass and refilling your friend's glass until all of a sudden, you've finished the whole bottle."

Penny laughed. "And you're drunk?"

"Well, geez, Penny, it's not bug juice."

Penny kept laughing. "You've really been around, Mr. Joines. A special life. A special man."

Jon looked up into her eyes. He smiled and looked back down at the small glass." Penny noticed his change. "Well, I better get going. It's been a lovely afternoon Jon. Thanks for inviting me up."

Oh . . . okay. Well, you're welcome anytime here."

Penny put on her jacket. "You think you will come to the art auction this weekend?"

"Yeah, do I need a ticket?"

"Well, yes, but if you are sure you're coming, I will get you one, and you can just pay me back."

"Okay, sounds good. I will plan on seeing you there, then."

Penny smiled. "Great."

Jon waited for the car to start down the driveway, then went inside and closed the door. He sat back in the booth. So, this is what it felt like to share a glass with another woman. You could give yourself to someone your entire life, continually falling in love, and when that person left your glass time sphere, then it was possible that someone else entirely, someone who didn't know the name of your favorite flower, someone with a different shape than your arms recognized, could come into your hourglass and leave their mark on its walls. They could leave the taste of shared wine on your lips. Jon twirled the small stemware glass around and around like a ballerina pirouetting. How? How could a body do this? How could the heart and the body be so in love with someone that it ached unceasingly, and yet the mind and that same body be crying out for companionship and to be touched?

It was like a limb without a branch collar. It was like the white pine that once stood full and proud when suddenly damaged, weeps unceasingly until the sap crystallizes over the causeway of its heart.

Jon wondered if he could find the letters he and Elizabeth had written about Queen Anne's Lace. He hadn't remembered seeing them. Which box could they be in? He hadn't looked at the old letters and the things in the great room for a long while. He really hadn't even been spending much time in the bedroom. It was all still so painful. Everything was still sitting where Elizabeth had left it.

This was different, though. There was something there. Something in those letters that he needed to find. What was it? Something in the words of Elizabeth that was calling out to him and would heal his wounds.

He pulled off his boots and left the kitchen to go upstairs. He turned all the lights on. He reached for the hat boxes and set them one by one on the bed. He felt panicked and short of breath as he dove into the sacred things, into the shrine he had maintained. If he could just find those letters quickly, then put everything back and retreat to the kitchen. He was anxious because being here, the place he truly wanted to be, the place where he had held Elizabeth's hand in his sleep for nearly fifty years, was no longer that place anymore but the trunk of a white pine, damaged, exposed, and weeping.

He carefully pulled out the photos and letters. There were so many that he moved the photos to the loveseat and then set the hat boxes on the floor. Spreading out the letters, he noticed a stamp with a dove on one of the letters. He thought of the cold night. He wondered if he opened a window would she come into the cabin. He shook his head. Tomorrow he would rip the vent screen in the eaves of the Sawmill so she could find her way inside the barn's attic.

He opened envelope after envelope. Drawing after drawing. He needed a system to organize them. He opened his notebook and tore out a blank page. He tore it into small pieces. He opened the drawer of the bedside table, looking for tape. There wasn't any. He left the bedroom and went down the stairs to look for tape. The great room was cold, and he knew he should start a fire to keep the house warm through the night, but he was in a panic now. He looked through the kitchen drawer for tape. His hands were shaking. There was something in the letter. Something Elizabeth had said. Something that could put the branch of the white pine back on. He closed the drawer.

He turned to the booth, stretched his arms, and leaned over it. His head was pulsing. He was in this place filled with beauty and loving memories, and yet at the same time, every beautiful and precious thing was like a love spear running through the atrium, the ventricles, crushing the stone chambers of his heart. He looked down at the bottle of wine and the shared glass, and for a second, he thought of swiping his arm and sending them careening across the small kitchen. Breaking them. Breaking the memory of sharing something as sweet as wine and conversation with someone different than Elizabeth. He breathed in deeply. He hated feeling his shirt tail out of his pants and the socked feet. He felt out of control and out of order.

He tucked in his shirt tail. He rolled up the ends of his jeans so he would not be walking on heels. He went into the great room to the buffet where his clothes were stacked, and he opened the cabinet doors and found a roll of tape. He added wood to the fire, then corked the wine and placed it under the counter behind the curtain. He washed the wine glass and placed it to dry. He turned off all the lights except one lamp beside the daybed.

There was something that Elizabeth had said. Something that she desperately needed to tell him now. She had written something to him nearly fifty years ago that seemed nice in a letter, but something that had been penned then for this moment now. He had to control the chaos in his mind. Something made him think of having a bourbon to calm his nerves, but he shook off the urge. He couldn't take the chance of something spilling on the letters. He closed the cabinet doors, and as he stood, he saw the cable knit sweater and pulled it over his head. He picked up the roll of tape and started up the stairs.

As he opened each letter, he scratched a descriptive word on a scrap of paper and taped it to the outside of the envelope. When he opened some envelopes, he knew the letter by the first word. Others, he found himself reading entirely. He was going through letter after letter, and he still couldn't find what he was looking for, the letter he had written to Elizabeth about Queen Anne's lace and another one she had sent back to him. He had hoped, but now he was getting to the last of the hat boxes. Had they been lost?

He looked across the room to where Elizabeth's purse was still sitting where she had left it. He knew she carried certain letters with her at times as if they were amulets against fears. He touched the bag and then slowly opened it. He could smell her fragrance. The lipstick, the lotions, the candy she would always give to children she saw in town but no letters. He returned to the boxes, now looking through the last remaining ones. He noticed the clock. He had been going through the letters for four hours and had ripped countless pieces of paper from his notebook. He was losing hope of finding the letter. It was like everything else in his life. The little things of Elizabeth, every tangible thing, everything except the memories, were constantly being taken away from him.

Jon heard a rush of wind, and the cabin seemed to shiver. Leaves of the ancient trees pelted the glass of the bedroom windows. Like the leaves, Jon felt abandoned and displaced, adrift on the sea of meadow grass. He carefully packed up and put away the letters, photos, and old sketches. He was exhausted emotionally and mentally.

He pulled off his clothes, defeated, helpless, the only solace for his heart in words he could no longer find. He turned out the lights and crawled into the cold bed. The leaves pelted the window and the wind ran across the open meadow and, hitting the granite walls behind the cabin, swirled upward in a spiral. Jon turned on his side and looked at the leaves, one moment against the glass and the next gone. He wondered if any of the leaves had been written on with tears. Words that only the dead could read.

He saw Elizabeth lying on her stomach in the field by the upper pond. The rug was like a magic carpet beneath her. He could see her laughing and smiling across the pond, the sun on her straw hat and her body warm in its glow. Leaves were spiraling and drifting around her. One lay down in front of her, and she picked it up and read it. She smiled. She turned and looked back at Jon across the field of Queen Anne's lace. He saw her touch her lips. He heard something behind him, and someone was there raking the leaves. He could hear them scratching the ground with a steel rake. "Gonna sack these leaves up and burn 'em."

Jon turned from Elizabeth towards the voice. "No, don't do that. Those aren't leaves; they're letters." He turned back towards Elizabeth across the pond.

"Ain't no letters here no more. Just leaves. Old leaves," the voice said.

"No, no, please, just sack them up; I'm gonna read them. I can read tears." Scratch, the metal tool raked. Jon looked back, and Elizabeth was reading another one. He could nearly see her blue eyes in the shade of the hat. Was she turning to smile at him again? Jon stood across the field gazing. "I will just burn these here. These leaves you ain't gonna read no more. This small pile first." Scratch again went the rake across his heart. Jon was torn between waiting to see if Elizabeth looked for him again and saving the leaf letters from being burned. He stretched his arm backward to stop the person from burning the leaves. He was waiting, waiting, her head turned slowly.

Her eyes met his. He could see her whisper, and she stretched out her arm and pointed passed him. He reached for her with one arm, smiling his heart full, and he reached behind him with dread to keep this unknown person from burning his memories.

Something hit the window. Jon opened his eyes. The dove was there. Walking slowly in front of the panes of glass. One of Jon's hands was stretched out to the glass, and the other behind him pointing toward Elizabeth's bedside table. Jon set up remembering the dream clearly. Someone trying to take all the cherished things of Elizabeth away from him and Elizabeth across the field of Queen Anne's lace, reading the words written on the leaves in tears. She had pointed behind him.

He leaned across the bed and opened the small drawer. There were the letters he had been looking for. They must have been the last letters she ever read. She had set them apart. Why? "Say?" Jon placed the envelopes to his lips and breathed in. He opened them and found one letter from him and one from Elizabeth, and a blue sun print of a Queen Anne's Lace. He opened his letter to Elizabeth. Inside the envelope was a carbon copy of a sketch he had made for her.

Dear Betts,
This flower is blooming on the edges of the field beneath my window. Like lace, it trims the places of the meadow where the spring grass is weak. Did you cause it to bloom? Like wheat, you turn to bread. Like tears, you turn to wine. Did this stalk in the field feel your joy and expose its brilliant heart to the sky? I did. I felt your heart and love within me bloomed.
Forever yours,
J

P.S. I sketched the flower. The peasants here call it Carotte Sauvage or Wild Carrot. I haven't seen it or at least noticed it on the mountain. However, now, in my convalescence, as I sit and ponder it and sketch it for you, it seems I feel a heartbeat within it. A strength that I've only seen in you. Something graceful, knowing, and yet loving. Do you know it, my dear? Because this flower, to me, says our love is strong even though it is apart. Even though I am weak within and hurting within, this flower says my woman is there. I find strength in this flower because it reminds me of you.
I went to H.Q., stole a carbon sheet, and traced it for you. I don't think the sketch will survive the mail. Find it, my love. Tell me it is you.

Jonny, My Love,
The flower you seek is in abundance. I have admired it and picked it for many years. It has even adorned our table many nights. Though, I must say, you haven't used it to make love to me. Stroked my lips and neck, the palms of my open hands, but tonight you did. However, you are mistaken. I did not cause it to bloom; love did. That wonderful and strong magic. We have much of it, sacked up, no doubt, in the storerooms built into the mountain of the rough-cut wood. The sap that hangs from it will profess. We have bundles and bundles, and if ever feeling weak or low, all we must do is go and pull out another bundle. My joy did not make this flower bloom, but it was love. Love is what we find within ourselves, yet it also surrounds our bodies. It is the nest of the dove as well as its corn and the seed. Me

P.S. This is a sun print of Queen Anne's Lace. That's its name, along with Wild Carrot. I wish I could send the flower, but it takes some time to press. I wish I was there to heal your wounds. I miss your touch too. Let this copy of the flower be something I can send you from afar. Place it in your window in place of me, and know that even though I cannot be with you, I have sent you this likeness of love like the nest of a dove. I will always be within you, and love, the independent flower, will always be there to surround you.

* * *

Penny woke up in bed and immediately thought of Jon. Throughout their afternoon and night together, she had watched him stealing glances. She wondered if the small glass of wine they shared would be the closest her lips would ever come to touching his. Was that the most her fingerprints would ever imprint on his heart? She dressed and set off on her morning walk around the lake. As she walked, she let her mind wander. How long had it been since she had given up on the thought of sharing life with someone? How had she given up on that dream? What was wrong with her that no one had scooped her up? Was it living in this small town? Was it that her soul mate had died in the wars, and therefore they had never met? Had she missed the right guy while in some silly relationship with some silly boy?

Or was it that love had just taken a very long time to reach her? Did love move any way it wanted when it wanted? Was it like a waterfall to some people gushing from the mountain, and for others, like sap from a tree? If love came now, she wouldn't be mad at it. No, she would appreciate it more. It would have a greater value.

She looked across the lake to the other coves. She could see people walking their dogs and working around their homes. She wondered what it would be like to have Jon there each morning she woke up. Would he walk with her? Would he plant flowers around the boat cottage and make each one bloom? She smiled at the image. She returned to the cottage and looked towards the firewood in hopes another letter or sketch would be waiting for her, but there wasn't. She touched the handle of the screen door and then stopped. She walked over to the firewood and looked around in case a note had fallen off.

She walked inside and prepared a smoothie. She picked up the framed photo of the flower Jon had drawn for her, looking into it for answers just as she looked deep inside her heart for explanations for this feeling. It was something that was on his mind. Something that he wanted to say to her but couldn't find the words to say, so he drew it. She set the picture down and looked across the lake. "Don't do this, Penny," she said aloud. "This is going to hurt you." What she was feeling for him could not be what he was feeling for her. He was hurting, he was lonely, and he needed to be touched. She shook her head. If she fell, if she did this, it would be the biggest chance she would ever take because her heart was getting ahead of her mind.

Her phone rang, startling her. "Hello?"

"Hey, Penny. It's Jon. Good Morning."

"Hi," she said, entranced by his voice.

"I was wondering what the dress was for the auction. My suit is at Brock's cleaners; I've only got one."

"That should work. I can go by and get it for you. You know if you aren't coming down the mountain until then." There was silence. "Jon?"

"I'm here. I was just thinking. Yeah, I could just pick it up from you and change at the Tea House or Theo's."

"Jon, just change here. I've got to set up things early, but you can just come in the house, and I will leave it in the spare room."

"Okay, I will come early and help set up."

"Okay," Penny said.

"Okay."

"See you then, Jon."

"Yep." The phone hung up. She was right. This wasn't going to work out. She was being foolish. What was this unstoppable feeling that she had to go and pick up Jon's suit from the cleaners in town? To be seen picking his suit up or heard saying his name at the counter as if she belonged to him or him to her. She wanted to feel the shirt and the jacket in her hands and imagine Jon's chest beneath the fabric, his hands holding hers, his arms around her waist, her arms reaching around his neck, and laying her head on his shoulders. All these things, something deep inside her wanted, hungered for. She touched her reflection in the window as if touching her own face.

* * *

"Morning Jon," Tom Cohen said. "Pull around back, and we will load up those cedar posts for you." Tom slid on a pair of leather gloves at the loading dock and lowered the tailgate. "These look good for you?" he asked.

"Good enough."

"Late in the day to get started on this. Why don't you wait until Monday, and I will have some of the boys come up there and help you put them in the ground."

"Thanks for the offer, Tom. I think I can handle it. Gets me out of the house."

"How's everything going for you, Jon? I know it can't be easy."

Jon quickly learned after Elizabeth's death that people didn't want to hear the truth about how he was hurting, so he lied to protect their lives and days. He looked into the eyes of his longtime friend and decided he couldn't trust him. "One day at a time." Tom smiled. "Good, good." Jon closed the tailgate. "You going to the auction tonight?" Jon nodded yes. "You going with Penny?" Tom snickered and looked at his feet. He removed the gloves and held up his hands. "It's none of my business. I just happened to see you cross the street with that bouquet of flowers the other day. Seen the two of you spending time with each other. It's ahh. Well, it's just a little quick and all. You know people in the town; they come in the store and say things about seeing you with another woman."

Jon was mad, but he was more hurt. "Penny is a very nice lady. It's very nice to talk to someone with intelligence and a sensible mind. We are friends. Yes, I am going to the auction tonight, and yes, Penny is going. We are not going together, but we will both be there. Just as I am sure you will be there and Theo and Alice." Tom was smiling and slowly nodded his head. "The flowers you watched me buy and carry across the street were laid on Ruby's grave." He stepped closer to the big man and looked him in the eyes. He leaned closer.

"Now, Jon. I didn't mean—"

"You remember my brother Ruby, Tom? My brother, that was murdered? That's where those flowers went."

"Jon, I'm sorry. I didn't mean to get in your business…."

"What's the matter, Tom? I mean, if you want to be a real son of bitch, then here's your goddamn chance." The man was backing up now, and Jon followed him, never breaking eye contact. "You want to be a goddamn bastard that tares open the wounds of hurting people? Here's your chance."

"Jon, stop now. You know I wasn't. I'm sorry. It was none of my business."

Jon poked him in the chest. "What you and all those other people don't understand is that if you don't empathize with the grieving, then you damn yourself to go through it."

"Don't say that, Jon. Please don't say that. I can't even think of losing my wife, our children." Jon turned and walked back around the truck. "That's your business. Stay the hell out of mine."

* * *

Driving around the lake, Jon thought about what Tom had said. He shook his head. How could people even begin to think that he could just disregard his life and love with Elizabeth? It made Jon feel sick to his stomach. "Damn it, and if I'm not here pulling up to her house, and she is getting my laundry for me." Jon shook his head and sighed. Life could be cruel. It was like one of his soldiers getting shot in the war, surviving yet succumbing to a quiet infection.

Jon knocked on the door, "Come on In." Penny walked over to the top of the stairs. "Jon, your suit is in the spare bedroom. Make yourself at home. I will be down in a minute."

"Okay, Penny." He pulled the receipt from the garment bag and left the cash and the ticket on the kitchen counter.

Penny came downstairs. "Hey," she said, smiling." She had both hands full and looked lovely. Jon smiled. "I'm going to run on to the Tea House." Jon nodded his head. He picked up the framed drawing. "You can just come over when you're ready." Jon smiled. He had forgotten what it was like to be in the room with a woman getting ready for a large party and event. "You okay?" She walked over and touched Jon's arm. She kissed his cheek. His heart surged. "You, okay?" She asked again.

"I'm good. Thank you for grabbing my suit. He motioned with the picture to the cash on the counter.

"My pleasure. I've got to run, but I will see you there."

The Tea House was full of people, and Jon slipped through the side door into the kitchen and said hello to Clarence and Theo. He pushed the kitchen door open slightly and surveyed the crowd. Everyone was sitting at the white-clothed tables, and the fireplaces were roaring. Art easels had been staged throughout the restaurant, and he could see Bobby and Penny making rounds throughout the dining room, thanking people for coming.

"You've got to jump, Jon. Never thought I'd be saying that to you." Jon looked back at Theo. "Remember jumping out of a plane into pitch darkness? Free falling towards the black Earth?"

Jon smiled. "About the most fun I ever had, with my pants on."

Theo chuckled. "You look sharp, Jon. They don't cut suits like this anymore." Theo brushed lint from Jon's shoulders.

"Never thought I'd be doing this alone. You know, Elizabeth loved events like this. I just loved taking her out."

Theo grimaced. "I know it's tough. Listen, just go out there and relax. Talk to people. Buy some art. Buy something that Elizabeth would love even if you gave it away, or let Bobby resell it. Look, there's a seat at the table in the corner. Sit with those folks. I know that guy he plays golf at the club."

Jon squared his shoulders, presented a smile, and began to walk purposefully to his seat. Penny caught his eye, and she lifted her head and watched Jon walk across the room. He reached the table and stood beside a white-haired man in a blue suit. "Good Evening. Is this seat taken?" The man looked over and extended his hand. "Please, sit. Upton Peace, how are you?"

Jon shook the man's hand. "Jon Joines, I'm well." Jon placed a white napkin in his lap and looked around the table.

"You live in Tryon, Jon?"

"Just outside of Town on Panther Mountain. How about yourself?"

"Saluda. Moved down here fifteen years ago from D.C. Wife rides horses and thought I'd be a golf sensation in this little Town, but I can't beat that Clark Benson at the club."

Jon smiled. He opened the program for the evening. "What I'm interested in is on the back page," Upton said. Jon flipped the program over and was amazed to see the photos of shiny gold coins. The man reached over and pointed. "Uncirculated Confederate gold. There's this legend in the community about a whole bunch of these coins going missing right before the end of the war. No one has ever found them." Jon looked over at Upton Peace. "It's another of my hobbies besides golf." The man shrugged.

"What do you do in Saluda, Upton?"

"I'm semi-retired now, but I do estate planning and wills. I'm an attorney."

"Do you have a card?" The man opened his wallet and gave Jon a card.

* * *

Later, Jon stayed to help Bobby and Penny clean up after the event. "Seems like it was a success," he said to Bobby. "Your coins sold quick."

Bobby smiled. "Yeah. It's Ruby."

"What do you mean it's Ruby?"

"It's Ruby. Ruby is the private benefactor of the clinic. I used his portion of the gold to start and fund the clinic." He laughed. "Isn't it something? Confederate gold. Owned by a grandson of slaves. Funds all this work that helps minorities in this Southern Town. He murdered by a racist." He looked into Jon's eyes. "They couldn't stop his song, could they?"

Bobby held onto Jon's hand. "Thank you for saying all this. Listen, Jon, remember when I told you and Betts that I left the mountain because I felt I was keeping you guys from fully enjoying your happiness?" Jon nodded. "Well, you know, I even wondered if I was the reason you never had kids." Jon cleared his tears and shook his head, startled. "Well, anyways. That was just half the truth, Jon. What I mean is that, well, I was scared."

"What do you mean?" Across the lake, the lights of the cottages were reflected in the water.

Bobby looked down and breathed in deeply. "I felt like everything I loved, truly loved in life, was going to die and be taken away from me. Like my Momma when I was a child. Then my friends during the war. Then, then, I thought all that was okay; you know I could get through because I had Ruby, and we had dreams and then . . ." Bobby shook his head and started to gasp for air. Jon put his arm around Bobby. They cried together this time, Jon weeping for Ruby and at seeing Bobby hurting. "I was scared that me being close to you and Elizabeth . . ."

"That we were going to die? Die just because you loved us so much? That's why you left? To save us?"

Bobby nodded. "I'm cursed, Jon. Everything I truly love dies." He was crying again, shaking his head. "I don't know why, but it does."

Jon again hugged Bobby. "Hey, hey, listen, I'm here." He turned Bobby's head. "It's not true. Not at all."

Bobby rubbed his head and looked bashful. "It's not all your fault. That's what I'm trying to say. I purposefully stayed distant. Loving yes. I love you and Betts with all my heart but just lived in fear that I'd lose you and cause you to die. And Wayne. I pushed Wayne away." He was quiet now, moving his mouth like he was remembering the sweet taste of love. He breathed out heavily.

"Probably the worst mistake of my life. Wayne was wonderful. You know he loved Ruby too." Bobby shook his head. He closed his eyes and leaned his head straight back as if under the gaze of God. "Forgive me," he whispered.

Jon closed his eyes too. He didn't know what to say. "Betts left me a letter."

Bobby looked over at him. "Yeah, she left me a letter. She's been leaving me all kinds of things. Notes around the house. Notes in that old book of Wordsworth I used to carry with me everywhere. I mean, not just a few notes, a bunch. In my clothes, in the drawers of the house, behind the salt."

Bobby smiled. "That gal."

Jon nodded. "Yeah, Special Woman. The notes are wonderful. It's like she is still just everywhere, and yet I can't touch her, which is killing me. I mean, I wish it would."

"Don't say that, Jon."

"Well, you know what I mean. But this letter, in this letter Bobby, she told me to chase love. To continually chase love."

"Hmm. Maybe that's what you need to do too. Elizabeth told me that too. Back when I was struggling. Of course, I wasn't honest with her. I mean, I couldn't tell her the reason I'd pushed Wayne out of my life was because I was scared that my love would cause him to die. I couldn't tell her I'd been distant from the both of you for the same reason." Bobby sighed and leaned his elbow on the car.

Jon looked over the lake. "So, where do we go from here?"

"Ahh, well, I'm too old for love. I mean," he tapped his chest with his large fingers, "my soul is too old. Too weary, too thin, for that kind of love."

"You've become a priest," Jon said. "You know, like the Cherokee, that is our roots. You were once a Chief of War, and those struggles and lessons brought you into being a Chief of Peace, and then now. Well, now you are a Priest to so many, Bobby. You really are the wisest man I've ever known."

"I still struggle, Jon. I doubt myself; everything I do, I doubt myself. It seems like my best intentions hurt people. I don't know what it is. Life would be so much easier if Ruby was still here."

"How can you say you hurt people? I mean, look around, Bobby. All these people adore you. They clammer to have a moment with you or to see your smile. Bobby, you mean so much to so many people. When you talk to people and respond to their questions, you make them think deeply about their lives. Your life has brought you through so much that people can feel it when they stand in front of you. It's intimidating in a way, but that is also what makes you a Priest to people. But I think you're lonely. I mean, you still have Ruby, who I'm sure is there for you in your memories, but he is not there to comfort you with his touch, with his voice. I think that is what Elizabeth was telling you way back then."

He paused for a minute. "I found these letters Betts and I wrote each other years ago. It was the first time I had ever seen the Queen Anne's Lace. I sketched it and sent her a copy, and then she did a sun print of one and sent it back to me. You know she couldn't send me the real flower, but what she sent in its place was unique and as special as the flower. Maybe Ruby sent you Wayne?

Bobby looked down, and Jon said, "I'm sorry; maybe I overstepped."

Bobby raised his hand. "No, no, that's alright." He sighed. "I let fear get in the way of fulfillment. And in the end, I still lost him." He looked at Jon. "Elizabeth was right. I should've chased love. I should've grabbed it, held it, fought for it."

Jon realized the advice he had given Bobby was the advice he himself found so hard to accept. He hugged Bobby. "I love you. I want to be a better Brother to you."

Bobby nodded. "Me too. I love you. You forgive me?"

"Forgive you for what?"

"Pulling away, being distant, not letting you share my burdens."

"There's nothing to forgive, Brother. Love is as constant as the fountain. It may have a drought, but it's never dry." Bobby smiled, and the two embraced again.

Penny walked out of the Tea House to where they were standing. "Who's the lucky boys? Clarence put together some care packages for both of you, Bachelors." She handed them each a small box. "Said you could pay him back by losing a hand at poker next week."

Bobby set the box in the car and then hugged Penny. "Thank you for all your help. You are an amazing woman."

Penny stood on her tiptoes and kissed his cheek. "Okay, well, I'm headed home. I'm worn out. Jon, I will see you in the next few days." "Sure thing, drive safe."

Jon closed Bobby's car door. "Night, Bobby, drive safe."

As Bobby drove off, Jon and Penny stood alone in the parking lot. "Did you drive?" Penny asked.

"No, I actually walked. You know parking is a little tight here."

"Well, come on, and I will give you a ride."

"You know, if you don't mind, I think I will walk back. Just want to think for a minute."

"Okay, but it's chilly, so don't make me worry. Come in the house when you get back, so I know you made it."

Walking beside the lake, Jon didn't notice the cold. He hated how much his own words, his own mind, his own body, were telling him to heal and how to heal. He wasn't ready. He still ached inside from the grief and loss, but everything seemed to push him forward.

Like everything around him was impatient, telling him constantly to hurry up, to move on. Everything happens for a reason. Wasn't that what people continued to say? He hated that saying. There was no reason for Elizabeth's death. Or the deaths of anyone that had spoken of a loved one at the remembrance ceremony. Was there a reason for Jared, a child, to contract AIDS through a blood transfusion? Was God's plan for him to die young? Just so he could mold a clay bowl with his hands and his Mother's tears that she could hold onto for the rest of her life? How about Jared just lived? Gotten married and had grandchildren for his Mother. Wouldn't that be God's plan, something that happened for a reason? A bowl? You took his life and gave his Mother a bowl? You took Elizabeth and gave me a box of ashes? "Fuck you. Fuck you." Jon raised his middle fingers towards the starry night sky.

    He was close to the Boat Cottage now, but he was angry. He was so angry he couldn't feel the cold through his thin suit jacket. He had never smoked, not even during the war, and yet, right now, he wished he could. It would give him a moment, a reason to be late while he collected himself before seeing Penny. He stopped and scratched his face. He needed to calm down.

    He desperately wanted to be touched. Just a hand on his shoulder, just a woman's hand touching his fingers. A moment where he could close his eyes and just be healed for a second. That was selfish. Wait, Is it selfish? The truth was that he wanted her. He wanted her in his arms. She was already in his mind. He remembered that line from Shakespeare. "If you love me, I will forever live in your heart, and if you hate me, then I will forever live in your mind." He did want her to love him, but he didn't want her to hate him. No, of course not, but he loved Elizabeth; he couldn't give his heart to anyone.

People would know and judge him like they already were. "Bastards, goddamn bastards." Did this mean he would be using Penny? He hurt, but if he used her to soothe his pain, didn't that make him a bastard? A liar? Jon thought of just getting in his truck and driving away. He shook his head. He was a man that gave his word and stuck to it. "Fuck." He breathed in deeply. He would just go inside, say thank you, and then be on his way. Just get his bag and leave. *Shit, why did I leave my bag?* Had he really wanted to come back and see Penny?

Jon pulled himself together as he reached her door. He knocked briefly and then went in. "Hello?" A bottle of wine and a small stemware glass were on the table. He didn't know if he could hide his emotions and do this. He heard Penny in the living room, making a fire in the art deco fireplace. "Hey, I'm in here." She smiled in his direction. Jon looked around the room and stepped inside. "Hi! How did you like the auction? Who was that guy you were talking to at the table?

Jon sat on the couch as Penny went into the kitchen. "He was an attorney from Saluda. Moved down here a while back. His wife is into horses, and he likes to play golf. Also, collects the gold coins Bobby was selling. I think he bought most of them."

Penny returned to the living room with a plate of cheese, crackers, and grapes. The bottle of wine she poured into the small glasses and asked Jon to try it. "Carmenere is my favorite grape."

"I think it is from Bordeaux." Jon sipped the wine. He got up, walked over to the fire, and moved the logs around. He straightened up and walked to the sliding glass door to look over the lake. She came over and placed her hand on his back.

"Jon, is everything okay?" Jon looked over and smiled, trying to hide his pain and anger.

"Yeah, I'm sorry. Just thinking about some things Bobby said."

"Anything you want to talk about?"

Jon looked down at his feet. Penny began to rub his back. It felt strange to Jon. His body used to only be touched by Elizabeth. "Well, I don't want to betray Bobby's trust in me." As soon as Jon said that, he thought about the gold coins. As young men, they had made a pact to never tell anyone about the gold they had found. But Bobby . . . Bobby had told Penny and even sold some through the charity auction without asking. Had time dissolved the bond? Jon looked back out the glass door. They stood side by side, reflected in the glass. "He thinks anything that he truly loves dies."

Penny stopped rubbing Jon's back. "What?"

Jon nodded. "He thinks everything he loves gets punished and dies because of him. Like a curse or something."

"Is that how you feel, Jon?"

"No, no. I mean. I never thought about it like Bobby. My mother died of Tuberculosis. I was sent to the orphanage because she was so sick and couldn't take care of me. I remember her, remember good things, but I was so young when it happened, and thankfully people were there who explained it to me and that it wasn't my fault. Then the war, you know, that was war. Even if a man who died of infection days later, it was still the enemy that killed them. At least, that's what I told myself. It bothered me and still does, but I've always said it was the enemy and not me. Then Elizabeth. We had fifty years together, and she died in her sleep. In my arms."

Jon looked over at Penny and saw a small tear running down her face. He pulled her to him. With his thumb, he touched her cheek and wiped away the tear. He realized that she had empathy for him. There was common ground. She had lost someone she loved to. A sun print of his own pain. She reached under Jon's suit jacket and wrapped her arms around his waist, drawing herself close. She laid her head on his chest, and Jon felt her fill the empty space in his chest with the love language of wanting hearts. "Bobby was different. His mother was his World as a child." Jon wrapped his arms around Penny, pulling her into his chest even more. He laid his cheek on the top of her head. "She was alive one day and gone the next. They lived on Main Street, and Bobby always played on the sidewalk. She had gone into the road to pick up a ball Bobby was playing with and never even saw the bus. It all happened so quick. Tore her chest right apart. Then later, as a young man, he was a medic in the war, just death after death of his friends. Then Ruby. Bobby blames himself for leaving the dulcimer on the porch. Ruby going back alone for it." Jon could feel Penny's tears soaking into his dress shirt.

She lifted her head from his chest. "I see now. His life has just been small glimpses of the sun but mostly pain, and grief, repeated over and over. Repeat trauma."

Jon nodded, and she laid her head back on his chest. "Yet, he is the strongest man I know." Jon ran his fingers through Penny's hair repeatedly, just letting the soft hair flow across his skin. He looked in the reflection of the glass and could see the two of them in each other's embrace, an image of the familiar feeling he had once known with a different flower.

Penny raised her head, wiped her tears, and looked into Jon's face. Jon moved the hair around her face with his fingers. She lightly kissed his chin. Jon felt the sweetness of the kiss. She stole a kiss closer to the corner of his mouth. Jon felt the moistness of her lips. She lifted on her toes and briefly kissed his lips. Jon closed his eyes, and Penny closed hers, and in the reflection of the glass, they embraced lips on lips, lives upon lives, humble cares, and delicate fears and sun prints consoling each other's hearts.

CHAPTER 19

"To be full and to be hungry, to abound and to suffer need"

Wanda Davidson sat down beside Marlene in the women's prayer room before the Wednesday night service. "I have some vegetables for you and your family in my van. "It's not much, just stuff that I put up in jars back in the fall, potatoes, beans, pears, kale. Not too many people eat kale in this church, I've noticed, but I thought . . . Preacher Skelton said that God had laid it on someone's heart to help your family. An old man that is close to Finn, I think he said?"

Marlene's head turned toward the humble woman. Could this be? Could God continue giving to them again, using this old man, Finn's labor from the summer? "He gave the Preacher money to buy Finn food and clothes. He said he would keep doing it, too, but people say that sometimes. Anyways, I guessed Finn's sizes, you know, from my own boys. I bought him some new jeans and some other clothes. I've got it all in my van. There's some cash too." She handed Marlene a church envelope.

Marlene placed it in her well-worn purse like it was a precious diamond. "Thank you." Wanda shook her head. "No need, Child." God provides for all of us in this world." Marlene lowered her head and thought she might cry. Sitting in the pew she watched as people moved all around her. Standing, sitting, walking, singing, and raising their hands in praise. She saw how healthy, how meaty they all looked. Everyone looked different from Reggie. Even the very old seemed strong enough to stand and walk by themselves. None seemed to be wearing diapers under their clothes or were jaundiced. Blisters were coming up on Reggie's lips. Sores were visible on his cheeks. His skin was like a yellow leather stretched taunt over sharp bones, and his teeth were like razors protruding under deep sunken eyes. Did these old people take coffee enemas each day? Did they dash off to the bathroom multiple times an hour? Did they frequently defecate themselves? Did they have to lay heavy towels over the bedsheets at night? Reggie was only forty-one years old. Marlene was still in her early thirties. Was this really what God intended for her life?

How could she have been so stupid as to have given an oath to love for better or worse, in sickness and health, for rich or poor? Why did she do that? What made her just throw all caution to the wind? She had stumbled into a second marriage too soon. Too soon after falling so hard out of love with the boy she had known from high school and lost her virginity to in the backseat of his coupe.

She remembered what it felt like to be young. To be pursued by a boy who was strong and laughed easily. The soft hair of his chest, the veins in his arms, the space between them heated with wanting. Would she ever know that again? She was only in her thirties, and yet it felt as if youth and happiness and spontaneity were all lost, old things, like the varsity jacket of her former husband that she had worn in high school and then after had hung in the closet. A relic, a trophy memory of the past. Something that could be slipped on inside but never worn outside again. How strange to be a young woman married to a middle-aged man who had become so old and frail before his time. To have lost all the sinew, the lust smells of youth and strength traded for weak flesh, the smell of aging skin, and shit, constant shit.

The house windows could not be opened to let fresh air in. The windows painted shut and covered with cheap storm glass, kept the disease and sickness in one's clothes and hair. The wood stove door could not be opened to let the smell of wood smoke drift throughout the house and cleanse the smell with aromatic cedar or pine. The ceilings were too low, and the home added on to carelessly that incense would not flow or circulate throughout the house. So, the smell of someone sick with diarrhea was constantly in her nostrils. The milk was spoiled, the air was tinged, her English muffins hidden and rationed out so long the edges turned green. She would cut the mold off and heat the stale bread.

Preacher Skelton used two passages for his sermon. He used Philippians chapter four verse twelve and Deuteronomy chapter twenty-eight. Marlene, in her stupor, followed along. Deuteronomy started so smoothly and comforting, then became horrible threats and fearful consequences. She felt as if that was her life. Something that started so sweetly. The image she had always had of herself of growing up and marrying her high school sweetheart. A warm, fulfilling dream. How it had changed. She felt so desperate, so old inside, clinging to a man who himself was an old, rugged cross. The image of Christ in her mind being crucified with his ribs showing, so thin, so frail, a crown of hope pushed like thorns into his head and bleeding. Bleeding from the wounds on his body. She could see Reggie now on the nightmare nights with his arms stretched like Christ, begging his father to let the suffering be finished.

Marlene stayed behind after everyone else when the invitational hymn was sung. She had watched Shane as he prayed and then lowered her head and closed her eyes. She slipped on the winter coat her mother had given her and gathered her things while waiting for Wanda to come down from the organ. They walked to the exit together, where Shane stood shaking people's hands as they left the auditorium. Marlene extended her hand to the large man. He took it softly. "Sister Marlene."

She nodded back. "Thank you." She said. "You know we live not far from Jon Joines's mountain. I could just go up there and get the money from him each week."

Shane looked over quickly to Wanda as if he needed her help. "Marlene, the lord does not want you to go up there to see Jon Joines at all," he said. "That wouldn't be right. The man's wife just died and that would look bad. A married woman going to a man's house that is not her husband. You see, the Lord is using Jon Joines right now to do his work. You know the Lord can use the unsaved for good. I think God is using Jon to draw him into the fold to use him for a bigger ministry. I want you to understand this is a delicate situation; we are talking about a man's salvation here. The fate of his eternal soul. Now Finn has certainly found favor in this man's eyes. Who knew that Finn would be such a powerful tool for God in all this?" Marlene was confused. How could the hired-out boy who needed so much of her correction and guidance actually be used by God?

"Brother Finn is an exceptional boy that needs to be cared for, Sister Marlene. Not only is he special to the old man, and to me obviously, and to Reggie's health, but he is special in the sight of God. Just imagine if we had a dozen more boys just like Finn. I don't know, but God is certainly showing me a new path of ministry. One that would abound in the rich blessings and yet keep us lean and focused on that path to Glory. Now, Sister Marlene, I have asked Sister Wanda to help me in this silent ministry. Each time Jon Joines bestows on your family a blessing, I will receive it from him and try, try without ceasing, to win him to the Lord. I will give that money to Sister Wanda, who will distribute it to you. Now, that's the Lord's will."

Marlene interjected. "But I feel like there is something I can do."

Shane raised his large hand. "Appearances, Sister Marlene. The devil will try to destroy this in any way he can. We must be careful. I cannot have direct contact with you because, as you know, it is wrong for a married man to be in contact with another woman. Can't even be in the same room with any woman that is not my wife." He raised his Bible to prove the statement as if the precept was in the book. "The devil has eyes and ears everywhere. Trust me now, this is what God wants." Marlene nodded her head. "Brother Reggie is not here tonight? I didn't see him."

"He's in Charleston on business. You know he has to go down there or up to Kingsport about every other week."

Shane responded with a sardonic smile. "Well." He extended his hand and received the slender hand of Marlene. "This is a secret ministry. Just the three of us know about it. I will not tell anyone, and no one else needs to know. God works in mysterious ways, often quiet ways. This money is meant for you." Marlene sighed deeply and felt as if she had suddenly been given a commuted sentence. She left the church and started home with her stepchildren and the boxes of food. She drove faster than usual, thinking of the meal she would prepare. Thinking of the bills in the church envelope. She reached the wheat hill house, immediately went into the bathroom, and closed the door. She set the large Bible on the vanity and opened its yellowed pages to the envelope. She tore it open and found a stack of twenty-dollar bills in front of her.

She felt cold inside. Colder than this part of the house. She felt like a killer. Like someone who was getting away with something. Here was the cash. The blood of hope for her life. How long would it last? She looked into the bathroom mirror and thought of the old man on his mountain of money. How far would she go for the old man to find worth in her as he did Finn? The faucet was dripping. How long would she have to patiently wait for there to be enough money for her to fly away? Couldn't the faucet just be opened? The money pour out of the old man like a fountain. Like a waterfall? What she would do to just to be alone with the old man for an afternoon. She could take care of him. Clean his house, and wash his clothes. He could sit and watch her. How much would that be worth to him?

She counted the bills and laid them across her Bible on the bathroom vanity. Power. Yes, this was power. Flexibility, strength, cash. She could buy English muffins and fill the car's gas tank. She could rent a hotel room and finally have privacy. She could buy something, maybe those Ferro Rocher chocolates that she always saw in the check-out line of BI-LO. She loved this feeling. This God. This God of money was real. You could hold it in your hands. You could tell someone to go fuck themselves if you had it. Maybe she wouldn't go back to her family in Kannapolis. Maybe she would save all this money up and then leave one night and drive all the way to Miami. Buy a string bikini with cash, and walk up and down the beach until the guys started talking to her. What would that power feel like? Strong men wanting her. Lusting after her.

She looked at herself in the bathroom mirror again and pulled the home-permed hair back with one hand. It fell behind her neck. She smiled into the mirror like she would smile at the shirtless men in Miami. Then she stopped smiling. She looked at the drab clothes she was wearing. The top buttoned up to her neck. The dress to her ankles with the wide belt. She breathed out in disgust at what she had become. She could change it if she could just hang on and be patient. She unbuttoned her top and pulled it down to see her breasts. She was still young. Reggie's hands still touched her in the night, but she wanted a man on top of her. A man hard and hot, and her wet, wanting to receive him. She gasped at the thought.

She turned from the mirror and leaned on the vanity. The thought of a muscular man and her hands on his ass pulling him into her and not letting him go until he was spent inside her . . . What kind of power would that be? What type of control this bit of money could bring her. God had sent this to her. God wanted her to enjoy life again. God had thought of her.

She put the money in the Bible. This was the safest place. She never laid it down. She looked back in the mirror, her face flushed, God's word in her hand instead of a young man's flesh. She felt ashamed of her lustful thoughts. She bowed her head and closed her eyes, searching but not finding the remorse that should be in her sinful heart. "God, forgive me." She prayed. Her stomach growled, and she remembered all the jars of potatoes and beans that Wanda had given her. She was hungry. She knew the kids were too. She flushed the toilet and washed her hands.

Finn had brought the boxes of food from the trunk of the car and laid them out on the kitchen counter. When Marlene leaned over the jars of food, she noticed her top was unbuttoned and stepped between the fridge and phone to button it. It wasn't long before Marlene called the kids to the table, and they feasted on white potatoes, green beans, and a loaf of homemade bread. Afterward, the dishes were cleaned and put away. It was late. Later than they normally stayed up. The house was cold, but they were full. Marlene wondered where she would hide the jars of food from Reggie. Would she have to lie? How would he react to someone from the church giving them food? Especially someone from the church where he wanted to portray an image. He couldn't handle that. What would he do? Would he stand up and testify to how much God had blessed him? Would he give away another month's rent?

She sat on the sofa in front of the wood stove with her head in her hand and the Bible on her lap. She would hide the jars of food in the bottom of her small closet and some under her side of the bed.

The dust ruffle would cover them. Tomorrow, she would go to BI-LO and buy a can of white potatoes and a large can of green beans. She would pay for the two cans with her own cash. She would open the cans tomorrow night for dinner but always leave them out on the counter like they had just been washed. Reggie would see them, and he would see the potatoes and beans on his plate and wouldn't ask questions. He'd just assume that she had found a good deal on the canned goods they were eating. He would actually be proud. Somehow, he was providing for his family. God was being good to them. It may actually help him feel better. Give him more self-confidence.

Marlene came to herself and realized the children were waiting for the traditional family devotion and then to be dismissed to their beds. Marlene called the children to her, and instead of sitting on the sofa, they chose the floor in front of her. She did not reach for the family Bible but decided to use her own tonight. She opened to the book of Proverbs, not far from the cash. It was not the thirty-first of the month, but she decided to read the thirty-first chapter. She read softly and wondered when Reggie might get home. She wondered why he usually came in so late at night. She used her finger to keep track of the lines she was reading and let them sink into her. "Who can find a virtuous woman? For her price is far above rubies."

When his turn came, Finn read, "Strength and honor are her clothing; and she shall rejoice in time to come."

* * *

Penny lay staring out the window at the moon and its rays sparkling across the lake. Jon kissed her lips and forehead. His fingers had traced rivulets of pleasure across her skin, and her whole body had come alive under him. He had kissed the side of her neck, and she instinctively kept turning into him and then ran her hand up the back of his neck and head and pulled him closer to her. She wanted him to kiss her chest. She didn't want him to stop. The fire blazed in the chimney just as she felt herself being consumed. She had never known how meaningful it could be to give yourself without expectation or reservation into the arms of someone you felt so secure with. She had brought him to the couch. She had wanted him to take her. Like a fawn shot through with an arrow, and in search of cool water, she, without hesitation, spoke her need. Hungry. Thirsty. His hands fed her. His mind seduced her. His voice was all she wanted to hear.

When she had sat on the couch, he had knelt, lifted her legs, and laid her out like Penelope in the arms of Odysseus. She was her own goddess becoming vulnerable in the arms of the man she hoped would love her. Sitting beside her, he covered her with a blanket. He said that he should go for tonight. That made her want him even more. She had asked him to stay. He seemed to think about it. Then he drew on her chest with the tip of his finger and up her neck and stopped. "I just need some time." He looked into her eyes, and she nodded. He had filled her to bursting and taken enough away to make her hunger again. He got up to leave, and her hand held his until he walked out of reach, and it fell back to the couch, and she watched him leave.

This was new territory. She had never been with a man who had just lost the love of his life and was desperately grasping for a way to hold on. She felt strange, bad in a way. As if she was robbing him from his grief. Stealing his attention away from his dead wife, but wasn't that the whole purpose? Wasn't that life? That death is the end. The old vows, the bonds done, completed? Weren't the living still supposed to go on and make the most of the time they had left? She wanted Jon, and she didn't like the feeling of competing for him, especially with a dead woman. How could she? Yet, she couldn't just let him walk away. She lifted the blanket and got up from the couch.

She walked to the door to lock it, but Jon had locked it before closing it. She wondered if he did that to be sweet or to stop all temptation to come back into the house for her? She had spent too much of her life hungry for love. She wanted him. She would give up everything to have him. She would leave the cottage, even sell it. She would sell CHIEF. She would move to Jon and his mountain, his cabin, and his vineyard. She would forsake all she had ever known to have one chance at true love. She felt her heart opening up a clear path to love, and she was bounding forward.

* * *

Driving home from Penny's, Jon could smell her fragrance on himself. He had kissed her, nothing more, but his heart had felt it was more. The moon was coming out behind the clouds, illuminating the fields like a searchlight sweeping the living crops for any who broke formation and were running away. He was old, yet the moon made him feel like a bastard. Like some teenager that had just licked the nipple of his girlfriend's breast and lifted his fingers to his nose to smell the scent of her sex again and again. "Goddamn, it." Jon lifted his eyes toward the moon that he had always associated with Elizabeth. The moon he had looked to on so many nights to connect with her while in far-off and dangerous places.

    He gripped the steering wheel, and it was as if he could still feel the soft flesh of Penny in his arms. It had been a different feeling, but it had been a wonderful and peculiar feeling. A part of him could have experienced that feeling in his arms all his life. That was a foreign feeling. Troubling and yet comforting. The way he could wrap his arms around Penny's frame and draw her into him. Something in the way she uniquely held on to him. Something that he wanted more of. He wanted to kiss every part of her. He wanted to know her, yet the moon shone on him. Seeing him. Would the shadows of the ancient trees hide him? "Goddamn it," he said louder.

He pulled into the driveway and got out of the truck. The wind blew so hard that it slammed the door shut. Jon closed his eyes against the wind. It reminded him of the old legend. The mighty wind meant some troubled soul had found a clear path to its love. "Fuck you."

He knew he should feed the fish children. He went for the barrel of corn, and as he passed the cabin door, he noticed a white envelope stuck in the door frame. He just stared at it and went to the barrel. He opened the lid and looked over at the paper. His first thought was that it could be Elizabeth's letter saying she was not dead, just like the letter he had sent to her after the gas shell had knocked him unconscious and over the ridge in the war. He looked at it as if it were a mirage in the distance. What else would she say? Would she say she forgave him? That if he came upstairs and made love to her and held her hand throughout the night just like the last fifty years, everything would be alright?

He walked to the pond and slung the corn wide into the moonlit sky. He watched it fall and spread out. The action seemed like the worth of his life now. Just one cast into the darkness hoping someone would stop and appreciate him. He never knew that he was so needy. He never knew that Elizabeth had done so much to keep him. She had treated him like some king, and he would just sit night after night in her glow and read, or draw, or write. How in the world did he not realize how precious every word and breath she exhaled was? He looked back at the door, and the envelope stuck in it. What could it be? No one came up to the mountain except for Bobby, and he was in town tonight. Jon walked back to the porch. He replaced the corn barrel lid, all the while looking at the note as if the wind would cause it to fly away. What was the deal with the wind lately, anyway? He had enough of it and nature's lessons. He pulled the envelope free from the door. He opened the door and turned on the light. The wind blew hard again. He shut the door, almost slamming it against the wind. Turning the envelope over, he saw in the corner "Beau Pre Baptist Church." Inside were receipts and a short note. Jon sat down in the booth and laid them out on the table. Receipts for food, clothes, and cash were given. For potatoes, beans, bread, and corn. The note, written in a shaky hand, said. "Hate I missed you. Just wanted you to know how the money for the boy was spent." Jon couldn't believe the pastor had taken him seriously and done what he had asked. Jon leaned back in the booth and saw the moonlight casting over the mossy yard. Elizabeth was smiling on him. She was happy that he had taken care of Finn. She knew Jon would take care of them in their next lives. He felt like this was enough to get him through the night, but he knew he would desperately be searching for more of something tomorrow.

* * *

Reggie turned off Hwy 26 onto New Cut Rd. He'd still have a few hours to lay in bed before sunrise. He'd shower and then lay down beside Marlene. Rub her back. She would roll over to him and lay her head on his shoulder. She was a friend now. Enough years had passed, and she had stayed with him. He guessed he could have spent more money and gotten a real diamond, but he didn't know if it would work out back then. Even on the wedding day, he had gotten up early and mowed the fields of the wheat hill house, not really having thought it would work out. He felt something would surely come up, and it would just be over. People would have seen him try with another woman and say it just didn't work out.

But then he got the call that they were about to leave. He had to call Pansy that morning and ask that she bring, his oldest son, to the church. Finn wasn't even there; too young. "And Pansy, would you mind picking up my house? I've got some guests coming this evening for a while." Reggie reached to the side of the seat and put more air into the suspension to ease the bumpy ride of the semi. The smell of diesel fuel was throughout the cab of the truck. Reggie looked back into the sleeper of the cab to where the cargo light was glowing. He could still see the sheets of the bed torn apart and smell the others' cologne. He stopped, as planned, at the next fuel station. He pulled the knob on the dash for the airbrakes, then reached back into the sleeper, gathered up the sheets, and threw them into the trash bin by the diesel pumps. He got back into the truck without refueling and pulled back onto the two-lane road that would lead him to the wheat hill house.

He looked up to the moon. A burst of wind hit the glass of the truck. He wondered where it came from. Looking towards the mountains, he could see faint lights in the distance. He felt a pain in his stomach and tried to ignore it. He shifted gears and then rubbed his torso. He wondered when the disease would win. This thing that he had been trying to ignore, to hide, to figure out. There was no getting away from it in his mind. He dreaded going home.

What was home? Every time he opened the Bible to read family devotions. He heard the Preacher's warning every time he went to church, even threatening to be sure your sin would find you out. Home was the debt of his past. Two marriages and children were an all-around failure. He slowed at the four-way stop. There were no headlights in any direction, and he just sat there behind the wheel of the giant truck, diesel fumes emanating from the leather binding of the steering wheel. He was alone in this disease. He always had been. Since the moment he refused, Dale Galimore invitation to backpack across Europe with him after high school. "They don't mind us there, Reggie. We can be normal, ourselves." Reggie shook his head. The idea and the place seemed so foreign. " I'm going to be late for my shift at the garage. You go, Dale, and let me know. Send me postcards."

What if he had gone? Just went and skipped it all. Skipped Vietnam. Skipped the social stigmas. What if he had taken that road? There would have never been a Pansy. Never would have been kids that needed so much food and money. No need for Marlene. There would have never been this disease because, well. "Dale would have been all I needed. There wouldn't have been others. But Dale's married now and seems happy. Well, he's not dying." He could see his thin reflection in the night glass and the glow of the dash lights. "Dale wouldn't want this. I don't want God judging him." Wasn't that it? God didn't make mistakes, so his being this way was his sin. Him pushing Dale away. Choosing Pansy as hopefully his cure. Choosing to have children as his cure. Choosing Vietnam as his cure. Divorcing Pansy as his cure. Choosing to be circumcised as an adult man as his cure. Marrying Marlene as his cure. And now this? A life of indebtedness leading to a horrible disease. God was chasing him down for something he felt he had no control over. He sat at the crossroads, the red light blinking in the dark night, alone.

Why not suicide? Why didn't he just shoot himself or hang himself? What was he really living for? A miracle? For Jesus to come back? For his family to finally find out the truth and hate him? For Marlene to leave him to waste away alone. For his kids to call him a Faggot and go to live with their mom, never wanting to talk to him again? Reggie let out the clutch, and the truck started rolling. What happens when the kids put it together? What would he say when they discovered why he had been discharged from the military? What would he do when they asked him if he had ever touched another man. What would they think of him when they envisioned him being with another man? Suicide looked so attractive. He could just go home. Get his pistol and walk out into the Moonlight of the wheat field. He could finally lay it all down. This pain in his abdomen would be gone. The hurting child within him would stop crying out. Reggie's lip quivered, and he felt a chill. He reached for the heater in the truck, but it didn't work. *Would the kids know then? I mean, really know the truth?* He began to think of what each would do in the wake of his suicide.

What if it didn't have to be that way? What if he could just stop, like the blinking red light at the crossroads. Just stop the business. Stop the lies. Just tell Marlene the truth. If she wanted to divorce him, then fine. If the kids couldn't accept him for what he was, then okay. Reggie could just be alone. Even move away, maybe to Venezuela. Lots of people like him moved away. That was the hope of freedom. He fantasized about freedom. Freedom to just be happy. It didn't change his love for his kids, or God, or Marlene, or even Pansy. He could probably love them all better.

He was getting cold. He was feeling weak. It was late. He turned on Mt. Lebanon Rd. The wheat hill house was just ahead. Reggie closed his eyes briefly, but then pain shot through his stomach. He was confused, like the moon and the stars were melting together. He pulled into the driveway of the wheat hill house, and the large tires of the semi rolled over the line of red rocks, crushing them into the fallow soil. He pressed the brake pedal, and the airbrakes brought the leviathan to a stop in the driveway. Like a long-distance runner collapsing before the finish line, he fell over the steering wheel, sweating yet shivering cold. With his head on the wheel, he reached for the dash and pulled out the airbrake knob. He choked the engine down and turned off the headlights. He opened the door and fell to the ground, trying to lower himself. He lifted himself from the steps built into the fuel tank and managed to close the cab door. Walking towards the house, he tripped over the pecan tree's roots.

He reached the door of the house and stumbled inside. Marlene came out of the bedroom in her robe. "I had a feeling." She said. Reggie looked at her and tried to smile. The thin man had left the day before somewhat stronger and taller and now had returned holding his stomach, sweating and shivering cold with fever. She helped him in. "Do you want to shower?"

Was it just the diesel she smelled on him? "Yeah, I better. Another fuel line busted. I'm so late." He said through clenched teeth. She helped him to the bathroom, and he stood leaning over the vanity, looking into the mirror as she undressed him. Steam began to fill the carpeted bathroom. The only way to wash him was to shower with him, so Marlene took off her robe. Carefully, tenderly, she cleaned him, and as she scrubbed away the grime, he leaned his head onto her chest and cried. His life was full of debt, yet his soul was so empty and cold it could only shiver in the steam.

She dried him off and helped him from the bathroom to the bed like a nurse helping a patient. Slow, shuffled steps toward his rest. She tucked him into bed and piled covers on top of him. The eyes rolled back in Reggie's head. The old friend of disease was coming around again. "Taxes, taxes, pay or debtors jail." The collector jingled his purse. "Taxes, beggars pay too. They breathe the King's air. Taxes for the King. Beggars pay an equal share or go to prison." How long would the hallucinations last? Another nightmare night? Another year at the NIH? He thought of the whole drawer full of medication in his bureau that didn't seem to be working again. Had he messed up and not taken them at the right time?

How long could he keep that from the kids? The thought of it was like a loaded gun pointed at his head. How long would the secret stay chambered like that? Maybe Jesus would come back before then. "Taxes, taxes for Jesus's love. Pay what's due or go to hell!" This disease of homosexuality was costly. What was wrong with him? Maybe he just wasn't truly saved. Maybe he just needed to be saved, right? Maybe call out to Jesus, and he would forgive the taxes, what was owed. People said they continually struggled with addictions until they were truly saved. He whispered in his delirium. "God, forgive me. Help me, please help me. Save me. I accept Jesus Christ as my personal Lord and Savior. Please, no more, no more, I can't pay. No more; just take me as I am or throw me away."

* * *

Finn woke up when his Father got home in the middle of the night. He could tell from the noises in the bathroom beside his bedroom that it wasn't good. He could tell he was sick. Finn always felt like he and everyone in his family were holding their breath, hoping Reggie wouldn't catch a cold or the flu. It affected him differently than other people. Finn had often tried to learn why this was, but he was always given the same generic response. Something had happened during a training exercise in the war. Some chemicals the Air Force sprayed had spilled and splashed up into Reggie's face. The substances had eaten holes through his liver. He just didn't have the same immune system as an average person. Finn would often have to repeat this over and over to people who wanted to know why his Dad was in the hospital again. Finn found himself repeating it now. "My Dad catches a common cold, and his body makes an antibody to fight it off, but instead of his white blood cells fighting the infection, they kill the antibody. So, the infection is allowed to run wild in his body. There are only thirteen cases even similar to it in the World. It's very rare."

The normal response was that people would say they hoped he would get better or they would pray for him. It just felt empty, like a lie. The only thing real about it was his hope for a miracle. Was hope the truth? His gut feeling said that it probably wasn't. He wondered if hope was the only thing that could make you forsake your gut feeling. Wanting something to be true and believing it to be true when it was wasn't true was like telling the World you were mixing mud pies in your wagon to sell as pancakes.

It was like Jesus weeping large drops of blood in the garden of Gethsemane, begging his Father to let the cup pass from him. He was distraught because he was mortal, fatherless, and passionately in love with the God who slept beside him, quelled his fears, and fed his immortal soul earthly food day and night. Jesus hoped he was immortal and that he was the son of God, even against his own gut feeling. He was afraid to die and to leave the God who had filled his heart with so much love.

Finn heard the door of the bathroom open. He could hear Reggie's labored breathing. The shuffling of his feet. He imagined a frail, pale man naked, shuffling down the short hallway to his bed. Marlene behind him, holding him up by his waist. A towel still in her hands to dry him once he lay down. Finn did not want to go through another nightmare night. He closed his eyes and prayed that God would heal his father. If a miracle was out of the question, then at least let him rest.

Later, Finn heard the door of his father's bedroom open. He could hear him struggling to the bathroom and then being sick. He could hear Marlene helping him back to bed and going to the kitchen for ice chips. He could tell it was not a good night, but he knew soon the sun would be up, and that would bring comfort to everyone. It was not likely that things would go really bad during the day. Usually, when the sun would come up in these situations, Reggie would finally be able to rest. As if the darkness of the night was a danger to be feared. Finn wondered why this was. How could a grown man panic in the dark? How could he only find the peace to sleep when the sun came up and he realized he had survived another day? He wondered how his father could be strong enough to travel out of town for a few days and then make his way back home only to become sick or at least depressed or remorseful each time he returned. It just didn't make sense. He was still lying in bed when he heard Reggie and Marlene make their way into the bathroom again. Finn got up and dressed. He could hear his father being sick. He wondered how it could even be possible for his father to have anything left inside him. Finn opened the door to his bedroom and looked down the hallway. He could see Marlene on her knees by the side of the bed with her hands folded, looking up into the eyes of God for mercy. Finn watched silently in the faint light of the early morning with the white plastic blinds still drawn. She was about to get up, and he moved back into his room to avoid contact with her, but soon a slight knock came at his door.

She came into the bedroom with the maroon Bible under her arm, and small handkerchief, and many tears in her eyes. She looked defeated and exhausted. "Finn." She said through tears. She walked over to him like a dog that had mistakenly bitten its master and sought forgiveness. Finn didn't say anything, but he stood almost as tall as she now. She laid her head on his shoulder and wept. Finn raised his arms around her shoulders, and she raised the handkerchief to wipe her tears. "I need your help." She looked up into Finn's eyes. "I can't lift him, and he's too weak." Finn looked into her bloodshot, defeated eyes and nodded.

"Okay." He said.

"I just need to get him back to bed. I will go in the bathroom and cover him up, then call you in." Finn nodded. The odor of sickness burned his nostrils and the corners of his eyes. He looked in his bedroom mirror, glimpsing his future. How could he do this without embarrassing his father?

"Okay, Finn."

The door opened, revealing Reggie sitting on the toilet. His bruised head rested on the window sill. Asleep and naked, the dawn lighted on him like the Earth remembered him as a child. Marlene had covered him partially with his robe. Finn took in the thin, rounded shoulders of his father. The soft skin that should smell sweet but had soured in fever. He walked over to Reggie and could see the fragile bones of his father nearly poking through the yellow skin. "How should I get him?" " Like this, under his shoulders like you're hugging him. Lift with your legs. Just watch the scars across his stomach. That's where they tried surgery and rerouted his biliary tree. The scars get really tender. Just mind them." " Okay, I will try." Finn's eye ran over the double rainbow arcing scars across Reggie's abdomen. "How could anyone survive that?" Marlene stood before Reggie in the narrow space between his knees and the tub. She looked at Finn, pursed her lips, and shook her head as if she didn't know. "Honey, Finn's here; he's going to help us."

Reggie looked up at Finn and started to cry. He turned his head towards the window and wept. "No, No, Oh no," he said. "Don't look, Finn. I don't want you to see me like this."

"I'm not Dad. I'm not. Hey, I promise. I only see the Giant within you." Finn put a hand under each arm of his father. To Finn's surprise, he could lift Reggie without much trouble. When he was standing, Marlene wrapped the robe around his waist and tied it. Reggie's arms were around Finn's shoulders now, and like two dancing in a tight embrace, they reached the promise light of the bedroom. As he laid Reggie down, he could feel the heat of his feverish body.

Reggie's hands found Finn's neck and fell down the arms. "You gettin' so big, son. You are my hero, boy." Finn looked into the sunken eyes beneath the feverish brow.

"I love you too, Dad. It's going to be alright. The sun's up now. You can rest." Reggie's eyes closed. He folded his hands across his chest as if practicing for a longer sleep. Finn turned to leave but Marlene blocked the door and hugged him immediately. In one way, he was as repulsed by her display of affection as the smell of sickness that stung the inside of his nostrils. In another way, having found worth in her sight was like a barbed lure being tossed in front of a hungry fish.

He left the room, but Marlene did not follow him. He expected her to say that it was time to start school for the day, recite the first chapters of Corinthians, and say the pledge of allegiance to the American flag and the Christian flag, but she had closed the bedroom door behind him. The house was quiet for several hours while Finn and his sister did their schoolwork. Occasionally they looked up at each other and couldn't help but look toward the closed bedroom door. Finn was happy that they both were sleeping. Maybe this was the way that Reggie would regain his strength this time. Maybe the fever would break, and he would be okay.

Near midday, the door opened, and Marlene said, "Finn." Finn got up, and as he approached the bedroom, Marlene gave him a hearty, rested smile and hugged him. "He needs to go back to the bathroom." Finn walked into the bedroom, and his father lay in bed, his robe tight around him like a medieval King laid out for burial. He opened his eyes as he felt Finn's presence. Ice chips melted in a glass on the table. Finn lifted his father's back from the bed and gave him a moment to get his feet on the floor. From hospital habit, Reggie's arms surrounded Finn's shoulders. Finn raised up, lifting Reggie from the bed. Too weak to walk, the frail man clung to Finn in a hugging embrace.

Along with chores and school work, Finn had to stay near to take his father in and out of the restroom. Marlene was willing to undress him and see to him while he was indisposed, but the lifting and lowering of the man, even in his diminished state, was too much for her. It troubled Finn to be in the bathroom with his father exposed and naked, having his bottom wiped for him. What if Finn inherited this unknown disease? What if Finn would be this frail at forty, having his bottom wiped for him? Finn decided that would not be the life he would ever have. He would never be old and frail. He would make sure to die young and strong. Finn was so afraid of this rare disease that he knew he would take his own life at the first sign of it in himself. He would go to Skyuka's Rest and jump.

Finn set Reggie down on the toilet and left the bathroom. A few minutes later, he was called for again. He returned, the smell stinging his nostrils, the window sill showing wear as the weary head lay there as all life seemed to flee from him. Marlene preparing praise for the future nurse. Marlene entered the kitchen with jars of beans and potatoes. He held his breath when she walked behind, knowing she was looking over his shoulder at the school book. Instead, she rubbed his back, shoulders, and arms. Her touch felt strange to Finn even though he had lived with her most of his life and called her Mother. Her hands felt hard and unpracticed in love for him. Like now, she was forcing it. Like some aunt who jerks your ears, messes up your hair, and doesn't know your birthday. It was not real. He remembered Jon saying that true love was like the water of the fountain flowing over you. Marlene's hands were like the sharp edges of wire-cut bricks.

She opened the jars and began to heat them on the electric stove. She took out the loaf of homemade bread and began cutting large toast slices. When lunch was ready, and bowls of steaming food were placed on the table, she extended her hand and asked Finn to say the blessing. He did so in a memorized and robotic way. Saying all the correct and acceptable things, and then he paused. He felt Marlene's hand in his. He decided to empty his own soul into the waiting ears of God. He asked God to let this cup pass from his Father. He asked to let the cup pass from Marlene and even from himself. He asked with desperate hope for a miracle. "But if not, God. Then I ask for strength and wisdom beyond my years. For if not my will, then thy will be done. In the name of the Father, the Son, and the Holy Ghost, Amen."

* * *

"Daddy, Daddy, can you hear me?"

"Jaime, you there?"

"I'm here, Daddy; the connection is bad. Where are you, Daddy?"

"I'm out in the Fellowship hall, son. I was looking for some privacy from these people down here."

"How's the revival going, Daddy? You and Momma enjoying Tampa again? I love that church down there. So many good memories. But why you out in the Fellowship building? Couldn't you use one of the church offices to call?"

The line was quiet on the other end, and Jaime Skelton looked to see the quality of the connection. "Daddy? Can you hear me?"

"Lord told me to come out here and pray awhile for y'all back home and the service tonight. That's actually why I'm calling you Jaime. How did everything go tonight, you know, with the service and all?" Shane prepared to hear his son's usual dramatic response.

"Daddy, oh, the Lord only knows where you get these Preacher Boys. Berry was going to preach tonight in your stead. The choir finished we had a special music; everything was going fine, and then he comes prancing up the altar steps like he's the new Pastor. Everyone in the congregation could see he went out and bought a pair of black Florsheim ankle boots like yours. Now let me tell you, he gets up there. Reads his passage, right. Begins to sweat and slings it over everything. Pulls his jacket off, takes his tie off, pulls out a handkerchief, sticks in his belt line, and hangs it down the front of his pants. Starts prancing around the front of the church like some whore in a mini-skirt. He preached for over an hour. I thought Brother Walker was going to die of hemorrhoidal distress. He stood up to say Amen and kept standing for ten minutes, holding on to the pew. Like a bumble bee was boring a hole through his seat. I thought we were going to have to take up an offering just to shut him up."

Shane could imagine the frustration that his polished banker son had to go through in his absence. "Jaime, did you do what I asked you?"

"You mean to lead the church while you are down there preaching revival?"

"Jaime, boy. Did you give that money to the Kindhart lady? Make sure Wanda got the food to her. It's important. Did you now, say?" "Yes, yes! Daddy, Daddy, what's got you all worked up? Yes, I took care of it. You know I always do. Though it disgusts me, uh, I just can't look at Reggie, and for the life of me, I don't understand why you are doing this. It wasn't just six months ago that you said the Lord would probably lead them elsewhere, and here now, you giving them money every week. I just don't get it, Daddy. You feed an old mangy stray, and he's going to keep hangin' around. I mean, God just hasn't called us to minister like that. You know to minister to people with infirmities. Especially to queer folk like that. God doesn't even send colored people to us. I see Beau Pre as a church of self-sustainable believers. You know, good Christian people that believe in how things used to be. Daddy, do you really want your grandchildren to be around people with diseases like that? Scabs all over them. They're just unclean to me.

Shane was satisfied to hear that Marlene had been given the money and vegetables. "You had sister Wanda give her the vegetables and money? Reggie wasn't around, though, right?

"Yes, Daddy. I just can't make sense of you most of the time."

Shane wondered how much he should tell his son. "Jaime, I know you are right about what you are saying, but God has been working on me. He's made me think different of late about that boy."

"What, boy Daddy?"

"Finn. I think God has something special for him. I think God might be working through him. We may need to consider that Finn might just be the young man we need to groom to take over the ministry at Beau Pre one day. Or at least we need to be thinking ahead. A continuance plan and such." "For the church, Daddy?" "No, rather, God's blessings on our Family's endeavors."

"I don't see how he plays a part in that picture, Daddy. That boy has a way. Some kind of way that gets under my skin. I don't know what it is, but I want to spit whenever I see him. I think he's dirty, just like his Daddy. That's disgusting. A man to let himself be sick like that."

Shane let his son finish his rant. He, too, had an aversion to anyone old, sick, or disabled, but he knew that Finn was the key to successfully acquiring the mountain from Jon. "Listen to me now, Jaime. Do you remember in Scripture about the lepers at the pool? You know the lepers were too weak to reach the pool when the Angel of the lord troubled the waters. You know, if they could get to the water and even just touch the water while the Angel troubled them, they'd be healed, but so many were too weak. They could see salvation, but they couldn't reach it on their own. They needed someone pure to help them. They needed a Samaritan, so to speak. Someone willing to help them reach the healing waters of Jesus. That's what I'm saying here, son. God may be asking us to go and be around these unclean so that he can use them for his service. Now this has been going on for most of the winter. I don't care so much about Reggie, but for some reason, God has been sending sustenance for that boy, and until there is a clear answer to his will, we must carry on in this work."

"The Lord's will you say, Daddy?"

"Yes, son. Now just imagine if we had a dozen Finns? Say, a whole home full of unwanted boys like him. Now just imagine what a powerful force for funding that would be? Especially at the camp meetings, people would see those boys as strong, mindful, and in need. They'd open their pocketbooks and support a ministry like that. Not to mention the government funding."

"Government funding. Like for a boy's home, Daddy?"

Pastor Shane turned around and looked across the empty fellowship hall. Satisfied he was alone, he said, "Yeah, I bet the government would send Eighteen hundred a month for each boy. Then think of the love offerings and monthly support from other churches. Besides that, you could organize them into work crews. Hire them out for love offerings like they do the chain gangs down in Texas."

"Oh, my Daddy. Now I never. My, who knew faith could bring in so much profit."

"That's what I'm saying, son. Here we've had all this infrastructure under our noses not being utilized. The old church building, the old fellowship hall, the dormitories. We've got the new place with a commercial kitchen and classrooms. Now, we have to start small, but just think about where the Lord will lead us. It's just like Lester Roloff and his girls' home down in Texas. I feel foolish now. God has been leading us to this ministry, and I just didn't see it until Finn came along."

"Now, Daddy, you know I admire Lester Roloff and what he's done with all those girls mixed up in drugs and prostitution, but you know the government is after him. Says he's chained those girls up and starved them. Some claimed to have been well, you know."

"Jaime, you know the devil is in the government. And you know that girl was possessed. They tried to help her kind, but it just wasn't God's will. Rollof said it himself that God wanted them to only minister to fairer-skinned girls. Brother and Sister Roloff have taken those harlots to raise like their children; God's blessed them for it. Brother Roloff's even got a private plane now. Imagine that, Jaime. Imagine how good God's blessings are going to be, son. You there, Jaime?"

"Yes, Daddy. What you say is, well, it's powerful, Daddy. You know I like the work at the bank, but I feel, well, I feel not entirely satisfied. Like there is more. Like more meant for me to do, Daddy. Hungry, I am. Hungry for God to use me. I work at the bank with all those disgusting sinners. Then even at our church, we have these people like David Childs. Moaning on and on about sickness and money. These people disgust me. Don't they know that God doesn't want to hear that mess over and over. They're just not Christian, not like us; you can't tell me they have faith. That they know God like us. I just want to lead and teach. Raise up an Army for God that think like we do. They'd blow up a building full of sinners if they had to. Just get rid of the filth." "God's going to use ya, son. We are going to be home soon. They going to take up the love offering Thursday night, then we will be on our way home."

"How much you reckon you'll get, Daddy?"

"Hmm, the agreement was twenty-two hundred for the week plus additional for every soul saved. We've had right many get right with God and about four saved. I believe that the Lord will lead them to see clearly.

"How's Momma doing?"

"Hmmm. The Woman about to poot herself silly eating all this Gulf seafood. Stabbed herself in the hand with a clam knife. She'll be alright. All these women down here doting on her taking her shopping and all during the days. So, Jaime. We can't lose sight here. This leper's son, Finn, is the key to all future blessings. God is using us to get him near that pool.

"I understand, Daddy. I will keep things going until you get back. Just remember, Daddy when God starts to pour on those blessings. I need more on my plate. Get off this dirt hill."

CHAPTER 20

"Draw me, and I will run after Thee."

Elizabeth led Jon up the path from the Salt pond. The setting sun was in their eyes, and occasionally, they stopped and shared water from a leather skin and turned back around to look over the azure water of the bay and the sailboats at anchor. They held each other's hands and continued over the hill and down the small rock path to the white sand streets of the Island town. On one side of the street was the white beach, fishing boats, and the open bay, and on the other side were small homes and some businesses selling fruits and vegetables or complete meals.

They made their way down the sand street to the white concrete customs house to check-in. Children ran up to them, and Elizabeth held out her hands and swung around in large circles dancing with them. Jon lifted her camera over her floppy straw hat, stood back in the white sand street, and snapped pictures of her dancing. He gave the children coins, and they ran back each to their own waiting mother.

The old customs house doors and windows were open, letting in the sea breeze. Street sand was sprinkled across the old, tiled floors. No one was in the office. They called out, and no reply came.

On the street, a local said the officials were napping and to come back later. They heard noises from the upstairs apartments of the customs house and realized that it housed the local brothel. With seductive eyes and sultry moves, Elizabeth began to flirt with Jon. She stood in the doorway and uncovered her leg from the Sarong around her waist. She bit the end of her finger. She stretched her arm up the door frame of the house, and Jon laughing, stepped back and snapped more photos of her.

He heard the bell of a lobster boat ringing from the surf. He turned quickly and looked down the long wooden pier stretching into the bay. He couldn't see the boat. He looked down at the camera window before him, but it seemed the image of Elizabeth was fading like sand was covering glass. He shook it, but it disappeared more. He looked up at Elizabeth to tell her to wait and not move, but the bell kept ringing, and he turned again to find the vessel. He stole a glance at her in the doorway, but she was being blown away, mixing with the sand of the street, her eyes full of fear and reaching out to him to save her.

Jon sat straight up in bed. The phone was ringing, and as he went to grab it, he knocked over the empty bottle of wine he had been drinking when he came to bed. "Jesus."

"Nope, sorry to disappoint. It's Upton Peace. I thought you may have forgotten, Jon. We had a meeting this morning at 8:30 to go over your estate planning. Is everything alright?"

"Oh shit. Sorry, Upton. I don't know how I overslept. I'm really sorry. Do we need to reschedule, or can I come over now? I can be there in about forty-five minutes." He hadn't forgotten the meeting. He assumed he would wake up with the sun or when the dove came to the window.

"Umm, yeah, Jon. If you can make it soon. I've got a tee time after lunch."

"Okay, Upton, I will be over directly." Jon slid out of bed. He briefly thought about the dream with Elizabeth. He remembered that day crystal clear. The part about her turning to ashes and blowing away was a recurring nightmare since he picked up her cremated ashes. The empty wine bottle had left small drops of red wine on the carpet. Jon knew he had to remove them. He went to the bathroom and he looked in the mirror. He almost didn't recognize the man he had become. He seemed unkept and wild. Like a thoroughbred horse who was brushed every day but suddenly turned out to be free.

He went back to clean the wine, and as he knelt down, he remembered the fine line of crimson blood that ran out of Elizabeth's mouth while she lay there. He closed his eyes and took in deep breaths. He lifted his head and kissed the wood box of her ashes on the bedside table. He let his mind drift back to the sailboat beneath the moon and how he had kissed her that night, moved her hair with his hand, and kissed her neck. Never had he known more serenity than when his lips touched her skin. "I love you, baby. I love you with all my heart."

He wondered if he smelled like wine. He remembered Penny was supposed to come over after her shift at the Bantam Chef. This was going to be the first night she stayed with him at the cabin, and he looked around at all Elizabeth's things that were still where she left them. He was sinking. This is not what he wanted. Why did he drink? This was all his own fault. How deep of a pit was depression, and why was he letting himself compound it with drinking?

He had wanted to spend an entire day just appropriately packing up Elizabeth's things. Did he really want to? No. Was he ready to? No, but having Penny in his life was something he felt like he needed. She was a life ring. Without her, he would never move forward. He was going to take a chance at healing; to do that, he had to put Elizabeth's things away. Maybe not away away but just out of sight so Penny would feel more comfortable. He looked at the purse and the hat boxes. It was all too much. He would have to come back after his meeting with Upton and do it.

He dressed, grabbed the paperwork he needed, and went downstairs and straight out the door onto the porch. The dove was there on the table, waiting patiently. Jon's hands were full. He was in a hurry, but no matter what was happening, he would always stop for her. He set everything down, went to the barrel, crushed the corn, and came back over and set down. The dove cooed for him. She ate from his hands and nuzzled them. He knew that today was the first step in getting back to Elizabeth. Today he would start his plan to secure the mountain and the sawmill as their home to be doves together. This was the start of his last hourglass full of sand, and when it ran out, he would be here beside her in the morning light. Jon whispered to the dove. "Does that sound good?" He waited for her cooing. "Say?" The dove, having fed, flew away.

The Lawyer's office was on Main St. in Saluda beside the old train station. Jon parked out front. A bell on the door chimed as he walked into the office, and Upton appeared. "Hey, Jon. Come on back and sit down." Jon apologized profusely, but Upton waved his hand and said, "I've got plenty to do. It's not a problem. My mother is elderly and still lives alone. I'm trying to line up some doctor's appointments for her, and then I will drive up there and spend a few days and take her to them. It's what children do for their parents, am I right?"

Jon looked at him and smiled. As an orphan, the thought of caring for aging parents had never crossed his mind. "I will take your word for it."

"No parents?"

"No. And no children. Actually, that's why I wanted to see you. I need a will or something of that sort. I really don't know what I need, but my wife passed away, and I was swamped with paperwork. I had no idea how difficult that would be, especially in a grieving state. I just want to have things done and easy. You know, so that when I pass away. Well, I don't want to be a burden to anyone."

"I see. I'm sorry for your loss Jon. Was your wife ill?

"No, never in her life. She died in her sleep. Died in my arms."

Jon could feel himself becoming emotional. He looked out the window of the office briefly. Upton gave him a second.

"Jon, in order to advise you on what you need, I'm going to ask you some questions. There is no right or wrong answer. I need to know about your assets and your general wishes." Jon listened and answered Upton's questions. The lawyer would scratch out information as it came from Jon onto a yellow legal pad. Jon kept noticing the clock. There was plenty of time before Upton's tee time. "Jon, it sounds to me that with what all you own and what you want to do, we need to set up a Trust for you. It's the best vehicle. We can tailor it to fit your needs specifically. Now one thing in a trust is we can define your medical care if you become incapacitated, say in an accident. You can designate someone to be your proxy. Make a decision about your care. Whether or not to give life support. A feeding tube, blood, oxygen."

Jon started shaking his head. "No, no, I just want to die. I don't want anything done to preserve or prolong my life. I want to move on."

"What now, Jon? I mean, there are times when life support can allow you to recover. You could go on living the rest of your life, Jon. I don't understand why you wouldn't want that. You look to me to be very healthy. Have you received some type of news from your physician?"

"Betts and I were married for nearly fifty years. I just can't." He stopped. "I don't want to live longer than I have to without her." Upton slowly nodded. He leaned back into his chair and pushed the pad of paper forward. "True love of some sort, huh? Some people live their whole lives without knowing what that really is. Listen, Jon. I am going to start drawing up this paperwork. Give me a couple of weeks. Then we will get together and review the other details of who, what, and where with your assets. I'm going to check into this preacher. That's an awful lot to leave to one person or group. You know, most people break it up over different charities. I will need some paperwork from them. I will give you a call when I've got things firmed up."

Both men stood and shook hands. "Thank you, Upton."

"Jon, you okay? You feeling alright? You haven't had a nervous breakdown or been declared insane by a physician? Are you feeling suicidal?"

"No, I'm fine, you know. Just dealing with grief. I miss Elizabeth very much. It's hard now just living with her shadow. Things that she used or touched and never will again. Trying to learn to walk or even learn how to breathe again. I feel like I'm stumbling. Every breath just seems deep and cold. Everything around me seems to be moving forward, and I'm standing still, frozen in time. I have these dreams where Elizabeth is in front of me, and then the next second is turning to sand and disappearing. I wake up underwater somehow, trying to collect all the pieces of sand and put her back together."

"Jon, you said you don't have kids or family?"

Jon shook his head. "Just my brother Bobby."

"I can't represent you if you have been diagnosed as insane. Since you haven't seen a doctor, we will move forward, but I want you to think more about the Living Will and life support. I also want you to consider the beneficiary of the mountain and the money. That is a tremendous asset to give to this preacher and church. You are not even a member there." Jon nodded his head.

Jon got back into the truck and stuck the key into the ignition but did not turn it. He could feel the red wine from the night before, but his mind seemed cold and clear as any stone knob on the mountain. He could think through his life, through his grief. He approached it just like he did the enemy in the war, but here he found himself ungrounded. He first had to know himself to defeat his enemy, and he was failing. He had come here today to plan the most significant moment of his life. A way to protect the mountain and the Sawmill, the future home of the doves where he and Elizabeth would be together in the afterlife but the only thing that came to his mind now was his obligations to Penny. Every nerve in his body was tender.

He had told her that he would prepare dinner for them at the cabin tonight, and they could spend a couple of days together. But how? Why? What was this inside of him? On one hand, he was literally planning out his afterlife with his deceased wife, who he dreamed of day and night, and then there was this part of him that was so concerned about now, about tonight, about being touched. He was concerned about keeping his word to this other woman whom he really wanted as company more than as a lover. That thought made him sicker than the wine had the night before. When did he start putting half-hearted concerns first ahead of his whole heart? What did Elizabeth think of him now? Did she still want him to always come back to the mountain? Did she still hope he could find someone he could be happy with? Was that it? Was she the only person he could still trust? Why did she say that so long ago, sitting on the wagon? " Why didn't she say. Find healing in the nature of the mountain? Or is that what she meant when she said there was a lot of love here?

Jon looked at the roof of the truck and scratched his head. And why did he drink? He used to draw and read in the evenings, but now all he did was sit and stare at the hourglass of his life and wonder why it wasn't moving. He wanted to see it nearly empty. He wanted to see those little plumes of dust swell up inside the glass of his life that said the end was near, but it didn't happen. His heartbeat was like a taut drum. He shook his head and wiped his nose.

Regardless, Penny was coming to the mountain in a few hours, and he needed to go shopping and then home to somehow pack away the sacred items of his love. How was he supposed to do that? Pack away the items someone you loved treasured and just put a lid on them, like an alabaster bookend on a basement shelf. Jon wasn't built like that. In a perfect world, he would be able to keep Elizabeth's things out in the cabin. The photos of the hat boxes, her godmother's journals. Jon could say to someone. "These were my wife's things. I love her very much, and I miss her. I understand that she is dead. I understand that finality, and I am trying to find my way forward. But you see, she was not only my lover but my best friend. These things bring me comfort. They don't really make me sad they make others sad when I tell them how much I miss her. So, is it okay if I leave them here? If I smile when I pass them or briefly reach out to touch them?" Why did he feel that he needed to ask permission from others to have his wife's things about their cabin? To Jon, Elizabeth's things were just as vital to the cabin as the door post or chimney flue. Her things were what made up the home for Jon. This was his home because Elizabeth had lived there because her things were still there. The truth was that Elizabeth was his home. If he removed all her things, he would destroy the shelter of his own heart. Without the amulet of Elizabeth, Jon would need to build shelter from the fragile walls of his heart. That seemed an arduous task. It may be cowardly, but it would be easier to just die and skip the demanding pain of looking inside himself and rebuilding a new home. "The Bedouin doesn't die from thirst. He dies because he loses his way to the next sacred well."

Jon looked into the rearview mirror of the truck. He saw the restaurants and grocery stores on Main Street. He picked fresh greens, lemons, garlic, onions, and pine nuts. A smooth cheese, flatbread, and balsamic. Wine, both white and red. A new bottle of bourbon. He looked at the cigarettes. Did Penny smoke? He had never smelled smoke on her or tasted it in her kiss, but he wanted to taste smoke in a woman's kiss again. He picked up a pack of the kind of cigarettes that Elizabeth had smoked. He thought that sometime when Penny wasn't at the cabin, he could light one and just let it smolder in the air to smell that fragrance again on the side porch. Everything fit into two brown paper bags. Jon placed them on the passenger side of the bench seat. The wind blew, and the heavy door of the truck pinned him for a moment. *Winter is really not giving up easy this year.*

Driving home from Saluda, he didn't listen to the radio. He would need to move Elizabeth's purse and probably the flannel shirts. He needed to move her ashes from the bedside table. He would place the small notes Elizabeth had filled the yellow book of poetry with back in the book and store it away. Change the sheets and wash the coverlet. Pack up Elizabeth's lotions, shampoos, makeup, and her robe. How could he do this in just a few short hours? How could he tear down the home that love built around his heart and pretend it was okay? Everything was sacred.

How would Penny feel coming to his home with a bag of her things? How would she feel lying down in the bed where Jon's wife had died? How would she feel looking in the mirror that had only reflected Elizabeth's gaze? How would Jon make love to another woman when his heart and mind were still in love with a dead woman? But he wanted Penny to come. He thought of the moment when she would arrive. Him walking out to meet her. Smiling at her sharing a small laugh. Leaning down and bringing her fully into his chest. Feeling the shape of her back in his arms while she embraced him hard. Her hands across his shoulders, not wanting to let go of him. In his mind, he could feel her hands touching him. Those hands knew the language of love, and they did speak to him. He wanted that. He wanted her lips, the soft skin of her neck and chest. He wanted the comfort and softness that she would bring. He wanted her presence in the house, around him, touching him, on him. Like a drug or a healing ointment, he wanted that. He wanted all that enough to tear down the old shelter of comfort that his heart had known for the hope of healing that maybe, just maybe, someone else could bring to him.

  Jon turned onto the gravel driveway and looked over the sea of grass. The sun had broken through the winter clouds, and as it descended upon the grass, the mighty wind from deep in French Valley moved across the grass like a wave. He wondered if it would ever blow again for him? He wished in some way that the mountain and the sea of grass could close their eyes. Maybe not have to see him be unfaithful to Elizabeth. That the ancient trees, the old root cellar, the fountain that never ran dry, all those living things could close their eyes and not see him reach for another woman's hands, take another woman in his arms to love. That the fish children and the wooden walkways, the moss-covered stone, and the limestone staircase wouldn't see the same warm glow of love coming from the cabin, and if they did, then hopefully, they would see Jon's conflicted heart also. Or did all of nature see it as a new beginning? Were they so old and wise that they had been there before? How many times had people fallen in love with someone in front of the fountain only to lose them in the meadow? How many times had the Fish Children escorted the glowing leaf of some Chief of Peace across the pond and over the granite dam? Didn't the Cherry trees always bloom on that last bitter cold day when it seemed nothing new could ever happen again? Was he lying to himself? The trees lost their beloved leaves and food source only to rebirth in tender green each spring.

With the groceries put away, Jon reached for the flannel shirts. He scooped them up in his arms and smelled them. Her scent was gone. The realization stopped Jon in his tracks. He smelled them again, but her scent had disappeared into the ether. They were just shirts now that she used to wear. That used to smell like her, but even the air was stealing her away. He decided he could leave them hanging there. He moved on into the great room. He didn't want to pack up the items she had on display, but he thought that he could at least remove some of the photos. Maybe set them over on the piano where they wouldn't be so prominent. He could always move them back when Penny wasn't there. He hated the idea of a double life but didn't know what to do.

He left those photos on the staircase that showed Bobby, Ruby, Elizabeth, and him together. He lifted one from the wall of Elizabeth, young, naked, curled up in the forecastle of the sailboat, looking longingly to the wine-blue sea. He held it in his hands and then kissed it as if kissing her body again just after he did when he took the photo. He looked at the empty space on the wall and then reluctantly, with his fingertips, pulled the small, slender nail from the wall. It was as if not only removing the memory of his beautiful love but also all hope of it ever being true again. He took the photo upstairs.

He took the wooden box containing Elizabeth's ashes from the bedside table and brought it to his chest. Every time Jon closed his eyes and kissed its cold surface, his mind went back to a night when he had undressed Elizabeth in the moonlight. He had turned her around. Moved her hair to the side and softly kissed her neck. This was paradise. He didn't need lips or the sense of touch to remember how it felt to have his lips against her skin that night, her body in his arms. Jon looked around the bedroom for a place to safely place her ashes. He thought of the Armoire, but locking her away in the dark closet felt wrong. He took the box carefully downstairs and over to the bureau where he normally stacked his clothes. This was a good spot in the great room beside the window. When Penny left, he would bring her back to their bedroom and place her beside him again.

There was a knock at the porch door, and Jon turned surprised because he did not think Penny would arrive so early. He hadn't put all of Elizabeth's toiletries in the bathroom closet. He opened the door and saw the wind making old leaves dance across the yard. Not seeing anyone, he stepped out the door, looking towards the driveway. "Preacher?" The large man was standing at the end of the porch and looking towards the sea of grass. His back was towards Jon, and it seemed he had not heard Jon's voice. The wind was cold, but Jon, still thinking about all he needed to do before Penny arrived, walked to the end of the porch wearing only his thin button-down shirt.

The large man turned and smiled at Jon like he was an old, trusted friend. He looked back at the large meadow like he was seeing the souls of all those who had called the meadow home for thousands of years. "Every time I see that field, I can't help but see its potential."

"Potential?" The wind pierced Jon's shirt, and the cold made his eyes water. "It's been a field since time immemorial. I can't think of—"

The preacher raised his large hand. "Potential is what you ain't done yet."

Jon wiped the tears from his eyes. His nose was running. The wind crossing the open field was biting, and yet here this preacher stood like Aaron telling the feeble children of Israel to forsake the God they knew for another they could create and, therefore, control.

"Jon, every time I see that meadow, I think of the giant pond it could be. Filled with spring water from the mountain. Full of fish, just like that small pond back there. Full of life and reflecting the sun. Reflecting the son of God."

The man seemed lost in himself, and Jon turned and looked into the wind and out across the field of grass he had always known and loved. He had never thought of digging it up and carrying the topsoil away. He pictured the steel blade of a motor grader turning corkscrews of earthbound grass over and over. Hundreds of yards of spiraled grass. Thousands of years of sedimentary gravity consumed.

"I see children out there." The preacher raised his hand as if smoothing out the field. "Canoes and paddleboats. Maybe a swim area for boys and another for girls." He looked over at Jon. "Potential. Potential is what you have the ability to do, but you ain't done it yet. You've got the ability to turn that old field into something incredible, Jon. I've seen what you can do. I've seen these ponds you've built. That vineyard you got over there in the valley." He lifted his leg, rested one of his ankle boots on the porch boards beside Jon, and leaned towards him. "I know that field is beautiful. Beautiful to any creature of God that drives up here and sees it, but what if hundreds of people could enjoy it. Do something there that would fill it full of life." The preacher reached into his pocket, pulled out a small envelope, and handed it to Jon. "Kids like Finn could come up here and spend time on that field if you turn it into a pond. You could turn that old Sawmill into dormitories and even build cabins up the mountain and over the valley. Now imagine how happy that would make your wife." Jon took the small envelope. "How's Finn doing?"

The preacher's face suddenly changed. "Oh, I think he's fine. You know he sings in the choir and sits on the front row at church. Now, he's quiet, you know. He has a few friends, but he's not like most boys. You know he's more serious-minded." Jon was rocking back and forth to stay warm. "I think he's got a serious life. You know he doesn't know when to stop working. Most boys his age are out throwing rocks in the parking lot and chasing girls. He always comes in and carries out the trash and then helps with the tape ministry we have." The preacher shook his head. "He even fixes people's cars in the parking lots." He ran his fingers over his black and white hair. "He came in the other week and had bandages on his hands. Folks say the boy was riding his bike home from raking leaves, and a school bus came flying up beside him, and all the kids piled off yelling, "Snake." Even the driver of the bus took off. They said Finn just walked inside the bus and hunted that snake down. The snake bit him three or four times, but he just came walking off the bus with it. Showed it to everyone and then turned it loose in the ditch." Jon laughed. "Sounds like Finn." The preacher started laughing. He seemed very relaxed around Jon as if the months of weekly meetings and conversations had built rapport with him and a trusting friendship. He stopped laughing and became serious. "Now, his Daddy. I'm afraid he's poorly. Reggie comes to church quite regular, but lately, he hasn't been able to. So, I went over and stopped by their house. Sister Marlene opened the door and uh," he looked down at his ankle boots, "well, I hate to say this about anyone. Especially church people, but uh, just a foul odor, foul, I tell ya. I mean unto death. She tried to invite me in. To come in and fellowship with Reggie. Again I hate to say it, but I just couldn't. My stomach was turning. I just gave her that money, and she took it and was very appreciative. I dare say that they wouldn't have nothing if it wasn't for you. Probably no food, either. She told me that Reggie may have one more opportunity to go back up to the National Institutes of Health in Bethesda."

 Jon knew he had to love Finn because Betts wasn't here to love him herself. He felt responsible for his care, and he knew Elizabeth would be proud of him for caring for her Skyuka Child that she was given in her last season of life. "You be sure to let me know if that happens," Jon said. He went into the cabin to retrieve another cash envelope for the preacher to deliver to Finn's stepmother. When he turned back around, the tall preacher was about to enter the cabin as if he had visited for many years. Jon said, "Sorry but I'm expecting a guest this evening." The preacher looked shocked. Jon stepped back onto the porch and closed the door. He held out the envelope. "For Finn. I trust you to get this to his people?"

The preacher nodded, taking the envelope. "Say you got a guest coming up? Didn't think you had any family."

"I don't, to speak of. My brother. This is just a friend."

"Uh-huh. A friend." The preacher slid the envelope into his pocket and stood there awkwardly. "Well, I wouldn't want to keep you from what must need doing before your company arrives." He turned to walk away at a snail's pace and paused at the end of the porch. "You know I love this mountain more and more." Jon nodded at him. "You know those two motor graders you got out there by the barn would make smart work of that field. Turn it into a pond."

Jon just wanted the man to leave, but he clung to the end of the porch like a wart on the edge of a hand. "One hasn't been cranked in a long while."

The preacher just nodded his head. "Looks like here comes your company. Your friends." He nodded to a car that had just appeared from the tree line and was on the gravel road at the far end of the meadow. The car was slowing.

Jon walked to the edge of the porch. He sighed deeply. He just wanted Shane gone, but he was lingering. Jon looked around his bulk and saw Penny's Opel coming up the gravel drive. "Well, I guess you better head out," he said. There was a sardonic smile on the large man's face. No one knew about him and Penny spending time together except for close friends. Having him there now with Penny coming to spend the night was embarrassing, and more, it seemed like a sin in front of this Preacher. Jon closed his eyes for a second. Why couldn't just one thing be easy?

He went back into the cabin and slipped on his boots. He could hear Penny's car pulling up in front of the cabin. Jon pushed past the Preacher to greet her as she got out of her car.

"My goodness. Haven't seen one of them Opels in years." The Preacher said, adapting to the moment like a Chameleon.

Penny opened the trunk, and Jon said, "He's leaving."

"Poor Man's Corvette, they called it. The Opel. Pretty neat car, I always thought. Say, why it's Penny from the Bantam Chef!" The Preacher looked at Jon with a mixture of surprise and respect. "This is your little friend?" The Preacher continued to laugh as if the older couple were naive teenagers. "Well, isn't that something?"

Jon helped Penny with her bag, trying to control himself. "Time for you to leave, Preacher." As they walked past the large man, Jon paused briefly and locked eyes with Shane. "You can leave now and come back, or you can never come back." The preacher's face turned entirely cold as if he saw the face of the Devil. He said nothing else but left immediately.

Jon walked with Penny up onto the porch and inside. He heard the dual exhaust of the preacher's truck rumble to life and the truck leaving the driveway. Once inside the kitchen, Penny turned to Jon, closed the door, and held her bag. Their meeting was all muddled, not at all what Jon had imagined. The preacher being there made their innocent pleasure seem dirty. She didn't say anything and tried for a smile.

"Hi," Jon said. He leaned forward and gave her a peck on the lips. "You must be chilly." Jon lifted the burner and added wood to the stove.

"Do you know that man?" Penny said.

Jon filled the tea kettle with water and set it on the stove to boil. "Yeah. I know him in a strange way." Jon moved towards Penny as if to take her in his arms, but she was distant. Jon leaned back against the cabinet. "Do you remember Finn? The boy who was with me in the summer? She nodded. "Of course."

Jon looked for tea bags. "I'm unsure how much I may have told you about Finn or his home life. It's not great, to say the least." Jon turned and looked at Penny. She was sitting in the booth now with her body turned towards him. "That's how he wound up here. He was supposed to only be here for a few days, and he stayed pretty much the whole summer. His people never even called or came up here to see him." Jon removed the tea kettle and poured water into two mugs. He picked both up by the handle with one hand, and with the other, he brought lemon and honey to the table. "Finn's Dad . . ." He pushed a mug over in front of Penny. She wrapped her hands around it. "He's dying of AIDS." Jon shook his head.

"I don't know; he's probably in his early forties but emaciated like a canvas bag full of odd tools. Finn doesn't know. They haven't told him the truth. I don't think they've come to terms with it themselves. Reggie and Marlene. That's his Dad and stepmother. They've told him some story of how it's a rare blood disease." Penny looked at her hands. "Finn lives in fear because he thinks that if it just happened to his Dad, then it could happen to him. Every time he gets a belly ache, he wonders if this is the end of his life. If he, too, is just going to be a bag of bones."

Penny looked like she was going to cry. "My God, these people are horrible. Don't they know what they are doing to that poor child?"

Jon leaned back in the seat. He took a sip from the mug. "I can't imagine what they must be going through. I certainly can't judge. I imagine pride and love play a part." He set the mug down but still held the handle. He stretched his arm over the back of the seat. "There's good pride, and then you have pride that can hurt someone. And love. The most powerful force in the world, and yet there is love of good things and love of bad things. War, ending people's lives in order to save other lives." Jon looked at Penny. Her hands were wrapped around the warm mug, yet Jon wished they would find warmth in his. "Finn's family goes to the church that man pastor."

"Seriously? That man is Finn's pastor?" Jon was surprised at her change. "Yeah, he's a preacher of some sort. A man of God."

Penny blew air out of her checks, set back, and folded her arms. "That man wouldn't know God if he got slapped in the face with his dick!"

Jon blew the sip of tea back into his mug. He set the mug on the table and reached for a napkin to wipe up the mess. He never expected Penny to talk like that. "What did he do to you?"

"That man is disgusting, Jon. He's repulsive." Penny shook her head and looked over at the Pine wood floor of the kitchen.

"Penny." Jon stretched both hands out towards her as if asking a question. She was obviously disturbed.

"He comes into the restaurant from time to time. Sometimes with his son." She was shaking her head and squinting her eyes like something was out of focus, and yet she was still trying to describe it. "They are both bad. They're like. They're like snakes. You know? Like with little forked tongues. Every word they say is veiled somehow. I don't know. I mean, sometimes, working in a restaurant, you can just feel the creeps. It was the same way dancing in clubs. Some men were just evil." She looked across the table at Jon, dipped her head, and lifted her eyebrow. "There's your two sides of things."

Jon just looked at her. He had never seen this side of Penny before. Her defensive side. Her combative side. Her reserve pool of strength was deep.

"So why is he up here standing on your porch?"

"Finn's Dad works for himself, and his stepmother does not work outside the home. Meaning they don't have much money at all. I don't think they really have enough for food." Jon paused. "I give the Preacher some money each week or so to buy food and clothes and things they may need."

"How much do you give them?" Jon was taken aback a little by Penny's question. It really didn't seem to be any of her business.

"Ah, I don't know. I usually just give whatever cash I have on me. It varies, I guess."

Penny crossed her arms again. "Well, I doubt very seriously that Preacher is coming up here for just a few bucks, Jon. You must be giving a pretty good amount." She looked at him as if she questioned his judgment. "How do you know it's getting to them? How do you know this Preacher is not taking the cash for himself?"

"Penny, I think he is an honest man. He may have some creepy looks or tendencies, but he seems to be honest enough or at least to follow through on someone's wishes. Anyways." Jon reached above him to the small shelf where he kept mail and retrieved the white envelopes Shane had brought to him. Jon handed them across the table to Penny. "He gives me the receipts. Shows how he spent the money. Look at it." Penny opened the envelope and pulled out several pieces of paper. Jon scratched his lower lip with the back of his thumbnail while he watched her investigate the papers. "Food, clothing, miscellaneous, and then cash. The church accountant, a woman named Wanda, manages it all. Seems legitimate to me."

Penny closed the envelope and handed it back. "And how long are you planning on doing this?"

Jon hadn't thought about that question. He had thought about asking Upton Peace to create some type of trust for Finn's family, but then he just assumed that the Preacher would just continue it even after his death. To him the Preacher just seemed like someone who would carry through with his wishes. Someone he could trust. "I don't know. I haven't thought about it. I just wanted to do something to make sure Finn was getting fed and was okay. That he was warm during the winter."

Penny's face changed. It seemed she could see Jon's good intentions, and Jon relaxed. "Seems like you're upset or something with me, Penny."

Penny took a deep breath and crossed her arms again. "I'm not upset with you, Jon. You have a big and good heart, and it is your nature to be sweet and fix things. Just like you fixed my heater. But I wonder if you may not be doing more harm than good. You have to consider that." She moved her hands across the table towards Jon's, but he pulled them back.

"Why?"

"You giving this money to his Family is kind and all, but is it enabling his parents to just maintain their lies to Finn or even to themselves?" It was something Jon had never considered. "If Finn's parents would actually be honest with themselves and be honest with Finn, then it would bring some resolution. There would be government assistance. They could even come and be a part of the clinic. Take all the food they want for free. Most of all, Finn would know the truth and wouldn't have to go to bed at night cold, hungry, and worrying about his future. It's child abuse, in a way."

Jon leaned back in the booth and rested both arms on the crown of his head. "You are a smart woman Penny. You've given me a lot to think about."

She nodded. "Well, good." Jon made it like he would stand up, and Penny reached for his hands. She grabbed him and held him. Jon was surprised and looked at her hands. She laid open his palm, and with her thumbs, she pressed and traced the lines in his hands. She closed her hand around each of his fingers in turn and pulled it, bending and twisting until the finger popped free. Jon let his eyes wash over her. He took in the frame of the woman. He took in the healing, the soothing comfort of the woman. He had heard her words' harshness earlier and admired that diligence. He had listened to the woman's intuition and had not discarded it. Here before him were all his favorite things in women. Jon was lost in these thoughts and mumbled, "A gift."

Penny stopped and looked up at him. "What?"

Jon realized he had said it in his daydream. "You have a gift with your touch."

Penny's smile softened as she continued to massage his fingers. Jon lifted his hands and pulled Penny from her side of the booth, and he slid to the edge and sat her across his lap. He kissed her long and softly. Their lips molding, making love to each other. He wrapped his arms around her body and pulled her into his chest. She wrapped her arms around his shoulders. He touched her cheek and pushed his fingers through her hair. "You're a beautiful woman."

Penny giggled. "You're a beautiful man." Jon smiled. His mind flashed back as if he had been absent-minded and gambled with something too precious. He always called Elizabeth a "Special Woman." He couldn't cross that line here. This had to be separate, different.

"What's a girl got to do to get a drink in this bar?"

Jon laughed. "Probably yell at the bartender." Penny wiggled her head and raised her eyebrows. Jon stood up. "Let me pour you a glass of wine. All that interruption before you got her left me a little behind in my preparations. I would like to go upstairs and get showered, and I need to change the sheets on the bed. So, I just need a few minutes. You can make yourself at home." Jon smiled and handed Penny the glass of white wine.

"You know I can change the sheets while you shower." Jon pretended not to hear what she said. He needed time alone in the bedroom. There were still sacred things that needed to be put away. "I will just be a minute." He moved quickly up the stairs.

He was somewhat panicked. He had delayed and delayed and put off the heart-wrenching moment as long as he could, and now that a new woman was in his house, he had to put Elizabeth's things away. He searched the room for things that would give away his conflicted heart. He moved the books Elizabeth had been reading from the nightstand and replaced them with a box of tissues. He moved to the bathroom and finally took down the bath towel that Elizabeth had last used. He also removed her white robe from the back of the door. A vision flashed through his mind of the last time he saw her wearing it, lying across the bed with the hat box, looking through their old letters. He closed his eyes. The memory was so vivid, and his current act so heinous that it was like a physical blow.

He turned the shower on as if he were in it. He opened the vanity drawer and saw her hair brushes and makeup. Hopefully, Penny wouldn't open it and realize the idols he was hiding. He wished he could just be honest. He thought of how Finn's parents continued to lie about the truth. He wondered if he was the same way. If hiding Elizabeth's things momentarily and bringing them out, later on was just enabling him to ignore the truth. By hiding all these things from Penny, he was, in essence, showing her his house and yet concealing what made it truly his home. He looked around the bedroom and the bathroom and was satisfied they were okay. He wished he would've had more time, but the reality is that it would have been too painful even if he would've waited for a new lifetime. Jon got in the hot shower. The steam filled his lungs as he took deep breaths. He thought of how Penny had sat there and rubbed the hard callouses of his hands, and it felt as if she was mending the tears of his wounded heart. He covered his face with the water. He wanted Penny; she was in his house, but his heart longed for Elizabeth. There were lovely things, lovely qualities about Penny, but his heart was in love with Elizabeth. "You are just not Betts." He whispered into the steam. When Jon came down the stairs, he passed the place where the photo of Elizabeth had hung, and he could see the hole left when the nail was removed. He remembered squeezing the head of the nail with his fingertips and how the whole significance of that photo seemed to slip right out of the timeline of their shared lives. How long could his home last if it was full of holes?

Penny was sitting on the daybed at the foot of the stairs. "Feel better?" she asked. She had removed her vest now that the house was warm, and she crossed her legs and patted the daybed for Jon to come and sit down. She was inviting, and Jon could smell her sweet scent. She had poured a glass of wine for him. She gave it to him and then kissed him softly. She placed her hand on his thigh, and Jon felt electrified by her touch. "I got you a gift." She said.

"You are a gift," Jon replied.

"You're sweet." She smiled at him, and Jon watched her move in the low lights of the night. She handed him a box.

Jon took it, and his hand dropped with the weight. "Wow, it's heavier than I thought." He leaned forward and took it with two hands. "What could this be?" He was flattered. Jon took out his pocket knife, cut the cardboard box's taped edges, and slid the heavy object out.

"It's a writer's box. Like a lap desk. I had it made for you."

Jon looked up at Penny. "It's gorgeous, Penny." He opened the lid, and inside, she had filled it with loose-leaf pieces of handmade paper. Fountain pens and drawing pencils. There was stationary that had been made by reusing old maps of Sicily. "Oh, my God. How did you find this?" Penny was glowing in the soft lamplight. She was smiling at him. Jon removed a letter from inside the case. He started to open it, and she laid her hand across his.

"Maybe save that for later?"

Jon looked into her eyes. "Okay."

"I just thought about the poems and the sketches that you do. I just thought that you could use this. You know, for those things." She paused for a second. "I don't know. Maybe it's silly. I just always imagine you at night up her writing or creating something that I know will be beautiful. Something that would make me feel beautiful."

Jon closed the box lid and leaned over to her. "You are beautiful. Inside and out. I could never capture something as beautiful as you already are." She blushed, and they kissed.

"There's something else in there too. Something new I thought you might like."

Jon looked surprised and then opened the box again. He pulled out a tin of oil paints and a packet of small canvases stretched on thin balsam. "Paints?" Jon looked surprised. "Wow! I've never painted before."

"I wondered whether or not you had or if it just wasn't your thing."

Jon smiled at her. "Penny, this is an exceptional gift. Very thoughtful. You are a great gift giver. That is something I'm not very good at."

"Oh, I wouldn't say that about you." She pulled him close and moved her hand behind his head, her fingers in his hair. She kissed him, controlled him, was laying claim to him. Jon was helpless. He needed so much of what she was giving him. His soul had always been with Elizabeth, but his body had been so cold and alone. Alienated from its caretaker's touch. Those two sides of love are within the body.

"Two things," Jon whispered in his kiss.

"What?" She said. "Two things. I should make us dinner before it gets too late, and I should pour you some more wine."

Her lips pecked his again. "Your lips are sweeter than wine to me."

"Come in the kitchen and keep me company," Jon asked.

Penny poured more wine from the spring box and leaned against the wood counter. She watched Jon move about his kitchen. He occasionally turned to look at her. "What were you saying earlier?" Penny tilted her head at him and pursed her lips. "You know about reading people. Men in the clubs that you danced in New York?"

"Oh. The pervs and creeps!" She shook her head. "Where do I start? Well, being a trained ballerina that broke her foot and became an exotic dancer is probably how every stripper's life story starts." Jon turned and laughed out loud. "What?"

"Nothing, nothing; I love how open you are about it."

"Well, it's the truth. I was an exotic dancer in New York City, and you know, parts of it were a blast. It was my art form. I mean, sometimes you see a guy walk through the door, and you just know that you are going to control him. You were going to soften him up or break him down, and by the end of the night, he was going to be putty in your hand. Most of the customers were good. Of course, you would get the obnoxious frat boys, but then you had some real sweethearts. I mean, guys that would come each week and just talk. It wasn't even like they came to see us naked or dance. It was like these guys just preferred the company or conversation of women. That was where they were most comfortable. Does that make sense?"

Jon turned around. "Yeah, guys who don't fart because they don't think it's the funniest thing in the world."

Penny shook her head. "What?" She giggled.

"Guys who have class and relish the intellect. That is more common in women than in men."

"Well, you said that better. Yeah, you would have these chummy sweethearts, and then you would have guys you would date. The other dancers, the bouncers, and then the creeps. Some guys you just had to look at once, and you knew they didn't have any respect for women. Just saw us as whores. Even called us that. But all in all, Jon, it was the time of my life. I wouldn't change any of it now. Not even breaking my foot. Sometimes I wish I would have kept a journal about my life then." Jon turned and took her glass of wine, and sipped it. "Well, you can always start now. You can borrow my writing box."

After dinner and they washed the dishes together. They stole glances and small smiles at each other. "Can I ask you a favor?" Penny said.

Jon looked over. "Sure."

"Will you draw me something? I just love drawings. I love your poems too. You can write me something."

Jon dried the last of the dishes and put them away. "It's not that easy." They picked up their glasses and walked back into the great room. Jon turned off the light in the kitchen. He knew the time was coming when he would ascend the staircase to his bedroom with another woman other than his wife. He didn't know how that would feel. They sat back on the daybed.

"Why not?" Penny asked.

"The poems just come out when they want. It's usually after I've been reading something and thinking about it or if I hear a phrase or two words together. Then it's instantaneous. It just comes out on the page. Then I let it sit a while. Then I usually go back to it and change something. You know, like sandpaper that's used to polish a coarse stone. I wouldn't call any of it great. It's layman's words. Blue collar poetry."

"Well, I love it. I mean, to be honest, I sometimes don't understand it all, but I love how it sounds."

"It lilts," Jon said.

"Yes, something like that. Well, sketch me something."

Jon looked at her. "I've kind of had a hard time with that. It's like I lost it."

"What do you mean lost it?"

"Ever since Elizabeth died, it's like I lost that part of myself. It's strange. It's like spending your life practicing and learning a language, and then something happens, and you lose it."

Penny was leaning forward curiously. "Like a stroke or something?"

"No, no. Like the trauma of Betts dying was so great and those moments and those days following her death so terrible, my mind had to make a choice without consulting me. It had to find the reserve strength, the calories, so to speak, to support what my body had to do. In those moments, no one could just take over for me. I mean, Bobby helped with the funeral arrangements, but I needed to carry her out of the house. I needed to follow her to the hospital. I needed to pick out her clothes for the funeral, and since my body was in such shock, my brain had to wipe away something vast and resourceful to sustain the mission of my heart at that moment. It's like trauma cost me a language I used to know and loved to speak."

Jon leaned back in the daybed, and Penny moved close, laid her head on his chest, and ran her fingers inside the buttons of his shirt to his chest. She unbuttoned them and placed her whole hand on him. They sat quietly for some time. She leaned her head up and stole kisses from his chin and neck. Jon wondered if it was time to climb the stairs. He placed his arm around Penny and ran his fingers inside the neckline of her top. He found himself looking over at her to identify the shapes his fingers were tracing. Her skin was different than Elizabeth's. Her bones and shapes were not familiar. She was relaxed. He moved in his position and leaned her over on the daybed.

He picked up her legs and laid them out. He stood back and looked at her. She looked at him curiously. It was as if he could see her naked in his mind as if he could see the dancer she was years ago laid out and posed.

He was kneeling now in front of her. He opened the writer's box and removed the small sketching canvases and a piece of charcoal. He moved the charcoal around the canvas with thin, quick strokes as if his mind was allowing him to regain his lost language. She rolled over slightly and lifted her hips. "Yes." Her almond-shaped nipples were becoming hard, and Jon could see them through the light top. Every curve of hers was coming out in the shading under his hands. He reached out and touched her legs and then thighs as if checking what he imagined was real. Jon again came back and moved over her body and lower back. He loosened her clothes, and his blind hands could see what his eyes couldn't, and he whispered, barely audible, "Yes." Jon stood, his shirt buttons were open, and his pants were undone. He showed her the sketch of her lying on the daybed naked, save for a thin blanket. Jon laid it down and moved over her. She smiled at him with her hand against his chest. "Jon, I don't look like that anymore. I don't have that body."

"You're beautiful to me." And he leaned over and kissed her neck. She lifted her neck, and he softly kissed the sides of it and slowly across her shoulders. "Jon."

He stopped. "Yes?"

"Turn out the light."

"Do you want to go upstairs?"

She shook her head no. "No, I want to have you here. Just the light." Jon kissed her neck again. She whispered, "Turn out the light, and we will be young again."

CHAPTER 21

"I have compared thee. Oh, My Love"

Jon sat at the booth and opened the writer's box from Penny. It was strange to have something new in his home. Something that was only his and his decision. Its home was here on the table. It looked slightly out of place, but like a healing broken bone, Jon nurtured it and rubbed its edges.

Over the winter months, Penny and Jon would see each other a couple of times a week. Seeing Penny here in his home was strange but welcome. She cared for him; that was obvious. They traded the words I love you, and Jon felt, in some ways, he did. He loved every flower, every tree, and even every view from the mountain.

Occasionally, they met each other's friends for dinner. The most comfortable meetings were with Bobby. The times he met Penny's friends, they were pleasant, and Jon felt that they liked him, but he could feel resistance. Something that was warning them that he may break her heart. He never felt that from Penny, though. She stood beside him and walked into any place. She was there to hold his hand or mend the loose buttons of his shirts. Never came to the cabin empty-handed or of mind or soul. She asked Jon to never drink alone, and he tried. She found letters at times when Jon was writing to Elizabeth still. She ignored them.

Jon opened the writer's box, and from it came sketches and paintings he had done over the months since she had given it. The letter that she asked him to read was now used as a marker in a blue notebook in the box. In the letter, she said that she didn't have the gift of words like Jon, but she thought that they could both use the blue notebook as a journal when they were apart and pass it back and forth each week. A different form of communication other than the phone, and Jon thought it was clever and her writing was broad and investing.

Jon smiled at the journal and her idea. It was sweet, but he could tell that only a portion of his heart could go along with it. The few days they'd shared were nice, but Jon was glad to be alone again. He would immediately take Elizabeth's ashes back to his bedside table even while Penny pulled out of the driveway.

Jon got up from the table and walked to the side of the porch closest to the pond. He set the coffee mug on the porch rail and opened the lid to the barrel of corn. He did not offer the corn both hands but grabbed a fist full and slung it at the pond in a straight line. He did offer the mountain or ancient trees a ritual arc of corn across the sky. He reached into the barrel again, and another fist full of corn was hurled toward the rising mountain. As if Jon was trying to force out the confusion that lay hidden inside himself. The water began to boil, but there was still no dove to watch him. The fish children hungry leaped and dove across and in front of each other to catch the food. Jon stood there and watched them. Lost in his own thoughts.

Jon heard a car tire's hit the gravel of the driveway. He turned quickly, still in the fog of his mind, and his sense rekindled. It was Bobby's sedan. He now remembered that the phone had rung and he was too slow to catch it. Jon walked to the edge of the porch. Bobby got out of the car with a big smile. "Morning," Jon said.

Bobby opened the trunk of the car. "Hoped I'd catch you. Eat breakfast yet?"

"No, just coffee is all. Can I get you some?"

"Oh, yeah, please. Got us a little surprise. Is Penny here?" Bobby seemed in a very good mood. Out of the trunk, he pulled two fly rods and his fishing vest. Then he lifted out a box from the French Bakery. "I'm kicking my vacation off right! Found us some of that thick-cut bacon and got everything to make some biscuits and eggs. Biscuits never tasted better than from Elizabeth's old cast iron Dutch oven."

Jon was smiling now. "It's great to see you. It's great to see you so happy." Bobby walked up the porch with his arms full and into the kitchen. He started cooking breakfast, and Jon moved his writer's box from the table.

"Now that's pretty," Bobby said. "That's different than your normal sketches."

Jon briefly lifted the charcoal sketch of the dancer. "Penny bought me this oil painting set and these canvases as a gift. I was thinking of maybe painting."

"That's new. That's good." Bobby said.

Bobby lifted the lid from the cast iron Dutch oven. "Oh yes, that's what I'm talking about." The two men set down to breakfast and divided the biscuits, each filling his with butter and jam. Jon looked up at Bobby. "So, this is your usual vacation. Down to Atlanta for King Week?"

Bobby's mouth was full, but he nodded and covered his mouth with a napkin, then set it on his lap. He raised his hand and showed two fingers. "Different, two weeks this time. I need some time. Going to start off different." He looked over and raised his eyebrows at Jon. "Thought we could do some fishing together in French Valley. You know, hit the old places up to the falls. Then I'm on down to Atlanta. They are dedicating the new museum, and I just can't wait, Jon. Can't wait to be back with the beloved community.

Why don't you come with me? You would love it. I've been asking you for years. Come down there and see everything at the King Center. Come meet Sister Coretta." He sat back and looked at Jon. His energy was so real.

"You could use a change of scenery, Jon. Not to mention being around the Beloved Community. People who know what loss is. What struggle and grief are. If it hadn't been for Sister King, I don't know that the clinic would be here today." " What does the Beloved Community mean, Bobby?" " Umm, that's a good question. I think people are afraid to ask sometimes. The Beloved Community means that every person has the right to their unique life experience." Jon nodded in agreement. " Freedom to exist." " Well said. Freedom to exist."

Jon wiped his mouth and sipped his coffee. "You know it's great to see you, Bobby. I wish we had more time together like when we were young."

Bobble opened the lid to the cast iron pot again. "That's what I'm saying. We getting old! Let's go get away for a while. Hear some good music in Atlanta. See some shows. Let's just laugh and have some fun."

Jon smiled. He did want to go in his heart, but in another dark and cloistered part of his heart, he felt like he needed to stay on the path to getting to Elizabeth as fast as he could. To fulfill her last request of them being birds together in the eaves of the old Sawmill. "Oh, maybe next year. You know?"

Bobby lifted his head. It was the same answer Jon had given him year after year. "Well, you know you are welcome. You know the Beloved Community is for everyone, not just minorities."

"So, who's watching the clinic for you while you're gone?"

Bobby arranged the food on his plate. "The deacons will take care of the church. We've got a visiting pastor to lead the services for two weeks. A very bright woman from Trinity College. The staff will take care of the clinic, but Penny will manage most of it. That woman is a godsend." Jon wondered if Bobby would make a reference to him seeing Penny. "Penny is a good woman Jon. A good friend, understanding, and strong

Jon nodded. "She is strong," he said. . " Penny is a wonderful woman. Hell, in a different life, I could even see being married to her and being in love with her even though she is very different than Elizabeth."

"How are you handling that? You've been seeing each other for a few months now. How were the holidays?" Bobby asked. " Nice," Jon said. " That's good," Bobby exclaimed. " And what about drinking?" Jon looked over in disgust. " There's no garden here, Bobby. I'm living indoors." " I gotcha; I'm just checking."

Jon leaned in as if they were in a crowded restaurant and not in the corner of a remote meadow. " Truthfully, I feel like a goddamn bastard." Bobby stopped eating and raised his eyebrows. The large man pushed back from the table and rested his clasped hands on his head. "I feel like a child stumbling between right and wrong. What my heart says is right, and what my mind says is wrong." Jon slid his chair back, leaned over his elbows, and rested on his knees. "I feel insane sometimes. Like a boat with no rudder. No direction." He was agitated and pressed his palms together.

"And not sinking?" Jon looked at Bobby. "A boat can be lost at sea Jon. With no rudder, no wind, and still not sink." " I guess, but that doesn't leave you much hope." " Well, Jon. Hope is reinforced by faith. If you are running short of faith in yourself, I will let you borrow some. The Beloved Community will let you borrow some. We collect and build up faith when we are with other like-minded people. That's why the great teacher said not to forsake the assembling of yourselves together. That's why your time with

Penny rejuvenates you. You are collecting faith in yourself without destroying anything to see if it can be mended." They sat in silence for a moment.

"There's like this side of me that is hungry. It's angry, it's frustrated, it's confused, even mean. Then there is this side of me that is completely in love with Elizabeth and is full. It's like I can talk to her anytime I want. I can be with her, in my mind, anytime I want, but I just can't touch her. I can't sleep with her at night. I can't kiss her lips or hold her hand. Does that mean I'm insane? Does that mean that I'm living in insanity?" They were quiet for a long while. "I'm not a guy who uses people, but I can't help but feel that I am using Penny, which disgusts me. I can't live with that part of me. "I just have always felt like I was a person who sustained others, and now I feel like I'm just taking everything. I feel like I'm just taking everything from Penny and not really giving anything real back to her. I'm just . . ." Jon shook his head and looked down at his boots. "Goddamn, it." He breathed out deeply, and Bobby said nothing. "She comes here, and I scurry about to hide pictures of Elizabeth or put away her robe from where it hangs in the bathroom." He rubbed his brow with his fingertips and closed his eyes. "I'm out of control, and yet I have this insatiable desire to touch and to be touched to be around her. It's like if I'm not around her, I would end up burning everything down. It's like I would destroy everything that is beautiful unless I feed this disgusting animal inside of me. It's like she's a refugee girl pulled out of a convoy for soldiers to blow off steam." Bobby moved forward and raised his hand. "Okay, Jon. That's enough. Let's bring this back to reality." Both men sat across the table in a long silence. Bobby was looking out over the wooden walkways to the fountain. Jon sat quietly like a teenager that had lost his virginity and was playing back in his mind sweet and sinister moments of intercourse. "Remember when you came back from the war?" Bobby looked over to Jon to make sure he was listening. "Remember that big brown book I bought you? That one with all the plants and trees in it. That's when we decided to build the grape vineyard as a surprise for Elizabeth, and we started studying the grapes and how vineyards are created?" Jon was smiling and nodding his head. The memory was rewarding. "Remember us thinking how much fun it would be to see the clusters of grapes hanging off the vines, everything we would do with them. Making wine or just walking the vineyard but remember how that book told us that the most important part of the grapevine wasn't the fruit, but those little suckers that come out each year from around the crown of the plant and root down in the soil. You know the book said that the fruit of the vine was sustained by the roots of the vine. It's like two sides of the plant opposite but necessary. That root is always sucking at nature's breast, constantly being fed and taking. The fruit is always giving the root is always receiving. The grape never says to the root be more like me. Humans, now, we do. We second guess ourselves and say we are doing wrong. My point is Jon. We all get hungry. We all have to eat; when we don't, we get angry, frustrated, and even mean. That doesn't make us bad it just makes us human. "You might see yourself as just taking or receiving from Penny because that part of you is famished, but you don't know how much you may be giving her, and that's not for you to decide. That's for Penny to decide. As humans, we are never more attractive than when we are hungry. Hungry for whatever it may be." He paused, and Jon was quiet, thinking of all he had said. Thinking of Penny lying on the daybed with her head nestled against his chest. "Just be honest with yourself and Penny. Sex is a basic need. It sustains us like water and bread. Just remember. If you cause her pain, you will cause yourself pain." Jon shook his head; still, the boy trying to make sense of his actions. "That's just it. If I'm truly honest with her, then I will lose her. I don't know if I can go through that loss." Bobby minced his face but was listening. "I just. I don't know, Bobby. I never realized truth would cost me so much." Bobby sighed heavily. "Those with conscience and character do the right thing and suffer the consequences."

* * *

Reggie Kindhart lay in mental and physical misery. He had no hope of peace or recovery. He couldn't sleep and was too weak to be awake. His mind was endlessly trying to problem solve. To piece back every conversation he could remember with his doctors. How far had he fallen in life against his will? If he was diseased, then it was a disease he was born with. People had spit on him as he came out of NIH. Called him a Faggot and reprobate without knowing what he was there for. And yet, here he was, part of a church with people that said he was choosing this. That his nature was a sin against his body and God. That God didn't make any mistakes. But if God didn't make mistakes, it was his fault. It was all his fault. He kept problem-solving until he reached a conclusion. Then his body would jolt awake only to recognize a new problem, another problem on the list.

He raised his hands in delirium and covered his eyes from the morning sun. In one semiconscious dream, he pictured himself standing on a Precipice looking over a dark valley of stars, but each star below him was a moment in his life that he had control over and could have changed the entire course of his life. Yet, as he looked over the critical moments of his life, he became increasingly horrified at its end. He needed salvation. He needed a miracle.

A knock at the door; Finn was there to take him to the bathroom, but he did not need to go. He could feel his butt raw from the constant wiping and diarrhea. Finn leaned over him and kissed his hollow cheek. Reggie's eyes briefly opened and then fell closed as if the morning light in the dim room was too much pain to take in. "Moma-lene's making breakfast. I think we may all have muffins, maybe even biscuits, today," Finn whispered, trying to give his father a reason to live. Reggie smiled, parting blistered lips over the bone teeth. "Want to try and sit in the chair? I can help you out there, and you can be with us while she's cooking." Reggie's eyes kept rolling and sliding open and then closed. He gave a slight nod.

Finn wrapped his arms around his father's shoulders. "Okay, I'm going to remove the blankets and then lift you up." Then I will swing your legs to the side of the bed. Just like I do when we go to the bathroom." Reggie nodded again next to Finn's head. "Okay, just rest a second, and then we will walk to the recliner when you are ready." Reggie's equilibrium was taking a moment to recalculate. Eventually, Finn hugged Reggie to his chest and stood up for both of them. Reggie's lifted his arms slowly around the shoulders of Finn, and he leaned what little of his mass was left on his shorter son. Finn walked slowly backward, and Reggie's feet stumbled and sometimes dragged along. Finn laid Reggie into the recliner and covered him with his favorite flannel blankets.

The exercise had made Reggie awaken fully. He could smell Marlene, the baker making something on the yellow electric stove. Somewhere in his problem-solving, he had determined how they could still have food and pay the mortgage even though he hadn't been strong enough to work in over a month. He couldn't remember the solution he had come up with now, but the baking bread smelled so good. Finn was kneeling beside him, and Reggie lifted a weak arm and laid it on the boy. He took a breath and seemed to swallow it. He said in an airy breath, "You getting so strong, Finn." He breathed out two short breaths like the phrase had exhausted him. Finn leaned closer. "I think that's from the pushups you got me doing. You know you said you should do one pushup for each year you've been alive, but for me, that's only twelve or nearly twelve. I can do a lot more than that. I normally do fifty in the morning and then seventy-five at night. It's easy. I'm not even tired at the end."

Reggie's eyes had closed, but he smiled again. He flopped a hand on the boy's arm. "You, my hero Finn. I'm proud of you. I'm going to get strong again, too." Reggie used the other arm and crossed his chest, pointing to it with a loose thumb. "Get me chest built up." The words came out in a choked-up cough, and he convulsed in pain.

"You are my hero Dad. I love you."

Air blew out of Reggie's nostrils, and his eyes flushed with tears. The sickness had made his emotions so sensitive. To hear his son's words even though Reggie was so weak, and the smell of his flesh pervaded the air. "You mean that?" Reggie tried hard to lift both arms and hug Finn. Finn lifted himself up from kneeling and leaned over the recliner to take the hug.

Finn knelt back down beside the recliner. His hand stretched out over the flannel blanket. "Absolutely. You've taught me everything now. I love it when after dinner, you talk to me about flying airplanes about what a Canyon turn is. You teach me about how motors work. I'll never forget the lesson about the center of balance. You are my best friend, Dad. You are a giant to me."

"You are a giant to me, Finn. You might be the Last of the Giants."

* * *

Marlene walked into the sitting room. Her baking apron was tied around her waist. She was dressed nicely and was wearing heels. Her hair was done. She was smiling, and she seemed secure in some unusual way. She came over and rubbed Finn's shoulders and his neck. She had been doing that a lot lately. She hadn't spanked him. She hadn't cornered him in his room when he was naked or changing clothes and accused him of misdeeds or sin. Finn wondered what the change was. He must have in some way grown-up or changed or become a child worthy of motherly love. Finn often found himself looking at her, wondering if he could trust her. He always wanted a mother. Someone who was nurturing, caring, and wanted him for just who he was. He had noticed that the milk was no longer spoiled, and the old cereal was no longer offered. English muffins were not hoarded or moldy but available, even offered to him. She often made the beans herself on Wednesday, and there was no backlash to Finn. She knocked on his door, asking if she could come in his room. The flashing eyes were gone. Something in her had been satisfied, like the meanness of those actions was just a result of some other hurt.

She leaned briefly over Reggie and pulled the blanket up over his shoulders. She put him to rest like an injured bird she was waiting on. Waiting for him to be taken, get better, or pass on. None, the less fragile while he was in her care. She leaned over and whispered in Finn's ear. "Breakfast is ready." The sound of those sweet words in Finn's ear was so nice. Was that what most children knew? A mother who didn't hit them? A mother whose lips didn't curl while she held the paddle and beat at their feet, breaking toes? Was that it? Was that all it took for her to love him? If so, he would have let her break his bones long ago. That would have been so much less painful than her mutilating his heart.

Reggie seemed to have fallen asleep. He got up and followed Marlene into the kitchen. She walked to the yellow electric stove and turned around. Finn walked up to her, his once horrible stepmother. Tears suddenly filled her eyes. Was she going to apologize to him? To say she was sorry? To say that she now found worth in him? He watched the tears trickle down her face; she was not holding her Bible for once. "He's going to have to go back Finn. Go back to Bethesda. He's not getting better, and his doctor may soon leave for a position at Duke University. He's going to be flying out in two days. She began to cry harder, and Finn didn't know how to comfort her. He felt uncomfortable being close to her and directly in front of her. For some reason, she was treating him as if he were her equal. As if he, the child, was half responsible for all the family decisions. Like he was her partner in this life.

She reached her arms out as if she needed comfort from him. Finn stood stiff and received her embrace. She began to weep on his shoulder. Through her sobs, she said. "I don't know if he will survive the trip." Finn began to cry. She hugged him harder.

* * *

"Preacher Skelton, this is Wanda. Marlene Kindhart called. Said Reggie is going back to the NIH in Bethesda. Said he has to leave the day after tomorrow. She wants to know if there happens to be any money for her." There was a pause in the voice message. "Just thought I would let you know."

Shane pushed the button on the answering machine to rewind the message and hear it again. There was money for her. There was probably enough money to buy the airline ticket for Reggie, but Shane was sure that clinical trials from the National Institutes of Health covered that expense for their test patients. The money was hers, regardless. He just didn't want to drive out there and give it to her. He didn't want to expose himself to that or to take the chance he may have to go in that house and pray with Reggie. Reggie would doubtless want that. This was an advantage, though. If Reggie was leaving, then Finn would have to go somewhere. Marlene never kept Reggie's kids around when he was gone for any length of time. "Lord knows where she'll scatter them now? I got to get on this." "Hmm, she needs that money now; that's a good thing. I need her fed but still hungry." He stood moving the pieces in his mind. If Finn went back to the mountain, then there was a chance, he could regain Jon's focus from this new woman. But if Finn went back to the mountain for the summer, then Jon may not be so inclined to continue sending money to Reggie's family. He crossed his arms and looked out over the pasture of cows to the lower area of his property, where he wanted to build a pond. *I'll stock my pond with Catfish. Bottom feeders will eat anything or anyone.*

He turned as he heard his wife calling for him from the guest bedroom. If he had to, he could request the church continue the little bit of money to Reggie's family. He could even just use the petty cash fund the church gave him for meals. It was insignificant. He just wanted to focus on tomorrow's meeting with Margot Bagsby. "Give me a minute Norma. Church business."

He closed the door of his home office and called Wanda back. "Wanda, I appreciate the call and your understanding of the delicacy of this church matter and handling Marlene. If you don't mind. Call her and let her know there is money for her, and we will have it for her at the mid-week prayer service. Beyond that, tell her that the church will help her and the family through this time and that if Finn needs a place to stay, then we can provide for that too. Jon may even have him back up to the mountain for a while. Uh-huh. Alright, you too now." He hung up the phone and sat in the high back chair of his office.

* * *

The following day the Nursing home service went smoothly. Shane seriously didn't know if any elderly wheeled into the home's recreation area even knew where they were. He slowly stacked the yellow hymnals one by one in the small podium and waited for the particular voice of Margot Bagsby to come echoing down the halls. He heard someone enter the room and looked over and saw her.

She was not loud, and she was serious. She crossed her arms and then looked down the large hall that turned into the cafeteria on the other end. "So, tell me. What is it?" The preacher looked at the businesswoman, who he hated being controlled by. "Say? I don't have all day here." She looked down the hall again and then back to him.

Shane gripped the edge of the podium. "Jon Joines is seeing another woman. Has her up there staying with him from time to time. It's been going on a while."

Margot looked intently at him and uncrossed her arms. "What? What woman? Do you know who she is?"

"She works at the diner." He looked sideways at Margot. "Penny is her name."

Margot made a face of disgust. "Oh, goddamn." She breathed out heavily. "You know her?"

"Yes, I know her. She's some common floozy. She was a country girl who moved to New York City and became a stripper. When she was used up, she moved back home. Moved in with her brother, who was a Fag."

"This could be bad. That little whore saw her opportunity, didn't she? Well, she's got another thing coming. I've got plans for that mountain." Shane heard a nurse coming. He looked towards the door of the Chapel and then back to Margot. "What should we do?"

Margot waited for the nurse to pass. They both greeted her with smiles. "How's things been going with that boy? You still going up there and collecting money and dropping off receipts?" Shane nodded. "You haven't missed any days? You've been careful?"

Shane nodded again. "He thinks of me as a friend. I've got him laughing with me." She turned and tapped the podium. "That's good. That's really good. We've got to keep that going."

Her positive comments bolstered Shane. "There may be a chance that the boy can go back up there pretty soon."

Margot nodded. "Good, good."

"And I planted the seeds in his mind about that mountain being turned into something."

She looked at him closely. "You didn't mention development, did you?"

"No, no I wouldn't do that. I've been playing toward his soft spots. He loves that boy and feels guilty for never having children with his wife because that is what she wanted more than anything. To be honest, I'm surprised he's even seeing this new woman."

Margot closed her eyes and scratched at an itch in a way that seemed unladylike to Shane. She was quiet for a long moment. "Well, maybe that's it. Use his guilt against him."

Shane frowned. "Guilt? His wife is dead. He's not breaking any rules seeing another woman."

She swatted off his comments. "I know that. He can sleep with any two-bit whore he wants. The thing is, and I know because I was at her funeral, he loves his wife deeply. He's a good man. Maybe, naive, but he's swallowed up by grief and probably guilt. You can go up there and make him think that him seeing this new woman, this younger woman is not appropriate, morally dirty. You can hit those soft spots you mentioned and get rid of this woman." She looked up at the drop ceiling of the nursing home. "Who knows. Maybe he will make it easy for us." She chuckled. "Maybe you can just lead him to the top of the mountain and show him an easy way off. Isn't there a story about that in the Bible?" She turned and laughed, delighting with herself.

"When the devil tempted Jesus?"

Margot slapped his arm and laughed. "Yeah, that's it. If anything changes, call my pager. Oh, and don't go planting seeds. You're not a fucking Farmer."

* * *

Jon sat down at the porch table with his paints and filled in the lines of the charcoal sketch of the dancer with color. He had not touched it or alcohol in the few days Bobby had been around. Now that he was gone, he mixed colors for the skin tones and shading. He used red for the silk draped over her body. It was okay, but it didn't fully resonate with Jon. The red seduced his mind, and he loved the body because he knew the body now.

He had traced the lines of Penny's body with his hands over and over in the dark of the night. They would make love and then both sleep, but Jon would wake up in his house but not his home. He would lie in the dark and kept returning to what the preacher had said about the field being turned into a pond. About him being the only one, the chosen one even, to bring about its full potential. Was this what he needed to prove to himself that life had meaning and could go on? Did he need to destroy something that was beautiful in order to see that he could rebuild it again with his own hands and mind into something that would be equally beautiful and useful for many others? Wasn't that what happened to him? His beautiful life had been destroyed, and it was up to him to make it beautiful again. That would be the ultimate test. The test was to see whether or not he was worthy of that life.

He went back to the painting. There was something that didn't represent what he truly felt. He wondered what it could be. The dancer resonated with him, but she was too prominent on the canvas. There needed to be something that hid her. That covered her in his heart. The frustration, the chaos, the grief that was masking her. He laid a newspaper over the table and put the canvas on the paper. He thinned some paint in a coffee mug and then dipped his fingertips in the paint and flicked it across the canvas. The splatters and drips covered the dancer and the white canvas. Jon stood back and looked at it in the light. He thinned another color. Again, he plunged his fingers and, this time, let wider lines of paint form on the canvas. In the place where the two paints collided, they started to bleed together, and Jon didn't like that. No, I want to control the chaos. He decided to let it dry, but the paint was not drying fast enough.

He thought of sketching a new one. Painting something new. He went to the cupboard and opened the bottle of bourbon. He poured himself a drink and went back to the canvas. "This is ridiculous." He poured himself another drink. Rarely in his life had any art like this consumed him. He didn't do modern art, especially not drip art. He didn't appreciate it. Finally, the paint seemed dry, and he thinned another batch and again spread it purposefully in shapes over the canvas and not just over the dancer. He decided to let it dry.

He went up the stairs, took off his clothes, and climbed into bed. *A boat lost at sea, with no rudder, can still float.* He thought about the letter he had written to Elizabeth. How he had been crossing the sea, and there was no wind or rain for days. How he could see a rain cloud in the distance, but it would never come. He was there now again. Holding to the lines of the boat. His lips blistered and split from thirst. How he fell to his knees and begged for the rain to just come, wash over him, cool his lips, satisfy his thirst. Then in his dream, she came quickly across the sea then all-encompassing flashing; her love soaked him at first, then sank his ship, enslaved the crew. Left his sea soul stray, split lipped, and dying for another drop of her.

The wrap on the window came at first softly. Jon felt like he was still on the beach watching the storm passing. The dove cooed, and Jon awoke. She was back. She forgave him. He put on his clothes and walked to the porch. He ground the corn and spread it across the rail. The dove came and ate in front of him. He smiled at her. Asked her where she had been. She fed and flew away, and Jon watched her leave, flying back towards the sawmill.

Jon started his coffee. He thinned more paint and applied another movement to the dancer. The canvas was fully covered with three base colors, yet if you looked closer, you could see the detailed painting of the dancer within the layers. The painting now resonated with him. It was something that could fill the empty nail hole left in his house. Under the chaos and frustration and confusion in his life, there was this spectacular being who was giving all of herself to him, and more than anything in life, he needed her, and yet he didn't feel like he could clear a path to run straight to that love. Jon flipped the canvas and wrote "The Dancer" on the back. He set it back down and then took out a piece of the old stationary map that Penny had given him. He began to write.

> *You dance inside my chest*
> *Where no one sees you,*
> *But sometimes I do,*
> *And that sight becomes this art.*

He wrapped the canvas with brown paper and secured it with red and white twine. He slid the card under the twine and set it to the side. Jon stood looking over the pond with his coffee and noticed that the red maples were putting out small leaves, and the tips of the dogwood limbs were swelling with pregnant buds. He heard the dual exhaust of the pickup before he saw it. He was still not entirely comfortable with Shane coming up to the mountain, but he thought of Finn each day and wanted to know he was okay.

Jon stepped off the porch and walked to the driver's side of the blue and silver Chevy. "Morning," Shane said.

"I haven't seen you in a while, Preacher."

The man looked down at his ankle boots and then out across the sea of grass. "Well, these days, I never know when you might have yourself a little company." He paused and spit on the ground. "Figured I give you a little privacy. The boy appreciates what you've been doing."

Jon received the jab. He turned towards the front of the truck and leaned against it. Shane said, "I got some news for you that I thought you may want to hear directly."

"What's that?"

The Preacher breathed in deeply. "Finn's stepmother called the other day. Said his Daddy, was headed back up to the Hospital. The NIH is up in Bethesda. Not sure how long he'll be gone this time or if he will survive the trip up there." Jon turned quickly towards the man. The Preacher raised his hands. "Now, it's all going to be okay. Finn is okay. I got Wanda from the church to look after them. I knew that would be your first concern and ensured they were financially and emotionally provided for. Marlene called asking if there was any money for her, and I authorized Wanda to cut her a check to take care of immediate expenses."

Jon reached for his wallet. "Let me pay you back."

The Preacher raised his hands again. "No, no, we don't need that. Beau-Pre Baptist doesn't let her church family go without. Not when God has been so good to us."

Jon returned his wallet to his pocket. "Well, I've got an envelope for them. It's just in the kitchen. He started walking to the porch, and the Preacher followed him. When Jon came back outside, he saw the Preacher standing over the wrapped gift for Penny with her name on the card stuck in the multi-colored twining. He was smiling.

"This here a little present for your new friend?" Jon said yes and held out the envelope. The Preacher took it. "You know, I just can't imagine doing that." He shook his head with a sardonic smile.

"If Norma Jean died, I just couldn't. I wouldn't know how to take another woman like that." He raised his hand. "Now, don't get me wrong. I'm not saying it's a sin, you know. Your wedding vows are only until death do you part, and I realize you got to go on, but after two have been married so long . . . Well, I just can't imagine, but that's me. I'm not saying it's wrong for you."

Jon looked at the man. He thought it easy to judge someone when you haven't walked in their shoes. He stepped back off the porch, and the large man followed. "You know Finn might need a place to stay while his Daddy's gone." Jon turned and looked back at the man. He hadn't really thought of Finn coming back up this summer. He never considered that he would have the opportunity. "I know he'd love to. Whenever I talk to him at church, he asks for you."

Jon felt his heartstrings being tugged on. He and Finn had a close connection being the only people to spend the last living day of Elizabeth's life with her. Jon dipped his head to the side. "Well, he's more than welcome anytime. He can come here and stay as long as he wants."

"That won't get in the way of your company. You know your new wife?"

Jon didn't like that slight at all. It made him mad, but he held his tongue. "Finn is no problem. Anytime he wants to be here, then this is his home."

He opened the door of the pickup and climbed inside. "Finn could help build that new pond." He gestured toward the beautiful field of grass. "You got two motor graders. The two of you could make quick work of it. Probably have it done in a few weeks." Jon shook his head. "I haven't made my mind up about that." The Preacher clued in on Jon's words. He realized Jon had been considering it. He pushed the door of the truck open with his ankle boot. He scratched the side of his black and white hair and waited for

Jon to say something else. He glanced in the rearview mirror to see if they were alone. "That field has been grass a home for people for thousands of years. I just don't know if it's my place to change that. You know, disturb its peace."

The Preacher chuckled. "Well, God even took seven days to create the World, and at the end of each, he said, "It is good," Then, every new day, he made more changes. You see, God lives in the space between man and what he desires most."

Jon looked hard at the Preacher. That was the first time he had ever heard him speak about God in a way he could understand. What Jon desired most right now was assurance that someone would keep the mountain and the Sawmill in place so that he could rejoin Elizabeth in the afterlife. If he could ensure that desire by destroying the field and creating a new pond where fish and people could live and enjoy, then that was a purpose, a reason for living, and if he could find some new meaning in it and a reason to keep living, then okay.

The Preacher let the door close and cranked the truck. He spoke to Jon from the window. "I'll keep you updated about Finn's Dad. I will stop by in a day or so." He tossed a wave and pulled away down the gravel driveway.

Jon stood looking at the grassy field. The wind was moving up the valley and across it. The words "New Wife" kept ringing in his ears. Like the old one could just die, and you could shrug it off and get a new one. Is that what he did? Was something wrong with him?

Jon climbed into the truck and drove across the mountain to the vineyard, between the stone columns and down the hill. He needed to be there. He needed to be close to Elizabeth. He needed her guidance, her healing words, and her friendship. He walked up and down the rows stopping to look at the brass tags with the author's names. He stretched out his hands and let the vines graze his fingers as he walked by. This was home to him. Elizabeth was here; she couldn't be packed up from here. When he thought about that, he stopped and looked up at the mountain's top, where Skyuka's Rest lay. All the sunsets and picnics they had shared there couldn't be packed up and taken away from him. He looked across the valley; soon, the trees would awaken and bloom against the blue mountain ridges.

He looked at the Gazebo anchoring that side of the hill and saw Daffodils near blooming in multiple short rings around the stone base. He laughed. He remembered planting the bulbs years ago. He had done that for his own pleasure, no one else. He had always thought of a Daffodil as a new beginning. Something that was long awaited and hoped for. He stood and admired them. He stepped onto the Gazebo and walked around its wisteria-covered columns that would soon be in full bloom. How he wished they could have celebrated their fiftieth wedding anniversary there. He read the brass plates with the poem on the floor. "My woman whose eyes are savanna." He read each one slowly and out loud. He closed his eyes and whispered it all again from memory to Elizabeth. He raised his hands in a prayerful shape and covered his face, and closed his eyes, talking with his Dove.

He sat on the blue soapstone steps and looked over the vast, deep, unending valley. "It would take God to destroy and rebuild all that." He shook his head, thinking of what the Preacher had said. God was the space between man and what he desired most. What the hell did that mean? "What I want most is to be with Elizabeth. So, you're saying God is between me and her?" He scratched his head and looked at the sun. He knew Penny would be up soon. He felt he needed to entertain or distract her with small things to distance her from his heart. " So, God is not between me and her? This is getting confusing." He took out his pocket knife and cut a dozen or so daffodils for a table bouquet.

When Jon got back to the cabin, the phone was ringing. "Hello?"

"Jon?"

"Penny, everything okay. You on your way up?"

"Um, no. I'm running late. Today has been a doozy between the restaurant and the Clinic. That's why I'm calling. I'm going to be late, and I still need to stop by the lake and pick up my bag."

"Okay." He looked over at the Daffodils and the present he had wrapped for her. "Well, take your time. Just be safe. I will have dinner waiting for you."

"That's nice, but I just want your arms wrapped around me right now."

Jon smiled into the phone. "Well, you have that too. I will be here."

He wondered how long she would be. Elizabeth had always just been at home. He didn't realize how he had always taken that for granted. Now the tables were turned. He was serving another. He was waiting at home and would be the one waiting on the porch when Penny arrived; he would be offering comfort, a meal, and an ear to listen to her day. Her day off the mountain. Jon would be required to make the meal, wash the dishes and ensure she had a shower and a good night's sleep. Elizabeth had always done that for him he didn't realize how much that required. How vulnerable it made you, how insignificant it could make you feel. He couldn't ever imagine Penny being that woman. He looked at the clock. He thought about going up to the rest for Sunset. Then he thought about the bottle of bourbon. He may have deserved one?

He poured himself a drink, neat, and the spirits warmed him. The second the liquid touched his lips, he felt loose. Like he lost all his inhibitions. He stepped out on the porch and thought he might need a bit more of a drink before sunset. He could sober up before Penny got there.

He looked around the house. He wanted to feel comfortable in his house if he couldn't truly have her in his home. He turned all the lights on and began to clean. He methodically removed small photos and items from the cases that may lead to uncomfortable conversations for himself. He didn't mind talking about Italy. He didn't talk about the war or even the years directly after the war. He didn't want to discuss why he and Elizabeth had never had children. He didn't want to talk about the time he and Elizabeth nearly broke up and divorced. The reason why they had been to the Salt Pond, and the Azure Island, the white sand street, with the children and the photos, it all was too painful.

Yet if he removed all those things from the list of what he wanted to talk about, then what was left? It was all intertwined like the layers of paint dripped over the dancer. He wanted to keep the most central parts of his life hidden and cloudy. They could talk about books, ideas, politics, languages. Any of those things. He had filled his mind franticly with noise that he may not have to hear the silence of painful things.

He looked again at the clock. He wanted to do something special for Penny. The wind had picked up, and the night was chilly. He looked around the great room and decided to rearrange a corner with a small table and candlelight. The Daffodils were placed in a clear vase in the center of the table. He set the table with formal dinnerware. He stuck a bottle of Prosecco in the spring box. He went upstairs, put fresh sheets on the bed, and smoothed out the coverlet. He turned Elizabeth's bedside lamp on. He placed small chocolates in front of the vanity sink so Penny would know they were there for her.

He returned to the kitchen, past the nail holes in his home, and prepared the meal. Risotto with roasted cherry tomatoes garnished with basil, pine nuts, and a drizzle of Spanish oil. The fish he would cook at the last minute. The bread he had sliced and lightly fried in butter and garnished with sea salt flakes and rosemary butter. He had melted grated Parmesan into crisps with chives and lemon zest. He had everything in its proper dish or vessel.

He went upstairs and changed from his usual jeans and button-down shirt to nice pants, a belt, and a blue dress shirt. He had a feeling, and he looked out the window and saw the pale blue glow of the Opel's headlights beyond the field and felt excitement. Excitement to take Penny in his arms and meet her needs. To give her the painting and the dinner and to be her hero. To feel that again. He wanted to tell her she was dancing inside his chest where no one could see, but he did.

He opened the door to the porch, and the wind blew hard. The lanterns on the porch stood straight out against the porch eaves. Did that really mean what the legend said? It passed, and he walked out onto the porch as Penny pulled into her spot beside his truck. She got out of the car with her arms full of her bags, purse, and file folders. Jon started to speak, but she spoke first. "Oh, I have got to pee, Jon Jr! All this planning on this mountain, and you couldn't put in a rest stop?" She dumped all the bags into his arms. She seemed very tired and almost in pain.

"Jon Jr?" He asked as she passed by. He watched her walk straight into the house and through the kitchen. Jon walked into the kitchen and placed the bags one by one on the booth. He thought this would be the right time to sear the fish and light the candles on the table. He pulled the ruffled apron around him and set the cast iron pan on the stove. Penny came out, her hair a little disheveled. Jon was over the stove, making sure the thin fillets did not burn. "So, what's the problem?" She said. Jon turned to look at her. She had not kissed him or even come near him. "I can tell you're a little upset. Because I'm late?"

"No problem here." Jon had his hands full, removing the risotto from where it had been warming and dressing the plates.

"You haven't even kissed me; hello, Jon."

Jon set the plates down. He walked over to Penny, the woman he saw as the beautiful dancer in his heart, and took her in his arms, the ruffles of the apron tickling their faces as they kissed. He moved his hands over her shoulders. "Listen, I'm thrilled you are here. I know you've had a busy week. Especially with Bobby being gone to King Week in Atlanta."

She looked down like she was a little wounded. "I've always wanted to go to that." She wiped a tear from the corner of her eye. "But I always have to stay and run everything."

Jon pulled her close to him again and said nothing for a while. Just comforting her. He pulled back and looked into her eyes. "I've made a nice dinner for us. There's some bubbly in the spring box. It's all going to be okay. Why don't you go upstairs and change? I will set the table for us." She nodded her head and turned for her bags. She wished there was another place, another home. She knew his bedroom was a sacred place where Elizabeth had died, and right now, she hated Jon was making her go there alone.

Penny came back down in an NYC sweatshirt and sweat pants with wool socks, something that Elizabeth never wore. When she was at home and comfortable, she was in silk and slippers. Penny had pulled her hair back with an elastic. She placed her hand on Jon's chest and kissed him. "I'm sorry, I'm just tired, and it's been one thing after another all day."

Jon took her hand. "It's okay. You're here now."

"I'm starving."

Penny dove into the food like she hadn't eaten all day. Jon poured her some wine. "Are you a sports fan?" he asked. Elizabeth was never into sports, but this was someone new.

Penny stopped eating and wiped her mouth. "I love sports. Wayne got me into it. We would go to all the games when he was in New York with me. Do you like sports?"

"Yeah, but I'm not really into football or basketball. I fish. I like to hike. I like to build and create things."

Penny scrunched her face. "Don't you hunt? Don't all men hunt around here."

"No. No, I don't hunt." Jon was quiet for a minute.

"Why not?" Jon looked down and took a bite of food. He wanted to ignore the question. "Say, why not?"

Jon looked across the candlelit table. "Because if you've ever been to war, then you really can't play at it."

Penny pulled her head back. They sat for the next minute in silence. They had finished their plates of food, and Jon turned his chair to the side. "I, uh, I got a present for you." Jon lifted the wrapped package from the side of the table.

Penny looked at it in surprise and pursed her lips. "Oh, that's sweet, and you made me such a wonderful dinner." She got up and came over to sit on his lap. Jon felt strange touching her through the thick cotton sweatshirt. With Elizabeth, he could always feel her body through her clothes. He adored that feeling like her body was all his, and the more of it he was given, the more she was given of him. Penny took out the card and read the poem. She tilted her head at the poem. She slowly took off the brown paper like it was a fine decoration. Jon was looking for her reaction. "Oh, wow. You used your paints. That is something. Very different than what I thought you would do. Where's the charcoal sketch you did?"

Jon was looking into her face. "That's it."

"What this?" She looked back and ran her hands over the hardened drip lines of the painting. Jon pointed to the center of the painting and traced the lines of the dancer so it could be revealed to her eyes. "Oh." She said. "I thought you would just paint that image."

Jon straightened up in the chair, and Penny moved with him. "I did. I did at first, but it just didn't feel right or finished in a way." Jon wondered if he should go on.

"So, you covered it over with all this? This seems chaotic."

Jon looked at the picture and then back up to her. "But don't you get it? I mean, with the poem? That you are the dancer that is in my chest where no one sees but me? You know, you are this beauty inside me even though my world is chaotic. I'm relying on you."

Penny nodded her head. "Did you write the poem too?"

Jon shook his head. "No, no, that's an old Rumi poem. After I finished the painting, I loved it so much that the poem became the perfect way to describe it."

Penny placed her hand on the painting and then on Jon's chest. "Well, it is very nice. Thank you." She moved the painting and the card off the table and out of the way.

Jon sat awkwardly with her on his lap. "You've had a long day. Why don't you get comfy upstairs, and I will clean things up." He moved to stand up, and Penny slid off his lap. They hugged and kissed. "I'm glad you are here," Jon said, trying to smooth out the hard edges of the night.

He remembered doing the dishes with Elizabeth each night. Standing beside her, sometimes talking, sometimes not. She would have been over the moon if he had made that meal for her. The evening would have lasted way into the night. "But she's gone, right? You are gone?" Jon reached under the counter and poured himself a shot of bourbon. He drank it while he dried the dishes. Returning to the table, he blew out the candles and slowly turned out each light leading to the stairs. Ascending to the bed chamber of his "New Wife." He did so laden with grief. Alone he climbed just as he had asked Penny to do earlier in the night. He passed the old outline of the photo that used to be on the wall, and he ignored it in his peripheral vision.

Penny was in bed and under the blankets. Still wearing the thick sweatshirt. Jon shot her a brief smile as he went into the bathroom to brush his teeth. He was surprised by her makeup bag on the counter. He said nothing. He opened the vanity's top drawer and was surprised to see Penny's toothbrush beside his. Had she opened all the drawers? Had she opened the closet and seen all of Elizabeth's things? Jon's heart started beating faster.

He came to the side of the bed where Penny was and sat down. He touched her face and pushed her hair back over her ears. She reached her hand up and touched his chest. "You have to go back to work tomorrow?"

Penny nodded. "You could come down and meet me for lunch."

Jon touched her hand. "Wish I could. Some men are coming up to work on one of my Motor graders. They are taking some lumber in trade for their labor. I got to be around, but we'll have tomorrow night together." She nodded. He leaned over to kiss her and then reached to turn out the bedside light.

"Jon." He stopped. "Can I ask you something?" He nodded. "Why did you cover up the sketch of the dancer with all that paint. Why did you hide her? I'm sorry, it's so different from what you used to do. I thought the sketch was sweet and so romantic the way it happened."

"I told you, Penny. It's new to me. The old form of art is something I lost."

She looked displeased by his answer. "Did you write that poem to Elizabeth?"

Jon furrowed his brow. "I told you it's a Rumi poem."

"But did you send it to her in a letter or something before?"

"No. I never have." Jon felt that Penny was showing jealousy of his life with Elizabeth. She looked unsatisfied but did not say anything. Jon turned off the light and got into bed beside her. He felt disconnected from her, confused at why his gift of art was not appreciated but actually hurt her. He had been honest in the art and assumed that she would see what he was saying through it, but Penny needed clear words, even if it was painful. She rolled over and laid her hand on his chest and her head in the crook of his shoulder.

"Why are you trying to hide me, Jon? Like I don't exist in your world except for some hidden secret place?"

"I'm not trying to hide you, Penny."

"Yes, you are. Your painting says that clearly. You can't even see me in it, and your poem says it too."

Jon raised his hands in the dark as if trying to plead his case. "I was just trying. I am trying." They were silent. Penny rolled over to the edge of the bed and with her back to Jon. He lay awake and stared into the abyss of his broken heart.

When the morning came, Jon rubbed Penny's back to wake her. Then he left and started making coffee and breakfast. Penny came downstairs, still wearing the thick sweatpants. Jon smiled and kissed her lips. Then handed her a mug of coffee. "Breakfast is almost ready."

"I normally just eat toast." She opened the door to the porch and walked out to sit at the table outside. Jon cut up fresh fruit and mild cheese and made eggs. He toasted the leftover baguette from last night's dinner.

"Go away. Go!" He heard Penny's voice from the porch. "Shoo, go! Get off the table. Go!" The words did not quit, and Jon looked quickly out the door to Penny. The Dove had come and lighted upon the table. She walked around and cooed like it was her table, porch, and breakfast spot. Penny had stood up now and was swatting the Dove away. She reached for the small cushion on the church pew to bat at the Dove.

Jon burst out and grabbed it from her hand. "Whoa, whoa, hey. She comes here every morning. I fed her. It's fine. Hey, stop!" He grabbed Penny's wrist.

She flashed a look at him. "You feed her? Birds like that carry diseases, Jon, and it's bad for them. You can't have that bird just walking around your table. Jon stretched out his hand, and the Dove so familiar with him stepped onto his fingers. He carried the Dove over to the corn barrel and ground the corn into meal, and then let her eat.

Penny stormed inside, returned with household cleaner, and sprayed down the table and the porch handrail. The Dove, having fed in the familiar safety of Jon's hands, flew away. Jon looked at Penny but didn't say anything. He went into the kitchen and came back with two plates of food. They ate silently, and Jon noticed that she did not touch any fruit or eggs but just buttered the baguette. "You're not going to eat?"

She looked over at him. "I told you. I just eat toast for breakfast. That's it. That's all I've ever done." Jon nodded. "Birds like that are bad, Jon. You can't just have them around on your table. It's disgusting."

"This is the mountain, Penny. There are wild things everywhere. We are not in the city. This is how it is. This is my life here. You know, I've had a life before you. It's not like everything is just going to be brand-new, a fresh slate."

She set her butter knife down and placed the napkin in her lap back on the table. "Oh, I know. I get it. This is your life. That's how it's going to be." She walked inside and back to the bedroom and prepared for work. Jon stayed on the porch until she came back. She appeared in the doorway dressed like she was when she arrived the night before.

Jon took in her beauty and forced a smile. "I assume you're working at the clinic today?" He gestured with his eyes at her clothes. "Yes, there is so much to do with Bobby gone. Clarence comes today and makes meals for all the shut-ins. I told Samson at the Bantam Chef that I needed to take a week off to handle everything until Bobby returns."

Jon stood up and walked closer to her. "I'm sorry, I didn't realize. Maybe tomorrow I can come down and give you a hand."

She nodded, leaned over, pecked his lips, then turned back and kissed him romantically and intensely, like she wanted him to think of her all day. She pulled away and said, "I'm glad I'm inside your heart. Because that's exactly where I want to be." He wrapped his arm around her waist, pulled her to him, and kissed her again.

He walked her to the Opel and opened the door. "I will see you tonight." He stood there as she backed up and drove away.

She hadn't taken her bags. Her makeup bag was still on the vanity counter. She was planning on returning, and in a way that gave him hope and dread. He thought about making space for her things. Cleaning out the bathroom for good and maybe even one of the armoires even though they contained all of Elizabeth's hat boxes and their greatest treasures - the letters and photos. He sat on the edge of the bed and looked at the place where the wooden box containing Elizabeth's ashes would be if Penny wasn't there. He felt embarrassed for not having it in the open. Not only was he hiding his feelings for Penny from the world and his own heart, but he was hiding Elizabeth. He opened the drawer that contained the small book of poetry filled with notes from Elizabeth. Why was he hiding from Penny his nearly fifty years of marriage with Elizabeth? Any reasonable person would know that he had obviously had a life before. A wonderful romantic love. The love of his life. How was he supposed to just pack that up and pretend he was happy with life moving on without it?

The truth was that he was coming apart. The beauty of his life had been destroyed suddenly, and anything that one loses suddenly, they will mourn, and he was helpless to do anything about it. Now he felt as if he were lying on a grenade, and when it went off, it would destroy not only him but everything else around him, and then he would see if the pieces could be put back together into something beautiful.

His love for Elizabeth was still more substantial than any other force in the World. He didn't have to clean anything out for someone new. It was too painful for him to deal with. If Penny didn't like seeing those things of Elizabeth's in the drawers, then she could not open the drawers. He could get rid of other things. He could clean out the sheds and maybe some of the Sawmill. He could load those items up and donate them in town.

He came downstairs and caught a glimpse of the Daffodils on the table. He was never able to tell Penny what the flowers meant to him. How they reminded him of her. He could load up items from the barn, drive into town, and surprise Penny at the clinic with the flowers. He could tell her what they meant to him, which might help smooth things between them. He remembered how she kissed him and felt in his arms. He wanted that again. He needed that again.

When he reached the clinic, he could see Penny in the parking lot directing the loading of meals that Clarence had prepared to be delivered to shut-ins in the community. She stopped when she noticed Jon's truck and smiled with surprise at seeing him get out of the truck with the bouquet of Daffodils. Jon walked up and kissed her. "Are these for me?"

"Yeah." He smiled. "I picked them yesterday. They're all blooming around the Gazebo. I planted them years ago." "They're beautiful."

Jon looked at her and smiled. "You're beautiful to me, and I want you to know that."

"I do." She said. "Daffodils are special to me because they come up and bloom before anything else on those winter days when you just don't think anything good can happen." He put his arm around her and whispered into her ear. "You are my Daffodil." She kissed him. "How's things going?" He gestured to the work.

"Good, better than I expected. I didn't think you were coming into town. I thought you had men coming up to work."

"I do. They're up there digging through stuff. I just realized how much stuff I've got lying around that Sawmill, and I wanted to donate some of it. And I wanted to see you." Her kiss had worked. She had been on his mind all day. "Is there anything you need me to do here?"

Penny turned, holding the flowers, and looked at the vans about to depart. "No, I think this is all going well. I will probably be home early." She smiled.

"How about at the Lake cottage? You need me to do anything while I'm down here?"

She thought for a second. "No. But I was thinking that I would like to put CHIEF in the water. The spring boat parade is coming up, and I thought we could put it in the parade to honor Wayne's memory." She paused. "And Ruby and Elizabeth, of course."

Jon nodded. "Yeah, I would love that. Just tell me when."

"This weekend? Maybe we could stay at the lake?"

"Yeah, yeah. That sounds good. I'll see you at the cabin." Jon waved to Clarence and then got back in his truck. He passed by the dump and looked over to see if the equipment and old tools were being picked up or just thrown away. He wondered how much of his and Elizabeth's life together would wind up in the dump. All of Elizabeth's God mother's journals about the walks in the garden with the King. And the story of Elizabeth's birth, the night it snowed across the desert, and the old wolves came down from the mountain and walked in the streets of the city but were tame because the old Mullahs were blessing and kissing the hands of the child. Who would take that and cherish it? "That's why you have kids," he said out loud. "Pawn that shit off on them."

He pulled in front of the Sawmill. The men had the motor grader running, and it was billowing out smoke from the exhaust. "Going to need a battery, Jon. Otherwise, you'll have to push start it with that other machine." Jon nodded. "Say what you are going do with that ole rotten wagon in there?"

"It's not that bad. I'm going to drag it out and restore it. Probably this summer."

"How much of this stuff are you getting rid of, Jon?" Jon looked around the old Sawmill that had become more or less storage. Elizabeth's old Cadillac was parked in one bay. Jon kicked the dirt with the toe of his boot. "About all of it, I reckon." The older of the two workers scratched his balding head. "You reckon? What, you moving or something?" Jon stuck out his lower jaw and shook his head no. "Say, Jon, you ever found any of that gold they say is up here? My Daddy used to tell me that story."

Jon looked him in the eye. "If I found any gold, you think I would've worked like this all my life?" It had become so easy for Jon to lie.

The men chuckled. "Heard tell you got a new lady. That what all this cleaning out's about?"

Jon looked over. "Nope."

"Well, Cohen said."

"Cohen?" Jon nearly shouted.

The man looked surprised. "It's alright, Jon. We'll come back up and fetch out what we done traded for from you." The man pulled the lobe of his right ear like a nervous tick.

Jon nodded. "All right."

Jon closed the large doors to the Sawmill, and Penny's small Opel pulled in the driveway as he did. He knew there was no hiding the vintage sports car from the two men. He turned, returned to his truck, and drove to the cabin. He pulled up as Penny was getting out. "Hello, Beautiful Lady." She smiled an easy and loving smile. "Want to come inside?"

They both climbed the stairs to the bedroom and once there, they embraced and kissed. Jon opened the window to the bedroom, and the cool spring air rushed in. They undressed and made love like lovers do. They fell asleep in each other's arms, and the cool wind that blew through the open windows kissed their skin.

They woke up tranquil and close. Penny got up and went in the bathroom while Jon dressed and went outside to pick her another bouquet of spring flowers. When she joined him in the kitchen, he said, "I thought we could take the staircase up to Skyuka's Rest for sunset. It's supposed to be a full moon tonight. We might catch both." She smiled and nodded. "Want a cocktail?"

She thought for a second. "I will just have some of yours." Jon pulled out the bottle of bourbon from the cabinet. "Oh, you're having that. Well." She squeezed her lips tight. Jon pretended not to notice and poured himself the drink. "I don't need anything."

"Okay," Jon said.

Unsure about her steps on the stone staircase, Penny asked if there was any poison ivy. Jon reached out to touch the trees, but she walked with her arms crossed over her sweater. Whenever Jon turned, expecting to see her close behind, he found he had to stop and wait as she carefully weaved around the plants hoping to avoid contact. "Okay, do I have ticks on me?" Jon stopped and looked at her. "No, seriously, I feel like I have something crawling on me." Jon chuckled. "I think you are good."

They sat at the Rest a while, Jon finished his bourbon, and Penny seemed enamored by the views. "I wish you would have brought your sketch pad to draw something she said." Jon looked at her, thinking she knew he wasn't drawing anymore. He didn't say anything.

The wind was picking up, and as the sun set, he knew they should be heading down. It took a while because, with each unfamiliar step, Jon was holding Penny's hand and guiding her feet. It was different with Elizabeth because she had been here for so long. She often climbed the staircase at night with no light other than the fireflies. Penny would never be able to muster the courage to do that.

Jon could hear the fountain and see the lanterns glowing on the cabin porch. He turned, thinking Penny could take the last step on her own, and when she did, she stepped to the mossy granite rather than the wood of the walkway. Her foot slipped on the spring lichen, she fell hard against the limestone stairs, and her thigh struck against the granite rock. "Careful!" She was hurt and scared, and the fall had jarred her emotions, but Jon having drank the bourbon, was loose and didn't realize how bad it had scared her. He helped her to the porch to make sure she was okay. There was a large black stain down the side of her pants. "Ugh," She said. Jon brought her a towel and one of the flannel shirts to keep her warm.

She took the towel. "I don't want that. It's not mine." She gestured with her facial expressions toward the Flannel. Jon went inside and refilled his bourbon. He came back out. "You're having more?" Jon pretended not to hear her. She was wiping the moss off her clothes. Jon leaned down to help remove her shoes. "You should power wash that shit. It's dangerous."

Jon looked up into her face from his kneeling position. "The moss?"

"Whatever the smutch is on that stone. Why do you even have that here? Can you bust it up and just have grass like normal people?" Jon turned and looked over the moss-covered granite to the fountain that had never run dry.

"Are you talking about my yard? The moss is a living thing. The stone is a living thing. It's how it's been for thousands of years." Penny was grimacing in pain and trying to remove her jeans. "We've never had a problem with that." He realized what he had said as soon as the words had left his mouth.

Penny stopped taking the dirty pants off and looked down at him. "You mean Elizabeth never had a problem with it. Elizabeth probably didn't have a horrible reaction to poison ivy or was worried about Lime's disease. Well, guess what, Jon, I'm not Elizabeth. I am a different intelligent, accomplished woman. You're constantly comparing me to Elizabeth." In her frustration, she raised her voice, echoing off the granite walls. "How am I supposed to compete with a dead woman?" All was silent, and for the first time since the day Ruby was murdered, the drop of sap from the rough-cut siding dropped into the waiting hand of gravity. Jon leaned back, and Penny turned hurriedly and hobbled away up the cursed memorial stairs to use the dead woman's shower.

Jon sat at the outdoor table and sipped his drink. He couldn't believe someone would say pressure wash the scum off his life. Bust up this rock that is the foundation of his home. He may destroy the beautiful things in his life, but he sure as hell wouldn't let someone else or some other force of nature do it. He finished the drink, and it made his lips tingle, and, at that moment, he began to hate her for encroaching on his life, for wedging in between him and his grief. Yet she was here, and she was hurting, and it was nighttime. He couldn't just send her away.

The full moon was coming up over the ancient treetops, and he could already feel the old souls of the meadow dead coursing up and down the mountain. The wind was moving through the tops of the trees, and he could feel the spirits of the bourbon coursing through his veins. He waited for Penny to come back down. "Can you come inside, Jon?"

Jon didn't look up. His glass was empty. "I'm good where I am."

"Please. I want to talk, and I'm in pain and don't want to be out here. Will you please come inside?" Jon made to get up, and she went in before him. He grabbed the highball glass with two fingers and poured a splash more before walking into the great room to see her.

He started to sit on the stairs, and she asked him to come and sit beside her on the daybed. He did. "I don't like it when you drink bourbon. It makes you act different."

He looked over at her. "Am I mean?"

"No, you've never been mean, but you treat me differently. You don't show me as much attention."

"Attention. You do like that." He turned and set the glass on the small antique light stand. He turned back around to face her. She was in her sweatpants again, sitting with the hurt leg before her.

"I get it, Jon. My whole life was shattered when I broke my foot in New York. I went through a hard time too. I did again when I lost Wayne but—"

Jon chuckled and held up his hand. "Hold on. You were a kid having the time of your life in New York who broke her foot and became a stripper. A career you said the other night that you loved." She started to speak, but Jon kept going. "When I was that age, I was in a war, killing men and watching a few of my best friends get killed." She shook her head and again tried to speak, but John plowed ahead. "And then you are trying to compare losing your brother to me losing my wife of fifty years. Guess what? I lost my brother, too, and it doesn't compare to losing your significant other." Jon sat back, shaking his head. He couldn't even look at this naive girl.

"It's all relative, Jon, to what we know. Of course, I wasn't in the war, and of course, maybe losing my brother wouldn't be the same as me losing someone I was married to, but I'm trying to say that I understand what you are going through or that I'm at least trying to put myself in your shoes. It's just really hard for me."

Jon stood up. "I had a very wonderful life with a woman I adored. And by the way, we didn't have this kind of stress."

"There you go again. Always comparing me to her."

"No, I don't!"

"Yes, you do. You can't even make space for me in your home. You can't even kiss me with your eyes open. You always close your eyes so you can envision her." "What? Have you taken leave of your senses, woman?" He spread his arms apart. "People don't kiss with their eyes open. Are you insane? You're the one that wants to make love with the lights off."

She looked at Jon. "No woman wants to look like some old hound dog in front of her new lover. And don't say I'm insane. You're acting drunk! Why are you being so horrible to me? You won't even let me speak."

"Drunk? Get the fuck out of my life." He pointed up the stairs. "Get your shit and get the fuck out of my life."

Penny burst into tears. She left the daybed and climbed the stairs. When she came back down, Jon was on the edge of the porch. She pushed passed him towards the Opel. "You don't have to be this way. I love you." Jon said nothing to her and just looked over at the ruff cut boards outbuildings. She got to her car and threw her bags inside. "You know Jon." She paused, and he looked at her. "Maybe

I was young, not some war hero, but just a floozy, an exotic dancer, a stripper, in your mind, maybe just a common whore, but you know what the difference is between you and me? Do you? When my world was shattered, and I lost all that I ever had and hoped for.... I didn't stop dancing."

CHAPTER 22

"What Mean These Stones?"

Jon watched the taillights of Penny's car fade into the night. He was steaming from what Penny had said and yet chastened by her words. "It doesn't matter." Jon slung the rest of his drink onto the gravel of the driveway and went back inside. He picked up the flowers he had picked and threw them in the waste basket. Without her in his house, maybe he could rebuild his home. He brought Elizabeth's ashes upstairs. He took the yellow book of poetry out of the table drawer, laid it in front of the wooden box, and pulled out the small notes she had left for him. He went to the armoire, took out the photo of Elizabeth, and hung it back on the staircase wall. He felt good. Felt like now he could focus on what was important. Like he had his time of self-pity where he needed to be coddled, and now, he was ready to just be the husband of one wife until death did her part.

    Still, the house seemed empty. He went to the porch and looked over the moss-covered stones to the waterfall in the moonlight. He thought of climbing the staircase again to the upper pond. He looked across the porch and down the driveway, but there were no Opel headlights coming back up the mountain road. He thought of going out to the Sawmill and counting all his gold. "Like that will do anything." He stepped back inside and reached for the bottle of bourbon, but it like his soul was empty. He tipped it up to get the last drop. He saw the moon coming through the window, and he knew he couldn't sleep without it. In anger, he grabbed the keys to his truck. "Shit." He hated driving down the mountain. The closest place to buy liquor was in Lynn. "If I'm going, I'm buying as many bottles as they have. I'm not doing this shit again."

Instead of backing up the truck to turn around, he ran through the field and back on the gravel road and gunned it. He leaned forward to look up to the moon and punched the windshield. He looked at the moon again, then took both hands off the wheel and flashed the middle fingers towards the sky. "Fuck you, God. Fuck you for taking her!" He slammed the steering wheel with the palms of his hand. The trees flew by. As he turned a corner in the gravel road, the back tires broke free of the gravel and threw up clods of grass and dirt. Jon oversteered and gunned the powerful motor again, and the truck fishtailed back and forth down the ancient tree alley where the wild azaleas would soon bloom.

He came around the next curve going too fast, and he saw yellow Daffodils blooming on the edge of the road. He jerked the wheel to run over them, but the front tire sunk into the soft soil of the shoulder, and the truck lunged off the road. Jon fought to correct it by applying power and then the brakes, but it was too late. He was heading straight for a tree, and if he couldn't control it, he hoped to go over the side of the mountain. The back of the truck jerked violently, and Jon punched the gas; for a few seconds, the truck left the mountain and just like its ancient dead, he was plunging down the slope. "So, this is how it ends?" He stilled his mind and tried to take in the beautiful last moments of his now miserable life. When the truck smashed into the side of the mountain, Jon's head violently hit the dash. The truck seemed about to flip end over end for a second, but then it found enough weight and settled like a baby's head against its mother's breast. Jon briefly had a moment of consciousness before everything went black.

Thunder Love Come
Few drops beg I for my lips
Smile flashing, blue eyed rain you came
Covered me, soaked me - then sank my ships
Left my sea soul stray, my heart split lipped,
Blistered, thirsting for another drop of you.

Daffodils dance inside my chest- My woman whose eyes are savanna
Whose tears are water I drink in prison
He who falls in love beneath the weight of grief
Disappears into emptiness with a thousand new disguises.
Daffodil your yellow flower only I can see - draw no injury cause no pain.

Sparks flying, who gave you those ribbons? Why did he do that? Jean Paul sleeps in a lined casket now. Was that lightening or a luminary, first platoon is dead? No Jean Paul. That's not my blood. It's not me. I see the sparrows in my window. I'm in my night season Jonny. Look up to the Rest. Is my Love really everywhere?
It's our meadow so chase love
What goes comes back. Come back we never left each other.
Yellow spring flower. See how the flowers of the field they grow? The grow inside my chest where no one sees but I do

THE BOOK OF SAY

I can't taste this wine. It doesn't matter, I'm in love
The spring box, the water, the fountain that's only business is to flow.
Thunder love, smiles flashing, I'm begging you.

The rain fell on Jon's face, and then the thunder came. The winter storm had taken the mountain by surprise. Jon's face felt badly bruised and bleeding. He didn't know if he could open his eyes and lay sideways across the bench seat. The windshield was gone, and the drops of water ran over his parched lips. He licked his lips. He kept his eyes closed and took in where he was hurt and if he could wiggle his fingers and toes. He tried opening an eyelid, and it was painful, and his vision was blurry. He drew short raspy breaths. It didn't feel like any ribs were broken, and there was no taste of blood. He pulled his legs up to his chest, reached for the shoulder belt, and wrapped it around his hand. He slowly pulled himself upright behind the wheel and groaned in pain; his shoulder was dislocated.

He twisted his head to see how far he was down the mountain. He judged it to be about fifty feet. He wondered what the chances were of anyone realizing he was down here and figured they were slim, especially with Bobby gone. He reached across his pants and dug into the opposite pocket for his knife. He held it to his lips and opened the blade with his mouth. He braced his foot against the dash of the truck and pulled out as much of the seat belt as he could. He held the belt in his teeth and reached up as far as he could and cut it. He repeated the process on the other side. He took the seat belt loop and lifted it above his head for a sling. He slowly and carefully lifted the forearm into it and then tied a slip knot into the end of the belt.

He didn't know how long he had been down there, but the sky was lightening, and he needed to move. He needed to gain as much on the sloped terrain as possible before the rain soaked the disturbed ground and turned it into mud. The door was too heavy to open, so he would have to go out through the busted windshield and across the hood. He kept breathing shallow breaths to control his core muscles and the pain. He slid off the wet hood and nearly under the truck. The pain in the shoulder and his head was enough to make anyone pass out.

He kept focusing on his breathing and one movement at a time. If he focused on his hand holds and foot positions, he felt he should be near the top within an hour. Anyways, it didn't matter. In an hour from now, his life would be much different than it currently was. He was using all his strength and his mind to try to stay focused. Bright lights kept flashing across his vision. He kept saying jumbled poems over and over in his mind. At one point, he thought he saw Elizabeth leading him. He definitely saw her hand reaching out to touch the bark of the ancient trees as she climbed the staircase to the upper pond in the moonlight. He kept following her hand. Touching the trees where she touched them. Stepping on the limestone where her bare feet had stepped. He reached a point where she was stopping, and he reached out to touch her to draw her near him. The poem. What is gone will come back again. Come back; we never left each other. He reached for her but only found the wet, cold stones of the gravel road. His blistered and bleeding hand dropped the rocks, and through his blurred vision, he cast his eyes all around, calling out to her, reaching for her. Then he heard the rumble again. The rumble came closer and then stopped in front of him. A man's voice was deep and booming, and he could feel large arms around his torso and lifting him. "Elizabeth. Betts?" Jon was looking around the gravel road and wondered why he was floating. Something in his arm exploded like a spear running through it. He gasped out. He briefly saw the truck's dash again, but he didn't seem to be falling. "Betty, we never left each other, so come back."

* * *

"Sir, I understand you found him?" Shane Skelton turned on his boot heel, surprised to see a female Attending Doctor at Saint Luke's Hospital. Not only was she a short woman, but her body seemed withered by a stroke on one side, and she used a crutch to help her walk. Her white coat hung to her knees.

"I'm happy to tell the Doctor all I know when he gets here, Mam."

"Sir, I am the Doctor. You tell me all you know starting now." She stopped writing on her clipboard and looked him in the eyes. "Go."

"Well, I'm a pastor, and I've been." The doctor stopped. "Are you family?"

"No."

"Do you know the patient's name?"

"Jon Joines."

"The condition you found him in?"

"Vehicle wreck."

"Was Mr. Joines still in the vehicle when you found him?"

"No, he had climbed out and up the bank. He was delirious on the road." The doctor took a moment to catch up on her notes. "This ain't going to be in court or something, is it?"

The doctor cast a glance upward. "Something you are worried about?"

Shane waved his hands. "Oh no, no, nothing like that. I've been coming up there to help him."

"Help him? So, I assume by that he lives alone?" The doctor had not stopped writing.

"He's a widower. Wife died middle of last summer."

"In your opinion, could this have been an act of self-aggression?" She did not look up.

"Self-aggression?"

"Is he depressed? Was this a possible suicide attempt?"

Shane put his hand in front of his mouth and just shook his head no.

"Do you know what his wife's name was?"

"Elizabeth. He kept muttering that on the way over here."

"Do you know his age?"

Shane shook his head. The questions were becoming too much. He didn't want this much involvement in Jon's life. "No. But I know he looks much younger than he actually is. Good genes, I guess."

"Who would be his next of kin? Does he have children?"

"Not to my knowledge."

"Does he have any siblings?"

"No, but why would that matter?"

She stopped and pulled the clipboard close to her crutch. "Mr. Skelton, when someone dies, and there is no immediate will or health care order, the law first looks above to see if there are parents alive. If there are not any, then it looks below to children. If there are none, then it looks to the left and the right for a next of kin. Do you know if he has a will or living trust?" Shane's mouth was open. In all his planning and attempts to become rich, even though he preached every Sunday about heaven and hell and the afterlife, this was the first time it had ever sunk in that he would die one day too. Norma Jean would have to handle the cows, the farm, and the property he had bought. At the very least, Jaime would have his hands full. "I don't have the answers to your questions. Like I said. I've just been ministering to him for about the past year. Is he going to make it?"

"Mr. Skelton. I can't discuss his medical condition with you because you are not his immediate family. However, I can speak on what is obvious since you were the one to bring him in. He has a severe blow to the head. He has severe trauma to the body, but upon examining him, I don't think he has any broken bones or lung damage. We will do initial scans to ensure there are no concussions or internal bleeding."

Shane interjected. "But the shoulder was all." He moved his hand. "We are going to put him under to let the body heal. We will help him sleep then we will be able to address the shoulder. Are you sure there is no one that would have more information about him than you do? Someone who would know if he takes medications or insulin?"

"He's got a girlfriend." He said in a whisper. Shane looked up and down the hallway to see if anyone was coming.

"That's great! Do you know her name or her contact information?"

He leaned closer. "Her name is Penny. She works down at the Bantam Chef." The doctor was writing again. "Is that in Tryon?" Shane looked at her like she was from a different planet. "Yeah, they got the Amish Haystack and the dip cones."

* * *

"Penny, you got a call out front."

"Okay, just send it back here." Penny turned in her chair in the Bantam Chef's office. She held her hand above the phone and turned the window unit air conditioner off so she could hear it ring. "This Penny, how can I help you?" "Good morning Penny. I'm the Attending doctor in the ER at Saint Luke's Hospital. We have a man that was brought in this morning that we believe you know, Jon Joines?"

Penny's heart stopped, and she gasped for breath. "Is he okay?"

"Yes, he's been involved in a single-vehicle crash. He's sore but stable." Penny could hear her heart beating in her chest. "We were told by the man who found him that you were a friend of his?"

"Um . . ." She felt tears coming into her eyes and a quiver in her voice. "We've broken up. We are not seeing each other anymore." She wondered if that were true.

"Does he take any medications that you know of? Any insulin?"

"No, no. He doesn't." "Does he drink alcohol?" Penny's mind flashed back to the full moon night when Jon carried the high ball glass. "How many drinks per week would you estimate?" Penny was thinking. "Not to excess, why? Was he drinking?" She couldn't believe that Jon would let himself get that way. "I can't answer that, Penny. You know we have rules and can't share anything with you if you are not family." That stung Penny's heart. She desperately did want to be Jon's family. "Did you know his wife?" The love spear rammed through Penny's chest as she leaned over the office's small, pressed wood desk. "Elizabeth was her name. Did you know her?" Penny was grieving. When was this nightmare ever going to stop? Through all this pain and now separation, Elizabeth was still at every corner of her life. Like her ghost was taunting her again and again as if it wasn't enough that she won Jon's heart back from the grave, but now she needed to flaunt her dominance over her. Penny set down the phone and clasped her hands together as if about to pray for strength. She could still hear the voice coming from the receiver on the desk before her. She could feel the tears starting to stream down her face. "Penny, you there?" Penny picked up the phone, but she could tell her voice was going to crack. "Does he have any other family besides his wife? Perhaps someone with his Power of Attorney?"

Penny cleared her throat. "His Attorney is Upton Peace from Saluda, but his brother is Robert Gunn here in Tryon. He's on vacation right now."

"Any way to contact his brother?" Penny hadn't thought about needing to contact him. She handled most of the planning for the clinic anyways. "Wait, Penny, you said Robert Gunn from Tryon? You mean Bobby?"

"Yes, Bobby Gunn, who runs the clinic here in town."

"What? This old guy is Bobby's brother?" The doctor's voice seemed elated. Penny couldn't help but feel her spirits rising. "You have got to be kidding. He's Bobby's brother." Penny could hear her telling the nurse's desk. "We adore Bobby. He comes in about once a week in the evenings, goes from room to room, plays his guitar, and sings for our patients. My goodness, to hear him play and sing Bill Wither's "Ain't no Sunshine when She's Gone" is my favorite. That man's sweet spirit and playing transforms this hospital. I sometimes come in on my days off to hear him sing." Penny's tears of sadness were turning to tears of joy. "Is Jon anything like Bobby?"

Penny smiled. "He has beautiful qualities too." She smiled, taking pride in the man she loved, but then her heart felt the love spear shift in her chest when she thought of Jon telling her to get out of his life. She ran her hand gingerly over her badly bruised thigh. It hurt, but he had hurt her much worse.

"You said Bobby is on vacation. Any way to reach him?"

"Well, he's at King Week in Atlanta. I supposed I can call and find someone in the office who can get up with him."

"Oh, of course, King Week. Bobby's always talking about it. We all want to go with him sometime, but we can't get our schedules coordinated. We can't believe that Bobby knew Martin Luther King. Marched with him, road with the Freedom Riders, jailed with Jon Lewis. Okay, so I'm going to level with you and walk the line. Jon is in stable condition. We are going to want to keep him for a good while. When he goes home is probably going to need someone to help him. If no one is available, then we can schedule a nurse to visit him. If you can, contact Bobby and just let him know but reassure him that it's not an emergency per se. He can call us here at the Hospital; I'm sure he has the number."

"Okay."

"Well, Penny, it was a pleasure talking to you; any friend of Bobby's is a friend of ours, so if you are by this way, please stop in and introduce yourself."

"You've been very kind; thank you, Doctor."

"Not a problem. We are going to take good care of Jon. Don't worry about him."

* * *

"Jean-Paul!" Jon lurched upright in the hospital bed, his thrashing arm blindly sending a cup of ice chips on the bedside table across the room. The pain shot through his chest and head, and he fell back into the bed with his eyes fixed on the large man sitting in the chair beside his bed. "What the hell are you doing here?" His voice was hoarse.

"Dear God," Shane said, "I thought they knocked you out."

Jon took in the room and realized he was in a hospital. "Stuff goes bad on me," he croaked. The preacher got up from the chair and walked over to Jon. Blocking the bright sun that was flooding the room.

"Do you remember what happened to you, Jon?" The sight of the Daffodils in the headlights growing on the side of the road and him trying to crush them flashed in Jon's mind. He closed one bloodshot eye to focus on the image. "You went off the mountain. Like airborne. Where were you headed anyways?" The preacher paused. "I pulled you out."

"You were there for me?" The preacher nodded. "You pulled me out?"

"Up the bank, well, cliff."

"Cliff?" Shane shifted, and the sun beamed harshly into Jon's eyes.

"Well, to be honest, you had found your way somehow to the road. I picked you up and got you into the truck." Jon tried to lean over in the bed, but the shoulder prevented him. "Now, now, easy, don't worry. The doctors have run tests on you. There's no internal bleeding, and the shoulder is not broken; it's just out of place."

"I know what it is. It's happened before. It's an old injury." Jon blurted out the words like they were blood in his mouth. "Who'd you tell about this?"

Shane sat back down. "Well, I didn't have much information to give. I've known you for about a year but realized you haven't told me anything about yourself. The only person that I know that you knew was your girlfriend." Jon's hurting head flashed the images of Penny getting into her Opel and the last words she said about him being too weak of a human to keep trying for love. In her words, to keep dancing. Making the most of her dreams in life. "I gave them Penny's name and told him where she worked."

Jon pushed his aching head back into the pillow and arched his back. He covered his hurting eyes with his hands. "Oh, shit!"

The Preacher immediately stood up and came over to Jon's bed. "What? What, Jon? Say? You can trust me, Jon. We are friends." He went to sit on the edge of the bed. Jon felt the weight on the edge.

"Fuck off, you goddamn Piss Ant." Shane flashed red, and his eyes twitched. He went and stood by the window. "I didn't ask you to bring me here. Hell, if you wanted to do me a favor, you should've just run over me." The pain in Jon's body was a compounding ache in his mind and the grief in his heart.

"Somebody else would have. Somebody that wasn't your friend. Somebody that might just want all the gold you got buried up there somewhere." He turned back to Jon's bedside. "Well, I ain't that person. I don't give a damn what you got. I thought our friendship was thicker than some three-inch cushion." He raised the tiny pillow that had been in the hospital chair. Jon looked into the former Police officer's eyes and was surprised that he would curse in front of him. "Now tell me what you need. Who do you want me to call? They asked if you had an attorney. Something about a Living Trust." Jon squinted his eyes, wondering what the importance was, and then he remembered Upton asking if he wanted artificial life support in the event of an accident. Jon's mind suddenly became precise.

"My attorney is Upton Peace in Saluda."

"You want me to call him? He got your will?" Jon shook his head. "No need to call him. It's being worked on."

Shane sat in the chair. "You going to need a new truck. That one is definitely totaled. They say they are going to keep you for a week or so. They reset your shoulder while you were out. Say you may need someone to help you while that shoulder heals."

Jon looked over at the man. "A week or so?"

"I guess your lady friend can come up and care for you?" Both men were quiet for a moment.

Jon looked at him. He was too embarrassed to call the only person he could trust and didn't want to interrupt his vacation. He shook his head. "No, we are done. Not seeing each other anymore." Skelton said nothing, just raised his head and turned to the window before the satisfied smile could cross his face. It seemed as if all this was going to be worth it. He took several deep breaths to let his pounding heart slow down. "What about young Finn?" Jon thought of how panicked Finn would be if he knew he had been in an accident and a hospital. "His Daddy left yesterday on a flight out of Greenville/Spartanburg for DC. I could make arrangements and have him up here when you're ready." Jon looked down at his arm in a sling. "He could help you a bit. You know, while you're getting healthy." The words rang in Jon's ears. Did the preacher mean while his shoulder was getting better, or had he smelled the alcohol on his breath? Had the doctors checked his blood and realized the accident was because he was drunk? Would they tell Bobby that?

"You and Finn could do a little fishing," Shane said. "Maybe restore that old wagon in the barn." He chuckled. "Maybe even teach him to build a pond so he can keep the legacy of that mountain going." He chuckled again. "That would be a great name for a boy's camp, wouldn't it? 'Legacy Mountain.'"

Jon imagined him and Finn sitting on the porch in the lantern light again. Talking, exchanging ideas, and even sketching. That's what he needed. Someone that had known and loved Elizabeth and his old life as much as he did. Together they could get back to it. If Finn was there, then Jon knew he wouldn't drink bourbon. He wouldn't need it. With Finn there, he could fill the emptiness with books, ideas, conversation, and happiness. He could forget about the numbing effect of the bourbon because Finn would restore some of the old truths, the good truths he depended on. Jon felt lost. Like the granite was power washed around his house, and his home had slid over the granite dam of the pond and disappeared into the ether. Like he had used everything in life to shield himself from facing the fears he had felt since childhood. This was too much pain, and Jon shook it away. "See what you can do. Finn can stay as long as he likes." Shane said. "Good, Good. Now that's some good news for everyone." Shane turned to collect his belongings. I will come back and check on you soon."

As he was leaving the room, Jon said, "No need to come back here. Just take Finn to the cabin. I will be there." Shane stopped when Jon said this, the doorknob to the hospital room in his hand. He looked at Jon and knew what he said was true. He slowly nodded and opened the door as the Doctor on the crutches was about to walk in. "Pardon me. I was just leaving." Shane tossed a wave of goodbye toward Jon's bed.

Jon watched the Doctor walk to his bedside. "The brother of Bobby Gunn; now that's amazing." Had he met her before? "We didn't realize because of the different last names and you being white." She rolled her hand out to Jon.

"We were orphans adopted." She folded her hands as if settling in to hear a long story. Her bedside manner was lovely. "I figured. I bet it is a great story."

She looked through his charts, and Jon wanted to tell her the story of his life with Elizabeth. He didn't. "Now we know Bobby is at King Week. Were you a freedom rider with him back in the movement?" Jon shook his head no. "Oh, my, he's got some stories. Being jailed, bitten by dogs."

Jon nodded. "They used to call us when he'd get locked up. We would offer to pay his bail, but he wouldn't leave." Jon used his good hand to scratch the back of his neck with his forefinger. "We weren't as close back then as I wish we could have been." The doctor smiled. "Well, Jon. You are alive and lucky to be so. The local sheriff went up to the mountain and took photos of everything. They lifted the truck, and we saw photos of that." She shook her head. "It's a wonder." She patted Jon's good arm. "How's the shoulder today? You must keep it resting for a couple weeks, maybe longer." Jon nodded. "You're past the window of concern for concussion. Though we did notice significant damage from the past." She asked a question with her eyes, and Jon did not see the need to answer. She scratched the space between her eyes. "Because of your age and the fact that you live alone, we want to keep you for about a week."

"But—"

"The rest will do you good. We serve three meals a day, and you can watch as many reruns of the Young and Restless as you want." She leaned in closer and patted his arm. "This is non-negotiable, Jon. Jon did not look at her. She turned and caught the bottom of the door with her crutch to swing it closed. Obviously, a well-practiced move. "Get some rest. My shift ends tomorrow night, so I will be back to check on you." The door closed.

Jon looked at the bandages and sling around his arm. He assumed his head looked as bad as it felt. He touched the sling. "Goddamn Velcro. We've come a long way, Lefty." He laid his head against the pillow to conserve his strength and looked around the room for his clothes. There was nothing around but the tv and the drab walls. There was no way he was staying here for a week. He had dealt with this injury before. He knew he would have a real fight on his hands with that doctor. And his truck was totaled. He closed his eyes and rested for a moment. Piecing everything together.

With his eyes closed, he reached over to the bedside table and slid open the drawer. His fingers fumbled over several items taking inventory. At the bottom of the drawer, he found the phone book. He laid it on his chest. He briefly wondered if he was too weak to stand. He set the book down and hit the button to raise his bed, slid his legs over the side, and let his head clear. Holding his breath for core strength, he raised himself up slowly and stood.

He set his goal as the bathroom toilet and slowly slid one foot in front of the other. Holding his good arm out when he got close to it. "Way to go, Jonny." He made several passes before going back to the phone book. He laid it on the bed while standing and, with one hand, turned the pages until he found the number he was looking for. He marked the number with his finger and repeated it over and over. He turned to the phone and dialed the number.

"It's a good day to own a Dodge! This is Texas Stanley. How can I help you." Jon pulled the receiver from his ear, the voice being so loud.

"This is Jon Joines. I bought a red pickup from you last summer. You remember me?"

The voice on the other end of the line was quiet. "I do. You're the only man that ever cussed me out in a whisper. That was fucking scary!" Jon couldn't help but laugh, but the chuckle bounced his arm in the sling. "How can I help you, Jon?" "That last truck you sold me wrecked itself. I'm in the market for a new one." "Okay, they do that sometimes. Well, the new models are on the lot. Just stop by and pick one out." Jon breathed out. He opened his mouth to speak and then wondered how to say it. "I want it brought to me." Texas Stanley looked at the phone. "Sight unseen? What do you want in the truck?"

"I want the best you got on that lot, and I will pay you 10% above your asking price if you have it here tomorrow at noon." There was quiet on the line.

"Do you like green?"

"Do you?" "I love green

What's the address?"

Saint Luke's hospital, pull up to the front door."

"Okay, I got it. You not robbing the place, are you?"

Jon didn't laugh. "If you can't be here by noon, the deal's off. Are we clear?"

"Crystal, pleasure doing business with you."

Jon hung up the phone and replaced the phone book in the drawer. He practiced walking again and then started walking up and down the hallway slowly. Making sure he passed the nursing station and saying hello to everyone. He made a point every hour to do that. His legs were sore. His whole body was sore, but he needed the nursing staff to get used to his face and see him exercising.

* * *

"Penny, it's Bobby; what's going on?" "Oh, Bobby. I've been trying to reach you for days." "Well, we've been dedicating the new museum. I'm sorry. What's going on?" "It's Jon." The phone line went silent. Bobby's heart stopped with fear that the last person alive on Earth, whom he truly loved, had been taken from him. "He's okay." With those words, Bobby breathed a sigh of relief.

"Thank you, God," he whispered.

"There was an accident."

"What now? Did he flip a machine? Cut his hand off?"

"No, no, okay, evidently. It was a vehicle crash. He was driving down the mountain late at night or early in the morning. He ran off the mountain, Bobby. I talked with the Sheriff. He was here for lunch. He showed me the photos of the truck. It was bad. Evidently, he just dislocated his shoulder and hit his head. They're keeping for a few days at the hospital." Bobby was taking in all the information. "Well, let me talk to him. Aren't you there with him? Penny turned her head and ran her hand up the back of her neck. She didn't want to tell Bobby this story. "No, this is the office phone for the restaurant I'm at work."

Bobby processed what was going on. "Well, who's taking care of Jon? Who found him?"

"The Preacher found him. That one that has been coming around up there and keeping Jon up to date about Finn?" "Finn? I haven't heard anything about this man." Bobby was quiet. "And what is it, Penny, that you are not wanting to tell me?" Penny was quiet. She didn't want to admit that she had lost Jon's love because she desperately didn't want to lose Jon's love. She wanted it more than anything, and this space that was now between her heart and him was the opposite powerful side of love that she never knew could be so cruel. "If I'm going to help Jon, then I need all the information, Penny." "We are not seeing each other anymore." She blurted out. Bobby pulled back from the phone because the news was disappointing to hear. "We had a couple of bad nights where we were just out of tune with each other. I don't know. And then we had this argument, and I was trying to be close and just wanted to talk to him about what I was feeling, and he just stood and said . . ." She was tearing up on the phone, and her voice was cracking

"He said to get the fuck out of his life, didn't he?"

Penny was sobbing now on the other end of the line. When he found out he had an emergency call, the people that went with Bobby laid hands on his back and prayed silently. Penny blew her nose and caught her breath.

"That's exactly what he said, Bobby. It hurts so bad." Bobby was quiet, tears welling up in his eyes not just for the pain Jon had caused Penny but for the repeated trauma that had continued throughout all their lives. "How did you know that, Bobby? How did you know that's what he said?"

Bobby exhaled heavily. "Because I've heard it before. I heard it when Elizabeth left him."

"Left him? I don't think I understand."

"Oh, yeah. Elizabeth left him. I don't mean packed up and said, 'We are getting a divorce, and I'm moving down the street.' I mean that women simply drove to town, left the keys in the ignition, got on a train, and left the country. Not a letter, note, a phone call, no trace of her. She booked passage on a boat headed to Malta and got off before it made its port of call. She never cleared customs anywhere. Never took a bank draft anywhere. Started over with the cash she had and sold the jewelry she was wearing. Jon had an idea of where she had gone but no real clue. He bought a sailboat and crossed the North Atlantic in the middle of winter. Started at the top of the Mediterranean Sea, looking all over for her. Even lost the boat in a storm and nearly died. He bought another boat and kept looking for her. Finally found her in some little beach town in Sicily. Some place she thought he would never find her. She had traded some of her jewelry for an old Sicilian cart full of handmade baskets. She was selling the baskets on the street. Pulling the cart each day to and from the beach park by hand over the cobblestone streets. Evidently, very content in her new life. You see, Jon's actions had hurt her very deeply. " Penny was floored. "In my mind, they had this fairy tale love that just magically happened and was perfect. I never thought in a million years that they could ever be apart. Bobby chuckled. "They were apart for a good while. I mean enough that Elizabeth had started over with a new man. That's always what's left out in the great love stories, but those experiences make them. They stayed in the Mediterranean for a couple of years and considered giving up the mountain. As if the mountain had triggered Jon's pain, but that wasn't true. A mountain cannot be good or evil, just as bourbon is neither good nor evil. It's our actions that are good or evil. Jon often recounts those years as a luxury experience skipping over the pain. I often thought about that. To be honest, we all do it. There's a period after devastation when only truth remains. When the lies we tell ourselves are exposed, we can begin again in truth. This is what all the world's religious traditions call rebirth or Nirvana. I call it Heaven. Jon remembers those years with such fondness because he found Elizabeth, and she gave him her forgiveness, and he began to live his life in truth and, for the first time, experienced Heaven. Penny was silent. She wondered if Jon would come searching for her. "When did all that happen?"

"When Jon came home from the war, he turned the area in front of the fountain into a garden of potted plants and trees. It started simply enough. I think they slept outside in the full moon one night, and then Jon decided to add a few plants to the area. Then he started adding truckloads of plants and then trees to the area. Then he and

Elizabeth started living in the garden, just like the story of Adam and Eve. Elizabeth would go inside and shower, but Jon bathed in the fountain. He started living in this fantasy Eden. It was beautiful, with walkways and carpets and tables and lanterns at night. Jon had set out the plants and trees in defense positions as if they were the spirits of his dead soldiers still guarding him. I don't know how many people realized this. Elizabeth, Ruby, and I discussed it, but it just seemed temporary and a way that he was trying to heal himself. All he did was tend to the garden, himself, and Elizabeth. He functioned, but he did not leave the garden. I finally got him interested in growing and building a vineyard as a surprise for Elizabeth. That was the breakthrough. He left the garden to build another one for the woman he loved. By the time we finished the vineyard, he was sleeping back inside. The garden was still there but a little neglected. Then it wasn't enough. His mind and hands had to be occupied constantly, or the old pains would start creeping up. Then, at night, he couldn't sleep. He started drinking bourbon to sleep, then drinking it to dull the pain. Around then, Ruby was murdered, and it was just too much stress. Jon felt he had to fix everything and protect us, but he couldn't. None of us understood it, and we didn't want to embarrass him, but he acted differently on that hard liquor. Elizabeth wanted a child, and on top of all the other things Jon was going through. He flew off the handle. He was never violent, but he has so many words and knowledge in mind that he can sling darts like Hercules." Penny was listening, fascinated by this love story she could relate to. It was the true version of Jon and Elizabeth. She didn't have to compete with Elizabeth because Elizabeth was already on her side. She heard Bobby breathe out slowly as if giving away something he really needed for himself. " The reason Jon doesn't talk much is not because he doesn't have anything to say. No, that's not it. He's scared to interrupt the peace of god." There was silence.

"I will come home, Penny. I will take care of Jon."

"I don't think you have to end your vacation early. They say they're going to keep him for about a week." Bobby laughed. "Oh, If I know Jon, he's already on his way home."

* * *

Finn stood at the outdoor terminal of the Greenville/Spartanburg airport and watched as his father, Reggie, was fitted into a very uncomfortable-looking wheelchair. The man's yellow skull-like face was strapped across the forehead, chest, lap, and feet. Then wheeled quickly to the plane, lifted by two men, and carried up the stairs. Finn watched with others gathered from his church while the plane taxied to the small runway. The silver wings lifted, and Finn wondered if he would see his father again.

Not being able to see the plane any longer, he turned to look for Marlene but could not find her. He assumed she must be downstairs, and Finn headed for the car alone, having been to the airport so many times to see his father escorted away in this fashion that he had become very used to the airport layout. When he reached the taxi stand, he still had not found Marlene.

A hand touched his shoulder. "You ready young man?" Curtis Brown was a tall man with kind blue eyes, and his wife Brenda was smiling as if Finn were a cute puppy at a shelter. Finn noticed the man was carrying his red fireman's bag. "Where did you get that? I'm not leaving, am I?" He turned to look for Marlene again and then realized that not only had the airport trip been to drop off Reggie, but it was also to drop off him. The people seemed kind. Finn smiled and nodded, " Okay."

Finn looked quietly throughout their small home, especially at the tall man's gun case. When the woman served dinner that night, she told him that he had come straight to this house when he was born and left the hospital, and his carrier sat upon this very table. Finn's face screwed up. "What was it, Curtis. Two to three months we kept him?" "No, it was six months, Brenda. I remember it like yesterday. Your first home was here in Greer, Son."

Finn looked at the man, and he was still smiling at him. "I loved it. You were the cutest little fella. Still are. Well. you are a handsome young man now." They all held hands before saying a blessing over the meal.

"Where's my stepmother? Do you know?"

"Um," Brenda said, "Well, best I know, she's gone to see her brother, she said. I guess he lives in Myrtle Beach?" Finn shook his head as if he didn't know. "Your sister is with the Wests over on Edith Drive."

Finn nodded. "Yeah, I cleaned out their well."

"Oh yeah, with Preacher Skelton," Brenda said?

Finn swallowed hard, remembering the experience. "Yes, ma'am."

She finished her plate of food and slid back from the table. "Well, from my understanding, we are supposed to take you to Panther Mountain in a few days to stay with Jon Joines. Would you like that? Preacher Skelton said you had a good time up there. Best of my knowledge Mr. Joines had a car accident and messed his shoulder up, so you will go up there and help him out a bit." Finn lost his smile. "An accident? You reckon he's alright?" The tall man leaned forward. "Jon, now, he's a pretty tuff fellow. Don't you gotta worry much about him. Right, Brenda?"

Later, they all three sat in the front seat of the man's small Toyota pickup truck. He let Finn change the manual transmission's gears for him since the shifter was in front of him. Finn breathed in his favorite places of the mountain and pointed out the waterfalls for them to see. He asked if they could slow down and try to find the glen with the blooming Azalea, but he couldn't find it.

When they came out from under the canopy of ancient trees, Finn cast his eyes across the beautiful sea of grass that never stopped flowing and waving in the breeze. Finn noticed the dark green Dodge in the current year's body style when they reached the cabin. Jon stepped off the porch, his arm in a sling. He raised his good hand in a wave. "My, my, the Flatlander returns!" Finn grabbed his red fireman's bag from the back of the small truck and ran over to hug Jon. "What's this now? No axe this time?"

Finn looked down at the bag, unaware of what was in it. "I didn't do my own packing this time. Otherwise, I don't leave home without it."

Finn showed the couple from Greer the fountain and corn barrel, opened it up, and fed the fish children. They drove to the upper pond, and all fished, and Jon watched from a place in the shade where he had stretched out the old rug that he and Elizabeth always used. Jon felt full in his soul, like Elizabeth was there in their meadow beside him, watching their Skyuka Child as he returned home. Finn laid out the fish on green herbs in the wicker basket, and when the sunset had finished, they came down from the Rest, they all said goodbye, and Jon bid them a safe trip home.

Finn and Jon got into the cab of the new truck. It was different. There was not a bench seat anymore but two separate seats. "You going to clean them fish and cook them up?" Jon raised his eyebrows toward Finn. "You know that's why you're here to care for this old man." Finn sat forward in the seat as they drove down the mountain ridge. "You are old. You are as old as a tree. That big tree right there. Moses planted that one, no wait Methuselah. How did you break your arm anyway, old man?"

Jon smiled. I didn't break my arm. Just dislocated it."

They cleaned the rods and fish. Jon had removed some baby spinach and carrots from the cupboard. He was doing everything one-handed. He was drinking water from the spring box. Even though the bourbon he had bought today was on his mind. He pulled out panko breadcrumbs for the fish and taught Finn how to fry them. They sat down at the porch table in the lantern light and ate. Finn was excited in his boyish innocence. "You know what I like about catching fish?" Jon smiled and waited. "It's not actually catching the fish but the whole experience." Jon didn't interject, just watched as the boy filled the night with self-taught philosophy. "You have this straight rod that bends when you cast. Then you have this line that can be made straight, but when you cast, it rolls through the air." Finn raised his fork and drew corkscrews rolling through the night air. "It's like what you said about straight lines and arches." He crisscrossed his fingers in front of him.

"Fusion," Jon said. "Maybe a better word is flow. You were experiencing the power of humans working with nature instead of trying to control it."

Finn thought about this and agreed. "I like the idea of this big fish just waiting for that right fly, and the moment it sees the perfect one, it can't even control itself. It just," he flicked all his fingers out, "goes for it. Grabs it and won't let it go even if it pulls out of its own." "Comfort zone?" Finn nodded. Yeah, the place it controls." Jon smiled at the boy. Finn was eating more of his meal. He sat back and looked at the lantern light. "I want to write a letter about that to my mother for her birthday."

Jon wiped his mouth and turned his chair out towards the fountain. He sipped his water. "To the woman I met or to your real Mother?"

"No, my real Mother, Pansy. I haven't felt like I could write while away from here."

"Why is that?"

Finn scratched his head. "Just doesn't feel safe in a way. Like no one would appreciate it. I can make mistakes around you. You are different. I wish everyone I knew was like you."

Jon pushed back his chair. It was a lot to hear. Especially after he felt like such a failure with Penny and Elizabeth. "Well, you are in luck." He went inside, brought back the writer's box to the table held by his good hand and hip, and set it down. "Go ahead, open it." Finn lifted the lid, removed the different stationary pieces, and looked at the strange fountain pens. "You can use all this to write letters to anyone you want. Here." Jon went into the kitchen and returned with a roll of brown paper. "Use this cheap paper to practice on. Write a draft of your letter, leave it alone, and return to it. When you get it to say what you want and how you want to say it, then you can write it on one of these nice cards, and we'll send it to her. We will send her flowers too. Decent people send flowers. If you ever show up at someone's house in France, you better have a bouquet of God Damn flowers." He looked at the floor and then away.

Finn smiled. With Jon's help, he could give his real mother a gift that she would see and value. Not one of the things he made by himself that disappeared or went into the outbuilding. With Jon's help, he could send her an adult gift, something she would keep and not throw away like his kindergarten drawings.

"Why don't you work on that, and I will do the dishes," Jon said. Finn was eager to use the items in the box and start creating his letter. Jon was happy for the diversion, and as he set the dishes by the sink, he reached under the cabinet and took a shot of bourbon. He looked briefly around the door and took another. He thought it would hold him over. He washed the dishes, making more trips than usual since he did everything with one hand. He returned and was surprised at how far Finn had gotten in his letter. He obviously had been thinking about it for a long time. Finn was still heavily concentrated, and Jon felt it was okay to pour himself a drink. He went back into the kitchen and poured some bourbon into a mug he used for tea. He came back and sat down, and Finn finished his rough draft and leaned back to think about it. "So? What do you think?" Jon said.

"You want me to read it to you?" "Of course." Jon listened to the boy's letter, and parts of it were truly beautiful. Finn described the lines bending and arcing through the air as he cast the fly and let it land on the water. The fish beneath the water and what he felt when it connected with all its power and never let the small fly go. There was a moment when Finn almost cried. He was passionate about what he wanted to say. He was almost desperate to connect to his mother in the way he wanted his mother to love him so badly. "What do you think?"

Jon raised his eyebrows. "I think it's beautiful, Finn. I'd be very proud to call you my son."

"But the words. I mean, should I change them somehow? Is this how you would write a letter to Mrs. Elizabeth?"

Jon thought for a second. "Finn, I've always thought that if you want to communicate with someone, you must take yourself out of the writing. When you are addressing a crowd, the moment you say I everyone stops listening. People want to have their own adventures, do their own problem-solving, and self-teach or arrive at the answer to their problems on their own. So, if you want to truly communicate with someone, your letter needs to be ninety-nine percent story and one percent experience. The last line may be, I was flung for thee. Finn was thinking about what Jon was saying. "When a rose blooms, it doesn't call out and say come look at me, come see how good I smell. It sits in the wind while someone stops and asks, 'What is that sweet fragrance?' They go searching and find their own rose."

Finn leaned back in his chair and smiled. "For an old tree, you sure are wise."

Jon smiled at the boy. "You know why, don't you? I've had a lot of shit piled up around me." Finn laughed heartily at the swear word.

Jon sipped at his mug. He nodded toward the letter. "That's good work, Son. Let it sit and think about it."

Finn moved it around on the table. "I finished that book, Flight Deck. It was really good. I would've brought it back to you if I had known I was coming."

"You should talk to Bobby. He served in Guadalcanal." "He was there?" "Yeah, sure was." "Where were you? Jon held the mug in his hand but did not drink from it. "Europe, France mostly."

"Is that why you named the valley before the vineyard the French Valley?" Jon nodded, and this time he smelt the spirits in the mug. "Why don't you ever talk about the war? Jon set the mug down. He moved his head sideways. "It was a job. I survived it; others didn't. It didn't define my life for others; it does." "What about Bobby?" Jon looked up at the lanterns getting uncomfortable. "You have to ask him."

"Did you have the same jobs?"

Jon shook his head. "No, Bobby was a corpsman. A medic. He went into combat without a gun. That's how much they thought of Black men back then."

"And you had a gun?"

Jon nodded his head slowly. He tapped his head. "I had my mind." Finn leaned forward and rested his elbows on his knees. He had a lot of questions in the lantern light, and Jon knew the deep one, the one he didn't want to talk about, was coming. . "What do you mean?" Jon, his tongue loose, and his pain dulled, felt free to talk. "The German Army was this massive, complicated machine and had been for over a hundred years. Everyone assumed them unstoppable. Especially the Nazis. There was this German general named Rommel. He was a tank commander in the Second World War, but he was a very efficient combat soldier in the First World War. He kept journals of all his exploits. His near misses, his defeats, and his failures. The German army made his journals into a book of small platoon tactics and based all their foot soldiers' training off of it. Anyways, we all knew the war was coming, and we were going to get swept up in it. I had always read military history. When I realized I would fight in Europe, I read everything I could find about my enemy. If you want to win a battle, you must first know yourself, and second, you must know your enemy. I had already learned to read and write in German. I had a good understanding of French. I read Rommel's journals in German. Nearly memorized them."

Jon took a sip from his mug and Finn realized it wasn't tea because of the wince he made around his lips and the tea would have long been cold by now. He smelled a fragrance in the air, and it was not that of a rose, but like syrup. "When we got in theater our Platoon leader was shot in the head the first day. I assumed command and knew immediately that if we were going to survive, we would need to fight in an unconventional way. So, we did." Jon wanted to end there but he knew the boy was longing for more. He tried to pivot the conversation. "What do you want to do tomorrow?"

Finn didn't need to think long. "I want to see the vineyard. I want to go back to where I got cut, see what I did, figure out my mistake, and learn from it." Jon was impressed that the child did not blame him. "I have a scar on my thigh, and since I will carry it for life, I want to understand it and carry the lesson of it as long as I have the scar." The bourbon in the mug seemed cowardly now. The boy continued. " I also want to reread the poem engraved on the brass plates. I want to see if what I have memorized is exactly what it says.

You know, test my memory, make sure it's accurate with the truth."

Jon thought of all the lies life had forced him to tell to shield his heart from the truth and how he began to believe them at some point. He rubbed his hand on his jeans. He stood and raised his eyebrows. "Better hit the rack then. Come help me make up your bed." The two got up from the table, and each blew out one of the hanging lanterns. Jon closed the door. Finn brushed his teeth in the side bathroom he had always used. He came out, and Jon was tucking the sheets around the corner of the bed with one hand. Finn helped. When they finished, Jon told Finn good night. "Last time I was here, I told you thank you for having me," Finn said. "For listening to me. Taking me seriously. If it wasn't for you, Mrs. Elizabeth, and Bobby, I don't know I would be here now." Feeling the damaged foot and the twinge of pain each time, he carried his Father. "I never thought I'd be back, and I'm going to enjoy every moment." Jon hugged him.

The vineyard was different now that Jon had finished cleaning and was maintaining it. They walked each row of grapes, and Finn recalled what he remembered from the pruning lessons and the branch collars with Jon. "You remember the different kinds of Pine trees on the mountain?" " Loblolly, Virginia, and White Pine. I guess this is the spot where I got cut?" Jon winced as if he was injured by the memory. Jon explained how the saw worked and the built-in safety features. " I should have explained this before." " Well, there is no wisdom without memory." Jon looked at Finn. " You reading philosophy?" " I don't know what philosophy means. It's just something I heard Bobby say. Where is Bobby?" "Busy, I reckon. You want to try and crank the saw and cut something?"

The base of the Gazebo was adorned in fading daffodils. They were no longer emerging stems but mature blossoms of sorrow that left Jon's heart alone like the picture nail in the cabin wall. A place where love could have hung its merit badge. Finn touched the wisteria vines wrapping around the green steel of the Gazebo. Kneeling in front of each brass plate, he read the poem again. " I brought this piece of paper to rub a copy of the inscription. It's something special." Jon nodded. "Lot said there. Poetry and all. Lot said there." When Finn traced the brass plates. He returned the paper to his pocket. Jon sat on the soapstone steps looking out over French Valley, and Finn joined him. "What does unconventional mean?" Finn repointed the pencil with his pocketknife.

"It means not scripted." Jon looked over. "Not by the book. Something different than what is expected." Finn looked at the pencil's point, holding it to the sun. "What did you learn from all those books that helped you fight unconventionally in the war?" Jon thought for a moment of the best way to proceed. "I led a squad of like-minded men. Where most squads or platoons are in constant contact or in need of resupply from a forward operating base, my squad lived off the enemy." Finn was listening. Not giving Jon too much direct attention. "If we needed food, ammunition, medical supplies, then we hunted our enemy and took it." Jon wanted to end here.

"And what else?" Finn asked.

"We approached the conventional tactics of the enemy in an unconventional way." He thought the answer would cause Finn to chew on it, but he didn't.

"Like what?"

Jon looked far out over the valley. "Rommel had set up his platoons with a heavy machine gun in the front and one in the rear. We would wait for a large fog to settle in and then run through their patrols, splitting them into two. Those in the rear patrol would stumble over the bodies of the soldiers in front of them and immediately think they were being ambushed. They would fire on the front of the patrol with the heavy gun. Those in the front would think they were being attacked from the rear and turn their heavy gun on their own troops." Jon exhaled deeply. "We would go a week sometimes and never fire a shot."

"Did you use guns?" Jon shook his head at the valley. "Not so much." "Did you come up with that plan?"

Jon looked over at him. "That was Lord Nelson in the Straits of Gibraltar. Pursued by two warships. He headed into the oncoming night. When darkness fell, he turned out all his lights and dropped sail. The two men of war passed his ship simultaneously, and when they did, he released full broadsides into both ships. The enemy's ships, still under sail, cleared his vessel, thought they were under attack, and immediately fired into each other, sinking with friendly fire. Unconventional."

"I want to read about him." Jon smiled and stood up, hoping they could leave now. "What was your best victory?" Jon looked at the boy, firmly sitting on the steps and not budging. "Winning the hearts of the people." Finn squinted his eyes. "How so?" Rome and Greece produced some of the greatest generals and leaders the world has ever known. Many won the war only to come home and be put to death or exiled. A good leader knows that the war is fought for the hearts of his people and battles are fought for the ground they call home. So, we met the needs of the people in the villages and countryside. Made sure they had food, and evacuation plans, proper bomb shelters. In turn, they did us favors and kept us operating and alive. Most people think to beat a Giant, you've got to meet it head on the battlefield. You don't. You just have to cut off his toes one at a time."

"What about Jean-Paul? Theo said he died for love."

Jon started to turn his back, and then he remembered Finn wanting to confront the chainsaw and give purpose to his scar. Did he have that kind of courage? He looked out across the valley to the setting sun. "He was a kid. Not much older than you. He had it rough. Nazis had taken his family, and he had been hiding under a shed floor for days when we found him, and he was praying with his hands clasped and his eyes shut. He opened his eyes and then smiled and said God answered his prayers. He always prayed a certain prayer before he ate. I still hear his voice nearly every meal. He'd clasp his hands and say. Earth, who gives us this food. Sun, who makes it ripe and good. Dearest Earth and Dearest Sun to you, we give our loving thanks." Jon looked as the sun slipped away. "He was a lover of many things." Jon's voice cracked. "Witty, quick, hard worker. Every time we had an opportunity to drop him somewhere, he would just march out with us." He faced Finn, finding the courage to speak about his grief. "We liked him. He was a good boy. Helped us dream of home and having children of our own. When I think of him, I whisper that prayer." "You reckon he hears it? You know now when you say it?" "I'd say yes. Right now, yeah, right now, I have to say yes."

"How did he die?"

Jon bit his lip to control the memory. "I don't have to talk about that." He began to leave. Finn stood up and trailed behind towards the new green truck.

"So, you always won?"

Jon smiled. "Every Hannibal has his Carthage. Even Napoleon had his Waterloo."

In the dusky silence, they drove back towards the cabin. Jon pointed up to the Eaves of the barn. "You see her?"

Finn leaned to the glass. "Is that the one that came to breakfast?"

"Sure is. She lives up there now." Finn lifted a palm to the Dove as if seeing a familiar face in a vintage frame. "I've got something to do here. Would you go up to the house and feed the fish? Be there directly." The boy turned again and smiled at the Dove, then ran beside the great sea of grass to the cabin. Plunging his hands into the corn and scattering the kernels in a wide arc above the pool. Then the fish children came from the deep like dark spears splitting the liquid night. He fell to his knees and watched the feeding. "There's a mighty river there. We just can't see it." Jon stood on the porch beside the corn barrel. He had the coffee mug in his hand.

Finn turned. "God lives in the space between man and what he desires the most." "What did you say?" The first sip of bourbon and Jon was drunk. "Something that Preacher said. God lives in the space between man and what he desires the most." " What does that mean?" " No clue." "Why did you say it?" Jon turned the mug with both hands and leaned against the porch column. " I just imagine that river sometimes. Wonder how it flows. I think about that granite rock that hides it, contains it. How mighty that stone barrier must be." "Is the river what you want?" Jon shook his head and looked down. " I'm fine with the rock." " Well, if the rock busted loose, we might be destroyed." Jon looked at the boy kneeling in the grass. " Might turn free." Finn looked back at the pond, then spun around and looked at Jon, who was leaving the porch. "Hey, where's the piano?"

"Having it restored." Jon lifted the coffee mug with his good arm. "I'm going to start dinner."

Finn stayed in the yard as the first of the fireflies were twinkling in the cool air of the night. Walking around the fountain, he pulled off his shoes, stepped into the small pool of water, and felt how smooth and worn the limestone had become with years of use.

"Dinner up."

Finn turned and saw Jon setting down a plate on the table, and he ran over, still barefoot. "Pizzas. So, you took a baguette and toasted it, then made a pizza. I think they call that Stouffers."

"Never heard of them, eat."

Jon refilled his mug and came back to the table. Finn placed the rubbings he had made at the Gazebo in the writer's box.

"How's the letter coming?"

Finn nodded his head. He was now standing at the table, eating with one hand and sorting his papers with the other. "How would you describe this fountain?"

Finn was interested in playing Jon's game. "I would say the Cherokee came here sometimes together and sometimes alone, but the fountain always listened and gave them understanding and wisdom. It gave them something Gold couldn't buy."

Jon smiled half-heartedly. "Gold?"

"Yeah, money can't buy."

Jon slid his chair back from the table. He leaned down and scratched his leg. "Did Bobby tell you that?"

Finn looked up from his papers. "When's Bobby coming by? I miss him?"

"Did Bobby tell you about the gold?"

Finn looked up at Jon, ready for another story. "What gold?"

Jon raised his head toward the pond. "The drought. The time we thought the fountain might run dry. Did he tell you too?"

Finn realized that Jon was being serious. "Tell me what? You're acting strange."

Jon rubbed his hand slowly over the hair on his head and breathed out. Like he unwittingly had let out the truth of a secret he had held for nearly all his life. John got up and refilled his mug. This time leaving the bottle out on the counter. He sat back down, and for the first time, he removed the sling from his arm. "Supposed to come off tomorrow anyways." He laid it on the table, out of character. "There's a legend about a payroll officer for the Confederate Army named Motlow that was taking a huge shipment of gold from the coast up to Richmond. The story goes that he was raised in these parts, and when two Northern Scouts started tracking him, he came to this mountain and hid the gold in an old clay jug factory the Cherokee started. People have looked all over. Hell, every year, we've got to run off a few. We, Bobby, Ruby, and I, first heard the story from the man who adopted us and brought us up here. He was a bad drunk. Blurted out that not only was he the wealthiest man in the county but that there was hidden gold on his land. He just had to find it." Jon sighed and rolled his eyes toward the ceiling. "He tried. He would get drunk and swear. Curse the moon and the mountain for hiding it from him. "We looked too. We were already all over the mountain sourcing timber, but we would spend all our spare time making maps and marking out places. The war came, and we gave up on it. Then we started building Elizabeth's vineyard. We would come home every night and bathe in the fountain or swim there in the pond." Jon stared into his mug of memory. He burped, and Finn jerked his head at the stench.

"This bad drought came one summer. No rain at all, and that's bad being up on a mountain because there's no water on top of a mountain, you see. That's what makes this mountain entirely different. There's like a huge spring or river that swirls up inside of this one." He raised his hand as if pushing off an unasked question. "I can't explain it." His words slurred slightly. He stretched his bad arm out. Finn was surprised. "We kept coming home, and the water in the pond was getting lower and lower. Then water in the fountain started to change. We figured it made sense. No rain, no water. All the foliage was turning brown. Even the field out there was nearly dirt. We came home one day, and the water had dropped so low that a small stream was barely coming out of the fountain. Ruby went over to wash off, and for some reason, he pushed a stick in between the rocks where the water normally gushed out, and when he did, a gold coin popped out and fell at his feet. He started hollering, and we all ran over there like he had been bitten by a snake. That's when another coin popped out, and then another. The water started flowing again like usual. "We sat around all night trying to figure out what this meant. There had to be a way inside the mountain. We had always thought that these pools were where the people who lived here washed their clothes and cookware, but could they have settled in this meadow because this was the Jug Factory? We went to work on the vineyard the next day, and that's when Bobby put it together."

Finn was leaning forward, hanging on every word. "What was that? What did Bobby figure out?"

"The space in the wall of the pond. The place that I used to pull myself down to and feel the cold water rushing out. That had to be the opening to the old Jug Factory. Then Ruby made a plan. He had been at Pearl Harbor trying to free sailors from sunken ships and knew a way for us to get in there safely. We came home and rigged it all up. Elizabeth had found two more coins while we were gone. Ruby had this balloon, and we rigged it with an air hose and a light that ran inside it. We put it in the opening, and then, using a compressor, we filled the balloon with air and turned the light on. I went down with a mask and peered into the opening and could see that it was a vast cavern." Jon pointed over Finn's shoulder towards the granite boulders on the far side of the pond.

Finn turned around to see and, in his mind, imagined it all.

"I surfaced and told them what I'd seen. Ruby said he would assemble everything safely and then instruct me on how to go about going in there. A few days later, the water dropped below the opening, and we could see inside. Ruby still insisted on the use of the equipment and not being rash. We hauled the gold out of that cavern for the next four days and across the pond. The day we finished, it began to rain, and I've never seen the opening to the old Jug Factory again."

Finn was mesmerized by the story. "How did Motlow know about it?"

Jon shook his head. "I don't know. When we went inside, there were several different sets of Civil War gear. Evidently, it was a safe place for deserters. At that time, you must have been able to dive under the water and come up inside the cave. I assume the underground waters increased and flooded the whole space at once. I guess that's why the location of the Factory was lost to history. No one thought to look underwater on a mountain." He poured himself water. "You are the only person I have ever told about this, Finn. It's a secret."

Finn nodded. "Do you still have it?"

Jon stretched his shoulder. "Not all of it but a fair amount. It's out in the Sawmill. You've passed it a hundred times."

Finn smiled. "Let's go see it."

They took their plates inside and grabbed flashlights. Entering through the apartment door, Jon turned on the lights and took Finn back to the wood shop. Jon raised his hands. "Here it is."

Finn looked around the shop at all the tools hanging on the walls, the benches, the cans of glue the old scrap wood of various lengths. He looked under the tables and drawers but couldn't find it. Jon was resting against a bench near bins of ruff-cut dimensional wood. Jon picked one up. "What are those for?" Finn asked. "These are stretchers. We lay these between stacks of wood so they can dry out. Just scrap material, nothing important." Jon laid one on a large butcher's block. "Grab that hatchet over there and chop it in half." Finn returned to the bench, unsure why Jon wanted him to chop the wood in half. He heaved the hatchet back and came down with force on the wood stick. It split in two, revealing shiny gold coins in each piece. Finn's mouth dropped wide open. "What?" That whole part of the shop was filled with scrap wood.

"Grab another," Finn repeated the process four more times. Each stick of wood was the same. Jon chuckled and went to a drawer and removed a wide chisel. He stood one of the chopped pieces on end and split it with the chisel. The pieces slowly split in half, revealing rows of gold coins. Jon took his finger and tapped his mouth. "These lips don't lie, kid."

After several minutes of looking at the coins and explaining their markings, Jon closed the shop door, turned off the lights, and they walked back to the cabin. "So, you all have the same amount?"

"Yeah, split it three ways."

"How much was there?"

Jon shook his head and was quiet for a moment. "Remember that picture in Bobby's office at the church. The one where Ruby is standing under the fountain, and the water is flowing all over him?"

"The black and white one?"

"Yeah, that's it. Those shadows? The black and white photo makes you think it's just large drops of water, but it was actually gold coins he was throwing in the air."

When they reached the porch, Jon said, "Finn, I've shared my life's secret with you. I'd appreciate it if you keep it to yourself. At least until I'm dead and gone." Finn nodded and held out his hand to shake. Jon took it and hugged him.

"I'm probably not going to be able to sleep tonight," Finn said.

Jon laughed. "Just dream, kid."

The following day, they made toast for breakfast. This seemed unusual to Finn, but he didn't question it. Jon drank his coffee and turned the pages of the small yellow book of poetry. On the last page of the book, he started sketching. Finn leaned over his shoulder to look and whistled.

"You being nosey?"

Finn sat down across the table. "You drawing you a girlfriend?" Jon stopped drawing, bit the half pencil's end, and looked up. Finn grinned at him.

"Finn, I've been thinking about building a pond beside the house in the grass field. Another pond full of fish like this one." Finn looked around. He was taking in the idea. "I thought we could do it together."

"I want to fix up the old vineyard cart so we could drive it over to the vineyard," Finn said. "That would be cool. When are we going to get started on that?" Jon was quiet for a minute. "Well, we will get to it. You know, this pond I'm talking about would be big enough to take a canoe out on. You could fish from the canoe."

Finn spread jam on his toast. "I can do that in the upper pond." Finn had a point, but Jon needed him to get on board. To get excited about his idea. "You can run the machine."

Finn took a bite of his toast and shrugged. "I run machines all the time. My Dad sells them."

"Machines that big?" Jon pointed over his shoulder with his thumb toward the Motor Grader by the Sawmill.

Finn looked at the machine unimpressed. "Piece of Cake."

Jon smiled. "Prove it."

The two giant machines ripped into the soft soil of the field of grass. Finn looked at the enormous straight blade as it spun endless spirals of dark red earth up and over like a plow. He could see earthworms, and small stones, mixed in with the large clumps of grass, tuberous roots, and wild onions. He could see hordes of grasshoppers of all different sizes holding on to the grass, and at the last moment, when all was certainly lost, they took flight, knowing they would never return. Some in anger flew straight at Finn and covered his face and neck to where he had to push them off his face. The machine still rumbled on with smoke flowing from its pipe and the giant rubber tires ever pushing the impending destruction of the once tranquil sea.

Jon led Finn with his own machine. The two leviathans, one slightly behind the other and to the side, like battleships on a mighty sea. Jon would occasionally stand looking over a flotilla and point to things that needed attention. Finn could not sit in the giant seat and still operate the foot pedals as required. So, he stood too, imitating the man he saw and idolized even though he didn't understand why they were doing this. Finn liked the field. It was an essential part of the mountain. He had always envisioned not just the grass field but, in ancient times, hundreds of dwellings scattered across it. Of animals milling around and being fed and small children running and playing between the dwellings. He had always imagined that the driveway would have been their main road to the community but also the fountain and the pond. On special occasions, they would gather there and ascend the stone stairs to the Rest to offer prayers and supplications to the Elder Fire. How the families would descend the staircase in the moonlight, reaching out to touch the ancient trees, and once the children's feet touched the moss-covered stones, how they would run in the moonlight to this red clay earth.

Jon turned his machine towards the center and motioned for Finn to continue on the perimeter. Jon was using his machine to push the topsoil out of the swale being created, and Finn continued tapering the outside edge of the giant bowl. Jon turned his machine, stretched far out of the seat, and tossed a thermos of water to Finn. Finn turned it up even with the grasshoppers clinging to his face and chest, and as the water poured over his mouth, he saw crimson rivulets streaming down his shirt and arms. He passed Jon again, and the man swirled two fingers around his head and then drew a thumb across his neck. Finn knew they would soon stop for lunch.

On the second go-round, the boy drove the giant machine up to the sawmill, where Jon was waiting to fill the beast with fuel. Finn pulled the choke on the machine, and the engine came to rest. Jon seemed spry as if the work was invigorating to him. He was speaking louder than normal. "Not bad for a morning's work." He stuck the nozzle into the machine's tank and pulled the lever. Finn could see the splashing fuel in the tank and dots of it outside. "Don't rub your eyes. Here, do this." Jon held a cotton towel under the thermos of water he had tossed to Finn. "Now then." He handed Finn the damp, cool rag, and the boy wiped his eyes. " Them grasshoppers latching on to you? They bothersome when they go to fightin'." Finn didn't respond. He felt sick for destroying their home. "Don't mind them. Few days more and will be down to chipping clay." He was still talking loudly and surveying the massacred field like a brutal man used to doing brutal things. "Probably going to hit some rocks. Shouldn't be a problem for these machines. They'll get pushed out to the side, and we will pick them up this evening. You can drive the truck. New truck and all. Yes, Sir." He tapped the end of the nozzle into the tank and then handed it down to Finn. " How's your arm? Shouldn't you rest it?" " Aww, good as new." He rotated it. "I got a spot for them rocks. I think I want to build a shed up by the rest. We will haul the good ones up there. Toss the other ones." Finn turned to replace the nozzle. " You don't mind tossing them rocks, do you? A little work like this is a good experience. You know, mountain living isn't all fishing and picnics."

Jon lowered himself down from the machine, and Finn noticed that the wrinkles on his face were covered in dark red clay dust. Finn smiled at him.

"Don't laugh too hard. You look the same." A truck pulled into the driveway. Jon leaned over to Finn. "Go make us some of those pizzas while I talk to this fella."

Finn started running towards the house when he heard Jon holler. "Wash up first." Finn threw his hand above his shoulder in acknowledgment. The smell of plowed earth pervaded the entire meadow as he ran down the driveway. Finn imagined all the earthworms plunging deeper into denser soils, looking for a place to sleep tonight.

He washed in the cool water of the fountain. He made their lunches and moved the plates to the table. Jon washed and joined, still in a good mood.

"Having fun driving that big machine?"

Finn took a bite and raised one eyebrow. "It's kind of what I do."

Jon chuckled. "Oh yeah? Been farming long, have you?" Finn shook his head. "Are you at least having fun?" Finn set down his homemade pizza. "I feel strange about it." He paused momentarily, and Jon looked at his lunch as if he hadn't heard the comment. "I mean, we could fill it all in. Probably wouldn't hurt anything."

"What feels strange about it? I thought you'd like to build a pond."

Finn took a drink of his ginger ale and sat back in his chair. "When we first moved to the wheat hill house, it was surrounded by peach trees. They were old trees not in great health, but they were laid out in terraced rows and formed big sweeping arcs over most of the acreage. They didn't produce a lot of peaches or great peaches, but there was always enough for us to eat in summer. The best part of having them there was that they would bloom these beautiful pink flowers in the early spring. All the fields for a few days would be like carpets of pink. One day we came home, and my dad hired a bulldozer man to push up all the peach trees. I can still remember that day. My stepmother told me to take a glass of cold water to the man running the machine. I remembered seeing all those beautiful trees piled up in a huge mound of twisted trunks and blooming branches. I watched the man drink the glass of cold water. He gave it back to me and thanked me. I stepped backward over the clods of soil and deep holes where the trees had once been held in place by their roots. The man with the machine dumped fuel on the twisted pile of trees and lit it on fire. He thought I would be amused, kind of like you."

Jon was finishing his lunch and did not look up from his plate. He was quiet. Finn finished his ginger ale. After lunch, they walked back to the machines. Finn saddled up and waited for instructions. Jon finally turned around. "I don't know what we will find in the soil, if anything. Like I said, the rocks we'll get out of the way at the end of the day. I put a bandana on your seat. Cover your face with it when it starts getting dusty." He cranked the machine, and Finn cranked his own.

The sun had dried out the top layer of soil, and Finn watched as it seemed like he was creating ample folds of ribbon with the blade of the machine. He saw the first stones. He watched as they rolled and tumbled but did not break into pieces. They eventually rolled off the blade and further into the basin. He hit something larger like fieldstone, and he watched as the piece rolled under the blade and made a furrow deeper in the soil. He was raising small stones now, and some very soft would break in many pieces, and he couldn't tell if it had been a rock broken into many pieces or just gravel in the soil. He made several more passes, occasionally looking at Jon pushing the topsoil up and out of the basin, timing the movements of his machine so it did not hinder Finn's progress. Occasionally, he gave Finn a thumbs up, but mostly, he looked very determined and concentrated on the soil beneath his machine.

Finn hit another grouping of dense stones, and he noticed that they had straight edges on them, and he thought that was peculiar. He watched them not rolling but being pushed and occasionally flipping hard onto the ground before becoming lodged under the blade and snapping. He was surprised when the dirty stone broke in two, and the inside of the stone looked bright and new. Like it had never seen the light of day. Finn watched it pass like a channel marker in the open sea. He stopped daydreaming when the machine was about to make its turn, and it started to strain, and the motor began to choke down. Finn looked at the blade, and no less than thirty stones had piled up in front of it, all being pushed because they had straight, squared edges. He stopped the machine and turned it off. He got down and pushed the bandana under his chin. He looked over at Jon, but he was still pushing topsoil from the basin. Finn touched the stones. They were wet with the moisture of the soil. Finn thought they were peculiar. Not like stones, he saw on top of the soil around the mountain. These stones had straight lines; he knew that was a sign of man. Man conforming and controlling something. He placed his hand entirely in the center of one rock and realized it was cupped out like a bowl. He removed his pocket knife and scratched at the clay. Inspecting other stones in the pile, he realized they were much the same, just different sizes.

Jon's machine choked down, and Finn stood up to see if he could get his attention, but Jon had hopped off and was getting in the new truck. He drove down into the basin and backed up to Finn's machine like he had expected the stones to pile up in this way, and it was time to move them. Finn was confused. This was something peculiar that should be discussed.

Jon got out of the truck and tossed Finn a pair of leather gloves too big for his hands. "Well, pretty good stopping point for today. We will get up early tomorrow and get started before it's too hot." He lifted one of the stones. "I figured we get them loaded and drop them off at the Rest. I want to build a shed up there to store things in. A place to camp out and cook dinner." Finn was looking at the rocks. "These stones have been shaped." Jon said nothing as he lifted one to the truck's tailgate. Finn laid his hand on it. "Look, it has a depression in the middle of it. Most of them have it. Jon went for another stone and was waiting for Finn to help him lift it, but Finn walked in front of him and around the blade of the machine. "So many of them like that." He looked back at Jon, who sat on the tailgate and was looking over at him. Beads of turmeric sweat rolled down his face into the buttoned-up shirt. "See, they were spaced out in a line, and I kept picking them up in front of the blade." Jon took off his gloves and drank from the thermos of water. "They were squared off; that's why they didn't tumble but got pushed."

Jon looked over at what green grass was still left in the field. He cast suggestions to Finn like bait to a fish. "What are you thinking? A rock quarry, maybe? Some Mason's scrap pieces? Maybe scrap from one of the old mansions. Maybe the old hotel foundation." Jon stood up and put his gloves back on. "What are you saying? I can't understand you." "Well, I'm saying people dump their leftovers. Square edges will make easy work for the foundation." He started lifting the dense stones one by one until the truck was full. He picked up all the round stones he could find from the basin.

They climbed into the truck, and both drank from the thermos. The truck climbed slowly out of the hole in the grassy sea and started up the arcing ridge road of the mountain. Finn could see that sunset would be soon. They were both filthy. Too filthy to enter the house without washing first in the fountain. Finn was almost too tired to think about cooking or eating dinner. The sunburn from the day felt hot on his face.

At the top of the mountain and they began unloading the stone. Finn was sore, but Jon seemed driven by determination. Finn rolled a stone over, and it pinched his finger. "Careful now," Jon said. Finn looked up at him, waiting for him to acknowledge the awkwardness of the whole situation, but Jon carried on with a blind eye. "I can't understand you. Can we talk about this? What you're saying doesn't make sense to me. "The nice square ones I want to put over here away from the Rest. The round ones, you can chuck them over the side. Just be careful, and don't throw yourself over the side."

Finn carried an armful of the round stones between the giant rocks and laid them down a few feet from the cliff's edge. " You said you wanted the round ones here? He sat down and removed his gloves. He had a purple blood blister forming on his finger. He looked down the undulating peaks of the Blue Ridge until he could see no further. He was mad at the contradictions he didn't understand in a man he idealized. A person who had given him so much clarity, understanding, and education was now muddling everything beautiful about life. Could he still trust him?

He nudged a round stone with his boot, but it only moved slightly and rested back in its spot. He sucked on his finger and then bit it slightly and stood up and kicked the round stone hard, and it sailed out into the air and fell into oblivion. He tried to kick another stone, but his boot rolled over it, and he spun around dangerously near the cliff's edge as if the stone was defeating him. He sighed in disgust, picked up the stone, and hurled it off the cliff, pushing it violently away from his chest. He picked up another and slung it hard with one hand, then another, and another until all were gone.

Jon walked up and dropped another armload of round stones by the Finn's feet. Finn sat down. Jon stood before the sun, and Finn shielded his eyes to look up at him. "You know you've said 'I' a lot today," Finn said.

Jon turned slightly. "What?"

"You've said 'I' a lot today." Jon sighed. "You said if someone wants to truly communicate with people, they must take 'I' out of the conversation." Jon nodded, walked back to the truck, and took out the thermos. Finn watched as he walked over to the area where he was considering building his camping shed. Finn looked down at the blood blister on his hand. Jon seemed like just another man. Someone greedy, proud, and consumed by what he wanted to do. Even if it was as silly as running loud and stinking equipment or throwing stones from a cliff. Jon had changed from the kind lover of art and beauty into a raw and uninteresting needy creature rooting through the remnants of life's onion skins and carrot tips.

* * *

They had been digging for days. Jon would walk out early into the basin each morning and pick up handfuls of soil like a Diviner. Casting it or balling it in his hand. Proclaiming whether they could make progress that day or would be delayed. Around and around, Finn went with the motor grader, and the basin got deeper with every turn. And every day, they talked less in a common language Finn could understand. Lunch was the same each day, and Jon was so tired at night that he opened a can of tomato soup for them to eat. Promising he would go into town the next day for groceries.

Finn asked about the odd-shaped stones they began to see. Picking his words carefully. The hard stones didn't break and moved strangely beneath the giant steel blade of the machine. Jon sorted through them, separating each pile and placing them in different places. Paying Finn daily with a pile of stones he could toss in frustration from the Rest where Skyuka had been killed. "How do you say wagon again in French?" " You ask every day." "I'm practicing. Practice makes perfect, right?" "No, practice makes permanent." "When are we going to work on the wagon?" "I want to stop this pond and throwing stones. It doesn't feel right, and the field is destroyed. You said that every heart recognizes truth, but this doesn't feel right. This needs to be corrected. We are destroying something beautiful, and you are ignoring me." "You said that wrong. I'm not ignoring you. I'm teaching you about life. Your life can be beautiful, and in an instant, it can be destroyed. It will be up to you to make it beautiful again. God lives in the space between man and what he wants the most. God is in the work it takes to get there." He thrust his finger at Finn, and the boy stared back. "God is not in this work. That's just the story you're telling yourself. You didn't just bulldoze peach trees and lite the blossoms on fire. You've ripped up the heritage of the Elder Fire, the homes of the Chiefs of Peace. There is a difference between Wisdom and Knowledge. Wisdom is round and all-encompassing. Knowledge is a straight line. Moses struck the rock, and God punished him." " God isn't punishing me." " No, God is not. You're doing that all by yourself."

At lunch, a blue-gray Chevrolet pickup pulled up the driveway. Finn recognized the truck, and his stomach sank. Jon didn't seem alarmed. The Preacher got out of the truck and walked over to the porch, and placed a booted foot on the smooth planks. "My, my, looks like a different place around here." The booming voice surpassing a large smile. His hooded eyes looked into the shade of the porch and fell open Finn like a corded noose, but he did not seem surprised that he was here. The Preacher looked again at the vast pile of topsoil that appeared to dwarf the earth-moving machines. He whistled in amazement. "Black Gold right there. Yankees buy that up in a heartbeat around Greenville."

Jon turned his chair so his back would not be to the Preacher. "Well, that's not for sale. I've got plans for it."

The Preacher chuckled. "Oh, I bet you do. I'm glad you do. This is good work you are doing."

Jon motioned to the table. "Make yourself some lunch if you like. We will find you a chair."

"Finn, how are you, son?" Finn reluctantly made eye contact with the man who had left him in a well for two days. He started to say good, but that wasn't the truth. He wanted to tell someone, anyone, who would listen, that this didn't feel right. Recruited to destroy something he had cherished on the slim hope that they could create something equally beautiful. It was like watching Jon set fire to the cabin, sorting through the remains with him, then planing the charred boards into something smooth and as beautiful as they once had been. He could just look the Preacher in the eye and give him several strong head nods like he was doing okay.

The Preacher cleared his throat. "I need to talk to you about your father."

Finn's heart leaped, and his ears burned. He pushed back from the table and stood, awaiting words that could determine the rest of his life.

"He's okay now, son. Sit down. You can sit down." The preacher stretched a hand out to the boy in the first act of compassion Finn had ever seen him offer anyone. Finn was on the point of tears. He sat back down. "He made it to the hospital, and after a few days, his fever broke. Now they did some type of experimental surgery on him. I don't know exactly what all that involved, but I know it lasted sixteen hours - and he survived that too. Evidently, he woke up and watched them close his stomach up. I can't imagine that. It's a long shot, but if he continues to get stronger, he may be home soon. Maybe in time for the July camp meeting at the church."

The preacher looked over to the vast hole in the earth and tossed words towards Jon, "Down to the chipping clay, huh? About halfway, you reckon?".

"Probably so," Jon said. "What's that now?" "I said Probably so."

The Preacher turned back. "You get finished up in time; we'd love to have you come down to the Camp Meeting."

"I won't be up here during that time. Just wanted to let you know. People come by the thousands from all over to that meeting. I put it together years ago. It's really something to see."

"I bet so." The Preacher twisted his head, puzzled at Jon.

Finn stood and cleared his bowl. He looked at the Preacher. "Do you know where my stepmother is? Will she be home for my father, you know, if it makes it and all?"

"See Marlene every Wednesday service. She's been spending the rest of her time with family down in the low country. I think Myrtle Beach, she said." That didn't sound familiar to Finn, but he got the information he wanted.

Jon took his bowl to the kitchen. Finn took the hint and did the same. He wanted to show the preacher the interesting stones he had gathered. He wanted to ask someone, anyone, other than Jon, what they meant. He walked off the porch and got the preacher's attention. "What's the meaning of these stones? They've got unusual shapes. Look at this one. It's round on the top but comes down into almost an axe head. Look at this one. It's like a bowl."

The preacher looked down at the small stash of stones the boy had collected. He huffed. "You got a clay pipe there. And this one. Look at this now. Son, you found yourself a tomahawk!" Finn's gut feeling had been true. He knelt by his treasures, picked them up slowly, and turned them over. He imagined the stone lashed to a piece of hard oak, flipping over and over in the air. What other treasures of the Chiefs of War and the Chiefs of Peace lay hidden in the sacred sea of grass?

"We better get back at it." Jon passed him on his way back to mount the metal steed.

"Can we stop and work on the wagon, please?"

Jon turned. "In time, Finn. I'm focused on getting this done. I promise I will push the wagon out this evening, and I will take a good look at it." Finn had lost again. He didn't want the wagon project to be an "I" thing. He wanted it to be a "we" thing together. Something that they could do in loving memory not just of Mrs. Elizabeth but of the beauty and love and life that had once been part of the mountain. Like the field, they were destroying.

Jon mounted the machine, and Finn slowly climbed the metal stairs to his and turned the engine of the beast over. It sputtered and then roared to life like a dinosaur who was startled sleeping. The clay of the basin had dried out since there had been days of no rain, and as the machines moved, a spiral column of red dust rose from the mountain. With every pass, the hole grew, and Finn's head was now lower than the top of the basin. He'd dug that far into the heart of the field he had always loved. To ever see it move in the moonlight again would be a memory. He noticed the Preacher standing on the bank above him with a satisfied smile, waving. Finn concentrated on the rocks coming up and rolling in front of his blade.

His mind became numb, lost in the roaring hum of the machine's engine. The Wordsworth poem that he had learned the summer before played over and over in his mind. "One impulse from a vernal wood may teach you more of man, of moral evil and of good, than all the sages can." Why had Jon turned into a brutal teacher?

A loud hissing broke Finn's daydream, and he looked back and saw that one of the axe-like stones had punctured the thick tire of the machine and was rolling over and over, determined to puncture the artery of the invading machine. Finn slowed and stood up, watching the tire. Jon passed by and yelled above the machine. "Keep pushing it, keep pushing." Finn nursed the wounded beast to keep moving. Jon passed again. "Push it! Keep going; you got other tires." Finn didn't know why his face flashed so much hate. Was it him, the machine, or the stone struggling to save its history? Finn watched the thick rubber of the tire succumb to the wound, slowly deflate, and begin to bend. Jon kept passing him and throwing his hand forward to compel him to maintain the charge. Finn altered the blade and saw the tire coming loose from the wheel and beginning to bind. He looked across the basin for instructions from Jon, but he saw only a man enraged.

* * *

As he rounded the first curves of the mountain road, Bobby noticed the sky was turning orange. Squinting, he saw what appeared to be a giant column of red dust. There was a large commotion in one area. Was Jon logging again? Bobby knew there were sections of the mountain that did need to be thinned out at times for the health of the trees, but he assumed they would talk about it first. Bobby anticipated the place where Jon was working, but with each bend, the cloud just got larger and dusted collected on the windshield. He slowed in the road, thinking Jon must be on the other side. When he did, he passed a blue-gray truck driven by a man with dark features looking intently at him through the window, just like John King Fisher had nearly thirty-six years ago when he hung Ruby in the effigy of Christ from the sycamore. Bobby felt evil wash over his entire body once again. Bobby locked eyes with him as he passed, and then, just like so many years ago, he gunned the gas pedal to the floor and broke out from the line of trees in front of the field and screamed out loud as he saw the giant cloud of red dust rising from the field beside the cabin. His car slid sideways in the gravel driveway and sped towards the cabin and the origin of pain. In some part of his mind, he fully expected to see Ruby's outstretched, tortured body swinging again. The car slid to a stop, and Bobby threw open the door, and his large frame ran to the edge of the basin in horror at the size of the crater.

Bobby shouted and flailed his arms, but no one could hear him between the machines' noise and the rising dust. Stumbling, he started down the slope and reached the bottom of the pond with tears of horror streaming down his face. Running to face the behemoths head-on. Swinging his arms wildly and screaming at the top of his voice, but as he sucked in his breath, his lungs filled with the red clay dust. He suddenly grabbed his chest, choking for air. He felt his pulse quicken, and a sharp sound filled his ears. He clutched his chest, his head stretched, desperate for air, but the red clay filled his mouth. Pitching forward, white froth spewed from his mouth. He was on all fours in the dirt when Finn reached him, yelling, but all Bobby could hear was the deafening sound of mechanical silence. Jon reached them, removed his bandana, and doused it with water. "He can't breathe he yelled." He stuck the wet cloth around Bobby's nose and mouth.

"Get his arm, Finn. We've got to raise his chest muscle and open the passage to his lungs. Like a boxer who fought a long, hard fight, Bobby was on his knees with Jon and Finn raising his arms as if in victory, but Bobby, felt the ghost of John King Fysher near, and his arms were the arms of Ruby being stretched out. As shadows receded, Bobby's held the wet rag over his face, and with the machines off, the dust of the basin subsided, and Bobby took long, deep breaths again. "Go get the truck, Finn; drive it in here." Finn took off. "Take it easy, Bobby. We will get you up to the house."

The green dodge topped the edge of the basin and plunged into what used to be the field. They helped Bobby inside, and Jon drove to the cabin. Bobby sat in the front seat of the truck in the shade, and Finn brought glass after glass of cool water to him.

After a long while, Bobby was breathing steadily, but he felt as if he had lost something he cherished violently and was searching for a way through it. He got out of the truck and went back to where Jon was. The two men were quiet. "Was that a heart attack?" Bobby shook his head. "Why Jon?" Jon didn't say anything. "Why are you doing this?" Jon didn't look at him. "Say?"

Jon slid off the tailgate. "It's my land. I can build a pond anywhere I want." He kicked the gravel in the driveway with his boot.

"That's not your land Jon. Hell, where you put the cabin isn't your land. You know this has been a sacred field for thousands of years. Why Jon, why? You've ripped this away from me, away from the entire world. Away from Finn, away from yourself? Do you understand that field will now only live in history in memory, and when we are lost, it will forever be lost?" Why must you destroy all this and cause so much pain?" He stepped closer to Jon and pointed over at the basin. "You digging out the heart of God trying to fill the hole inside yourself." He returned and stood before Jon leaning on the tailgate. Bobby dwarfed the thin creature Jon had become in his stupor of grief. " You'll get to die for love, Jon. You may live to be a hundred, and you may die of cancer or another car accident, but in that last moment of your life, it will not be those things that will kill you. In that last moment, you can succumb to the pain in your soul and pay whatever debt you feel you owe. But now and for the rest of your days, you don't have to be attached to it. You don't have to keep returning to it in your mind for self-abuse. You hearing me? You lost Betts suddenly and violently, and I get that. You didn't have the time to say goodbye, and you will always carry that pain, but you don't have to destroy the world or others' love for you to punish yourself. That's what you're doing here." He pointed to the empty hole. "That field out there, Jon, was your heart. It was enchanting, full of history and spiritual wisdom, and now you feel guilty for not realizing how fragile the lives of our loved ones are of how precious each moment is. Elizabeth was a gift. Every day you have left is also a gift. You can live each day as some huge drama trying to justify the story you're telling yourself." He stopped and drew a line in the red dust with his shoe. " But in doing so, you will be wasting your life. I wasted so much of mine I can't afford to waste anymore. Just air to breathe is enough to be joyful." He paused again and looked into the ancient canopy of the trees. "You'll get your chance to die for love, so why not forgive yourself, forgive others, forgive the past for dealing you this shitty hand of cards, and keep living."

Jon turned towards Finn. "Go fill up the machine for me."

"Leave that boy out of this business, Jon. He doesn't want no part of this foolishness." Finn walked away from the two men and sat in the shade where he had collected his stones.

"I'm just building a pond, Bobby. It doesn't concern you."

"It doesn't concern me? I grew up here, Jon. Know every part of this mountain. Damn, near every tree. I've got right to this land just as much as you do." Jon tried to interrupt him, but Bobby raised his voice. "And this is wrong. This is shameful, Jon. How many homes. How many hearths did you push up out of the clay? How much of these sacred people's lives did you destroy here, and for what? To hurt somebody as much as you hurt?"

Jon ripped off his gloves and threw them in the back of the truck. "It's just a damn pond, Bobby. I will fill it full of fish and let children come here and enjoy it. I'm building it for Elizabeth!"

"Bull shit, you are Jon. I know what it is to hurt. I know what it is to lose the love of your life. To ache all over your body day and night. To have a longing to be with them wherever they are. Just to be able to touch them again."

Jon huffed and turned his head. "No, you don't. It's different."

Bobby lowered his head and looked into Jon's eyes. "Excuse me? You want to say that again?"

"I'm going to build it. Hell, I already got most of it done. It's my land, Bobby."

"No, no, you are not going to do any more of this, Jon. This is not just your land. It's our land. Hell, it's not even our land. It belongs to history. It should be preserved."

Jon spit on the ground. "Well, my name is on the deed." He pushed away from the truck.

"Oh yeah, Jon? Is that where you are headed. Is your name on the deed? And so what? Are you going to tell me to fuck off? Get the fuck off your mountain?"

Jon was quiet, his face red. Bobby pushed a finger into Jon's chest. "Why is it just your name on that deed Jon? Hmm? Tell me that. Better, ask yourself that.

Jon turned around and faced the basin. "I told you to fill up that machine!" He yelled at Finn.

"Leave him out of it," Bobby said.

"He's eaten my food. He will do what I say.

"Oh, you own him too. Is he one of Jon's boys?" Bobby was coming closer to Jon. "You know what it was like for me and Ruby to live our entire lives not as Jon's brothers but as his boys? Every time we go make a delivery. Every time we go set up for a garden party and play. They didn't pay us; they paid Jon for his boys. Every time we go get some food. Ruby and I would have to go wait at the colored entrance to get the same food you just walked inside to get. We'd ask you to get us a cup of water when the colored fountain broke, and no one cared to fix it." He was diving closer to Jon's face now. Trying to get him to look him in the eyes. "Why aren't our names on that deed Jon?" He thumped Jon's chest with his finger. "Let me tell you. Because if two adopted black boys went to the judge in Polk County and said the old man who adopted them had been missing for 10 years and that the whole mountain with all its gold was theirs, making two colored boys the richest men in the county, you think he would've gone along with it?" Bobby shook his head. "No, they'd hung us from the nearest oak tree for that man's murder. But you now, born with the white man's credit," he raised his hand and pushed the sweat from Jon's cheek. Jon smacked his hand away, "You walk in there with your pal Bagsby and a little cash, and your name is on the deed. Now, isn't that nice? Now look where we are."

THE BOOK OF SAY

"You had plenty of opportunities to get your name on the deed too. You've had just as much opportunity as me, Bobby."

Bobby shook his head. "Don't know about that. A black man digs up an ancient piece of ground. They'd shoot him in a heartbeat. Very least, beat him and run him out of town."

Bobby reached out to grab Jon's shoulders, and Jon pushed him away hard. "Leave me alone." Bobby reached to pull him in again. "Get the fuck away from me and get the fuck off my land."

"Or what, Jon?"

"I call the police and get you thrown off. I won't be there next time to bail you out of jail."

Bobby looked hard into Jon's eyes and shook his head. He turned and walked to his car. Finn came running and threw his arms around Bobby. "Stay, Bobby." " You feel safe, Finn?" Finn pulled back and contemplated. " I just don't understand." " Yeah, how long has he been speaking entirely in French?" " More than a week." " When did you learn French?" " He taught me some words last summer, and then I took a vocabulary book home, but this well, he teaches with his eyes and movements. He touches everything and names it. He asks a question and expects an answer. It's been exhausting on top of all this." He turned a clay stain arm toward the pit. "Jesus, that's brutal." " Why is he doing that?" " Destroying the field trying to build a pond?" " No, why is he speaking in French, and he doesn't realize it?" Bobby opened the car door and sat inside. " It's the language of his heart. It's his base form of communication. It is the language he dreams in and what his mind reverts to when cavitating." Finn knelt in front of the man. "When our bodies lose something violently, they go into shock. They start devouring stored calories. That's why he's got so thin. In the same sense, his mind is working overtime to find a solution to this problem, and it's failing to find a way to bring Elizabeth back to life. His mind has to give up space it once held for something else, and in doing so, it is collapsing and reverting to its base form of communication." Finn stood and drew a Dove in the dust covered car. "Come here, Finn." " I'm proud of you. This is not something that you should go through, and I don't know why you have to experience so much as a child." Finn began to cry and hugged him. " There, there now. It's going to be okay. We will figure this out. We just need to be careful; things are delicate." " When will I see you again?" " Anytime you need me or feel scared, call me Finn." Bobby started the vehicle and drove away.

Jon walked over the basin and to the mangled tire of Finn's machine. Finn filled up his thermos and peered over the side of the rim. He saw Jon mount the hobbled machine, planning on forcing it out of the basin. When Jon cranked the engine and was about to raise the blade, the Dove came and lighted upon the steering wheel. Jon sat in the empty basin's sunlight and stared at the Dove. "Shew. Go on now. This ain't the time." The bird did not move. Jon raised his hands and tried to blow it away, and it just turned on the steering wheel and looked at him. "Go on!" He said forcefully, not wanting to touch it. "Shoo. Go on, Betts, let me alone." He yelled. He waved his hand towards the bird, and it picked up and flew away. He jammed the huge tractor into gear, and it lurched forward, the tire flopping over.

The Dove dropped from in between him and the sun like an eagle and swarmed his face with her wings. Jon stood up and threw the machine out of gear, and flailed his arms. "Goddamn it!" The bird flew off, and he leaned over again to push the machine into gear; the Dove dropped from the sky and, with her claws, grabbed the cheek of Jon near his eye and tore the flesh. The razor-like claw caused Jon to twist his head and lose his balance in the foot pedals of the machine, and he tumbled from the machine and fell hard to the packed red Earth. He lay there with his head on the dirt and touched the cut place beneath his eye, and pulled back a finger covered in blood. He slowly got to his knees and looked for the Dove. He grasped one of the smooth, dense stones from the Earth, and just like the Warrior who drew the bow and loosed the arrow that pierced the Eagle heart of the Elder Fire, he threw the stone with uncanny accuracy, and the Dove, taking the wound full in the breast, rolled over and over in the air until it plunged out of sight over the edge of the basin. Jon stood slowly, having killed his own Idol of love, and climbed back on the machine and straddled it like the Warrior who plunged the first knife into Skyuka's chest.

Finn watched in horror as all this played out below him. The Bible verse he had heard so many times echoed in his mind. "I was hungry, and you gave me food. I was thirsty, and you gave me drink. I was a stranger, and you took me in." How could this be the same man? Jon did not reach the basin's top before the tire came entirely off the wheel. He abandoned the machine, and Finn could tell he was angry. He came over to him. "Keep working on that one while I'm gone. I've got to go into town to find a new tire and someone to fix it."

Finn shook his head. "Je ne veux pas." " You don't want to?"

Jon closed the tailgate on the truck. "Fine, go fishing, do something else."

Finn leaned in. "I want to work on the wagon. I wanted us to do it together."

Jon nodded his head and walked to the Sawmill, and pushed back the heavy doors. Finn followed along behind him at a safe distance. Jon pulled the wagon out of the Sawmill and into the sun. He pulled the oiled tarp off of it. He grabbed a scraper and held it in his hands. Finn walked up. Jon shoved the scrapper under the chipped paint and removed it. "This what you wanted?" Jon handed him the scraper. "Scrape all the paint off it, and I will give you a gold coin." "I don't want your gold. I wanted us to do this together. For memory's sake." Jon shook his head. The blood from his cheek had nearly dried.

"Don't want my gold? Got plenty of your own, do you?" He paused, and Finn started working.

"Who you think has been feeding you all winter?" Finn didn't understand the statement and did not say anything. Jon walked to the truck and left in a cloud of dust.

Finn scraped paint from the wagon until the gravel under it was littered with flecks of color. He thought Jon would be back by sunset, but he wasn't. He covered the wagon with the tarp and left the scraper inside. Then the dove landed on the wagon. Finn saw where the stone had hit it. The purple wound in the beating breast was stark in the late afternoon light. He was thankful it was alive. He took her in his hands to the cabin and ground the corn, and poured water for her on a shallow plate. She cooed softly, snuggled his hands, and then flew away.

Finn fed the fish children, then washed and made himself something to eat. He kept looking for Jon, but he didn't come. He was worried and thought he would call Bobby but when he went to the phone all the little pieces of paper around the phone had been removed. He scratched his head. He decided to go up the staircase to the upper pond. As he climbed with his rod in hand, things almost seemed hopeless. He pulled out the leader on the rod and began to cast, the line at times straight, at times bending, at times rolling continuously in the wind, every movement a choice of his own hand.

CHAPTER 23

"Who walketh upon the Wings of the Wind"

After fishing in the upper pond, Finn lay in the grass and became mesmerized by the fireflies in the treetops. He didn't know if he had ever seen something as beautiful and considered spending the night there.

But then he thought of Jon, Bobby, his father, his sister, his real mother, and Marlene. He was worried, and it didn't feel right to enjoy this moment of tranquility when he didn't know where they were. Bobby had nearly died in the pit that Finn helped create. Jon was bleeding, and the Dove was wounded. He wondered if he could just slip under the water of the upper pond. Slip into another beautiful world. One where everyone was kind and at peace. What would they call a place like that? Heaven? Bobby had said that Heaven and Hell were periods we went through in our lives here on Earth. This loneliness, this heartache, this confusion seemed that way. Bobby also said that when we reach the bottom of hell, then heaven surely awaits us.

Finn walked back down the staircase in the dark. He wondered when it would be time for them to stop living in hell and begin living in heaven? Was he at the bottom? Was Jon at the bottom? The porch lanterns had been turned on, but Jon was upstairs. There were three large bottles of Alcohol on the counter. Finn washed his hands and went to bed. Jon's bedside light was on, but Finn could hear him snoring.

When Jon woke up, he looked out the bedroom window and could see the great hole that had been dug. It seemed as empty as the room did now without a woman. His head was hurting, but it did not match the hurt in his heart. He thought of Elizabeth and had a hard time to keep from crying. He didn't want Finn to see him this way and decided to stay inside. It seemed like more and more each day, the small things, the tangible things of his life with Elizabeth, were being ripped away. The things he was trying to do to prove to himself that life was going to have beauty in it again, even if that beauty was different, were a battle to complete.

Late in the morning, he walked to the kitchen to smell the flannel shirts, but they were gone. He walked to the sea salt container, and it was empty. Finn had topped all the pizzas with it. He went outside and put his boots on. Walking to the sawmill where Finn was scraping the wagon, he saw that the dove was with him. Hopping from area to area, following the boy. Finn was talking to the dove.

Jon was happy to see it and quickly approached, and the bird fled and flew up to the safety of its nest. He didn't say anything to Finn, just looked over the wagon. He could see the rotten wood. He could see the rusted hinges. He could see where Andiamo had nibbled on the wood of the back gate. Finn moved from around the wagon and removed his gloves. "I'm going to make a sandwich." Jon didn't say anything. Finn turned towards the cabin and started walking away.

"Want to go to town and mail that letter to your mother?"

Finn turned. "I haven't found the right words yet."

"Why not?"

Finn didn't say anything. Jon looked at him, knowing why the boy hadn't been inspired to write. He hated himself for it. He could feel himself coming apart. He was spiraling out of control and didn't want to do that in front of the boy. He needed Finn to go just like he had pushed everyone else out of the way in the past. Just like he had Elizabeth, then Penny, and now Bobby. If his life would implode, he didn't want to cause more pain to the child he loved. "What about that church meeting? Do you want to go to it tomorrow? The one, the Preacher, was telling us about?"

Finn shrugged his shoulders. "I don't really buy into that shit."

Jon laughed at the boy's swearing, but he didn't mind it because Finn had already proven to be mature in his eyes. A young man who already had grown legs to stand on and would face anything the world threw at him. Finn turned again towards the cabin. "They called." Finn stopped and turned around. "Your Dad is back home. They said he would be at that church meeting tomorrow." Jon had cast the words before the boy like a fly, but he was uninterested. He just walked away.

He looked at the old wagon and saw how the worms were eating the wood. He felt angry like everything in life was out of his control. Like worms were eating every moment of his life to the core. He grabbed the wagon's edge, and it broke off in his hands. "Goddamn it." He threw the broken piece inside the wagon and then kicked the side of it, and the panel broke in two. If he was going to lose everything, then he was going to be the one to destroy it, sell it, or give it away. Without giving it much thought, he stormed into the Sawmill and came out with a can of gas, and emptied it over the wagon. He watched as the soft dry wood soaked it up. He leaned back and, without hesitation, struck a match and flicked it into the wagon.

Within a flash, the entire vineyard cart was engulfed in flames. Finn came running, screaming at the top of his lungs, "No! No!

No!" He dashed over to the hand pump and started filling buckets relentlessly. Running back and forth back and forth to the flames that had to be one hundred feet in the air. He kept working and working while Jon, having stepped aside, was glad to watch his old memories burn by his own hand and not be stolen away by something he could not see or control. Finn ran past him, and he reached out and grabbed the boy's shirt. Finn turned and started beating Jon about the head and chest. Jon took the blows, never taking his eyes off the flames of the wagon.

The wagon shifted and broke in half, and he wrapped up both of the boy's arms and dragged him away from the flames. Finn kicked at the ground and caused both of them to fall, but Jon was stronger and held the arms of the boy, not wanting him to hurt himself in the flames. Finn was inconsolable. Weeping and weeping. Crying out as if in pain. Jon jerked Finn to his feet, and the boy fell again on the ground weeping. Jon slapped him across the face. "Get yourself together. Finn went to strike him back, and Jon grabbed his arms and spun him around to his feet. "This is not the worst thing that will ever happen to you in life. Do you hear me?" He was shouting in the weeping boy's face. "This is not the worst thing that will happen to you." Finn tried to get away, and Jon pinioned his arms.

The death of the wagon left only hardware and hinges. "Get a hold of yourself. The thing was ruined, eaten up with worms. It would've been a waste of my time."

Finn retreated to the edge of the barn beneath the Dove. "You are horrible."

Jon barely glanced at him. "It had to be done, kid. You will understand when you're older."

"No, it didn't. You know I wanted to restore that for Mrs. Elizabeth."

Jon shook his head and waved the comment off with his hand.

"She's better off without you," Finn said.

Jon looked hard at the boy. Finn had hit his target. "Yeah. You're probably right, and Bobby is too."

Jon raised both hands and rubbed his head. "Don't forget Ruby. My brother Ruby. I'm sure that's my fault too."

"I don't know how Jean-Paul ever loved you. Why would he ever die for you?"

Jon pointed his finger at Finn. "Don't go there, you little Son of a Bitch."

"How did he die?"

Jon turned and walked towards the boy. "I'm warning you." He pulled back his fist as if he would strike Finn in the face.

Finn screamed in Jon's face, "You killed him, you killed him, didn't you!" The boy lunged with all his might knocking Jon to the ground. "You killed Jean-Paul. You're a murderer, and you tried to murder the Dove."

Finn retreated to the safest place he knew. As he ran, he thought of how he often disappeared into the wheat fields of his home for safety. If Jon didn't want him anymore, he wished he could live in the Gazebo at the vineyard or at the Rest, where he could see the whole world. He could live in Bobby and Ruby's old apartment in the Sawmill and be near the Dove. He could take care of her, and she could care for him. He felt hopeless and lost.

He watched the sunset, and when night fell, he snuck into the Sawmill to sleep. He knew in the morning, Jon would want to drop him off. He probably had his bag packed for him now, just like the Preacher had done. Finn wanted to cling to the only home he had known for as long as he could. Leaving this way was not what he wanted.

Jon was waiting in the truck the next morning. Finn walked up and climbed inside. They pulled out from the cabin. The destroyed field on one side. The ashes of the vineyard wagon on the other. Finn looked back towards the cabin when the truck turned onto the gravel road. "You should call that driveway Tomahawk Lane. The other road, Eagle's Rest." Jon looked at Finn. The cut beneath his eye was turning black. Silent as a tomb, they rode along.

The parking lot was congested with church vans and buses when they reached Beau-Pre Baptist. Men milling around in suits and the women in long skirts in the summer sun. Jon pulled up in front of the Fellowship Building, and Finn got out. He started to pull away but then stopped, put the truck in park, and came around the side to where Finn was standing with the fireman's bag. "I just want to." He reached out to hug Finn but stumbled, trying to stick cash in his pocket. "Just take this." Embracing the boy hard. " I love you. I want you to know that I will always love you." He tried to say other things, but his words were meaningless. Finn just nodded. Jon wanted to hug him again, and Finn half-heartedly placed his forehead into his chest. He watched the truck disappear down the road, then set his red bag against the wall and began to change the trash bags while the Righteous ate from plastic plates.

* * *

"Good morning Upton."

"Come on in, Jon. How are we doing today? I'm sorry this has taken so long. I didn't think we would be into the fall before finishing it. Sit down. I've got all your paperwork right here."

Upton reviewed Jon's power of attorney designation and went over his wish for no heroic measures to be taken should he die or otherwise become incapacitated. "Regarding your health wishes, have you changed your mind, or is that still how you want it?"

"No, that's good. I want to go as fast and quick as I can."

"Okay. Now I just want to talk with you about your living trust, considering its size." Upton Peace took off his glasses and leaned back in his chair. "You want to leave everything to this Preacher and his church? You've given that a lot of thought?

Jon nodded. "He's the only person in my life anymore. We don't see eye to eye on everything, but he is the only person I can trust."

"Uh-huh. And this is his name and the name of the organization he is affiliated with?" Jon leaned forward and confirmed the name. "Jon, you are making this one man and one entity incredibly wealthy. Not only in money but real estate. Normally people with assets equivalent to yours break them into donations to an alma mater or Charities, those types of things. A large contribution to one person raises eyebrows." Upton Peace paused for a long moment and chewed the edge of his reading glasses. "Jon, I hope you don't get upset with me, but this Preacher contacted me back when you had your accident and were in the hospital. He had somehow gotten my name or information through the hospital or a conversation with you while you were there. Anyways, he reached out to me. Now, all our conversations are confidential, and I did not give him any information, but he did introduce himself and told me of his church and this large meeting they have every year. Invited me down there. I went. Lots of people from all over. I wanted to see for myself who this Preacher was and his church. Now, Jon, again, it's none of my business. I'm just here to counsel and do as you direct me, but I can't say that I agree with everything I heard from that man. Now, I'm not a religious person or an evangelical by any means, but some things were unsettling. Also, Jon, this man, was arrested not too long ago. Even had to go to court. Now they acquitted him of the charges, but regardless, that is unsettling. My point, Jon, is to make sure you are doing this with full knowledge of who this man is and faith that he is going to fulfill your wishes."

"Upton, I understand and appreciate your concerns. I have given it a lot of thought. Nearly constantly. I am one hundred percent sure that this man will follow through." Upton drew a deep breath.

"Okay, Jon. Well, it's all ready. We will go into the next room with the witnesses and sign the paperwork. It will be filed at the Polk County courthouse this afternoon."

* * *

Jon spread the topsoil out across the banks of the new basin. He thought of Elizabeth sitting on the yellow tractor in the big sun hat. He smiled, and then his eyes filled with tears. He walked across the soft soil and sowed grass seed. He thought of Elizabeth lying on the rug in the field and had to stop and cry.

He laid plastic pipes from the small pond downhill to the new basin. It was crude, not his best work, but even so, it began to fill the void and scab his sin. He threw the remnants of the vineyard cart into the basin so no one except Finn would know what he did.

The blue-gray pickup truck with dual exhausts came by. Poking, prodding, reminding, daring, in much the same way Satan had tempted countless prophets in the desert or on the mountains. Using other words to say, "Cast thy self down."

With each passing day, the cabin became a tomb. His tomb, one he had built for himself. The exterior adorned with ponds and fountains and memories, even ancient tales. But inside the tomb, nothing was left to resonate with memory, and Jon feared being alone. On those nights, he pretended to live a normal life. Once again filled with lovely things. He tried to read, he tried to write letters of apology. To explain why he had acted this way through a hidden meaning in an obscure poem. The bourbon helped affirm excuses.

But the dove would come in the morning, and he felt that her forgiveness was all he needed. The letters, some stained with bourbon, others with genuine tears, were burned in the morning's fire. He stopped shaving or combing his hair. Often he wore the same clothes for days. In time he stopped going upstairs. He slept on the daybed and once it was gone the floor. The book he was reading beside his head. The last bottle of bourbon conquered by a small glass.

    The cut stones that had been pushed up from the basin Jon laid for the foundation of his shed. Carelessly in his new disheveled way, he built the structure by the Rest. He built it out of old wood left in the Sawmill. He faced the small door to the cliff view of the Flatland below. He planted rows of Daffodils there and flanked the shed with two Cherry trees he knew would bloom first in the spring. He drank throughout the day, and he often stopped his work and began to wander down the mountain and the old trails. Stopping at the ancient trees. Hugging them, kissing them. He wept on their bark and leaves and asked forgiveness if he had ever hurt them. "Betts loves you too."

    When it rained, Jon did not go indoors. The rain soaked his head and ran down his beard, and Jon watched the drops of water drip off his fingers and ruin a painting or make a nail too slick to hold. Those were minor pains like the cold. It didn't matter. On the full moon nights when the wind blew hard, he walked. Walked all night with the moon, twisting his head to see if she was still looking for him. He'd walk between the vineyard's rows and struggled hard to remember the work by the authors on the brass plates. Near morning he would lay on the soapstone floor of the Gazebo and sleep until the dove came again to fetch his heart home.

    He walked the gravel road, picking what grew there, passing the cabin and the Sawmill, and walking up and up until he reached the safety of the small shed. He dragged a table inside and pushed it against the wall. There was enough room left for a cot. One night after toasting the stars, he reached and closed himself in his cell, wondering if he would rise the next morning. When morning came, he opened the shed door, and the dove was there in the soft dirt where he had planted the Daffodils. He took out a carpenter's pencil and sketched her amongst hopeful blooms on the inside of his cell wall.

He went back to the cabin that day and went inside. He retrieved two wooden boxes that had both been in the bedroom the dove and the daffodil. He closed the door of the cabin and never returned. He walked across the wooden walkway and did not look back. He climbed the staircase to the Rest. In the shed, he placed the wooden writer's box on a shelf at his head and the other wooden box of Elizabeth's ashes on a shelf near his heart. The wind came at night, and sometimes the shed door would fly open, swirling the leaves and dust about his reddened eyes. In his stupor, he would reach out and close himself in again.

Some nights he stumbled to the Rest and lay upon it with his arms outstretched with his bourbon in one hand. He would sketch out his favorite shapes in the stars until sleep found him. Then the Dove came and woke him from his momentary rest.

In time, he laid more stones and built another room just as small as his new home. Here he hung a sink, a mirror, and a shower curtain nailed to the boards. He hung a light and dug a well. When the Wind came, it shook the prison, but each day Jon made sure it wouldn't fall. The snow came, and like the rain, he didn't notice. He used charcoal from his fire and drew on the walls. He called out to the Dove for forgiveness, and she told him to cast stones. That each stone would become a new dove. Then one night, the cell door blew open. Jon got up from his prison cot. He looked at his sketches of all he loved. He took a piece of coal and wrote above the door, "My Skyuka Child will return," and he stumbled towards the place of Rest and flung his granite soul out upon the eternal wings of the Wind.

CHAPTER 24

"Use Your Freedom to serve one another in Love"

Finn pushed open the rarely used front door of the house and stepped lightly out to the front porch. The peach trees across the road from the Wheat Hill House were in bloom. His gaze took in the peach tree's blossoms covering the foothills up to the Blue Ridge and the one distinct peak he knew best. He sat down on the porch steps and remembered what spring was like on the mountain. Looking across the flatland and seeing the pink carpet of blooms all the way to him. Did Jon ever do that?

A car turned at the intersection, and Finn waited for it to top the hill, but as it came closer, it pulled in the driveway between the clay-colored stones and stopped at the place a walkway should have been. When Finn realized Bobby was in the car, he stood in disbelief. Bobby stepped out, and his smile was as big as his heart. He was wearing a winter coat with a sheepskin collar. His smile turned to pinched lips, and tears welled in his eyes, and at that moment, Finn knew that Jon was gone.

Finn sat on the steps hard and cried loudly, tears streaming down his face. Bobby wrapped Finn in his arms just as he had clasped Jon in the dirt off the porch when Elizabeth had died. They cried on each other's shoulders for a long time. Bobby pulled out a handkerchief and dried Finn's eyes. Finn felt run through with the love spear. "He's gone?" Bobby slowly nodded and wiped his tears. "How?"

Bobby sat beside Finn. "He threw himself off the Rest." Finn covered his mouth and began crying again. Bobby bit his lip but couldn't hold back his own tears. He wrapped his arm around Finn and drew him near.

"Are you sure? "Why? Why would he do that, Bobby?"

Bobby was quiet for a while. "He was hurting. He thought he was alone." He looked over at Finn. "It was his free will. That is what makes us part of God."

Finn nestled into the strong arms of Bobby. "I will always love him and Mrs. Elizabeth." Finn kept shaking his head. "I didn't need to lose them. I don't need the machine, Bobby."

"Finn, look at me, son. We never lose the ones we love. We never lose them." He tapped Finn's chest. "They are always here." Finn nodded his head.

"Look, Finn, I don't think I've ever shown you this." Bobby stood and removed the wide leather belt with the brass buckle from around his waist. "Look here. See what's burned into this belt. I started doing this nearly forty years ago." Finn stretched out his hand and took the weathered belt. On it, Bobby had taken the time to use a wood burner and write all the names of the loved ones and friends he had lost. Finn touched the newest names of Jon and Betts. He saw other names like Wayne and Ruby. All around the belt in different places and sizes were the names burned like tattoos into the leather that Bobby wrapped around himself daily and carried with him. "They are with me every day. Every morning when I put this belt on, I imagine them making me stronger, like they are holding me up. Their love, their memories their lives are always with me each step I take, son. Jon and Elizabeth will always walk with you for as long as you live."

Finn was wiping his eyes with the handkerchief. "I hurt to think of him being so sad. His pain was everywhere last summer. I'd look at him sometimes and couldn't even recognize him. I couldn't even talk to him, and he was so mean to you, Bobby."

Bobby nodded and sat back down, and put his arm around Finn. "Hurt people hurt people, Finn." He was silent for a long time. "Finn, I was much the same way as Jon after Ruby died." Finn heard those words and pushed away from Bobby in disbelief. The large man looked over and slowly shook his head. "It's true. The second year is often harder than the first for people in grief. The first year you have an overwhelming feeling to tell everyone you see about the person you love. When that doesn't heal the hole in your heart and your life, many people begin to beat themselves up.

"A year after Ruby died, I left the mountain. I left my home with Jon and Betts and participated in the Civil Rights movement. I was passionate to right the wrongs of how many African Americans like Ruby were murdered. Our society viewed us as inferior, so I joined the Beloved Community. The movement that Dr. King led. I marched with him and went to jail with him. I led sit-ins and freedom rides. I remember the day we marched in Selma. The dogs unleashed, tearing into my legs." He looked over at Finn. "The pain of grief was so real inside me that when those dogs had their teeth in my legs and were mangling the flesh, I couldn't even feel them. I watched them tear me up and nearly asked them to do it again. I would see those white police officers coming with their sticks and wouldn't flinch. Not out of courage, Finn, but because I felt I needed to be beaten. I needed to be punished for letting Ruby die. I would wake up every morning, get on one of those buses, and hope that day would be when some Klan member would put a bullet through my head. I got so low, Finn, if one of them had held out a noose for me, I would have put my neck through it."

Finn shook his head. He couldn't help but grab onto Bobby's arms while hearing this story. "I was in jail all the time. They'd drench us down with fire hoses and then offer us bail. They'd even call Jon and Elizabeth. Jon would drive through the night to find me in some Mississippi prison. He'd post bail and say he was taking me home to get cleaned up, but I'd just stayed in the cell. They'd bring food, and I wouldn't eat it. I was punishing myself and punishing myself. It went on for nearly ten years that way, Finn. Even after Dr. King was murdered. I saw sister Coretta, one of the strongest women I've ever known, deal with grief. I tried to learn from her, but I rationalized it out differently in my mind. I was keeping myself down."

"What changed, Bobby?"

"Jon."

"What do you mean?"

"I was in this jail. Had been for a while. I had served my sentence and was free to go. Guards came and opened my jail cell door. Left it wide open and walked away. I closed the door back on myself. I stayed inside. I stayed inside my own prison, Finn. The guards didn't mind. Jon wrote me a letter. He always did, but sometimes I didn't read them. Sometimes I would read them and couldn't respond. But I read this one. One out of a hundred that made a difference. He wrote me about the Bedouin fighters in the desert. He described them and the desert and how they could sometimes travel more than a hundred miles across the uncharted desert with just one pint of water. The reason they could do that was because there were these sacred wells in the desert that had never run dry. These Bedouins were not large men, not incredibly strong men, but they had this compass within themselves that led them to the next sacred well, even at times when they could not physically see. In sandstorms or delirium, they would find the sacred well. Jon said in the last line of the letter that the Bedouin fighter didn't die from thirst in the desert. He died because he lost the way to the next sacred well."

Bobby paused and wiped the tears from his eyes. "Because of that letter, I stood up and opened the cell door, and I found the strength that day to walk out of my own prison."

Finn shook his head and sat quietly for a long time. "Jon was drinking." He looked over at Bobby, and the man grimaced and nodded.

"Yes, addictions last a lifetime."

"What do you mean?"

Bobby stretched out his long legs. "Did you ever hear about Jon's Garden, the secret garden he created?"

"Just a little."

Bobby sighed. "Jon had a very different experience in war than most. He once told me that at night he had this recurring dream of being marched out in a line of men in the snow, and each face in front of him and behind him were people he had killed. He said the line in both directions never ended. When he came home from the war, he had seen so much death and destruction that all he wanted to do was create things of beauty. He took the area around the cabin and planted a few flowers in pots, setting them on the granite. Then it exploded, and he brought in trees, weeping willows, and River Birch, all in huge pots, massive. Before too long, you couldn't even see the cabin or the fountain or the pond. He had massive boxwoods in pots that formed a complete wall. Now, let me tell you, it was beautiful. I mean, he had lights and rugs and furniture. He and Elizabeth started pretty much living outside.

"For nearly two years, Jon did not leave that garden. He didn't even walk out to the Sawmill. He didn't get in the car and go to town. Finn, he did not leave that garden. He had set up all the plants as if they were platoons of soldiers protecting him. Elizabeth took care of him like he was a child. She knew how hard he was hurting, and she healed all that pain and never even said a word about how strange it was. She just played along with his insanity. Let me tell you, Finn. Jon loved her at first sight, but he fell deeply in love with her then.

"They would throw parties in the garden. Ruby and I would play all night. People and children were all dancing on the stones. Playing in the fountain. You could go into Jon's fantasy world, but he would not step a toe into your reality." Bobby paused, and Finn sat patiently. "The military didn't help. They were always calling Jon, asking him to come back. Then ask him to teach. There were times when men in long cars would come up the mountain to talk to him. His answer was always the same. We were all worried. Elizabeth, Ruby, and I would talk about what to do. We didn't know.

"I finally bought Jon this big brown book of plants and trees for his birthday. He loved it. Plants were his thing. He studied that book day and night. I came to see him, and we sat on the chaise lounges in the garden and showed him plans for the vineyard I wanted him to help me build. I told him it would be a surprise for Elizabeth. It worked. He left the house a few days later like it was no big deal. Started clearing the spot where the vineyard is now. It worked so well that he started taking some of the plants from the garden over to the vineyard to plant, and slowly, one by one, the secret garden was dismantled, and the cabin reappeared.

"But then the old pain reemerged. Betts' wanted to work in town, and he couldn't take that. It was like he needed her around constantly. Like she was his distraction from the hurt. He was a man who could master the chaos of war but could not control the chaos within him. He started drinking liquor. A little bit at first just to sleep and then all the time. He became this different person. He considered going back into the Army to train soldiers for Vietnam. He pushed us all away. When Elizabeth tried to intervene, he pushed her away. Told her to get out of his life. She did. The smart woman she was. She told him she was going to town, and she left. I mean, left the country. Disappeared. Jon nearly lost his mind. He thought that he could treat her how he wanted just because they were in love and that she would never leave. But control is not love, Finn, you remember that. He bought a sailboat and swore to cover every inch of the Earth to find her."

Finn looked into Bobby's eyes. "Heaven and Hell?"

Bobby smiled and nodded. "Heaven and Hell are things we experience here on Earth. Understanding that allows us to forgive and be good to one another."

Finn said, "Love is patient, love is kind, it forgives all, it bears all."

Bobby nodded his head and smiled. "Amen, brother Finn, Amen!" They shared a laugh.

"Can you forgive Jon?" Finn asked.

"Oh, gosh, yes." He laughed heartily. "We are brothers Finn. My goodness, we had knockdown drag-outs all our lives. But you know what? Jon Joines is one of the finest men I have ever known."

"But even after what he said, Bobby?"

"Finn, do you know how you tell the difference between a real diamond and a fake one?" Finn shook his head no. "The real diamond has flaws. Jon gave me so much love and kindness. I wouldn't have traded him on his worst day. I'm very proud to call him my brother."

"Bobby, you said that Jon's heart language was French. That was what his mind reverted to for solace." A car drove past the Wheat Hill house, and Bobby watched it pass and then nodded to Finn. "What's your heart language, Bobby?" "Mine? Oh, mine is music. I play music, sing music, listen to music. I do it when I'm happy, and I do it when I'm sad. Like Jon would describe a flower in French when he was happy and at his lowest, begging for forgiveness and understanding. All hearts recognize the truth. Truth can manifest through music or words, reading, and swimming. What do you think your heart language is?" Finn looked back at the view of the peach blossoms and the blue mountains in front of him. My heart language is nature. That is where I've always run to for protection. Whether here in the wheat fields or on the mountain by the upper pond. Hiking, fishing, casting the fly, and seeing it land on the water." Bobby nodded in agreement. "I love that Finn. You know Elizabeth's heart language was nature. She was picking wildflowers the first time I saw her. That's probably why you have such a strong connection with her." "So, a heart language is not the same for every person?" "No. No one can tell you what your heart language should be; only you know. That's the meaning of the Beloved Community and what we teach at the clinic. Every person deserves their own individual life experience."

Finn took heart in this comment.

"What happens now to the mountain Bobby since Jon is gone?

Bobby stiffened and ran his hands down his legs.

"Oh, Finn."

Finn leaned forward with concern. "Bobby, tell me. Say?" Bobby crossed his arms and looked at his feet. "Bobby?"

"Finn, he left it all to me and the clinic." Finn smiled. "You know that book, the one I bought him about plants. He left me a letter in there. He left you one too." Finn's eyes teared up, and tears rolled down his face. Jon's love for him was real. "Jon left me the whole mountain except for ten acres surrounding the Rest.

Finn wiped his tears, still emotional about Jon leaving him a letter. "What about the Cabin?"

"The cabin is fine. It's empty. In Jon's last days, he did some strange things. He got rid of nearly everything. All the furniture, the tools, the old boxes of books. He explained in his letter that he didn't want to leave that stuff as a burden for me. He wanted me to go on in peace and happiness and not be weighed down by his passing. The other strange thing he did was build a shed by the Rest. I guess he needed a change of scenery but was too attached to the mountain to leave. He built it entirely from old scrap wood he had stored in the Sawmill this ruff cut lumber. He was creative and used every stick of it. It's a tiny shack but built like a fortress."

Finn laughed. "Fort Knox?"

"Yeah, something like that. You know Finn, I'm going to need some help up there. We are going to use the mountain for the clinic programs. We will host gatherings up there and hold the remembrance ceremonies twice yearly in the vineyard." He breathed out hard. "It's important for people dealing with grief and pain to know they don't have to face the road alone. They, too, can decide to get up and walk out of their own prisons. We are going to call the new clinic the Live for Love Foundation. We are going to turn the Sawmill into the Jean-Paul Center for Hope. I will need you to help me, Finn."

Finn was crying and wiping the tears from his face. Bobby hugged him. "Did you fill in the basin?"

Bobby shook his head. "No, Finn, I didn't. It is part of the story of the field now. The murder of Skyuka is a part of the history of the Rest. It will remind us of how we can, at times, go wrong in life. Remind us that if we injure others, then we injure ourselves."

"It's like my scar from the chainsaw. Something to learn from." Bobby smiled. "Did Jon die alone?"

Bobby nodded his head. "In a way. When Jon cleaned out the house, he started living in the shed. He started surrounding the Rest with rows of Daffodils and Cherry trees. You should see it all in bloom. He was creating another defensive wall of beauty around his heart. He began sketching things on the walls and left some things for you there. He left you the Rest, Finn, and that little shack. He left you the Rest because he always saw you as a future Chief of Peace. Finn buried his face into Bobby's chest. "I just want him."

"I know you do, son. He will always be with you."

The door of the Wheat Hill House opened behind the two men, and slowly, Reggie stepped out on the porch. Finn and Bobby turned around. "Finn, son, why are you crying?" Bobby turned and introduced himself. "Bobby? Finn talks about you all the time. You've given him so much that I couldn't." Bobby took the thin hand of my Father and held on to it, letting him know that he wasn't scared of his illness. That he saw God within him.

"Reggie, we have a large meeting twice a year at my church. People come from all over and share their burdens and their strength. I would really love for you and Finn to be my guest. It is a remembrance ceremony. Gives the Beloved Community a chance to gather and, in a healthy way, share each other's burdens. I would love for you to come."

I stood up and went to my Father. He wiped the tears from my face. He looked up at Bobby with sunken eyes and smiled. "We would love to, Bobby."

Bobby reached out and gave me one more hug. "Good, good. All who love are born of God. Everyone is welcome in the beloved community." We watched the giant of a man leave the porch. When he got to the car, he turned back and looked at me.

"Oh, Finn, forgot to tell you. Two doves are showing up to be fed every morning now. I know you will love them."

The End

EPILOGUE

The majority of this story is true. I have classified it as fiction because a few things are untrue.

The Preacher and his Son are real people. I do not believe the Son killed anyone, but they both are evil people, and the World will be a safer place when they are gone. I was close to the Preacher, and I know things about him and his Son's lives that would devastate their families and grandchildren. I have chosen not to share those stories for their protection.

The Wheat Hill House, my Father, my Stepmother, and our living conditions are real. The couple from Greer are precious to me. When I was forty years old, the Lady told me that they were going to adopt me as a newborn, but my Father, having met my Stepmother, backed out of signing at the attorney's office. I've often wondered how different my life would have been.

My Father died when I was 21. We scraped fifty dollars together and bought a cemetery plot in a local Church graveyard near the Wheat Hill House. I dug my Father's grave by hand. When the people gathered left the gravesite, I retrieved my shovel from behind a tree and buried him. In death, I hope he found peace.

My Stepmother went on to marry again. I did not keep in touch with her, and I do not know if she is still alive. I have forgiven her, and I do not need an apology from her. I tried to show that she was trapped. Under different circumstances, she may have been a different type of person.

My real Mother has always been a mystery to me. We have yet to find common ground. She is an intelligent and accomplished woman whom I admire. I will always be grateful for the respite she gave me as a child. It's hard to imagine that I would have survived without it. Mrs. Elizabeth was the first woman to show me a mother's love, so I bonded with her quickly.

The mountain, Cabin, fountain, ponds, fish, children, porch, and walkways are all real, but they are no longer the same. The Cabin is now part of a five thousand-square-foot home. I wonder if the owners have any idea of the field. The old places are still there but covered over. That's what happens when we replace wisdom with knowledge. I am the only person who knows this place's story, so I sought to share its history with my readers.

Jon and Elizabeth were real people. They were less well-traveled than I made them to be in the book. Mrs. Gertrude Bell was not Mrs. Elizabeth's Godmother.

The Cabin was decorated in an opulent fashion. The piano, daybed, and porch are accurate.

Jon's relationship with Penny is made up and came from my experience of trying to date while still dealing with grief.

Jon did run his truck off the mountain. He struggled very deeply with the loss of Elizabeth.

The gold legend is true, but its location is about fifteen miles from the mountain. I learned the story from two men who had dedicated their lives to finding it. I worked on a tree farm beside Motlow Creek in my early teens. One of the men weighed about four hundred pounds, and his friend had designed a crane on the side of their truck that would pick the man up, lower him, and retrieve him from the creek bed. There, he would grovel on all fours, panning for gold. The story they told me during their lunch breaks was interesting, but money has never been a god to me. I kept planting trees.

On March 6, 2011, my fiancé and our daughter Aria died in my arms at The University of Chapel Hill Hospital. We met and lived on the small island of St. John in the United States Virgin Islands. Someone can read about Kristi Lynn Hansen from St. John USVI online. Over one hundred and fifty handwritten letters sent between Kristi and me cannot be found online. These are the letters, word for word, that are in the book. Most of these letters crossed oceans. Kristi and I agreed that no matter where we were in the World, we would be together every full moon and spend that night outside and in each other's arms. My flight back from Italy to St. John was our most extended trip to fulfill this promise.

The inspiration for this book came to me when, in grief, I did something as a man that I remembered seeing Jon do in the second summer I spent with him on the mountain. I knew then that I needed to make a different choice. I was planning my suicide, and Estate planning was holding me up. I went to Maine to build a chimney for my friend during that period. Paul Pono said a few things to me that gave me a reason for living. Paul and his family are dear friends of mine. Paul is a brother to me.

The story of Elizabeth's passing was our story. The story of Jon's grief was my grief. I found Kristi nonresponsive in our driveway. When told that I could not touch her, I began to rip tree roots from the ground. Today, I am a survivor. Tomorrow, I may not be. However, I am very thankful for every moment of this beautiful life, just as my beloved taught me to be.

The University of Chapel Hill holds a remembrance ceremony every year. That moment had an enormous effect on my life. What I described in the book is exactly what happened that day. I encourage everyone to seek out this ceremony in your local hospital. It will open your eyes and heart. Please participate if this is the first time you have experienced this ceremony. You do not have to undergo significant loss to strengthen the Beloved Community.

Writing the book was very cathartic for me. It has taken ten years of my life and has undergone many changes. I, too, went through many changes. In writing, I realized that I did not just need to heal over the loss of Kristi and Aria, but I needed to process and heal from my childhood. Today, I am a survivor of traumatic grief, which means that since childhood, I have experienced tragic events every few years of my life. Ninety percent of people who share this take their own lives.

I am a supporter of the Beloved Community. Every person has the right to live life any way they want.

Every chapter title of this book is a phrase from the Bible. I struggle with the Christian tradition. In writing this book, I realized that the source of a lot of the emotional abuse I endured as an adult is the result of being attached to the emotional pain I experienced as a child. Writing this book taught me to let go of the attachments I was clinging to justify my life. I realized that everyone I've known and will meet is living their own story. What is truth for me may not be the truth for them. I realized this was the root of the drama in my life. Clinging to these relationships and painful memories was causing me to waste my life. I found the courage to live with awareness, which has given me the strength to let go. I hope that people needing healing, whether it is grief or addiction, will read this book and join the Beloved Community of people for support and gather the courage necessary to change their lives. If I can ever be of service to anyone, please do not hesitate to contact me.

I have worked my entire life as a stonemason and a stone sculptor. I worked the majority of my career up until Kristi's passing under the Pen Name A. Tew. I had to stop my work in the years of my grief, and during that period of my life, I lived in Charlottesville, Virginia. There, I did minor masonry repairs - I fixed loose bricks and broken things, and People know me as Ben the Stonemason. Now, I live in Sicily. I split my time between the city of Ortigia and my Olive Grove in the Castiglione di Sicilia. I harvest Sea Salt and Sea Glass from the Ionian Sea.

    If you are struggling with grief and trauma and are short on faith in yourself, then I will let you borrow some. Feel free to contact me.

Thank you,
Ben Shepherd
WheatHillHouse@gmail.com

CREDITS

I thank loved ones who have read this manuscript many times and have encouraged me through these years of my life.

I want to thank my editor, Robert Kenney, for his hard work and advice.

I thank Jon and Elizabeth for letting me stay with them in their beautiful home as a child. It was a place where I felt safe, loved, and alive.

I want to thank my Father. Even though he was misguided, he was a beautiful person with a beautiful voice. He taught me many valuable lessons.

In this book, I drew inspiration from many other Authors. I want to thank and credit every one of them.

Louis de Bernieres. His words are like butter. I've listened to his novel "Birds Without Wings" so many times that I've nearly memorized it. His work "Dust That Falls From Dreams" and his book of poetry "Of Love and Desire" have meant so much to me. One of his poems about the man falling in love with the moon was the inspiration for the second to last chapter of the book. In speaking of Jon roaming the mountain at night following the moon and picking what grew by the road.

Thank you, Mr. Louis de Bernieres, for having such a tremendous and beautiful impact on my life.

Don Miguel Ruiz. His book "The Voice of Knowledge" has been committed to memory. For two years, I've listened to this book's recorded version twice daily. I can't explain why. Every single time I heard it, I learned something new. It has radically changed my life for the better. His words are echoed throughout my book—the points of wisdom and knowledge. Of stories, people tell themselves of attachments and letting them go. Of not trying to make other people's beliefs right or wrong. His work is powerful, and the truth of his words resonates. Thank you so much for your life's work.

The poetry of Rumi was like a Bible to me in my grief. I value this truth and wisdom—the poem "The Dancer" and his words about Roses not seeking attention.

William Wordsworth has always been a favorite of mine. I also have a small yellow book of his poetry committed to memory.

Susan Sontag and her book "Illness as Metaphor and AIDS and its Metaphors" helped me put into words so much of what I experienced and saw as a child while visiting my Father at the National Institutes of Health.

Thomas Mann and his book "Magic Mountain" helped me understand lung disease's effects on one's emotions. This book gave the idea of the dead being bobsled down the mountain past the living. While writing this book, I developed a lung condition myself, which really brought his words to life.

Mrs. Gertrude Bell. I thank you for being an astounding human being. You have inspired and encouraged me in how you faced so much grief and used it all positively.

I thank Janet Wallach for her book Desert Queen. Talking about Gertrude Bell's life, Villa, and rose garden.

I thank our Native Americans. The beauty of your lives and the respect for humankind, animals, and the Earth is something I have learned from.

I thank James A. Michener. The imagery of the snow on Baghdad and the old Wolves coming out of the mountains was from his book Caravans.

I thank Andre Breton and his beautiful poetry.

:

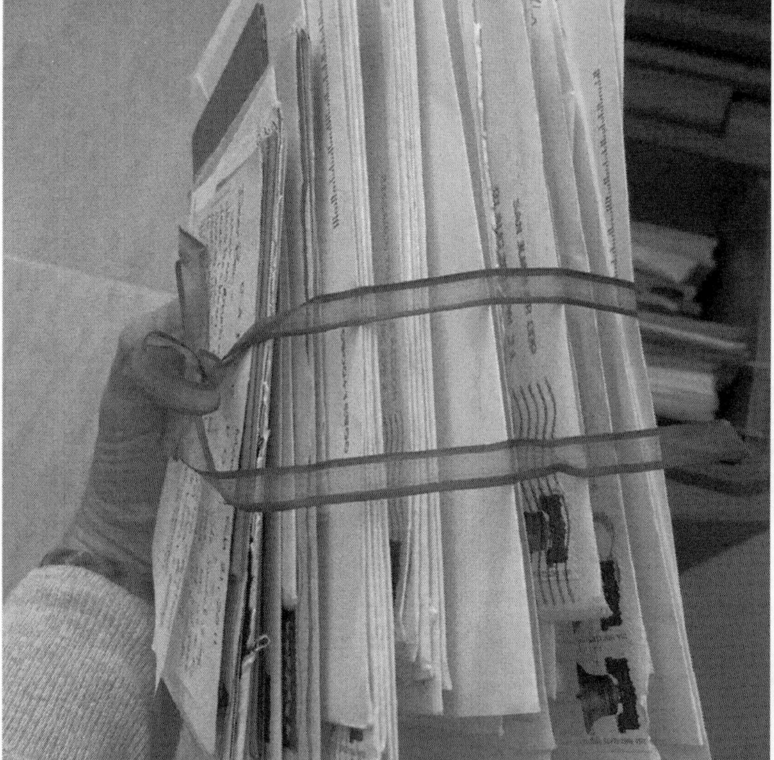

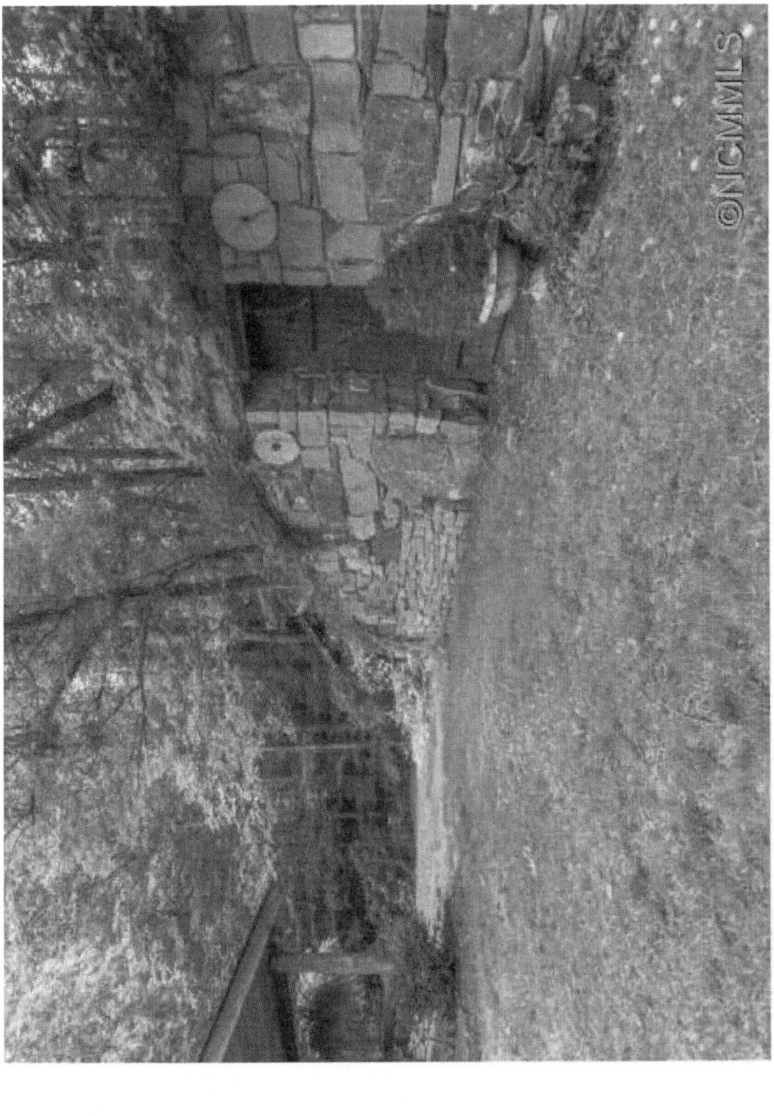
©NCMMLS

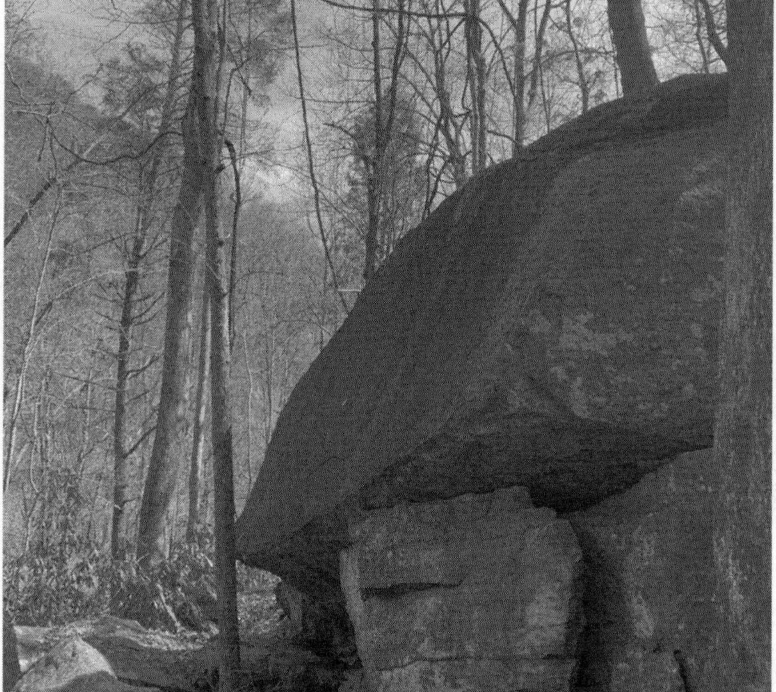

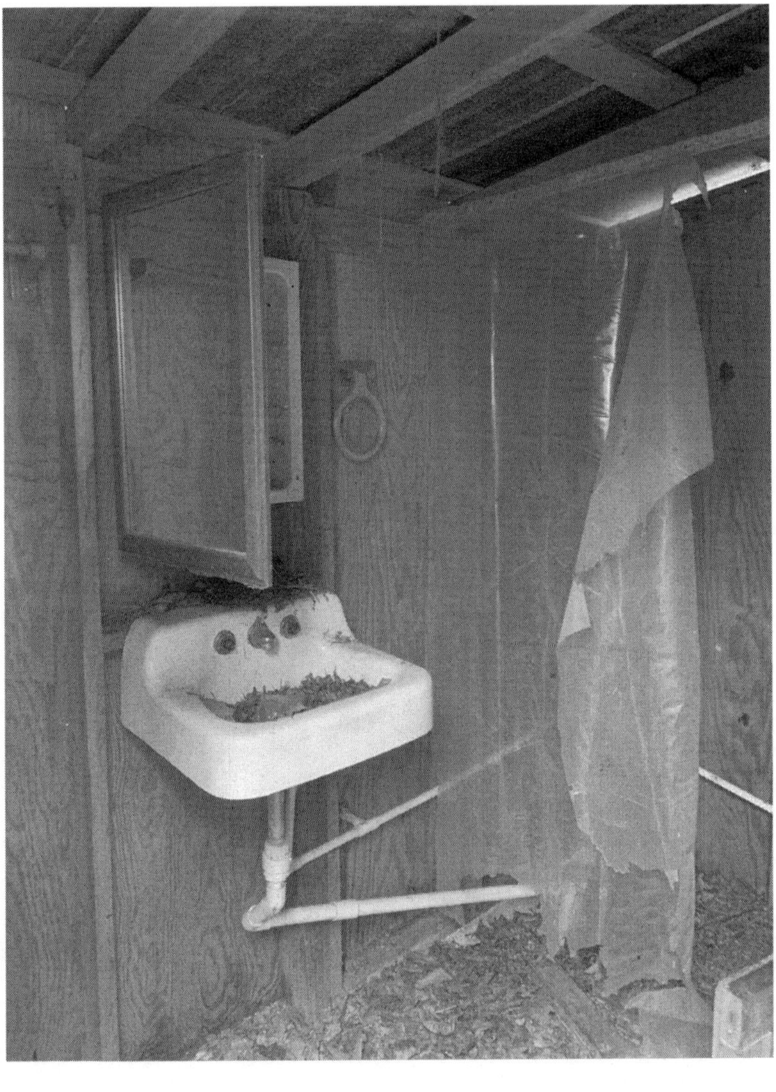

The Shed Jon spent the last days of his life living in.

THE BOOK OF SAY 563

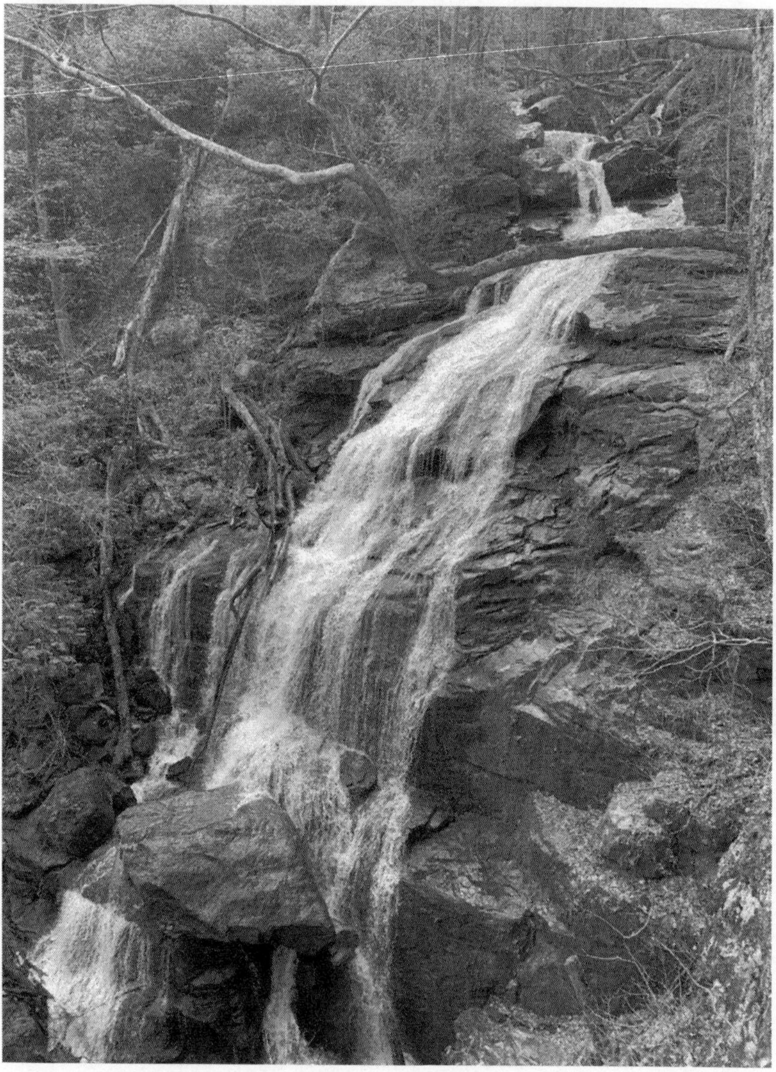

THE BOOK OF SAY

Made in the USA
Middletown, DE
24 June 2024